CW00529982

STUDIES IN IMPERIALISM

general editor John M. MacKenzie

When the 'Studies in Imperialism' series was founded more than twenty-five years ago, emphasis was laid upon the conviction that 'imperialism as a cultural phenomenon had as significant an effect on the dominant as on the subordinate societies'. With more than seventy books published, this remains the prime concern of the series. Cross-disciplinary work has indeed appeared covering the full spectrum of cultural phenomena, as well as examining aspects of gender and sex, frontiers and law, science and the environment, language and literature, migration and patriotic societies, and much else. Moreover, the series has always wished to present comparative work on European and American imperialism, and particularly welcomes the submission of books in these areas. The fascination with imperialism, in all its aspects, shows no sign of abating, and this series will continue to lead the way in encouraging the widest possible range of studies in the field. 'Studies in Imperialism' is fully organic in its development, always seeking to be at the cutting edge, responding to the latest interests of scholars and the needs of this ever-expanding area of scholarship.

British Imperialism in Cyprus, 1878–1915

MANCHESTER
1824

Manchester University Press

British Imperialism in Cyprus, 1878–1915

THE INCONSEQUENTIAL POSSESSION

Andrekos Varnava

Lecturer in Modern History,
Department of History,
Flinders University,
South Australia

MANCHESTER
UNIVERSITY PRESS
Manchester and New York
distributed in the United States exclusively by
PALGRAVE MACMILLAN

Published by MANCHESTER UNIVERSITY PRESS
OXFORD ROAD, MANCHESTER M13 9NR, UK
and ROOM 400, 175 FIFTH AVENUE, NEW YORK, NY 10010, USA
www.manchesteruniversitypress.co.uk

Distributed in the United States exclusively by
PALGRAVE, 175 FIFTH AVENUE, NEW YORK, NY 10010, USA

Distributed in Canada exclusively by
UBC PRESS, UNIVERSITY OF BRITISH COLUMBIA,
2029 WEST MALL, VANCOUVER, BC, CANADA V6T 1Z2

British Library Cataloguing-in-Publication Data
A catalogue record for this book is available from the British Library

Library of Congress Cataloging-in-Publication Data applied for

ISBN   978 0 7190 7903 0   *hardback*

First published 2009

18 17 16 15 14 13 12 11 10 09   10 9 8 7 6 5 4 3 2 1

Typeset
by Graphicraft Limited, Hong Kong
Printed in Great Britain
by the MPG Books Group

CONTENTS

[v]

ACKNOWLEDGEMENTS

As with life, it is not possible to successfully complete a project of this magnitude without the lives of other people touching it.

This book began as a PhD dissertation at the Department of History, University of Melbourne. I would like to thank my principal supervisor, Richard Pennell and my associate supervisor, Paul Nicholls for their persistence, advice and guidance; Patricia Grimshaw, at that time the Head of the Department, for supporting my application, as a 21-year-old, for an Australian postgraduate award; the two postgraduate officers, Kelly Angwin and Ron Baird; the two postgraduate coordinators, Professor Chips Sowerwine and David Goodman; and the Head of the Department, Charles Zika, for their great support. I also wish to thank the other postgraduate students who went through the PhD adventure with me and were a constant source of support: Kwabena Adou-Boahen, Ian Coller, Roland Burke, Nell Musgrove, Jenny Spinks, Tim Goldsmith and Emily Turner-Graham. The staff members of the Baillieu and Education Resource Libraries at the University of Melbourne have been excellent, especially those from Inter-library Loan, who I bombarded with a record number of requests during my first two years; and Norm Turnross and Blanca Pizzani.

I am very grateful to the A.G. Leventis Foundation for granting me $US3,500 and to the Arts Faculty at the University of Melbourne for the $AU3,000 grant for archival research in the UK in 2003. I am grateful for the services of various institutions and people, during my three months of research in London: Royal Holloway University of London, Egham Hill, Surrey; the National Archives, Kew; the British Library; St Anthony's College, Oxford, and Debbie Usher, its archivist; Richard Schofield, my supervisor at King's College; Robert Holland, Professor of Imperial and Commonwealth History, Institute of Commonwealth Studies, University of London; and Klearchos Kyriakides and Tim Reardon for their advice and hospitality.

I have a number of people and institutions to thank for their assistance and advice while in Cyprus from October to December 2002, and since my move there in September 2006: the Cyprus American Archaeological Institute; the Archbishop Makarios Library; the Cyprus Research Centre; the State Archives of Cyprus; Ruth Keshishian of Moufflon Bookshop; Thelma Michaelidies of MAM Bookshop; George Georghallides and his wife Joan; Maria Roussou and Antonis Hadjikyriacou, who are responsible for my application for the Leventis Foundation Scholarship; Rita Severis, who shared with me her incredible knowledge of Cyprus; and finally, but by no means least, to the historians of City Pride Pub, who I hope will form the future Cyprus Historical Association, Nicholas Coureas, Christopher Schabel, Hubert Faustmann, Colin Heywood, Simon Phillips and Ken Owen Smith. I would also like to thank a number of other people who have been very helpful: James

ACKNOWLEDGEMENTS

Cameron, Christalla Yakinthou, Kynan Gentry, Yigal Sheffy, Jan Asmussen, Ersi Demetriadou, Eleni Apeyitou, Altay Nevzat and Nicholas Doumanis.

I would also like to thank the two referees of my PhD and the three referees for Manchester University Press, especially Costas Constantinou, who provided me with invaluable comments that significantly improved the quality of this study. I also thank the team at Manchester University Press, especially Emma Brennan.

My family has been a constant support. I thank my parents for their patience and the quiet environment. I thank my Auntie Katina and Uncle Andreas for taking me in while in Cyprus. I also thank my cousins Michalakis and Andreas for driving me to and from Nicosia to undertake archival research. I thank my uncle Kyriakos for leaving me his place in London while I was there. And finally to my beautiful wife Helen – thanks so much for your encouragement, support and patience.

Having acknowledged that all these people and institutions have touched this study in some way or another, it is only proper for me to recognise that any errors and shortcomings are entirely my own.

LIST OF FIGURES

GENERAL EDITOR'S INTRODUCTION

Imperialism often represented the temporary triumph of hope over reality. The Victorian belief in progress was so profound that progressive expectations of economic or strategic value were invariably wildly overdrawn. This was very much the case with Cyprus. Acquired in a mood of just such enthusiastic aspirations, it soon became apparent that the island was going to deliver neither the commercial nor the geopolitical value expected of it. Seldom has an imperial possession produced so quickly such a declining fall in its reputation for productivity, for its climatic and health properties, and its military advantages. Soon seen as a Tory folly by the Liberals, many politicians came to view it as an unnecessary blot on the imperial landscape. Abandoning it, as with the Ionian Islands earlier in the century, seemed like the best course of action, but the British discovered that they had become deeply implicated in, and had perhaps exacerbated, communal tensions. Cyprus had remained no more than a lease from the Ottoman Empire, but returning it to the Turks was inconceivable and handing it over the Greeks was fraught with difficulties. They were landed with the 'inconsequential possession' until later in the twentieth century, when a violent and messy decolonisation only served to stir up more hostilities and apparently ratchet up the scale of conflict.

Andrekos Varnava's book deals with these issues in illuminating ways. The author rightly demonstrates the manner in which Cyprus played a significant role in the imaginative culture of the British, through the fascination with the ancient world in the nineteenth century, the archaeological developments, which often constituted major news, the new invoking of the medieval crusades and the exaltation of heroes in that period, the philhellene passions of the time, and the various literary manifestations that had kept Cyprus at the forefront of their consciousness. The acquisition of Cyprus in 1878 was, therefore, rooted in romantic predilections, which may well have influenced Disraeli as much as hard-headed practical concerns. But Cyprus was soon overtaken by other events in the Mediterranean, notably the British move into Egypt in 1882 – again theoretically under the aegis of the Ottoman Empire creating the co-called 'veiled protectorate' – a development which seemed swiftly to render Cyprus redundant. It was certainly no longer important on the route to India and its significance in respect of the Aegean and Asia Minor was dubious in respect of the nature and scale of British interests there.

From the point of view of the British search for 'added value' from the island, it was unfortunate that Cyprus was locked into Ottoman debt, that medical and sanitary advances capable of overcoming its health problems had not yet occurred, and that neither the military nor naval establishments could find (despite much debate) anything to recommend it. The great irony is that Cyprus only seemed to offer advantages once air power had entered the equation and once the hostility of nationalist politicians had rendered the British position in Egypt untenable. By then, Cyprus was on the verge of becoming, despite its record of communal conflict, a highly significant tourist destination. Now its climatic and physical attractions would come to the forefront of the British consciousness in new ways. Only in modern times have the possibility of resolution and reconciliation become more real, perhaps in association with the European Union.

The author has shifted the historical centre of gravity on the island from the decolonisation years (which have received a great deal of attention) to the earlier era of British rule. He has done this through a remarkably detailed examination of official documents and other sources. He has also looked in detail at the British efforts to hand over Cyprus to the Greeks before and during the First World War, analysing the reasons for the failure of these early attempts at *enosis*. The book greatly increases our understanding of British dispensations and disappointments in respect of Cyprus, setting political and military arrangements into wider cultural and ethnic contexts.

In all of this we should never, of course, forget the people of Cyprus themselves who have been so often caught up in political and diplomatic events beyond their control.

John M. MacKenzie

ABBREVIATIONS

AC	Army Council
AMH	American Historical Review
BLC	Biographical Lexicon of Cypriots (Koudounaris)
BMGS	Byzantine and Modern Greek Studies
BS	Balkan Studies
CAB	Cabinet Papers
CAOG	Crown Agents for Overseas Governments and Administrations
CDC	Colonial Defence Committee
CHBE	Cambridge History of the British Empire
CHJ	Cambridge Historical Journal
CIC	Commander-in-Chief
CICMS	Commander-in-Chief Mediterranean Squadron or Station
CID	Committee of Imperial Defence
CMO	Chief Medical Officer
CO	Colonial Office
CP	Comparative Politics
CR-1	Contemporary Review
CR-2	Cyprus Review
EHR	The English History Review
EIC	Editor-in-Chief
EKEE	Επετηρίδα Κέντρου Επιστημονικών Ερευνών (Annual Review of the Cyprus Research Centre)
ERS	Ethnic and Racial Studies
ESS	European Studies of Sociology
FO	Foreign Office
FR	Fortnightly Review
GED	General Engineer's Department (later PWD)
GOCE	General Officer Commanding Egypt
HJ	Historical Journal
HOC	House of Commons
HOL	House of Lords
HR	Historical Review
HSANZ	Historical Studies Australia and New Zealand
IA	International Affairs
ICCS-1	Proceedings of the First International Conference on Cypriot Studies
ICCS-2	Proceedings of the Second International Conference on Cypriot Studies
ICQ	Irish Church Quarterly
IGF	Inspector-General of Fortifications (WO)

ABBREVIATIONS

IHR	International History Review
IJMES	International Journal of Middle East Studies
IJSL	International Journal of Society and Language
ILN	Illustrated London News
IO	India Office
IOR	India Office Records
JAH	Journal of African History
JCH	Journal of Contemporary History
JHS	Journal of Hellenic Studies
JICH	Journal of Imperial and Commonwealth History
JMA	Journal of Mediterranean Archaeology
JMGS	Journal of Modern Greek Studies
JMH	The Journal of Modern History
JWH	Journal of World History
KL	Kypriakos Logos
KS	Kypriakai Spoudai
LC	Legislative Council
LK	Laografiki Kypros
LO	Law Officers
MAS	Modern Asian Studies
MES	Middle East Studies
MM	Macmillan's Magazine
MO	Medical Officer
MRC-I, MRC-II, MRC-III	Military Report and General Information Concerning the Island of Cyprus (1907), (1913) and (1936)
NC	The Nineteenth Century
NN	Nations and Nationalism
NR	National Review
ODNB	Oxford Dictionary of National Biography
OHBE	Oxford History of the British Empire
PSQ	Political Science Quarterly
QR	Quarterly Review
RE	Royal Engineers
RMA	Royal Military Academy
RN	Royal Navy
SA	Secretariat Archive
SEER	Slavonic and East European Review
UE	United Empire
USM	United Service Magazine
WD	War Department
WO	War Office

Introduction

On 12 July 1878, the future admiral and governor of New South Wales (1902–09), Captain Harry Rawson, raised the British flag in Nicosia, the capital of Cyprus. The special artist of the *Illustrated London News* (*ILN*), Samuel Pasfield Oliver, depicted bemused, animated and scruffy natives, whom he contrasted with the solemn and pristinely lined British and Indian soldiers. Admiral Lord John Hay, who had taken possession of Cyprus in Queen Victoria's name, salutes the Union Jack.[1] A month later, Oliver drew 'Greek Priests Blessing the British Flag at Nicosia'. After Mass, they huddled under the hoisted flag outside the entrance in an act of benediction before a large crowd. Three cheers followed for Queen Victoria, Sir Garnet Wolseley, the High Commissioner, and the British nation. Wolseley stood before a throne especially placed for him, which he refused to use. The other British officers stood beside it, clearly indifferent.[2] Wolseley wrote in his journal that the ceremony was 'such a mockery of everything sacred', conducted by 'dirty greasy priests' and 'was like a penny peep show very badly done by very inferior showmen'.[3]

The scenes show the contradictions in the British rule of Cyprus between 1878 and 1915. The martial presence reflects the British aim in occupying Cyprus: strategy and power. The local reaction, especially of the clergy, reflected their support and even reverence of the British. The Cypriot Eastern Orthodox Christians welcomed the British with the hope that they would bring equality to Orthodox Christian and Muslim alike. The indifferent – even rude – British reaction contrasted with the British strategic aims behind the selection of a place with docile inhabitants. That the British ultimately failed was no surprise.

During the Anglo-Turkish Convention of June 1878, Lord Beaconsfield's Conservative government demanded and got from the Ottoman Sultan Abdul Hamid II the right to administer and occupy Cyprus. The island was to be a *place d'armes*, a term Beaconsfield used when he suggested seizing Cyprus in April 1878. A place of arms is an offensive base and thus needs a harbour capable of berthing warships for the disembarkation and embarkation of an army, especially in the case of an island. Such a base, the Conservatives hoped, would end the threats to British interests, both strategic and economic, in the Near East and India, arising from a weak Ottoman Empire and an expansionist Russia.

Figure 1 'Raising the British flag in Nicosia, Cyprus'
Source: Illustrated London News, 10 August 1878.

A generation later, in December 1912, the Liberals, Winston Churchill, the First Lord of the Admiralty, and David Lloyd George, the Chancellor of the Exchequer, with the consent of Sir Edward Grey, the Foreign Secretary, and the Prime Minister, Herbert Asquith, told the Prime Minister of Greece, Eleutherios Venizelos, that London wanted to cede Cyprus to Greece. Cyprus was of no value to the British except as a pawn. In 1915, a formal offer was made to Greece's government, but it was rejected.

This study examines Cyprus' progress from a perceived imperial asset to an expendable backwater, explaining how the Union Jack came to fly over the island and why after thirty-five years the British wanted to lower it. It deals with British imperialism and the problem of the worthless territorial acquisition. Ultimately, Cyprus' strategic, political and economic importance was always more imagined than real and was enmeshed within widely held cultural signifiers and myths.

The reader may ask: Why is it important to study the history of 'the inconsequential possession'? Most studies examine the importance of possessions to an imperial power. By showing their value to the imperial centre, imperialism and, in some cases, the reluctance to decolonise them in the face of rising nationalism, can be justified. Oddly, given this study, Cyprus also falls into this category in the traditional literature and received wisdom (see Chapter 1). This study shows that Cyprus was not always a valuable imperial asset. More broadly, examining the inconsequential possession reveals much about reasons of state, construction of policy and the contingencies of imperial governance. States do not always come to decisions logically or through evidence-based reasoning; decisions are often wrong; reasons for bad decisions can be twisted and turned to justify them differently; and there is a great reluctance to admit a wrong move, let alone to reverse it. Imperialism is especially difficult to reverse. Positive vibes and future value and prosperity usually accompany the occupation of new territory. It is not always easy to reconcile this with a sudden failure to realise this. Such failure hits at the pride of the imperial centre and the judgement of those politicians that decided on the move. But what is clear, and Cyprus is not the only case (for example, the Ionian Islands, Weihaiwei), is that a generation or two down the track, politicians are capable of critical reflection and reversing a policy that resulted in the acquisition of a failed possession. Personal identification with a policy, thus, plays a great part in 'reversing' a 'wrong move'. Whether succeeding in reversing a wrong policy or not, it is the intention that is important.

Examining the inconsequential possession also reveals a great deal about the ambiguities and unintended consequences that often remain unaccounted for in deterministic and monolithic accounts of the past. What does an imperial centre do when it occupies a place, once marketed as a pearl, that turns into a millstone? Does it fumble around to create a value for it? After all, it must justify its continued occupation. Conceptual and organisational confusion best characterise British perceptions of Cyprus' value and its administration between 1878 and 1915. Put simply, British governments whether Conservative or Liberal, did not know how to put Cyprus to any use within the wider imperial structures. Thus the 'inconsequential possession' can be seen as a deconstructive tool for demythifying policy and geopolitics.

In this respect, 'strategy' is also as an ambiguous discourse. At different periods or in different governmental quarters Cyprus was officially viewed as both important and inconsequential. Party politics and ideology, especially with respect to imperialism, influenced these differing views. But there came a point when even those that had been involved in the Conservative government that had occupied Cyprus did not know what to do with it. Thus it was possible for the arguments of those that considered Cyprus inconsequential from the beginning (the Liberals) to gain ground and result in the island becoming an expendable pawn.

Understanding how and why the British found themselves in such a position, that is, saddled with an 'inconsequential possession', and their response, which culminated in efforts to lower the Union Jack that had been first raised in 1878, is the main preoccupation of this book.

Sources and methodology

This book has an unconventional structure, combining a chronological with a thematic approach. It is structured chronologically until William Gladstone comes to power in 1880, when the structure takes a thematic approach, so that the focus is on the fundamental issues, leading to the final chapter, which examines Cyprus' eventual place as a pawn. Chapter 1 provides the necessary historiographical, thematic and historical context from which the chapters to follow can be situated and also draws upon other similar cases within these contexts. Chapter 2 explores the English/British imperial imagination relating to Cyprus from the time of Richard *Coeur de Lion* to Benjamin Disraeli (Lord Beaconsfield), with a focus on the strategic perceptions and cultural aspects of imperialism. Chapter 3 examines the occupation of Cyprus from a more conventional approach – the aims, interests and decision-making processes of Lord Beaconsfield's government. It attempts to draw links between the decision-making processes and the imperial imagination. Chapter 4 investigates the policy in practice from its reception to the realities in Cyprus. It reveals the difficulties encountered and London's reaction. Beaconsfield's loss in the April 1880 elections, when the Liberals came to power under Gladstone, forms a break because the opposition of the new government to the Cyprus venture resulted in a different approach to the island. It would no longer be treated as a potential strategic asset, but as an ordinary colony, in so far as who would run it (transferred from the Foreign Office to the Colonial Office), but also it would be more overtly considered part of the Greek world. It was during this time, with Gladstone as prime minister, that policy in Cyprus was set, until after 1915 when changes were forced on the imperial centre because of Greece's rejection of Cyprus, French imperial interests in the region and the rise of nationalism within the Greek Cypriot elite. The subsequent chapters are thematic. The themes explored are finance/economy, governance and identity, strategic value and international position. An important or at least a successful possession must be financially/economically viable, relatively easily governable, and developed through public works and its resources, hence the choice of these themes. If economically viable, easily governable and developed, the place would have an important position within imperial structures and internationally it would project the power of the imperial centre. This international aspect is explored in the final chapter. But far from projecting power, Cyprus was considered useless as a British possession not only by the British but also by key European powers. That it became a pawn was not sudden and not a surprise.

Few historians have covered Cyprus between 1878 and the First World War, let alone its strategic place within the British imperial imagination, politics and structure. Volume IV of Hill's *A History of Cyprus* covers Ottoman and much of British rule, but it was written from an imperialist perspective (remembering also that Sir Harry Luke, an old Cyprus hand, edited the volume) and focuses on the friction between the British and the Cypriots.[4] In *A Political and Administrative History of Cyprus, 1918–26* George Georghallides outlines the period 1878–1918, but does not explore the issue of Cyprus' strategic role and place within the British imperial structure as thoroughly as he does for 1915–26.[5] More recently two excellent studies on the period after 1878 look at the Cypriots rather than the imperial power. Rolandos Katsiaounis' *Labour, Society and Politics in Cyprus during the Second Half of the Nineteenth Century*[6] and Rebecca Bryant's *Imagining the Modern*[7] were both timely accounts of the development of national and political consciousness. There are few other secondary works worth mentioning. The lack of secondary sources means that archival sources must be used to tell the general history of the island as well as to address the questions this study seeks to shed light on.

This study, being about British perceptions and policy, relies on British records. Most of the archival material was accessed at the National Archives in Kew, London. The Foreign Office ran Cyprus until 1880 when the Colonial Office took over, and most of the material in the section on the Ottoman Empire (FO881) was transferred to the Colonial Office (CO67). Scholars have not examined the files in the Colonial Office relating to Cyprus' strategic disposition or its political and economic viability within the Empire from its occupation until its annexation in November 1914. Much data were also found in the Foreign Office classmarks for Greece (FO371) and the Ottoman Empire (FO881), the War Office, Admiralty and Cabinet Papers.

Examining only one archive, however, limits any study. In this case, it would present only the bare bones of policy-making without the meat behind it. Men on the spot and locals informed policy. This is evident in the collection of the Secretariat Archive (SA1), in the State Archives, Nicosia, which contain the papers of the chief secretaries during British rule. The SA1 series present the circumstances in Cyprus and include correspondence between London and the Cyprus government; the latter and its local officers; and local officials and the population. But military and personal files of officers are empty or missing.

Scholars often view unpublished unofficial correspondence, such as journals, diaries and letters, as complementing official correspondence, but this underestimates their value. The views and emotions of men on the spot and decision-makers alike are more freely expressed in private than official correspondence. History is not only about the official; it is also about the individuals and the importance of their perceptions, ideologies, prejudices and emotions, which are often suppressed from official correspondence and reports. They provide a private avenue to understanding Cyprus' place within the Empire and are useful in pursuing the secret diplomatic discourses and departmental debates.

Public sources, such as memoirs, newspapers, parliamentary debates and travellers' accounts, are equally vital in understanding contemporary perceptions. Such literary sources provide the public with those views that authors wish and agree to make public. Thus they must be contextualised. They also often help to understand shifts in government policy, the importance of issues and the views of the wider public beyond the politicians. Fictional references also have an important role to play, hiding messages that the author might otherwise not wish to overtly disclose – or more overtly disclosing messages, thus giving importance to them. Although many of these sources are readily available, most have not been used before in a study covering this period of British rule of Cyprus.

Images, no less than words, are vital. John MacKenzie correctly observed that 'a full understanding of orientalism requires some comprehension of the extensive range of artistic vehicles through which representations of the orient were projected'.[8] Despite this, images have seldom been taken seriously. From the caricatures of *Punch*, the sketches in the *Illustrated London News*, to photographs, such as those of John Thomson, the image has an important story to tell, politically, culturally and of course aesthetically.

The British were masters at analysing and visualising their Empire and educating those at home about it. Historians have significant records from which to understand the place of Cyprus in British imperial imagination, politics and strategy.

Notes

1 *ILN*, 10 August 1878.
2 Ibid., 18 August 1878.
3 Wolseley Journal, 18 August 1878 (ed.) Anne Cavendish, *Cyprus 1878: The Journal of Sir Garnet Wolseley*, Nicosia, 1991. Hereafter Wolseley Journal, with entry date.
4 Sir George Francis Hill, *A History of Cyprus*, IV (ed.) Sir Harry Luke, London, 1952.
5 G.S. Georghallides, *A Political and Administrative History of Cyprus 1918–1926*, Nicosia, 1979.
6 Rolandos Katsiaounis, *Labour, Society and Politics in Cyprus in the Second Half of the Nineteenth Century*, Nicosia, 1996.
7 Rebecca Bryant, *Imagining the Modern: The Cultures of Nationalism in Cyprus*, London, 2004.
8 John MacKenzie, *Orientalism: History, Theory and the Arts*, Manchester, 1995, 14.

CHAPTER 1

Historicising the British possession of Cyprus: the contexts

There was once a little lady, who had lodgings in a shoe,
She had so many babies that she didn't know what to do,
Queen Victoria's the lady, Old England is the shoe,
And the latest baby's little Master Cyprus.
> (The chorus of an 1879 comical and topical song, written by
> E.V. Page, composed by Vincent Davies and sung by Arthur
> Roberts, J.W. Rowley and H.P. Matthews)

Queen Victoria, so this song goes (see Appendix IV for full song), has added another baby (possession) to her collection – an extensive collection she does not really know what to do with. The new possession is Cyprus, thus implying, about a year after its occupation, that it too will be as useless as the others. No doubt, some of the others were not so useless, but then again some of those of value were not babies, such as Australia, Canada and India. Nevertheless, the song is clear enough: it argues that once occupied overseas possessions become ornaments that have no real value and it is not known what should be done with them. This song extract challenges the received wisdom of Cyprus' strategic importance and throws down the challenge to situate the occupation and subsequent retention of the island within the various theoretical contexts. So the main aim of this chapter is to examine the historiographical and theoretical contexts, ending with a section that provides a narrative of British imperial and foreign policies from which to better understand the chapters that follow.

Historiographical context

Historians have not included Cyprus in explanations of imperialism. This is understandable, as colonial expansion saw vast amounts of territory occupied in the last quarter of the nineteenth century and Cyprus was only a small part. Yet the politicians (namely Beaconsfield and

Lord Salisbury) who selected Cyprus placed great value on it. So it is odd that Cyprus is mentioned only eight times in the relevant volume of the sweeping *Cambridge History of the British Empire*.[1] The volume, published in 1959, coincided with agreements granting Cyprus independence after the violent EOKA (*Εθνική Οργάνωση Κυπρίων Αγωνιστών*/ National Organisation of Cypriot Fighters) revolt since April 1955. It had been front-page news for four years, so the omission is surprising, but Cyprus has always been more important for scholars of decolonisation than of imperial expansion.[2] Forty years after the *Cambridge History* appeared the *Oxford History of the British Empire* was published as 'a major new assessment of Empire'.[3] William Roger Louis, its editor-in-chief, claimed that it was broader in scope than prior studies.[4] Even so, in its 800-page *The Nineteenth Century*, Cyprus was mentioned a mere three times, in contrast to the *End of Empire* book and television series, which had a chapter and a documentary on the messy decolonisation.[5]

Cyprus did not became a stronghold after its occupation, consequently, it is not mentioned in most imperial defence studies, such as in W.C.B. Tunstall's two chapters in the *Cambridge History of the British Empire* (*CHBE*) and Peter Burroughs's chapter in the *Oxford History*.[6] Donald Schurman mentions Cyprus only three times in his study[7] and although Quentin Hughes mentions Cyprus more often in his study of British Mediterranean naval stations, his view reflects the received wisdom of the so-called importance of Cyprus.[8]

Because Cyprus is centrally located in the north-eastern Mediterranean Sea, where Europe, Asia and Africa converge (Figure 2), it seems extraordinary that it was never really a stronghold. It is 45 miles from Anatolia, 60 miles from Syria, 240 miles from Port Said and 350 miles from Crete. Most European and Near Eastern civilisations had occupied it partially or wholly: Greek, Phoenician, Assyrian, Egyptian, Persian, Ptolemaic, Roman, Byzantine, Arab, Genoese, Frankish, Venetian and Ottoman. For many historians this suggests that it was coveted as a strategic island vital to obtaining hegemony in the Near East.[9] Clearly it was coveted – because it changed hands so many times – but few commentators have perceived that it seldom served as a military bastion or offensive base.[10] It also suggests that having acquired it, no power exerted itself much to retain it.

Historians of Cyprus have taken for granted the island's strategic role to Britain because of its central location and subsequent role in Middle East defence policy after the Second World War.[11] Sir George Hill, the director of the British Museum (1931–36), spent thirty years on his monumental *A History of Cyprus*. Sir Harry Luke, a Cyprus Colonial Government officer (1911–20), edited the last volume. They

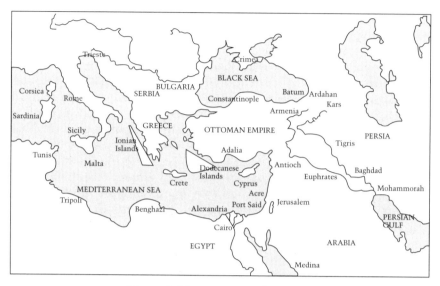

Figure 2 The Location of Cyprus
Source: © Dr Andrekos Varnava, 2007.

argued that the desire to make 'a *place d'armes* and not merely a coaling station . . . completely justified' Cyprus' selection.[12] This became the received view. The British journalist Nancy Crawshaw, who had covered the EOKA revolt, later wrote: 'Britain's interest in the Cyprus question has always been strategic.'[13] John Reddaway, the chief secretary of the Cyprus government in the 1950s, more recently wrote that this was 'indisputable'.[14] In 1964 T.W. Adams and A.J. Cotrell, American political scientists, claimed that Cyprus was a 'valuable . . . link in British imperial defence policy after the turn of the [nineteenth] century'.[15] In 1988 the historian George Kelling wrote that the island's 'value to the Empire always related to defence'.[16]

Historians of the British Empire and the Near East also accept this view. David Cannadine included Cyprus in his list of naval stations that the British had founded to encircle the world.[17] In 1999 Afaf Lutfi Al-Sayyid-Marsot, a historian of Egypt, claimed that the naval base of Alexandria, added to Malta and Cyprus in 1882, boosted British power in the eastern Mediterranean, implying that Cyprus was a stronghold.[18] Andrew Porter, Professor of Imperial History at King's College and former editor of the *Journal of Imperial and Commonwealth History*, backed this view.[19]

Two Greek Cypriot historians also adopted this view in discussing why Cyprus had changed hands so often. P.N. Vanezis argued that

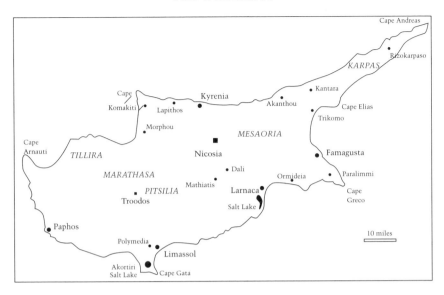

Figure 3 Map of Cyprus
Source: © Dr Andrekos Varnava, 2007.

Cyprus became a military base in 1878, while Stavros Panteli claimed that it was Britain's turn to exploit its strategic advantage.[20]

But these claims exposed a paradox: if Cyprus was such a strategic prize, why did the British not realise its value? In 1931, Harold Temperley observed that it was 'not easy to see that the occupation of Cyprus, which has never been fortified or made a naval base, was a real advantage to England'.[21] Christopher Woodhouse, who served in Greece during the Second World War, also thought 'Cyprus played virtually no strategic role at all, despite the circumstances of its . . . occupation' from 1878 to 1954.[22] Also, the aide-de-camp to King Constantine, General Victor Dousmanis, observed that Cyprus had not been strategically valuable to Britain as Egypt, Malta and Gibraltar had been.[23]

Most commentators refer to William Gladstone's return to power in 1880 and Egypt's occupation in 1882 to explain why Cyprus did not become a strategic base. These ideas have a long history, starting with the men who served in Cyprus. In 1885 Major Benjamin Donne, a commandant of the Cyprus *zaptieh* (military police), wrote in the first English book published in Cyprus that 'had Lord Beaconsfield's Government remained in power there is no doubt that Cyprus would have been made a coaling-station for the Navy and a suitable harbour and defences would have been made at Famagusta'.[24] In that year, Horatio Kitchener, who surveyed Cyprus, claimed that Gladstone stopped public works, which stalled development.[25] Colonel Hugh

[11]

Sinclair, the private secretary (1881–86) to Lieutenant-General Robert Biddulph, the second high commissioner (1879–86), agreed, believing for the rest of his life that Beaconsfield 'would have made it into a really important place of arms and developed its resources and harbour'.[26] In 1908 Basil Stewart, who helped build the Cyprus railway in 1906, argued that since Egypt's occupation, Cyprus had been 'practically neglected'.[27] A decade later, Sir Charles Orr, the Chief Secretary to the Cyprus government (1911–17), elaborated.

> By the garrisoning of Egypt with British forces the safety of the Canal was far more effectively secured, and Cyprus, at the same time, lost most of its value as a strategical point of vantage.[28]

In this view, the superior naval facilities at Alexandria rendered superfluous the development of Famagusta harbour (the only place for a naval or coaling station). In April 1927 William Bevan, the Colonial Commissioner to the Cyprus government, agreed with Orr in a speech at the Royal Colonial Institute, presided over by Sir Charles King-Harman, Cyprus's High Commissioner from 1904 to 1911.[29]

Hill and Luke included the Gladstone and Egypt explanations in their three reasons for the failure to establish Cyprus as a base (the third reason was that Britain's uncertain tenure stunted private enterprise, so necessary for economic development).[30] These reasons became the consensus view of historians, with one or both claimed as the reasons why Cyprus did not become a base by: D.E. Lee in 1934; W.L. Burn in 1936; Philip Newman in 1940; Doros Alastos (Evdoros Joannides) in 1955; Ronald Robinson and John Gallagher in 1961; T.W. Adams in 1962; Daniel Wosgian in 1963; Susan Rosenbaum in 1964; Robert Stephens in 1966; Quentin Hughes in 1981; Woodhouse in 1984; James McHenry in 1987; Klearchos Kyriakides in 1996; Rolandos Katsiaouinis in 2000; and in 2003 Anna Marangou.[31] In 1976, Richard Patrick asserted that, after occupying Egypt, London 're-evaluated Cyprus' value to Britain's imperial interests [and] downgraded the island's former strategic importance in relation to Suez'.[32] This study shows that Cyprus had no strategic value before Egypt was occupied.

The few historians who have noted the paradox that Britain occupied Cyprus for strategic reasons but did not turn it into a base, offer mis-directed explanations. In 1935 L.E. Lawrence, in a neglected thesis, thought it was clear by 1880 that 'Cyprus could not play the part in British policy anticipated in 1878'. Lawrence claimed that Cyprus was too far from the theatre of war in Ottoman Asia, but in fact, Cyprus was only forty miles from Anatolia. He asserted that the harbours in Cyprus were too poor to permit development; yet British harbour engineers found that it was not too expensive to redevelop Famagusta harbour. Lawrence also suggested that the failure to redevelop Cyprus was due to the Porte refusing to implement the reforms it promised in the Anglo-Turkish Convention for Asia Minor, but this was not it; indeed the Conservatives reinvestigated redeveloping Famagusta harbour after Constantinople's intransigence.[33]

A year earlier than Lawrence, D.E. Lee suggested that the decision not to make Cyprus a stronghold resulted from the failure to build the Euphrates Valley Railway, connecting the Mediterranean and India, and the British failure to establish an informal empire in Ottoman Asia.[34] In 1963 Daniel Wosgian outlined the implications of this:

> Cyprus has not substantially contributed to the development of an 'alternative route' to India, nor has it proved . . . the first step in the establishment of a great Near Eastern Empire. As to its use as a *place d'armes*, it can be pointed out that by an irony of fate, the first time after the Convention, that it served as a *place d'armes* was in 1915, during the Dardanelles campaign, when it was used as a British base in support of Russia and against Turkey.[35]

Cyprus did not have a role as a stopover on route to India and the failure to develop a place for it in British imperial structure contributed to the failure to seek an informal empire in Ottoman Asia. But the question of informal control did not hinge on Cyprus' development. As for the 'irony of fate', Cyprus had served as a base in the 1882 Egyptian war, but Lemnos filled that role in the Dardanelles campaign.

Wosgian also asserted that Cyprus had 'some positive value as a secondary strategic base at all times, during . . . British domination, whenever conditions in the Near East were unsettled'. He added that 'strategically Cyprus was of some use to the British' because it was denied to an enemy.[36] Thus, Cyprus had 'only a sort of residual importance', as Susan Rosenbaum claimed a year after Wosgian.[37] George Georghallides, formerly the director of the Cyprus Research Centre, shared these views. In 1979 he argued that Cyprus had a 'negative strategic significance' and was held as a 'reserve *place d'armes*, lying on the periphery of an area of vital concern to Britain'. He thought that the 'principal strategic consideration militating against' the satisfaction of the Greek Cypriot leaderships demands for *énosis* (union of Cyprus with Greece)[38] was the fear that it would fall to a power that could challenge British interests in the eastern Mediterranean. Georghallides claimed that when Winston Churchill, the undersecretary at the Colonial Office, visited Cyprus in 1907 and declared that the British government could not grant *énosis* because Cyprus did not belong to Britain, he was obscuring the real reason: 'the political and strategic usefulness of Cyprus to the British Empire'.[39] But this conclusion was wrong: Churchill's push to cede Cyprus to Greece five years after his visit and the 1915 offer, contradict it.

Cyprus' place in British imperial strategy and defence is not simply explained. A grand imperial strategy did not govern policy towards Cyprus before 1912; policy oscillated between ad hoc perceptions of advantage, non-advantage and disadvantage. Cyprus raises the question of the ability of historians to test the overall theories of imperialism.

Theoretical contexts

Mainstream justifications for imperial expansion

G.N. Sanderson asserted that it was the historian's task to explain imperial expansion.[40] Until now, there has been no effort to do this with Cyprus. This study presents a different – although not new – approach to the understanding of British imperial expansion, revising the understanding of economic and strategic theories by distinguishing between actual and imagined benefits. This brings into focus the 'Eldorado' or 'Promised Land' motif in accounting for expansion in the case of the inconsequential possession, and presents a cultural explanation to account for imperial expansion and failure in Cyprus' case.

Imperialism is a frame of mind or policy that dominates the politics, society, economy and culture of foreign entities by informally or formally controlling them without significant settlement from the metropolitan centre. R.J. Horvath believed that the last point was the difference between imperialism and colonialism: the latter occurred when significant numbers of colonisers settled in the dominated place.[41]

There must be a historical context for this mindset: European imperialism was not new to the nineteenth century – Spanish, Portuguese, Dutch, French, Russian and British expansion had transpired over four centuries. The label 'new imperialism' was given to a period starting in the 1870s when European powers dramatically began occupying territory, culminating in the 'scramble for Africa'. Ronald Robinson and John Gallagher distinguished 'informal' empire (in the mid-Victorian era) and 'formal' (in the late-Victorian era)[42] and claimed that the later period was no more imperialist, thus questioning the concept of 'new imperialism'.[43] Why then did Europe expand so suddenly starting in the 1870s?

In September 1877 the journalist Edward Dicey wrote that

> our Empire is the result not so much of any military spirit as of a certain instinct of development inherent in our race . . . 'To be fruitful, and multiply, and replenish the earth,' seems to be the mission entrusted to us, as it was to survivors of the deluge. The Wandering Jew of nations, it is forbidden to us to rest.[44]

[14]

Dicey implied that the British were the modern Chosen People – chosen to create an Empire. In a lecture five years later Sir John Seeley, a noted historian, claimed that the British seemed to have 'conquered and peopled half the world' in a 'fit of absence of mind'.[45] Seeley implied that the British had awoken to find themselves controlling an empire on which the sun always shone. His aim was to draw attention to the empire and not to account for how it came to be. Through time, many contemporary commentators and historians have invested much time in explaining imperial expansion.

The economic impulse theory was the earliest offered. The British economist, John Hobson, writing when the Empire was a hot issue during the Boer War, argued that after the 1870s, industrialised Europe needed new markets.[46] Capitalist greed, for cheap raw materials, profitable investments and exploitable places, underpinned imperialism. He influenced Lenin's thesis that imperialism was the logical growth of capitalism, but Lenin emphasised finance capital.[47] Nearly a century after the 'new imperialism', Eric Hobsbawm agreed that the 'convincing' motive for expansion was the search for markets.[48]

Non-Marxist historians destroyed these models by showing that investors and financiers did not influence policy to the extent claimed and that many territories, especially in Africa, were not economically important.[49] But in the 1990s, P.J. Cain and A.G. Hopkins linked material forces to socio-political developments to account for imperialism. They argued that it was the capitalist interests of elite gentlemen, which convinced the British nation of the necessity of imperial expansion.[50]

Cyprus does not fit so easily into the economic theories. The island was occupied for economic reasons, but the justifications for its occupation were couched more in terms of the economic advantages of the Levant. Cyprus was to open the trade of the Levant to British investors. At first, and then periodically, British investors were interested, but the British did not develop the once famous Famagusta harbour and few British firms made their way to Cyprus, let alone establish shop there. Those that thought that Cyprus offered economic advantages based their assessments on a past that preceded Ottoman rule and on the British ability to renew the glory days of a once economically thriving island, which had fed the Crusaders and was one of the main Western emporiums in the Near East before the Ottoman rise. But the British made little effort to revive the island. They did not concern themselves with exploiting Cyprus' resources or location. Yet the island was exploited. The Cypriots paid a tribute of nearly £100,000 per annum, nominally to the Porte, but actually to the British Exchequer, which retained it to pay the bondholders of the 1856

Crimean War Loan, which the Porte was in default, and to which London and Paris were liable. This was not achieved through developing Cyprus' economy, but through high taxation.

J.A. Schumpeter proposed a different theory: that sociological and psychological forces were at work. An overtly jingoistic nationalism propelled imperialism. The 'new imperialism', he claimed, was a 'temporary reaction of political sentiment and of threatened individual interests'. Industrialisation and liberalism at home threatened the traditional aristocracy.[51] They focused imperialism into active propagandist associations and pressure groups in order to publicise and promote territorial expansion and interest in colonies. In 1883 British Conservatives founded the Primrose League and in 1884 the Liberals founded the Imperial Federation League. In 1882 a German Colonial Society was formed and, in 1883, the Society for German Colonisation.

Commentators have argued that Schumpeter's theory is difficult to sustain because it implies that imperialism was popular, when it seems otherwise. David Cannadine showed that the British aristocracy played only a subordinate role in the building of the Empire.[52] In the 1930s, W.L. Langer argued that imperialism was not so popular in France and Italy as to allow the elite to get away with such a sudden expansion of territory.[53] More recently, Jonathon Rose claimed that throughout the nineteenth century most Britons were unaware of 'their' empire.[54] Bernard Porter agreed, showing that at least into the 1880s the working classes – about 80 per cent of Victorians – knew little if anything about it.[55]

Schumpeter's theory does not present the cause(s) of imperial expansion, but rather it offers a contextual basis from which to understand it. His explanation does not answer the question why specific territories were selected; it merely explains the circumstances and climate within which expansion was possible. No doubt there existed an extraordinary climate of jingoism before and after Cyprus' occupation, making it easy to justify, but this does not explain why territory, or indeed why Cyprus, was chosen.

J.S. Galbraith and D.K. Fieldhouse argued that the periphery, and not merely the metropolis, was central to imperial expansion. They believed that the activities of explorers, missionaries, merchants and government representatives created a 'turbulent frontier'.[56] Sir Stamford Raffles, a clerk for the powerful British East India Company and the lieutenant governor of Java, founded the British colony of Singapore in 1819. There were the Frenchmen Du Chaillu and De Brazza and the Englishman Sir Samuel White Baker in equatorial Africa; the Welshman Henry Stanley in the Congo; and the German Karl Peters in east Africa. The London Missionary Society and later the government sent David Livingstone, a Scottish missionary, to Africa to open a way for commerce and Christianity. When he vanished while seeking the source of the Nile, Stanley went after him and they met on the shores of Lake Tanganyika. Livingstone's funeral was a celebrated event and his discovery of Nyasaland (1858–63) resulted in it becoming a British Protectorate in 1889. France was the most active in organising 'mission civilisatrice'.[57] The idea that modern civilisation would improve humanity was imbued with racial beliefs of inferiority (the native) and superiority (the white European). The influence of 'men on the spot' was perhaps most evident in the Liberal government's decision to intervene in Egypt in 1882.[58]

The 'pericentric' or 'men on the spot' theory applies to Cyprus in an interesting way. It was not men in the island or in the vicinity in the 1870s that called for its occupation, but consuls that had lived in Cyprus in the 1840s. Beaconsfield's government used their reports when researching into Cyprus' potential. Those justifying the choice of Cyprus drew on the report compiled from the old consular reports to make their case and to convince themselves that they had chosen a future pearl of the Empire.

Robinson and Gallagher offered another explanation. Strategy and security had led British politicians to seek an African empire. The British had expanded informally by exerting commercial, diplomatic and cultural influence. The scramble for formal annexations in Africa during the 1880s aimed to preserve the security of these informal interests and wider imperial interests, specifically the routes to India (the Suez Canal) and Australasia (the Cape of Good Hope), from local movements in Egypt and South Africa. In short, local factors pulled European powers into expansion. In taking Egypt, London started the scramble, inviting the jealousy of other powers, notably France, to seize territory to balance the strategic equilibrium. London reacted to secure these new acquisitions and France and other European powers followed with counter-annexations.[59] Thus they argued that policy to protect imperial interests – imperial strategy – was the main reason for imperialism. This involved occupying strategic positions where coaling stations and harbours of refuge could be established to protect imperial strategy. British supremacy had largely been founded on maritime trade.[60] Ships in wartime required sheltered waters for repairs and replenishment of supplies, and as maritime operations increased, possessing natural harbours became more vital. Naval bases were established. Steam resulted in the need for coal, so coaling stations were established because steam needed coal depots. Initially servicing trade, they came to supply naval needs. By 1880, Britain had the largest overseas empire and biggest mercantile and naval fleets.[61] Fortified or garrisoned territories defended imperial interests in wartime, so sea power, empire and strategy were linked. Imperial defence was the first problem that involved all the Empire in the age of 'new imperialism'[62] and Robinson and Gallagher argued that formal expansion aimed to defend such bases.

No doubt Cyprus was primarily occupied for strategic reasons. The local crisis was not on the island, but numerous crises raged around it: in the Balkans, Asia Minor and Egypt. British political and economic interests in the Ottoman Empire, Egypt and India were thought in need of protecting. But why select Cyprus, especially when it did not become a valuable strategic asset? How does one explain the fantastic disparity between the justifications that underpinned its occupation and the outcomes and what impact do these explanations have on explaining its occupation in the first place?

One criticism of Robinson and Gallagher's theory came from a pupil of theirs, A.S. Kanya-Forstner, who, with C.W. Newbury, claimed that the 1882 crisis in Egypt did not trigger the 'scramble', because in 1879 the French conquest of Senegal was well progressed, London and Paris were vying for the African west coast and King Leopold of Belgium had taken the Congo.[63] Kanya-Forstner offered the 'mythical' or 'Eldorado' thesis to explain French expansion in Africa. He attributed French expansion to the myths and delusions of the official mind, primarily of men on the spot, who convinced the politicians back home of the value of the resources of western Africa.[64]

Thus, it is exaggerated perceptions of value that explain imperial expansion. The French recreated medieval legends about the wealth of Senegal when contemplating informal control in the 1850s, and men on the spot revived these in the 1870s to justify formalising control. The economic illusions took the form of fantastic official estimates of the resources and population of western Africa, which were used to justify turning it into 'the India of the French empire' in 1879. Kanya-Forster claimed that the French saw the Western Sahara as an 'Eldorado' of boundless wealth. But that was a fallacy. The perceived threat to French strategic interests and prestige after the British occupied Egypt motivated French expansion into the Upper Nile, aiming to remove the British from Egypt. After diplomacy failed, the French decided on force in the 1890s, setting their sights on Fashoda. The move nearly resulted in an Anglo-French war. However, Kanya-Forstner showed that the aims behind the Fashoda strategy were based on unrealistic illusions and a perceived importance in its strategic vitality. The move on Fashoda aimed to scare the British into negotiations, but instead ended in the humiliating French withdrawal.

The 'mythical theory' was heavily criticised. It was claimed that Kanya-Forstner failed to place the decision-making in a socio-economic context or to link it with 'a frame of mind' of imperialism.[65] G.N. Sanderson thought the evidence to support the 'mythical theory' was not persuasive and it did not explain why the myths suddenly took control of French policy in 1879. Robert Tignor wanted to know when and how the myths of wealth originated and why they were held in the face of accumulating counterevidence.[66]

Yet, there are other examples of the 'Eldorado theory'. John Wright showed that explorers, missionaries, politicians and intellectuals created myths to justify the Italian occupation of Libya. They wanted Italy to secure economic resources, settle a growing population (ten million had migrated from 1896 to 1915), increase prestige after losing a war with Abyssinia in 1896, and obtain a strategic position in the Mediterranean to end the perceived suffocation from France and Britain, especially the former, which had taken Tunis, the point in Africa nearest Sicily. All the territory suited to colonisation and Mediterranean strategy was taken except Tripolitania and Cyrenaica. A lobby consistently promoted their advantages and in March 1911, Italian nationalists launched a newspaper to promote Tripoli as the 'Promised Land'.[67]

There were also British examples. In 1898 the British leased Weihaiwei from China to convert it into a naval base. First under the Admiralty, then the War Office, it proved a poor base and in 1901 it was handed to civilian administrators. Successive British governments considered it worthless, but did not relinquish it to China until 1922. Two historians called Weihaiwei's occupation the 'irrationality of empire'[68] and it is a good example of occupying territory based on misguided perceptions of advantage. An earlier example (not identified by historians), was the British occupation of the Ionian Islands in 1815. They were perceived as strategically vital, but the British did not fashion a strategic role for them and ceded them to Greece within fifty years (see Chapter 3). Palestine was another case. Although it did not figure in British strategic plans at any level – official or popular – it was built up as the Promised Land within a popular culture that associated it with the family Bible, Sunday school and home. But British soldiers and officials ruling it after 1917 were shocked that its appearance was so different from the biblical imagery and yet the religious impulse was still drawn upon.[69]

This study shows that Cyprus fits very well into the 'Eldorado' theory of imperial expansion. Beaconsfield's government perceived it would be a great strategic asset to the Empire based on its location and past role during the Crusades. It was also claimed that Cyprus' location would open the Levant's resources to British investors. Also, the British would show the Porte how to rule over mixed races. Three centuries of Ottoman rule were ignored. Britain, a great power, would make Cyprus strategically and economically valuable as it had supposedly once been, and which its location dictated it should be. Cyprus' future value was based on a mythologised distant past.

Eastern Question

The raising of the Union Jack in Cyprus differs from most cases of British imperial acquisition because the island does not lie in the traditional areas of British expansion, namely in Asia and Africa. The case must be situated within the Eastern Question because the British occupied Ottoman territory. The Eastern Question relates to two historical developments between 1774 and 1923 in the Near East: the conflicts of the European powers over protecting and expanding their interests, informal or formal, real or imagined, in the Near East; and the creation of 'ethnic' nationalities in the Ottoman Empire and the formation of nation-states (Greece, Romania, Serbia, Montenegro, Bulgaria, Albania) or desired nation-states (Egypt, Armenia, Israel).

The debates on the Eastern Question focus on whether the crises were imposed on the region from outside – from the European powers – or whether the Ottoman system was at fault. In mainstream historiography, European attitudes and views dominate, as Ottoman failure to keep up with European modernisation caused Ottoman decline.[70] Thus, it is often forgotten that Ottoman governments desperately tried to preserve the empire from external and internal threats. Reforms to modernise military structures began in the late eighteenth century and progressed to political, economic and social structures. Eventually, in 1876 a constitution and a parliament were instituted. However, traditional forces rejected Westernisation and many resented European interference. Sultan Abdul Hamid II dismissed the constitution and ruled despotically; believing that only the state's power could arrest weakness and unrest. The legacy of authoritarianism further weakened Ottoman credibility (to European appearances), especially during the Armenian massacres of the 1890s. Not even when the Young Turks declared equality for all Ottoman subjects in 1908 was Ottoman weakness arrested; within four years they lost territory to Italy and a Balkan alliance.[71]

Abdul Hamid consented to the British occupying Cyprus as a defence measure. From Cyprus, the British promised to protect Ottoman territorial integrity from further Russian aggression. Abdul Hamid also agreed to implement reforms in Armenia to prevent further instability there and London agreed to pay the Porte Cyprus' surplus revenues. In the event that Russia returned Ardahan, Batum and Kars to the Porte, the British would also return Cyprus. The Sultan soon regretted handing Cyprus to the British. In the first instance, the British had agreed to the cession of Ardahan, Batum and Kars to Russia, which made Cyprus' retrocession unlikely. Secondly, in agreeing to implement reforms in Armenia, Abdul Hamid also agreed to allow new British consular representatives to oversee the restructuring. He soon believed this would be an intrusion on internal affairs, especially when he did not seem so willing to discuss, let alone implement, the reforms. Finally, there was the Cyprus tribute, which the British retained to pay the bondholders of the defaulted Ottoman Crimean War loan. Cyprus' occupation, far from giving rise to an informal British Empire in Ottoman Asia, had the opposite effect – the withdrawal of British support and influence, which eventually resulted in German support of, and influence, in Constantinople.

By the mid-nineteenth century, Europe had significant commercial, financial, spiritual and political interests in the Ottoman Empire. In the eighteenth century, France and Russia had led the way – the former in the Mediterranean and the latter in the Black Sea. Britain increasingly became involved as French and Russian hegemony threatened to become absolute. Later in the nineteenth century, the Germans replaced the British. European leaders and observers perceived that the Porte could not control its vast territory and instability was a menace to European imperial interests. European attention turned to the perceived untapped resources of the Ottoman Empire. European powers wanted influence over the Ottoman Empire, which appeared near to disintegration, because of interests in it and its location at the crossroads of Europe, Asia and Africa. Thus, European governments were deeply involved in Ottoman fortunes.[72] Cyprus' occupation was a perfect example. The island played no part in the Eastern crises between 1875 and 1878 and yet the British plucked this obscure Ottoman island to become a base from which to protect British interests from the threat of Russian expansion and Ottoman collapse.

For the European powers, the Eastern Question had a number of geographic areas of interest: Greece, the Slavic Balkans, the Holy Land, Egypt and, to a lesser extent, Armenia, Assyria and Mesopotamia. All these places belonged to the Ottoman Empire and European powers, to varying degrees, fought over them, particularly Greece, Egypt and the Holy Land. Why was this so? Once Britain and France had taken informal and then formal control of India and Indo-China, and Russia had extended its hold over parts of central Asia and the Caucasus, they required easy access to, and in the Russian case beyond, these places of control. All these routes led across the Ottoman Empire. Control over the vast Ottoman Empire meant that imperial interests could be extended at the same time as protecting against expansion of rival powers.[73] Bernard Wasserstein offered another explanation. He described the diplomatic intrigues between the French, Germans, English, Greeks and Russians over Jerusalem, the holiest city to all of Christianity's competing sects, as 'spiritual imperialism'.[74] The European diplomatic involvement in Egypt and Greece could be similarly termed, without the religious connotations.

Cyprus is, of course, centrally located to all the crisis zones of the Eastern Question. However, the culture emanating from the Holy Land, Greece and Egypt has most influenced the island. Europe saw the Holy Land and Greece as their spiritual ancestors. The modern places were not important, but the appropriation of 'ancient Greece' to intellectual and political life, and the 'Holy Land' to religious culture and social behaviour, made them important places of interest in modern times.[75]

Nationalism and identity formation

As mentioned, nationalism is a major component of the Eastern Question and the Ottoman Empire presents an interesting case in understanding identity formation. The question of identity is important because if the British occupied a place that would not be easy to govern, it would be much harder to create a strategic base.

Broadly, there are three approaches to explaining nation formation: the primordial, which believes that nations are intrinsic to human nature, necessary for humans to live and timeless, existing in every epoch;[76] the perennialist, which asserts that the roots of nations and nationalism pre-date the modern period;[77] and the modernist, which argues that nations are products of the modern age and that, as Ernest Gellner stated, nationalism 'engenders nations, not the other way around'.[78]

The modernist approach is most convincing. The primordial view implies that historical development does not affect national identity, since nations naturally exist. Primordialists confuse collective identity – which in pre-modern days could have been fashioned by class, religion, geography, kinship, culture and society – with nationalism. Perennialists hold that nations are rooted in ethnic groups, which have always existed albeit in different social or political environments from those of the modern world. I do not believe in the continuum of cultural community: in a script that ethnic groups wrote through epochs and employed in the modern age to free themselves from oppression.

There are various definitions of the 'nation'. I define a nation as a people that identify with a common historical ancestry, which results in a unitary socio-cultural self. I believe, like Walker Conner, that national consciousness must reach the full spectrum of society. He demonstrated that the French nation did not exist until the late nineteenth century. Stathis Gourgouris showed that the Greek nation existed only because it was dreamt, disseminated and institutionalised during the nineteenth century. 'Identify' is the distinguishing word in my definition. National identity is predicated upon perceptions not facts: on a script of the past imagined or dreamt and written and disseminated in a present. Such a consciousness only evolved in the nineteenth and twentieth centuries.[79]

Contemporary views rejected and revised the lived identity of Ottoman subjects because they were not an 'ethnic' nation. Harry Luke, a major figure in the history of Cyprus, both as an official and researcher, shows that:

> The Byzantine Empire had been no more national from the Greek point of view than its Ottoman successor was to be national from the Turkish; and its official designation of 'Roman' which was maintained to the end of its life, tended to become an artificial, non-national term exactly as the term 'Ottoman' was to become in its turn . . . To this day Orthodox peasants, not only in Greece, but even . . . in Serbia and Bulgaria speak of themselves as 'Romans' . . . The word 'Roman' thus included not only the Greeks of Hellas, the islands, the capital city and the various Greek centres of Asia Minor, but also the Serbs, the Rumanians and the Bulgarians of the Balkan Peninsula and the Arab-speaking Orthodox communities of Syria, Palestine and Egypt. The history of the Christian populations of Turkey in Modern times is to a great extent the history of disintegration of this artificial unity.[80]

Luke identifies an Orthodox Christian identity into the twentieth century, but believes that identities other than national identities are artificial. This was the British approach to the Near East at the time of Cyprus's occupation.

Most historians of Cyprus approach its history from a position that it is Greek.[81] But a growing literature, from Ottoman specialists and socio-cultural historians of Cyprus, argues that the Ottoman Empire was – to use a contemporary term – multicultural. People of different cultures lived together peaceably and were integrated socially and culturally. This gave rise to 'multiple identities'; identities formed by socio-cultural integration between each 'mother-culture'.[82] 'Political modernity' – rule by modern institutions of the state, bureaucracy, and capitalist enterprise[83] – completely altered the way Cyprus' inhabitants viewed themselves and ultimately it had a detrimental effect on the relations between the two main religious groups in the island.

Political modernity, which developed during the European Enlightenment and the nineteenth century, introduced concepts such as the state, civil society, public sphere, equality before the law, social justice, and national and civic identities.[84] As Dipesh Chakrabarty argued, 'The European coloniser of the nineteenth century both preached this Enlightenment humanism at the colonised and at the same time denied it in practise.'[85] Unlike Indians, Africans, and others not considered 'civilised enough' to participate in representative government, the Cypriots were civilised enough to have some part, but the principles of 'political modernity' were applied to an extent.

Nevertheless, political modernity allowed for the development of nationalist elites.[86] They competed with the elites in Cyprus that combined pre-modern and modern ideas. In this struggle, the nationalist elites rehearsed to their own subaltern classes the script of the past, which Europeans had created to base political modernity. Their opponents, being associated with the colonisers, lost ground. The peasants, however, were not introduced to the concepts of citizenship and civil society, but became members of the nationalist discourse and as such recruits into the nationalist ideal.

The development of national identities did not threaten Cyprus' growth into a strategic asset because it had no such value. Instead, the fact that Cyprus was not strategically important, afforded the Colonial Office the chance to do nothing when nationalism manifested itself as a challenge to British rule and to the excellent Muslim and Christian relations. Furthermore, when contemplating withdrawal from the island, only its cession to Greece was considered.

The imperial encounter

Chapter 6 shows that identities in Cyprus were evolving in confusing ways and that the interesting element was the British involvement. Although Europeans constructed identities for peoples throughout the world, including in Europe, there were few instances when a European country formally occupied a European space. Most of the British non-settler possessions were 'Oriental', that is, in Asia or Africa. Only Gibraltar, Heligoland and the Ionian Islands were in Europe, with Malta and Cyprus on the periphery.

The Ionian Islands were the only other place with an Eastern Orthodox Christian majority to come under formal European rule. Thomas Gallant found that there the British created identities for the Ionians through chains of analogies with familiar colonised cultures, such as the Irish and Indian.[87] The British created 'Aboriginal Europeans' and 'Mediterranean Irish' to account for the perceived awkwardness of the Ionians not clearly being 'European' or 'non-European'.[88] Gallant drew on the Orientalist paradigm – the process whereby the

West created an image of the East – that Edward Said and the reaction to his work created.[89] But Gallant challenged Said's bi-polar dichotomy paradigm by arguing that in the Ionian case the imperialists selectively applied the analogy of stock stereotypes of various groups to categorise 'the other'.[90] He highlighted Orientalism's shortcomings, situating the Ionian case within the Balkans by referring to Maria Todorova's 'Balkanisation' model – the argument that Western Europeans did not see the Balkans as Occidental or Oriental, but Christianity set it apart from the Islamic cultures of the Middle East.[91] Gallant showed that because Greece was between East and West and no obvious Occidental or Oriental identity applied, the British could construct contrasting identities based on various familiar stereotypes and dis-associated the Ionians from the ancient Greeks in order to deny them a place in the idealised ancient Greek world.[92]

Cyprus' case was different. First, the British had 'learned' from their Ionian venture – this will be subsequently shown. Second, Gallant does not seem to offer what the 'official mind' constructed and applied, but rather what was offered by travellers and the local British colonial authorities. Those on the ground were able, as 'witnesses', to construct identities based on experiencing the colonised: those in the metro-politan centre very rarely ventured to these far-flung places, even those in Europe or its periphery. In London they could create identities drawing upon their own perceptions and education, variously ima-gining a world of the Phoenicians, Greeks, Romans, the Bible and the Crusaders. It is often the case in postcolonial studies that the 'official mind' is enmeshed with the views of the local authorities, settlers, travellers and others, forgetting that it is the official mind that makes decisions about instituting governmental, societal and economic struc-tures, often ignoring the advice of the men on the ground. This study offers a postcolonial re-reading of the imperial encounter between the British and the Cypriots, covering local and metropolitan authorities and settlers and visitors. It focuses on the 'official mind' because the aim is to determine why Cyprus went from being a gem to being deemed worthless and a trade option to Greece.

The methods of colonial rule and responses to local reactions to, and demands of, the imperial centre, are also aims of Chapter 6. Scholars focus on the idea that European conquest resulted in resistance from the colonised, but this was far from universal. Many territories were acquired during or after wars or by force of arms. Once military control was established, economic, cultural and political control evolved. Military authority gave way to civilian control, often by indigenous police and politicians in cooperation with officials of the coloniser state. European powers thought it was the 'white man's burden' to rule those people whom they viewed as immature and backward. European methods of colonial rule, especially British, were based on co-opting local elites. Colonial regimes limited the political representation of the colonised to lower administrative levels or symbolic positions that had little or no effective decision-making power. The exception was indirect rule, which the British employed in some colonies, but in practice was based on loyal locals.[93] The famous examples of 'collaboration' were in India, Malaysia and various parts of Africa.[94] However, such practices were not isolated to Asia and Africa: the British also co-opted the elite in the Ionian Islands.[95]

Of all the British overseas possessions, the Ionian Islands may appear to compare best to Cyprus, but there are crucial distinctions. By 1815 the Ionians had been introduced – or were in the process of being so – to modernity and the ideas of the nation from their connection to Venice.[96] They had never been under Ottoman rule, as Cyprus stands alone as the only place the British occupied from the Ottomans that had a Christian majority. The Ionian Islands are a stone's throw away from Greece – Cyprus is not. Lastly, there was no violence involved in Cyprus' occupation.

To appearances, Cyprus was different from most overseas possessions: it was primarily Christian and geographically on the periphery of Europe, Asia and Africa. The broad concepts of 'West' and 'East', 'Occidental' and 'Oriental' and what constitutes 'European' and 'non-European' are not easily delineable when studying Mediterranean people.[97] Where do Asia, Europe, Africa and indeed the Mediterranean begin and end? How do the islands of the Mediterranean fit in? Grappling with these complex considerations, which were not at play in the traditional imperial setting, is one of the challenges of this study.

Much has been written about the British rule of Cyprus and that the British instituted the 'divide-and-rule' structures of India so that they could more easily rule.[98] But in India the British used co-option and created the Indian Princes in the pursuit of 'divide and rule', whereas in Cyprus the British did not practise co-option. The British created divisions that had not previously existed, but the reasons why have not been explored. This study shows that London determined that the island belonged to the unitary ideal of the modern Greek world that Europeans had fashioned after creating a unitary ideal of ancient Greece during the Enlightenment. Co-opting Europeans was not in line with modern politics. Consequently, the British introduced modern structures and approaches in Cyprus – as far as they did not impinge on their control of affairs – and in doing so assisted in importing the national identity being created in the Greek state.

The anatomy of decision-making

Placing these questions in an imperial framework means understanding that perceptions generate reality and inform policy: perceptions of interests, value and identity. How were policies and decisions made? Who and what informed the perceptions that resulted in decisions? Theoretically, civil servants of the departments of state, the Foreign, War, Colonial and other offices, would advise the secretary of state, who would recommend a policy to the Cabinet or take a decision himself. The interplay between personalities and ideology is inherent in such a system. But there were other forces informing policy, from diplomatic and colonial representatives (men on the spot) to the opposition and backbenchers. The Crown also had rights and powers, which the Cabinet only absorbed towards the end of the nineteenth century. The press was equally important in policy formation and its defence. There were also the influential persons behind the scenes, the peers and magnates, who had an ear at Whitehall and the palace.

There is no theory of policy-making or studies that explore all the forces informing policy for the period 1874 to 1914, but there are studies on the individual forces: on the departments,[99] consular and colonial service representatives and other men on the spot,[100] influential politicians, the newspapers,[101] the Crown, associations, and influential men.[102]

The departments underwent transitions at the turn of the century. Change was forced on the Colonial Office before 1900 and many territories in Africa and Asia run by the consular service were given to the Colonial Office after the precedent of Cyprus in 1880, thus adding to its workload. By the end of the nineteenth century, the Colonial Office was in the public eye with various colonial incidents (namely the Jameson Raid) and the Boer War.[103] Zara Steiner argued that the Foreign Office became more professional after Lord Salisbury left it and even more when Sir Edward Grey arrived in December 1905.[104] The War Office was also transformed after the Boer War, especially after the Liberals came to office in December 1905 and overhauled its structures.[105] Under the Conservatives, especially during Disraeli's tenure as prime minister, the Admiralty was less important, in relation to the other military departments, than it was under the Liberals.[106] Change was also later in coming; indeed, it was rather rushed in the wake of the German naval scare of 1912. Political heads of departments influenced structure and policy, but so did the unelected civil servants. Understanding the latter – who they were and where they came from – is vital in grasping the influence of the 'official mind'.

Many men who had served or travelled overseas influenced policy as much as politicians and civil servants and many later became politicians themselves. Lord Cromer and Lord Kitchener are good examples for the period after 1880. Cromer dominated Egypt and policy there whether Whitehall was Conservative or Liberal.[107] In 1914 Kitchener became the first military professional to become War Secretary. He started in the Royal Engineers, served in Palestine, Cyprus and Sudan, then led the British army in 1898 to win back Sudan and served as Chief of Staff to Lord Roberts in the Boer War, before becoming Commander-in-Chief in India and Consul-General of Egypt. These self-made men, who presented themselves as world-weary imperial experts, were influential in Whitehall.

Pressure groups outside political parties constituted another import-ant tier of stress on policy. These pressure groups included societies and associations that pushed their common economic, ideological and humanitarian values; gentlemen, mostly London based, with inher-ited or self-made wealth, who had substantial financial investments, such as bondholders of loans to foreign countries; and newspaper men, like Frederick Greenwood, who was instrumental in the purchase of the Suez canal shares in 1875.[108]

Policy did not happen in a vacuum and policy-making relative to Cyprus was informed by the often conflicting views of men in vari-ous departments (such as the Colonial, Foreign, War and Admiralty), various men of the armed forces, local representatives and officials, and members of Cabinet and parliament. In choosing Cyprus, the prime minister and foreign secretary convinced the Cabinet, but thereafter the departments of state and the civil servants primarily dominated policy. This was until it was decided to cede Cyprus to Greece – a decision that had nothing to do with civil servants, but with the polit-ical heads of their departments.

The historical context

In order to understand the various aspects of British policy on Cyprus, which will be the focus of the forthcoming chapters, it is necessary to understand the wider British political and imperial context, with specific emphasis on the Near East.

From the mid-1850s until the First World War, the parties of gov-ernment were the Liberals and the Conservatives. The Conservatives and then the Liberals had healthy majorities from 1874 to 1885, but afterwards they frequently required the support of a third force or minor parties. The rivalry between William Gladstone, a four-time Liberal prime minister (1868–94), and Benjamin Disraeli (Lord Beaconsfield from 1876), a two-time Conservative prime minister (1868–80) domin-ated politics.

Divisions between Liberal and Conservative approaches to imperial expansion were defined in the 1860s and 1870s. As a rule of thumb, Gladstonian and Radical Liberals opposed expansion, while Conservatives supported it. The Liberals were therefore more parsimonious with taxpayers' money when it came to imperial expeditions and the cultivation of colonies. They were also more willing to grant local representation to natives. But these principles were not always applied, partly because there were various strains in the Liberal party – Radical, Whig and the Peelite or Gladstonian – and because of the influence of minor parties and distractions. In the case of the Liberals, the Irish National Party and Irish Home Rule split them. The Radical Joseph Chamberlain and most Whigs formed the Liberal Unionists after rejecting Home Rule. They wanted a stronger Empire through investments in colonies and thus had more in common with the Conservatives.

Maintaining the Ottoman Empire had been British policy since the early 1800s. By the late eighteenth century, as territories were lost to Austria and Russia, and Egypt became nominally independent, the Ottoman Empire was being challenged. Its leaders responded. However, reform was not sufficiently widespread[109] and the structures to establish a free market economy did not exist. Reform focused on remodelling the army and the government on European lines. In 1839 Sultan Abdul-Mejid I issued the *Hatt-i Sharif*, an edict outlining reforms that were partly a reversion to Ottoman concepts of government and partly a remodelling on European lines. The reforms attempted to reorganise the empire; hence they were known as the *Tanzimat* (reorganisation). Many reforms grafted successful European practices, including universal conscription and corruption's elimination.[110] However, the reforms proved too costly and were being implemented while external and internal threats threatened the empire.

In the eighteenth century, Russia emerged as the major Ottoman antagonist because of two interests: religion – sympathies with the Orthodox Christians – and strategy: the desire to dominate the Black Sea and have access to the Mediterranean. The Straits Question thus became important. Controlling the passage through the Dardanelles was an Ottoman prerogative so long as the Black Sea remained its lake, but when Russia gained a foothold there in 1774, the rules governing the passage became contested. During the 1780s, Catherine the Great designed the 'Oriental Project' to expel the Turks from Constantinople. In response, the Porte declared war on Russia in 1787 and lost. The Treaty of Jassy (1792) saw Russia become the dominant power in the Black Sea.[111]

British interests in the Near East were as important as the Russian and indeed the French. From the early sixteenth century, the English traded with Cyprus, Crete and Syria. Henry VIII had consuls at Chios and Crete.[112] But within decades, Ottoman power ended the trade.[113] In 1580 Queen Elizabeth negotiated the same rights for English traders in the Ottoman Empire as for French merchants. By the end of her reign, the Levant Company had rights to trade with Venice and the Ottoman Empire and appointed consuls.[114] London also sent an ambassador to Constantinople. The flag followed the trade.

British strategic interests were another reason not to allow Russia or France to increase their power in the Near East. Men on the spot were concerned about safeguarding the route to India. When living in Cyprus, George Baldwin, a Levant Company merchant, suggested linking the Mediterranean and Red seas in 1771. He moved to Egypt, but failed to convince Whitehall to retain the Egyptian consulate in 1794.[115] Yet his career was important as one of the first of many British agents in the Near East to link the region with the Indian Ocean 'by painting strategic and other alluring fancies' for his superiors.[116]

In the 1820s the Greek revolt precipitated Russian expansion at the expense of the Ottoman Empire and forced Britain and France to create a Greek kingdom (1832). Its borders were restricted to ensure that it would not emerge as a power. Russia threatened British interests, especially after the Treaty of Unkiar Skelessi (July 1833), which made the Russians the principal Ottoman guarantor and ensured that the Straits would be closed to foreign vessels, except Russian, in wartime.[117] Another threat was Muhammad Ali, Egypt's ruler. In 1839 Britain joined Russia, Austria and Prussia in expelling his forces from Syria, thus nullifying Russian influence at Constantinople.

Over the next thirty years, successive British governments encouraged investment in the Ottoman Empire. London backed the Ottomans against Russia in the Crimean War (1854–56) and with Paris guaranteeing them a £5 million loan. Investment in the Ottoman Empire increased after the war as British, French and Austrian businessmen arrived to rebuild the economy. A national bank, a public education system and railroads were established.[118] Reform aimed to found a modern and centralised government, but it lacked funds and personnel to implement and 'ethnic' nationalism and the resilience of conservatives hampered efforts. In the 1870s, Grand Vizier Mahmud Nedim Pasha opposed reform,[119] while Sultan Abdul-Aziz (1861–76) used revenue to build grand palaces to match those in Europe. The army was enlarged, but unlike European armies, it was used for policing, so a large standing army was required. This was costly and the

Porte took out more and more loans. By the 1870s, it had huge debts and became bankrupt.[120]

The Crimean War changed British imperial strategy. Malta was a major port of call for grain from the Black Sea and the Levant and British military advisers considered its strategic importance equal to that of Port Mahon, Gibraltar and Corfu. But its operational value as the main supply base during the Crimean War resulted in the British deciding that Malta had a superior strategic position, leading to a defence plan around its enclosed 'Grand' harbour that took thirty years to complete, and which superseded Corfu, which was ceded with the other Ionian Islands to Greece in 1864. The opening of the Suez Canal in 1869 made the Mediterranean an important maritime cross-road, giving Britain faster access to the India Ocean and focusing attention on the eastern Mediterranean. Valetta became the essential coaling station for the steam-powered vessels that were replacing sail, and a staging post for warships, troops and stores on their way to the east.[121]

Strategic and financial interests in the eastern Mediterranean did not result in the imposition of formal British rule; rather, British financial hegemony increased. In the 1870s the Egyptian and Ottoman inability to pay their debts, combined with the Russian threat, threatened those interests. This forced Disraeli's government to change policy.

Because the French had greater financial interests in Egypt than the British, Egypt's financial collapse carried the risk that French domination would ensue. To prevent this, Disraeli's government purchased the Khedive's share in the Suez Canal Company. Increasing British financial and administrative control over Egypt culminated in its occupation in 1882, ironically by the Gladstone government – a prime example of the continuity of policy and the power of streams in the Liberal party, in this case the Whigs.

Between 1876 and 1878, the threat of an Ottoman collapse grew because of Russian aggression, precipitating various changes of government in Constantinople. Ministers under Midhat Pasha, a liberal, deposed Abdul Aziz. His nephew, Murad, a well-educated man, became Sultan, but he was an alcoholic and was replaced with Abdul Hamid II. He dismissed Midhat's liberal constitution and the first Ottoman parliament that had opened in 1877, and began ruling despotically. Russia sought to capitalise on Ottoman instability, supporting the Slavic-led revolts in the Balkans and then attacked the Ottoman Empire.[122]

In December 1876, Disraeli (now Lord Beaconsfield) started looking for a Malta in the eastern Mediterranean. He considered Cyprus from the beginning. Lord Salisbury, the India Secretary, also thought

Cyprus was suitable to protect British interests after the imminent (and to his mind desirable) Ottoman collapse. But army and naval advisers wanted Stampalia, one of the Dodecanese Islands. In mid-1877, Beaconsfield's government became alarmed as Russia occupied Ottoman territory in Europe and Asia, fearing that if Armenia was occupied it would be the first step to India. The Cabinet and its advisers thought that informal control of the Levant might stop the threat to Armenia.[123]

The Cabinet chose Cyprus as the lynchpin for this informal empire and the base from which to resist further Russian aggression. After considering an invasion, it was occupied by agreement in the June 1878 Anglo-Turkish Convention, which was extracted from Abdul Hamid in return for protecting his Empire. Although defending the Porte was the official reason for occupying Cyprus, that was incidental to the government's aim to secure British strategic and financial interests in the Near East and India. It is unclear if Cyprus was chosen before or after a report was made on its value, but the report was based on consular reports dating back thirty years. Although there was opposition from defence advisers and others, Famagusta in Cyprus was perceived as the site of a great naval base, a potential trade centre in the Levant and a laboratory where the Ottomans would be shown how to rule over 'mixed races' in light of instability in Armenia.[124]

Abdul Hamid thought Cyprus was cheap in return for British protection. The Sultan retained sovereignty and the surplus revenue in the Anglo-Turkish Convention, ceding only the right to occupy and administer Cyprus to Britain for as long as Russia kept territories in Armenia. But Whitehall had already agreed to Russia keeping these territories permanently.

The trade-offs over the division of Ottoman territory were an early manifestation of the formal imperial expansion 'new imperialism'. London realised that occupying Cyprus would incite reaction from the other powers and so agreed that Russia could keep Ottoman territory in Europe and Asia, Austria-Hungary could occupy Bosnia/Herzegovina and France and Italy could take Tunis and Tripoli, respectively. In 1881 France cashed in, with Italy following in 1912. Thus Cyprus was part of the first large-scale imperial trade-off that resulted in further European expansion, yet the island played little part in that expansion.[125]

Beaconsfield's government and many commentators thought that, beyond dredging Famagusta harbour, little was needed to make Cyprus the stronghold and commercial hub they thought it had been under Lusignan (1192–1489) and Venetian (1489–1570) rule.[126] They were wrong.

The Liberals quickly attacked the policy: the agreements violated the Treaty of Paris; they thought Cyprus was useless strategically; and they questioned the garrison's size (having instituted, when last in power, a policy to reduce colonial garrisons, under the War Secretary, Edward Cardwell). Radical newspapers, especially *Punch*, supported them.[127]

Liberal scepticism was boosted when it appeared that much work was needed to make Cyprus a stronghold and entrepôt. The troops suffered from 'Cyprus fever' and the commanders, shocked by the poor sanitation and water supply, and the lack of roads and forests, became frustrated and thought it was too hard to establish Cyprus as a base. The first high commissioner, Major-General Sir Garnet Wolseley, left within a year of arriving because of disappointment and boredom.[128]

Within weeks of the fever making headlines in British newspapers, the War Secretary and the First Lord of the Admiralty visited the island and realised that it was no place to keep troops, certainly not the 10,000 originally sent. By 1879, only a wing of a regiment and two companies of Royal Engineers remained. The Conservatives postponed redeveloping Famagusta harbour, officially because they first wanted to make its site healthy, but really because they had decided that its development was not a priority. Subsequent reports on the harbour found that such works were beyond Cyprus' finances, which were reduced to pay the tribute.[129]

One reason for selecting Cyprus was its perceived political advantage: unlike Crete, it was considered peaceful. Its population was about three-quarters Orthodox Christians and about one-quarter Muslim, with a sprinkling of Maronites, Armenians and Catholic 'Latins'. The Muslim and Orthodox elites, comprising the landowners and clergy, ruled over a semi-integrated society. Archbishop Sophronios III led the Orthodox elite in welcoming the British and asking for the protection and advancement of the Orthodox *and* Muslim society. The men on the spot did not know what to make of this. Modernity, which identified races, had no explanation. The politicians applied preconceived notions: Cyprus was after all Aphrodite's birthplace. A small but vociferous Greek nationalist element influenced them. It aimed to spread the topological dream of Hellenism to Cyprus. Tiny Greece had great ambitions of a greater ethnically pure Greece, a task made hard because the people called and thought themselves *Romiee* (Romans). Whitehall treated Cyprus, at least partly, as European. The Conservatives rejected the idea of co-opting the willing local Cypriot Orthodox elite, contrary to policy elsewhere, because they thought it was responsible for the loss of 'Greekness'. British rule not only created the space for the introduction of Hellenism, it planted its seeds. This divided Cypriot society and made British rule difficult.[130]

In April 1880 Gladstone became prime minister with a good majority. Having assailed Beaconsfield's expansionist policy, he transferred Cyprus from the Foreign to the Colonial Office and in 1882 it received a partly elected legislative council. Other colonies, especially in the West Indies, had similar councils, but Cyprus was not a settler colony and the locals were in the majority over the British. This exemplified the perception that Cyprus was European. A power vacuum resulted after the British rejected recognising the church as leaders of their community. Because the legislature was split along 'racial' lines, it politicised non-existent divisions between the Orthodox and Muslims, aiding the small foreign and local agitators wanting Cyprus' Hellenisation and union with Greece (*énosis*).[131]

British economic policy in Cyprus also created grievances. Conservative and Liberal governments decided to retain the surplus revenue to pay for the defaulted Ottoman loan of 1855, for which the British and French governments, in having guaranteed, owed bondholders £41,000 a year. The tribute was fixed at £92,799. For an overtaxed agricultural society that produced less than twice that in revenue, it was a heavy burden. In order too pay it, London provided annual grants-in-aid and the Treasury and the Colonial Office introduced a restrictive budget, which curtailed expenditure on public works.[132] Accordingly, nothing was done to correct Famagusta's insalubrity or improve its harbour. The Colonial Office realised that if military advisers wanted Famagusta as a coaling or naval station the island would have to pay to make it healthy. This would jeopardise paying the tribute. Therefore, it was decided that no imperial funds would be made available for Famagusta. Also, Gladstone's Liberal and Salisbury's Conservative governments ignored the Royal Commission (1879–82) on the defence of British overseas possessions, which made recommendations on the fortification of Famagusta harbour.[133] Local revenue was diverted elsewhere. In 1886 it was decided to redevelop Kyrenia's tiny harbour, which was not a natural outlet for Cyprus' produce and which went over budget, hindering other projects, including making Famagusta more salubrious and dredging the harbour.

Between 1882 and 1885 a series of events caused public concern, but not even this series of crises in the vicinity forced British action over Cyprus. A popular Egyptian nationalist movement under Ahmed Urabi threatened British (and French) financial control of Egypt. Gladstone's government was split over whether to intervene. But with Paris wavering and Abdul Hamid rejecting involvement, London sent troops under Wolseley, which defeated Urabi. Egypt became a 'veiled protectorate', much like Cyprus; it was under British control, but remained apart of the Ottoman Empire. However, in Egypt, control was exercised through a consular representative, the Consul-General, and the formal institutions of local authority were maintained.

In September 1884 William Stead, the *Pall Mall Gazette*'s sensationalist editor, questioned the fleet's strength and the security of coaling stations in his 'Truth about the Navy' articles.[134] Gladstone's government was forced to act, but only outlined spending £1 million – well short of the £2.5 million that the Carnarvon Commission had proposed.[135] Then when the 'Mahdists', under Mohammed Ahmed Ibn Seyyid Abdullah, who had been in revolt against Egypt's presence in the Sudan since 1880, threatened the British position in Egypt and the Liberals withdrew, General Charles Gordon stayed, but his relief at Khartoum in 1885 was too late to save him, sparking a public outrage.

Cyprus had a role in the Egyptian and Sudanese wars (1882–85) as a base for depots, a spot to rendezvous the forces, a place of refuge for Europeans fleeing Egypt and as a sanatorium and rearguard hospital for the forces. A decision was made to withdraw the troops from Egypt and the Conservatives decided to station them at Troodos, but when this did not happen, they flirted with using Troodos as a summer station. Cyprus' government, after much wrangling, gave territory to the War Office,[136] but never used it, preferring that troops return to England to recuperate. Cyprus was again neglected. British control of Egypt and Cyprus ran parallel, but Egypt was far more vital to the Empire than Cyprus and imperial defence was focused there.[137]

In 1888, the Colonial Defence Committee, which the Liberal government formed in 1884, decided that Cyprus not only had no role, but was a defence liability. Salisbury's government halved the garrison to four companies in 1888 and in 1892 the Liberals proposed to remove the entire garrison, and succeeded in removing much of it in 1895. The Colonial Office tried but failed to create an issue of potential Orthodox and Muslim Cypriot disorder and thought the *zaptieh* (the semi-military police composed of Orthodox and Muslims) was capable of policing.[138]

The troop withdrawal manifested divisions between an Orthodox-Cypriot-centric/pro-British faction and a Helleno-centric/anti-British faction. It is understandable to assume that the Orthodox-Cypriot-centric leaders would want the troops to stay to guard and maintain them, but this faction believed (and influenced the British to believe) that the garrison was superfluous because of excellent Orthodox-Muslim relations. The Hellenists wanted the troops to stay for fear that Cyprus would be returned to the Porte. This shows their weakness in the 1890s.[139]

In 1895 Joseph Chamberlain became the Colonial Secretary in a Tory-Unionist coalition and started redeveloping Cyprus. Irrigation works were undertaken in the Mesaoria, the vast plain between Famagusta and Morphou; the inner harbour at Famagusta was improved; and a railway was built from Nicosia to Famagusta.[140] But the works were unprofitable and finances were further strained to pay for the interest and sinking fund.

The works did not aim to alter Cyprus' strategic place. One proposal that could have done so was the raising of a local Christian and Muslim regiment. The high commissioner thought it could reorientate the Cypriots as both Orthodox and Muslims served well in the *zaptieh*. Whitehall's military advisers saw the proposal in imperial terms and restricted it to Muslims after applying the martial races theory, because the British considered the 'Turks' a martial race, but not the 'Greeks'. The question was defending Egypt, not useless Cyprus.

By 1900 the Conservative-Unionist coalition (1895–1905) was too preoccupied with the Boer War (1899–1903) to worry about a backwater, let alone combating the rise of Cypriot Hellenism. A major turning point in Cypriot Orthodox Hellenisation occurred in 1900: Sophronios died. A decade-long violent conflict resulted between the Bishop of Kyrenia, who belonged to the Orthodox-Cypriot-centric faction, and the Bishop of Kitium, who led the Hellenists. The British had not halted the rise of a generation of Cypriot Orthodox imbued with Hellenism through the control of education and the misuse of newspapers by foreign and local Hellenists. The Orthodox-centric/pro-British faction was marginalised, allowing for the imposition of Hellenism. Hellenists presented *énosis* as *the* solution to economic hardship. In 1908, the British helped the Hellenists win the archiepiscopal throne, which ironically led to the church adopting an anti-British policy and presenting *énosis* as the only solution to society's problems.[141] In April 1912, the Cypriot Orthodox members resigned from the legislature and formed a central committee to agitate for *énosis*, whipping up a nationalist fervour that contributed to the first Orthodox-Muslim disturbances.[142]

Outside forces also came to influence the Cypriot Muslims. Those loyal to Abdul Hamid wanted to preserve and progress the multicultural structures, but were challenged by Young Ottomans and Young Turks, who attacked the Sultan. All opposed the rise of Hellenism and *énosis*. They wanted British and Ottoman protection. Instead, the local officials increased divisions: one high commissioner supported the Hellenists (Charles King-Harman, 1904–11) and another (Hamilton Goold-Adams, 1911–14) the Muslims. So as the divisions within each religious group lessened the divisions between each became more pronounced. Cyprus was becoming politically dysfunctional.[143]

When the Liberals came to office in 1905, imperialism was secondary to the growing economic and social inequalities in Britain.

They embarked on an ambitious programme of social reform that would last until the First World War. Chamberlain's colonial schemes had gone. Social inequality and economic equilibrium at home was reflected in the colonial sphere. Winston Churchill reflected this when, after visiting Cyprus in 1907 as under-secretary at the Colonial Office, he argued that economic hardship had stimulated *énosis* agitation.[144]

But the polarisation of the two European blocks – the Triple Entente and the Triple Alliance – diminished the prospect of solving economic and social inequalities in Britain. In 1882, Germany, Austria-Hungary and Italy formed the Triple Alliance, agreeing to support each other if attacked by France or Russia. This alliance threatened the French. The British felt threatened by the growth in the German Navy, which was manifested in one of the great novels of the period, *The Riddle of the Sands* (1903). In 1904 the French and British governments signed the *Entente Cordiale* (friendly understanding) after formal and informal imperial boundaries were agreed upon. Three years later, Russia, fearing German and Austro-Hungarian expansion, joined Britain and France to form the Triple Entente.[145]

Cyprus, strategically worthless, also became a pawn in this geo-strategic chess game. It had been a pawn before 1878 and that it became one after was no surprise. In 1880 and 1881, Gladstone's government mulled over ceding it to Greece to resolve a Greco-Ottoman territorial dispute – exemplifying the Liberal view that Cyprus belonged to the 'modern Greek world' and that it was strategically useless. Returning Cyprus to the Porte – an empire with pre-modern systems – was contrary to political modernity.[146]

The increasing despotism and oppression of Hamidian rule also made returning Cyprus to him anathema. Hamidian rule disillusioned London, which gradually withdrew its support and influence.[147] The Armenian massacres (1894–95) precipitated European revulsion, but no action was taken to prevent their recurrence. Nothing changed when the Committee of Union and Progress (Young Turks) organised a coup in 1908 and then removed Abdul Hamid. Their proclamation of equality for all Ottomans did not defuse the crises involving European powers in Crete and Macedonia. After a brief period of constitutional rule, power became vested in the triumvirate of Mehmet Talat Pasha, Ahmet Cemal Pasha and Enver Pasha, who through secretive negotiations courted Berlin.[148]

In 1912, the rise of a German naval menace, which had manifested in British and French perceptions during the Agadir crisis over Morocco, resulted in the Admiralty reducing the British naval presence in the Mediterranean to protect home waters. This left interests in the

Mediterranean exposed to the growing navies of Germany's allies, Austria-Hungary and Italy.

In this context, Cyprus became a pawn. Churchill, now the First Lord of the Admiralty, determined to cede Cyprus to Greece in exchange for naval rights at Argostoli harbour on Cephalonia, one of the Ionian islands. Once made into a flotilla base, Argostoli would prevent the Austro-Hungarian fleet from exposing British weakness in the Mediterranean. Meanwhile, Greece would be developed into a small naval power to patrol the eastern Mediterranean, allowing the British to focus on Austria-Hungary and Italy from Malta and Cephalonia. Talks between Churchill, David Lloyd George, the Chancellor of the Exchequer, Prince Louis of Battenberg, the First Sea Lord, and Greece's prime minister, Eleutherios Venizelos, were held in December 1912.[149]

Venizelos, an Anglophile, started modernising Greece when he became prime minister in 1908 and during the Balkan Wars increased Greece's territory by nearly 70 per cent.[150] Talks scheduled for January 1914 were postposed until August, but the war superseded them. Yet, within weeks of its outbreak, the Cabinet agreed to cede Cyprus to Greece, but when a chance presented itself, the new War Secretary, Lord Kitchener, objected. Kitchener had not only recently been the consul-general of Egypt, 1911–14, but was an old Cyprus hand. However, in October 1915 the offer was made – the fifteen-month war had not made Cyprus strategically important. The offer was rejected. Nevertheless, Cyprus' strategic worthlessness had made it a pawn in the greater game of international politics.[151]

The great expectations of its strategic, economic and political value were never realised. Even as a pawn it failed.

Notes

1 E.A. Benians, J.R.M. Butler and C.E. Carrington (eds), *The Empire-Commonwealth 1870–1919*, Cambridge, 1959.

2 Stephen Xydis, *Cyprus: Conflict and Conciliation, 1954–1958*, Ohio, 1967; Leontios Ierodiakonou, *The Cyprus Question*, Stockholm, 1971; Stephen Xydis, *Cyprus: Reluctant Republic*, The Hague, 1974; Nancy Crawshaw, *The Cyprus Revolt*, London, 1978; Evanthis Hatzivassiliou, *Britain and the International Status of Cyprus, 1955–1959*, Minnesota, 1997; Robert Holland, *Britain and the Revolt in Cyprus, 1954–1959*, Oxford, 1998 (repr. 2002); Andrekos Varnava, *The Cyprus Problem and the Defence of the Middle East, 1945–1960*, Melbourne, 2001.

3 Andrew Porter (ed.), *The Nineteenth Century*, Oxford, 1999, front jacket.

4 William Roger Louis, ibid., vi–vii.

5 Brian Lapping, 'Cyprus', in Brian Lapping (ed.), *End of Empire*, London, 1985, 311–51.

6 W.C.B. Tunstall, 'Imperial Defence, 1870–1897', *Cambridge History of the British Empire (CHBE)*, III, *The Empire-Commonwealth 1870–1919*, Cambridge, 1959, 230–54; 'Imperial Defence, 1897–1914', (*CHBE*), 563–604; Peter Burroughs, 'Defence and Imperial Disunity', *The Nineteenth Century*, III, 320–45.

7 Donald M. Schurman, *Imperial Defence 1868–1887*, ed. John Beeler, London, 2000, 97, 110, 122.
8 Quentin Hughes, *Britain in the Mediterranean and the Defence of Her Naval Stations*, Liverpool, 1981, 183.
9 S. Panteli, *A History of Cyprus*, London, 2000, 46–7; Ch. Hitchens, *Hostage to History*, London, 1997, 29–32.
10 Robert Stephens, *Cyprus: A Place of Arms*, New York, 1966, 20.
11 Varnava, *The Cyprus Problem and the Defence of the Middle East*.
12 Hill, *History of Cyprus*, 274.
13 Crawshaw, *The Cyprus Revolt*, 22.
14 John Reddaway, 'The British Connection', *International Affairs* (*IA*), 1985, 531; John Reddaway, *Burdened with Cyprus*, 1987, 11.
15 T.W. Adams and A.J. Cottrell, 'The Cyprus Conflict', *Orbis*, 1964, 66–83, 69.
16 George Kelling, *British Policy in Cyprus, 1939–1955*, PhD dissertation, Texas University, Austin, 1988, xiv, 2.
17 David Cannadine, 'The Empire Strikes Back', *Past and Present*, CXLVII, 1, 1995, 183.
18 A.L. Al-Sayyid-Marsot, 'The British Occupation of Egypt from 1882', *The Nineteenth Century*, Oxford History of the British Empire (*OHBE*) III, Oxford, 1999, 651–64, 654.
19 Andrew Porter, 'Introduction: Britain and the Empire in the Nineteenth Century', ibid., 1–28, 12.
20 P.N. Vanezis, *Cyprus: The Unfinished Agony*, London, 1977, 7; Panteli, *A History of Cyprus*, 9.
21 Harold Temperley, 'Disraeli and Cyprus's, *English History Review* (*EHR*), XLVI, 1931, 274–9, 279.
22 C.M. Woodhouse, 'The Cyprus Problem', in P. Thayer (ed.) *Tensions in the Middle-East*, Baltimore, 1958, 193–214; C.M. Woodhouse, 'Cyprus: The British Point of View', in J.T.A. Koumoulides (ed.), *Cyprus in Transition 1960–1985*, London, 1986, 82–94.
23 Victor Dousmanis and K. Alexandris, *Μεγάλης Ελληνικής Εγκυκλοπαιδειας – Κύπρος*, Athens, *c.*1926, 39.
24 Benjamin Donisthorpe Alsop Donne, *Records of the Ottoman Conquest of Cyprus and Cyprus Guide and Directory*, Limassol, Cyprus, 1885 (Nicosia, 2000), 108.
25 PRO30/57/1, A/13, Kitchener papers, Kitchener to George Saunders, journalist, 6 June 1885, unpublished.
26 Hugh Sinclair, *Camp and Society*, London, 1926, 67. Sinclair died in 1924.
27 Basil Stewart, *My Experiences of the Island of Cyprus*, London, 1906 (revised 1908), 239.
28 Sir Charles W.J. Orr, *Cyprus Under British Rule*, London, 1918 (1972), 44.
29 William Bevan, 'Cyprus, Our Newest Colony', *United Empire* (*UE*), May 1927, 261–70.
30 Hill, *History of Cyprus*, 274.
31 D.E. Lee, *Great Britain and the Cyprus Convention Policy of 1878*, Mass., 1934, 77–80, 113–38, 165; W.L. Burn, 'The British Occupation of Cyprus', *UE*, XXVII, 3, 1936, 134, 138; Philip Newman, *A Short History of Cyprus*, London, 1940, 200–1; Doros Alastos, *Cyprus in History*, London 1955 (1976), 307, 310; R.F. Robinson and J. Gallagher, *Africa and the Victorians*, London, 1961, 93; T.W. Adams, *Cyprus: A Possible Prototype for Terminating the Colonial Status of a Strategically Located Territory*, PhD dissertation, University of Oklahoma 1962, 29–30, 34; D. Wosgian, *Turks and British Rule in Cyprus*, MA dissertation, Columbia University, 1963, 43; S.B. Rosenbaum, *'Peace with Honour': British Policy in Cyprus*, PhD dissertation, Yale University, 1964, 21; Stephens, *Cyprus*, 71; Hughes, *Britain in the Mediterranean*, 183; Woodhouse, 'Cyprus: The British Point of View', 83; J. McHenry, *The Uneasy Partnership on Cyprus, 1919–1939*, New York, 1987, 19; K.A. Kyriakides, *British Cold War Strategy and the Struggle to Maintain Military Bases in Cyprus, 1951–1960*, PhD dissertation, Cambridge University, 1996, 18;

R. Katsiaounis, *Η Διασκεπτική, 1946–1948: Με Ανασκόπηση της Περιόδου, 1878–1945*, Nicosia, 2000, 17; Anna Marangou, *The Seas of Cyprus*, Nicosia, 2003, 226.

32 Richard A. Patrick, *Political Geography and the Cyprus Conflict: 1963–1971*, Ontario 1976, 5.
33 L.E. Lawrence, *The British Administration of Cyprus, 1878–1914*, PhD dissertation, University of Wisconsin, Madison, 1935, 2.
34 Lee, *Great Britain and the Cyprus Convention Policy*, 125–65.
35 Wosgian, *Turks and British Rule in Cyprus*, 24.
36 Ibid., 43.
37 Rosenbaum, *'Peace with Honour'*, 23.
38 Georghallides, *A Political and Administrative History of Cyprus*, 14.
39 G.S. Georghallides, 'Churchill's 1907 Visit to Cyprus: A Political Analysis', *Epeteris*, III, 1969–70, 186.
40 G.N. Sanderson, 'The European Partition of Africa: Coincidence or Conjuncture?' *Journal of Imperial and Commonwealth History (JICH)*, III, 1, 1974, 1.
41 R.J. Horvath, 'A Definition of Colonialism', *Current Anthropology*, XIII, 1, 1972, 47.
42 J. Gallagher and R. Robinson, 'The Imperialism of Free Trade,' *The Economic History Review*, VI, 1, 1953, 1–15.
43 Robinson and Gallagher, *Africa and the Victorians*.
44 Edward Dicey, 'Our Empire in the East', *The Nineteenth Century (NC)*, September 1877.
45 John Robert Seeley, *The Expansion of England*, London, 1883, 8–10.
46 J.A. Hobson, *Imperialism*, London, 1900; J.A. Hobson, *The War in South Africa: Its Causes and Effects*, London, 1900.
47 V.I. Lenin, *Imperialism: The Highest Stage of Capitalism*, 1917; N.I. Bukharin, *Imperialism and World Economy*, NY, 1929 (Russian, 1917); L.S. Woolf, *Economic Imperialism*, London, 1920; A. Viallate, *Economic Imperialism and International Relations During the Last Fifty Years*, NY, 1923; R. Lambert, *Modern Imperialism*, London, 1928.
48 Eric Hobsbawm, *The Age of Empire, 1875–1914*, London, 1987 (1994), 66.
49 Robinson and Gallagher, *Africa and the Victorians*; D.K. Fieldhouse, '"Imperialism" – an Historiographical Revision', *Economic History Review*, XIV, 2, 1961–2, 187–209; Sanderson, 'The European Partition of Africa', 10–11.
50 P.J. Cain and A.G. Hopkins, *British Imperialism: Innovation and Expansion, 1688–1914*, London, 1993; 'The Theory and Practise of British Imperialism' in Raymond Dumett (ed.), *Gentlemanly Capitalism and British Imperialism*, London, 1999, 196–220.
51 J.A. Schumpeter, *The Sociology of Imperialism*, 1919 (trans. 1951).
52 David Cannadine, *The Decline and Fall of the British Aristocracy*, New Haven, 1994, 420–5, 558–605.
53 W.L. Langer, *The Diplomacy of Imperialism*, New York, 1935.
54 Jonathon Rose, *The Intellectual Life of the British Working Class*, New Haven, 2002, 321–64.
55 Bernard Porter, '"Empire, what Empire?" Or, Why 80% of Early- and Mid-Victorians were Deliberately kept in Ignorance of it', *Victorian Studies*, XXXXVI, 2, 2004, 256–63.
56 John S. Galbraith, 'The 'Turbulent Frontier' as a Factor in British Expansion', *Comparative Studies in Society and History*, II, 1960, 150–68; D.K. Fieldhouse, '"Imperialism" – an Historiographical Revision', *Economic History Review*, XIV, 2, 1961–62, 187–209.
57 K.L.P. Martin, *Missionaries and Annexations in the Pacific*, London, 1926; Sir Charles Lucas, *Religion, Colonising and Trade, the Driving Forces of the Old Empire*, London, 1930; R.J. Hind, '"We Have No Colonies" – Similarities within the British Imperial Experience', *Comparative Studies in Society and History*, XXVI, 1984, 23; John Laffey, *Imperialism and Ideology*, Montreal, 2000; Catherine Hall, *Civilising Subjects*, Cambridge, 2002.

58 A. Scholch, 'The "Men on the Spot" and the English Occupation of Egypt in 1882', *Historical Journal* (*HJ*), XIX, 3, 1976, 773–85.
59 Robinson and Gallagher, *Africa and the Victorians*.
60 John MacKenzie, 'Lakes, Rivers and Oceans: Technology, Ethnicity and the Shipping of Empire in the Late Nineteenth Century', in David Killingray, Margarette Lincoln and Nigel Rigby (eds), *Maritime Empires: British Imperial Maritime Trade in the Nineteenth Century*, Suffolk, 2004, 111–27.
61 David Killingray, 'Imperial Seas: Cultural Exchange and Commerce in the British Empire, 1780–1900', *Maritime Empires*, 1–12.
62 Schurman, *Imperial Defence 1868–1887*, 152.
63 C.W. Newbury and A.S. Kanya-Forstner, 'French Policy and the Origins of the Scramble for West Africa', *Journal of African History* (*JAH*), X, 1969, 253–76.
64 A.S. Kanya-Forstner, *The Conquest of the Western Sahara: A Study in French Military Imperialism*, Cambridge, 1969; 'French Expansion in Africa: The Mythical Theory', in R. Owen and R. Sutcliffe (eds), *Studies in the Theory of Imperialism*, 1972, 277–94.
65 Kanya-Forstner, 'French Expansion in Africa: The Mythical Theory', 293.
66 Sanderson, 'The European Partition of Africa', 14; Robert L. Tignor, 'Review of *The Conquest of the Western Sahara*', *American Historical Review* (*AHR*), LXXV, 6, 1970, 1755–6.
67 J. Wright, 'Libya: Italy's "Promised Land"', in E.G.H. Joffe and K.S. McLachlan (eds), *Social and Economic Development of Libya*, 1982, 67–79.
68 Clarence Davis and Robert Gowen, 'The British at Weihaiwei: A Case Study in the Irrationality of Empire', *The Historian*, LXIII, 2, 2000, 87–104.
69 Eitan Bar-Yosef, *The Holy Land in English Culture 1799–1917*, Oxford, 2005, 81, 88, 209, 247–94.
70 J.A.R. Marriott, *The Eastern Question*, Oxford, 1924; M.S. Anderson, *The Eastern Question 1774–1923*, London, 1966; G.D. Clayton, *Britain and the Eastern Question*, London, 1971.
71 M. Yapp, *The Making of the Modern Near East*, London, 1987.
72 Ibid.; M. King, *Oil and Empire*, London, 1976, 3–4.
73 Emmanuel Sarides, 'Byron and Greek History', *History Journal Workshop*, XV, 1983, 127.
74 Bernard Wasserstein, *Divided Jerusalem: The Battle for the Holy City*, New Haven, 2001.
75 For Greece refer to the voluminous work of Michael Herzfeld; for Palestine see Bar-Yosef, *The Holy Land in English Culture 1799–1917*.
76 E. Shils, 'The Virtue of Civil Society', *Government and Opposition*, XXVI, 1, 1991, 3–20; E. Shils, 'Nation, Nationality, Nationalism and Civil Society', *Nations and Nationalism* (*NN*), I, 1, 1995, 93–118; S. Grosby, 'The Verdict of History: The Inexpungeable Ties of Primordiality', *Ethnic and Racial Studies* (*ERS*), XVII, 1994, 164–71; S. Grosby, 'Territoriality: The Transcendental, Primordial Feature of Modern Societies', *NN*, I, 2, 1995, 143–62; S. Grosby, *Nationalism: A Very Short Introduction*, Oxford, 2005.
77 J. Armstrong, *Nations before Nationalism*, Chapel Hill, 1982; A. Smith, *The Ethnic Origins of Nations*, Oxford, 1986; A. Hastings, *The Construction of Nationhood*, Cambridge, 1997.
78 Elie Kedourie, *Nationalism*, London, 1960; Ernest Gellner, *Nations and Nationalism*, Oxford, 1983 (quote, 55); B. Anderson, *Imagined Communities*, London, 1983; A. Giddens, *The Nation-state and Violence*, Cambridge, 1985; E. Hobsbawm, 'Introduction: Inventing Traditions', in E. Hobsbawm and T. Ranger (eds), *The Invention of Tradition*, Cambridge, 1989.
79 W. Conner, 'When is a Nation', *ERS*, III, 1990, 92–103; S. Gourgouris, *Dream Nation: Enlightenment, Colonisation, and the Institution of Modern Greece*, California, 1996; W. Conner, 'The Timelessness of Nations', *NN*, X, 1/2, 2004, 34–47.
80 Harry Luke, *The Old Turkey and the New*, London, 1936, 76.

81 Alastos, *Cyprus in History*, this can be seen from the titles of chapters and the titles of the sections to the chapters; Panteli, *A History of Cyprus*, 57–9; Holland, *Britain and the Revolt in Cyprus*, 5–6; Katia Hadjidemetriou, *A History of Cyprus* (trans.) Costas Hadjigeorgiou, Nicosia, 2002, 362–4.
82 K. Karpat, *An Inquiry Into the Social Foundation of Nationalism in the Ottoman State*, Princeton, 1973; R. Davidson, 'Nationalism as an Ottoman Problem and the Ottoman Response', in W. Haddad and W. Ochsenwald (eds), *Nationalism in a Non-National State*, Columbus, 1977, 3–24; Bernard Lewis, *The Multiple Identities of the Middle East*, NY, 1999; M. Yashin (ed.), *Step-Mothertongue From Nationalism to Multiculturalism: Literatures of Cyprus, Greece and Turkey*, London, 2000; S. Anagnostopoulou, *The Passage from the Ottoman Empire to the Nation-States*, Istanbul, 2004.
83 Dipesh Chakrabarty, *Provincializing Europe: Postcolonial Thought and Historical Difference*, New Jersey, 2000, 4.
84 Ibid., 4.
85 Ibid., 4.
86 Ibid., 9.
87 T. Gallant, *Experiencing Dominion: Culture, Identity, and Power in the British Mediterranean*, Indiana, 2002, 16–17.
88 Gallant, *Experiencing Dominion*, 15–55.
89 Edward Said, *Orientalism*, New York, 1978.
90 Gallant, *Experiencing Dominion*, 17.
91 Maria Todorova, 'The Balkans: From Discovery to Invention', *Slavic Review*, 53, 2, 1994, 453–82, 454–5.
92 Gallant, *Experiencing Dominion*, 18–19.
93 R.E. Robinson, 'Non-European Foundations of European Imperialism: Sketch for a Theory of Collaboration', *Studies in the Theory of Imperialism*, 117–42; Hind, 'We Have No Colonies', 3–35; David Cannadine, *Ornamentalism: How the British Saw Their Empire*, London, 2001.
94 J.M. Gullick, *Malaya*, London, 1964, 38–40; Ian Copland, *The British Raj and the Indian Princes*, Bombay, 1982; A. and B Isaacman, 'Resistance and Collaboration in Southern and Central Africa, c.1850–1920' in G. Maddox (ed.), *Conquest and Resistance to Colonialism in Africa*, I, New York, 1993, 113–44; J.D. Graham, 'Indirect Rule: The Establishment of "Chiefs" and "Tribes" in Cameron's Tanganyika', *Conquest and Resistance to Colonialism in Africa*, 23–31.
95 Gallant, *Experiencing Dominion*, 77–8, 92–3.
96 Ibid.
97 Dimitris Xenakis and Dimitris Chryssochoou, *The Emerging Euro-Mediterranean System*, Manchester, 2001, 25–6.
98 Panteli, *A History of Cyprus*, 72.
99 H.C. Gordon, *The War Office*, London, 1935; H.L. Hall, *The Colonial Office: A History*, London, 1937; Z.S. Steiner, *The Foreign Office and Foreign Policy, 1898–1914*, Cambridge, 1969; B.L. Blakeley, *The Colonial Office, 1868–1892*, Durham, 1972; N.A.M. Rodger, *The Admiralty*, Lavenham, 1979; K.M. Wilson (ed.), *British Foreign Secretaries and Foreign Policy: From Crimean War to First World War*, London, 1987.
100 R. Huessler, *Yesterday's Rulers: The Making of the British Colonial Service*, Syracuse, 1963.
101 Stephen Koss, *The Rise and Fall of the Political Press in Britain*, I, London, 1981.
102 David Cannadine, *Aspects of Aristocracy: Grandeur and Decline in Modern Britain*, New Haven, 1994.
103 R.B. Pugh, *The Records of the Colonial and Dominions Offices*, London, 1964, 8–9.
104 Zara Steiner, *The Foreign Office and Foreign Policy, 1898–1914*, Cambridge, 1969.
105 John Gooch, *The Plans of War*, London, 1974; J. Gooch, 'Haldane and the National Army', in I. Beckett and J. Gooch (eds), *Politicians and Defence*, Manchester, 1981, 69–86.
106 J.F. Beeler, *British Naval Policy in the Gladstone-Disraeli Era, 1866–1880*, California, 1997, passim.

107 Roger Owen, *Lord Cromer: Victorian Imperialist, Edwardian Proconsul*, Oxford, 2004.

108 Howard LeRoy Malchow, *Agitators and Promoters in the Age of Gladstone and Disraeli*, New York, 1983; B.H. Harrison, *The Transformation of British Politics, 1860–1995*, Oxford, 1996.

109 Thomas Naff, 'Ottoman Diplomatic Relations with Europe in the Eighteenth Century: Patterns and Trends', in T. Naff and R. Owen (eds), *Studies in Eighteenth Century Islamic History*, 1977, 96–7; Yapp, *The Making of the Modern Near East*, 102.

110 Kemal Karpat, 'The Transformation of the Ottoman State, 1789–1908', *International Journal of Middle East Studies* (*IJMES*), III, 3, 1972, 243–81; Carter Findley, *Bureaucratic Reform in the Ottoman Empire*, Princeton, 1980.

111 Clayton, *Britain and the Eastern Question*, 26–8.

112 R. Hakluyt, *Voyages*, V, Glasgow, 1904, 62–3; A.C. Wood, *A History of the Levant Company*, London, 1964, 2.

113 Wood, *Levant Company*, 2–3.

114 Ibid., 20.

115 Ibid., 168–9.

116 Yapp, *The Making of the Modern Near East*, 102.

117 The Treaty of Defensive Alliance between Russia and the Ottoman Empire, signed at Constantinople, 26 June (8 July) 1833, *Consolidated Treaty Series* (*CTS*), edited and annotated by Clive Parry, New York, 1981; Afaf Lutfi Al-Sayyid-Marsot, *Egypt in the Reign of Muhammad Ali*, Cambridge, 1984; J.C.K. Daly, *Russian Seapower and 'The Eastern Question', 1827–41*, Basingstoke, 1991; Matthew Rendall, 'Restraint or Self-Restraint of Russia: Nicholas I, the Treaty of Unkiar Skelessi, and the Vienna System, 1832–1841', *International History Review* (*IHR*), XXIV, 1, 2002, 37–63.

118 Karpat, 'The Transformation of the Ottoman State, 1789–1908', 243–81; S.J. Shaw, 'The Nineteenth Century Ottoman Tax Reforms and Revenue System', *IJMES*, VI, 4, 1975, 421–59; Zafer Toprak, 'Modernisation and Commercialisation in the *Tanzimat* Period: 1838–1875', *New Perspectives on Turkey*, 7, 1992, 57–70; Sevket Pamuk, 'The Evolution of Financial Institutions in the Ottoman Empire, 1600–1914', *Financial History Review*, XI, 1, 2004, 7–32.

119 Butrus Abu-Manneh, 'The Sultan and the Bureaucracy: The Anti-Tanzimat Concepts of Grand Vizier Mahmud Nedim Pasha', *IJMES*, XXII, 3, 1990, 257–74.

120 C.G.A. Clay, 'Western Banking and the Ottoman Economy before 1890: A Story of Disappointed Expectations', *Journal of European Economic History*, XXVIII, 3, 1999, 473–509.

121 Henry Frendo, *Party Politics in a Fortress Colony: The Maltese Experience*, Malta, 1979, 6; Peter Elliott, *The Cross and the Ensign: A Naval History of Malta 1798–1979*, London, 1980 (1982, 1987), 78.

122 See Chapter 3.

123 Lee, *Great Britain and the Cyprus Convention Policy*, 39–40, 59–65.

124 See Chapter 3.

125 Ibid.

126 See Chapters 3 and 4.

127 Andrekos Varnava, '*Punch* and the British Occupation of Cyprus in 1878', *Byzantine and Modern Greek Studies* (*BMGS*), XXIX, 2, 2005, 167–82.

128 See B.C. Lyssarides, *My Old Acquaintance: Yesterday in Cyprus*, Nicosia 1999, 45–8, 64–72.

129 See Chapter 5.

130 See Chapter 6.

131 See Chapter 6.

132 Diamond Jenness, *The Economics of Cyprus: A Survey to 1914*, Montreal 1962, 118–91.

133 See Chapters 5 and 7.

134 *Pall Mall Gazette*, 15 September 1884; 16 October 1884.

135 A.J. Marder, *The Anatomy of British Sea Power*, London, 1964, 121–2; Schurman, *Imperial Defence*, 130–1, 135–6.

136 Varnava, 'Maintaining Britishness', 1127–8.
137 See Chapter 7.
138 A.G. Harfield, 'The Cyprus Pioneer Corps and the Cyprus Military Police During 1879–1882', *Bulletin Military Historical Society*, XXVI, 101, 1975, 1–8; A.G. Harfield, 'British Military Presence in Cyprus in the 19th Century', *Journal of the Society for Army Historical Research*, 1978, 160–70.
139 See Chapter 7.
140 Robert Kubicek, 'Joseph Chamberlain, the Treasury and Imperial Development, 1895–1903', *The Canadian Historical Association*, 1965, 105–16.
141 Anagnostopoulou, *The Passage from the Ottoman Empire to the Nation-States*, 191–3.
142 See Chapter 6.
143 See Chapter 6.
144 G.S Georghallides, 'Churchill's 1907 Visit to Cyprus', 167–220.
145 P.J.V. Rolo, *Entente Cordiale*, London, 1969, 205–70, passim.
146 See Chapters 6, 7 and 8.
147 S. Deringil, *The Well-Protected Domains*, London, 1998.
148 Frank Weber, *Eagles on the Crescent*, Ithaca and London, 1970.
149 See Chapter 8.
150 Richard Clogg, *A Short History of Modern Greece*, Cambridge, 1986, 103.
151 See Chapter 8.

CHAPTER 2

Cyprus from Richard *Coeur de Lion* to Disraeli: the imperial imagination

Europe in 1860

Victoria I, Queen of the United Kingdoms of Great Britain and Ireland, India, and Mesopotamia, acquires the Island of Cyprus and the course of the Euphrates, which is the shortest road from the British Islands to the Great Indies.

The change to Britain according to a map 'Il Europe en 1860', circulated in Paris.

(*The Times*, 14 February 1859, 14ff.)

Europeans, in driving towards Jerusalem during the Crusader centuries, construed the Mediterranean as part of their space and the Enlightenment and Romantic movements reinforced this conviction. This chapter traces the links between England/Britain and Cyprus since Richard *Coeur de Lion* and situates these links within a tradition of Romantic adventure, strategic advantage, spiritual imperialism and a sense of possession. Cyprus occupied a romantic and strategic place within this English and later British imagined imperial space. Many Britons saw the island as the ideal place to establish a stronghold from which to project British power in the eastern Mediterranean. As the epigraph shows, the British occupation of Cyprus was predicted nearly twenty years before it happened and, as will be shown, this prediction was based on the imperial imagination of Benjamin Disraeli, who was eventually responsible for its occupation.

Richard I and the Crusader tradition

Of all the English monarchs, Richard I was the most romanticised and, with the exception of the mythical King Arthur, the most fictionalised. References to Levant trade and the Crusader story were accessible in seventeenth-century England,[1] but the 'chivalric revival' of the

Romantic period secured Richard's place in British culture and identity as a gallant and chivalrous soldier. It began with Sir Walter Scott's *Ivanhoe* (1819), the story of a Saxon noble family at a time when the nobility was overwhelmingly Norman. The Saxon protagonist, Wilfred of Ivanhoe, is ostracised by his father because of his allegiance to the Norman king Richard I, who is secretly returning from the Crusades amidst the plotting of his brother, Prince John. Scott shaped the modern notion of Robin Hood as a cheerful and chivalrous outlaw and popularised his linking with Richard. This became a cardinal point on the script of the British nation. Eleanor Anne Porden then wrote a historical epic poem, *Coeur de Lion, or The Third Crusade* (1822), which recounts Richard's adventures on the Third Crusade. Three years later Scott returned to Richard in *The Talisman* (1825), which finds a sick king being prevented from completing the crusade because of schemers within the alliance. Scott's historical novels were enormously popular as cheap editions sold well throughout the nineteenth century.[2] Every British child that had an education grew up with the chivalric ethos and Richard's 'story' as it was disseminated through such popular fiction (Scott inspired other authors, G.A. Henty, *Winning his Spurs* (1882) and Rider Haggard, *The Brethren* (1904)), illustrated journals, societies and schools.[3] Cyprus has an important place in this story. In May 1191 Richard, before going to 'liberate' the Holy Land, seized Cyprus and married Berengaria of Navarre at Limassol.[4]

In 1912 *The Times* claimed that Richard had planned to use Limassol as his *point d'appui*,[5] but traditionally historians and the popular 'story' claimed that he had not planned to stop at, let alone conquer, Cyprus.[6] This fits well into the chivalric ethos. A recent biographer of Richard I convincingly argued that he did plan to take the island,[7] smashing the myth that he occupied the island when storms forced him to stop there and when Cyprus' ruler Isaac Comnenos' treatment of Berengaria and Joan, Richard's sister, forced him to defend his honour. In the wider scheme of spiritual imperialism, strategic imperialism became a necessity. Isaac, the self-proclaimed 'emperor' of Cyprus and the great-nephew of the Byzantine Emperor, Manuel Comnenos, had rebelled against Constantinople in 1183.[8] Richard wanted him removed because he suspected that Isaac had a pact with Saladin.[9] Cyprus was assured a romantic place in British history after Richard routed Isaac's forces. Images of Isaac begging for mercy continued into the nineteenth century, such as in Cassell's encyclopaedia edition of 1898. Richard seized much of Isaac's treasure, including his imperial standard, which he dedicated to St Edmund and placed on his sepulchre in Suffolk.[10] After marrying Berengaria at the chapel of St George, he was crowned King of Cyprus and she Queen of Cyprus and England. Thus, Cyprus became the first and only location outside Britain for a wedding and a coronation of an English monarch.

Cyprus became a valuable supply and fallback base to crusaders. Weeks after leaving Cyprus, Richard sold it to the Knights Templar for 100,000 bezants; 40,000 were paid up front. But they could not handle the Orthodox Christian population and a year later begged Richard to take it back. He, unable to repay them, sold it to Guy of Lusignan, a French nobleman and titular King of Jerusalem, who had helped him seize Cyprus. The Lusignan dynasty ruled for nearly 300 years, when, for as long as there were crusades, Cyprus acted as their base. In 1249, France's King Louis IX wintered there before going to the Seventh Crusade with Henry I, the King of Cyprus.[11] In 1268, Hugh III claimed the title of King of Jerusalem and in 1271 Edward I stayed with him before they went to war. In 1291, the Hospitallers and Templars retreated to Cyprus after Acre fell. The island was the sole outpost of western Christendom in the eastern Mediterranean until the Hospitallers seized Rhodes in 1310. When the Pope dissolved the Templars in 1312, Limassol virtually became a Hospitaller fief. Cyprus was a base for the capture of Smyrna in 1344.[12]

In the thirteenth century few in England were ignorant of the crusading movement and even the poor who joined it were passionate about reaching Jerusalem.[13] The Holy Land was internalised and because Cyprus belonged within this context, it also was. There were English claims to Cyprus during Lusignan rule, which were repeated in 1878. Roger of Howden, the royal clerk of Henry II who had accompanied Richard on the Third Crusade, claimed that Richard had given Cyprus to Guy only for the remainder of his life. The thirteenth-century author of *The Crusade and Death of Richard I* believed this and the fourteenth-century compiler of the Meaux Chronicle claimed that the Lusignans held Cyprus as an English dependency.[14] Hepworth Dixon, a journalist and traveller, claimed this in 1879 and thought this explained why Guy was not crowned king: 'Cyprus, in the view of English king and English council . . . never ceased to be an English fief . . . [because Cyprus] never passed legitimately from the jurisdiction of the English crown.'[15] But Henry of Champagne, to whom Richard had ceded his rights to Cyprus, cancelled them as part of the dowries of his three daughters, who married the three sons of Amaury, Guy's brother and successor, whom Emperor Henry VI crowned king.[16]

English royalty and the Lusignans were close, but the latter were subordinate to the former. In 1256, Henry III negotiated the marriage of his second son, Edmund, to Plaisance, the Queen of Cyprus and regent of the Kingdom.[17] During the reign of Edward I (1272–1307), the Lusignan arms were included in English armorials,[18] illustrating the political link between Cyprus and England. In 1363, Peter I of Cyprus visited England to muster support for a new crusade. Edward III amused him at a tournament at Smithfield and Henry Picard, London's mayor, entertained Peter, Edward, France's Jean I, Denmark's Waldemar and Scotland's David in the 'Feast of the Five Kings'. Edward allowed some of his best soldiers to participate and demanded Cyprus if Peter took Jerusalem.[19] Peter failed, but did temporarily seize Alexandria in 1365 – a feat that gave him a place in Chaucer's celebrated *The Canterbury Tales*. Edward's claim to the island shows the continuity of Cyprus in the English imperial imagination. In 1392, his grandson, Henry Bolingbroke, twice visited Cyprus[20] and four years later, Richard II, also a grandson of Edward's (Bolingbroke overthrew him in 1399), sent a diplomatic mission to Cyprus. Edward IV included the Lusignan arms of Cyprus in his wife's shield.[21] Then James I erected a monument for Elizabeth I in the chapel of Henry VII and included the arms of Cyprus in the shield with those of England, France and six other kingdoms.[22]

Western European orbit

In the late fifteenth century, Cyprus came under Venetian control and they modernised the fortifications and built new ones – the most sophisticated yet built by Europeans. At Famagusta they spent enormous amounts to replace the walls and construct new bastions.[23] Nevertheless, the fortifications only withstood the Ottoman onslaught for a year.

English Orientalist texts of the Elizabethan era fed the imperial imagination. Shakespeare's *Othello* was a tale of conflict on the Christian–Muslim frontier with an Oriental mercenary, who did not belong to his adopted Occidental land, trying to hold out against the Muslims during the Ottoman conquest of Famagusta in 1571.[24] Although *Othello* is not remembered for its military setting, Shakespeare understood the geopolitics of the day and had one of the senators say: 'when we consider the importancy of Cyprus to the Turk'.[25] With the European failure to hold Cyprus, Shakespeare was depicting the incompatibility of the Occidental and Oriental Mediterranean through Othello and the tragedy of the two lovers. *Othello* was a very popular play during the Victorian era. In 1861, when Charles Fechter and John Ryder alternated the roles of Othello and Iago, the *Illustrated London New* published 'Scenes from *Othello* at the Princess Theatre: The Town and Harbour of Cyprus'.[26] The scene, however, had nothing to do with the geographical reality of Famagusta harbour, but the imagined setting. If the Crusades and the Lusignan kingdom had brought Cyprus closer to English people, its Ottoman conquest achieved the opposite. The Ottomans were advanced in many ways, but closed Cyprus to the West and represented an 'otherness'. It was left to the imagination as Cyprus was incorporated within the Victorian spectacle every time *Othello* was played.

Western European kingdoms with a connection to Cyprus dreamt of retaking it from the Ottomans. In the seventeenth century, some members of the Cypriot Orthodox clergy appealed to Savoy's Charles Emmanuel and Tuscany's Ferdinand I to seize Cyprus in exchange for recognising the rights of the Orthodox Church. Louis, the Count of Savoy, had become titular King of Cyprus after his marriage to Anne Lusignan, the daughter of Janus, Cyprus' king (1398–1432). His second son and namesake married Charlotte, Queen of Cyprus (1458–64). The title was transferred to subsequent dukes of Savoy so when Charles Emmanuel agreed he was merely trying to reclaim what was his; yet he abandoned the project.[27] The Duke of Tuscany sent a fleet to Famagusta in 1607, having determined to use Cyprus for operations in the Near East, but it turned back.[28] In 1604, Sir Anthony Sherley, an English adventurer and Spanish spy, told Spain's King Philip III to occupy Cyprus to protect interests in Algiers and a report was prepared two years later on invading Cyprus.[29] In 1630 Henry, Duke of Rohan, the Protestant leader under Louis XIII, discussed buying Cyprus with the Oecumenical Patriarch, but the venture did not materialise. Then in 1669, Bernardin Gigault de Bellefords, one of Louis XIV's marshals, devised a plan to seize Cyprus for France and the Duke of Savoy, but nothing came of it.[30] Cyprus, despite the West's claim to it, remained Ottoman.

British men on the spot and the break-up of the Ottoman Empire

Cyprus' appeal for the West remained when, in the mid-eighteenth century, Ottoman stagnation provided European powers with the opportunity to partition it. In 1772 Russia and Austria aligned against the Porte and the Austrian chancellor Prince von Kaunitz proposed to partition the Ottoman Empire, with Crete, Cyprus, the Morea and certain Aegean islands going to a king of Austria's choice.[31] Russia would control a Greek kingdom, but another plan allowed for Habsburg control, with Cyprus going to Venice.[32] Catherine the Great encouraged Russian expansion into the Aegean and in 1782 proposed to create a Greek empire from Peloponnesus to Albania with Constantinople as the capital and Venice taking Cyprus.[33] In 1790, *The Times* reported that negotiations for commercial treaties were taking place in Constantinople and England would receive Cyprus.[34] Schemes for Western European expansion at Ottoman expense were a part of the Eastern Question and they positioned Cyprus in the Western, not the Greek, orbit.

The British interest in Cyprus came from 'men on the spot', not from the government, and especially from East India and Levant Company employees, who wanted to safeguard the route to India and increase trade. Cyprus was significant in trade: in January 1785, it exported 1900 lbs of raw silk to London, compared with 600 lbs from Alexandretta and 450 lbs from Smyrna.[35] While residing in Cyprus (1760–73), George Baldwin, a Levant Company merchant, suggested linking the Mediterranean and Red seas in August 1771.[36] In the early 1790s, John Taylor, a captain in the Bombay Establishment, proposed opening communications via Suez by acquiring Cyprus.[37] These men emphasised the importance of the eastern Mediterranean to India.

France knew its importance too and ordered Napoleon to take Egypt as a prelude to moving on India. When Lord Nelson stopped him, Napoleon turned on Syria. In August 1798, *The Times* reported that Napoleon planned to attack Aleppo from Cyprus.[38] Nelson sent Captain Hood to report on the island's harbours and obtain bullocks, lemons and onions.[39] Nelson was informed that 'the best anchorage' and place for procuring produce was Larnaca, where the English vice-consul could assist.[40]

Then an extraordinary event occurred that demonstrates the power of historical continuity. In May 1799, the flamboyant Sir William Sydney Smith, commander of the *Tigre* and the brother of the British ambassador to Constantinople, Spencer Smith, raised the siege of Acre, thwarting Napoleon's Syrian venture. As a reward, the Sultan commissioned him to command his forces and patrol the eastern Mediterranean.[41] In July *The Times* reported that there had been a violent insurrection in Cyprus and taxpayers had been massacred.[42] Then, in November, Smith intervened after janissaries murdered the Ottoman vice-admiral.[43]

> I landed on the instant, and exercising the delegated authority of Sultan Selim, as if he had been there . . . and wearing his imperial aigrette or plume of triumph, I restored order by re-establishing the hierarchy of authority and causing the disbanded troops to go down to the beach, like sly slinking wolves.[44]

The Archbishop of Cyprus, Chrysanthos, received Smith as a saviour and hung on him a cross that he claimed was the 'Templar Cross' of Richard I.[45] The event shows the power of historical continuity from a local dimension.

Through war Britain had won many vantage points, some of which were converted into naval or coaling stations. The French threat found strategists wanting more. For one, collecting islands was almost a hobby. John Barrow, a self-taught navigator and geographer (remembered for *Mutiny on the Bounty*) and a secretary to the admiralty (1804–46, with a break in 1806–07), advocated pre-emptive territorial aggrandisement to expand the empire by occupying way-stations to protect the shipping routes on which he believed British power rested.[46] He advocated taking Malta, Sicily, Crete, the Ionian Islands, Zanzibar, King George Sound, Western Port, Melville Island, New Zealand, Fernando Po, Ceylon, Singapore, Hawaii, the Ryukyu Islands and the Falklands.[47] Britain occupied all but two (Crete and the Ryukyu): some temporarily, others only informally, and most during Barrow's lifetime. The only island Barrow did not want was Cyprus.

It was left to John Macdonald Kinneir, a captain in the East India Company and a diplomat, to propose that idea. He visited Cyprus from 2 to 24 January 1814 and asserted:

> Cyprus would give to England a preponderating influence in the Mediterranean, and place at her disposal the future destinies of the Levant. Egypt and Syria would soon become her tributaries, and she would acquire an overawing position in respect to Asia Minor, by which the Porte might at all times be kept in check, and the encroachments of Russia, in this quarter, retarded, if not prevented. It would increase her commerce in a very considerable degree; give her the distribution of the rich wines, silks and other produce of that fine island; the rice and sugar of Egypt, and the cotton, opium and tobacco of Anatolia. It is of easy defence; and under a liberal government would, in a very short space of time, amply repay the charge of its own establishment, and afford the most abundant supplies to our fleets at a trifling expense.[48]

In the same year, Captain Henry Light of the Royal Artillery at Malta, visited Egypt and Cyprus and echoed Kinneir. He asserted that if Cyprus was wrested from the Ottomans it

> would soon become a flourishing country: the population would be increased by swarms of Greek emigrants from Asia Minor . . . [who] would soon fertilise the barren waste overrunning . . . half the island. The unwholesomeness of the air may be remedied by draining the marshes that cause it. In the time of the Venetians this was done, and the malaria was not felt. Circumstances may hereafter oblige Great Britain to strengthen herself in the Mediterranean; and for the richness of soil and general advantages to be derived from it, Cyprus may be considered more valuable to her than either Syria or Egypt.[49]

But Whitehall wanted to maintain Ottoman territorial integrity and did not aid Greek insurgents against Ottoman rule in the 1820s, despite the strong Philhellene climate in London and Paris. In December 1821, ten Cypriot Orthodox notables, who had escaped to Europe after the governor's massacre, issued a manifesto pledging to free Cyprus and sent agents to European capitals to raise funds. In 1823 General Comte Demetrius de Wintz, a Montenegrin, was asked to raise a loan and head an expedition.[50] Thomas Love Peacock, the poet, Philhellene and an official in the East India Company, aided him. Louis Comtesse, a London watchmaker helped by asking a Mississippi landowner to get a loan in Paris to cover the expeditionary force.[51] But they were disorganised.[52] Then in May 1826, Laisné Villévéque, a French Philhellene and Orleanist, proposed to Lord Granville, the British Ambassador to Paris, that Britain seize Cyprus and Moldovia. Prime Minister George Canning thought it 'wild and absurd . . . [because] both imply acts of war' and he wanted to 'avoid any new disturbance of the peace'.[53]

During the Greek insurrection, Cyprus was under Egyptian occupation. In 1827 when Captain Charles Frankland came to Larnaca he found Cyprus was uncultivated because of 'the rapacity and tyranny of the government' and the Cypriots 'ripe for revolt upon the appearance of . . . an auxiliary force', but Muhammad Ali was 'a formidable obstacle'.[54] The British worried about Muhammad Ali's power, but the French wanted him to extend it. In 1829 the Baron Félix de Beaujour claimed that it 'would be better to attack Syria by sea than from Egypt', but Cyprus was needed because

> Cyprus is to Syria what Zante is to the Morea; it would serve as a depot for the army and a harbour for the fleet. Larnaca and Famagusta are the most favourable points for naval stations.[55]

So Muhammad Ali believed. After his son Ibrahim defeated the Ottomans in Syria in 1832, he demanded independence, and Syria, Crete and Cyprus.[56] William Engel thought that without Cyprus and Syria he could not 'assure the independence and stability of his realm'.[57] The Sultan then offered Cyprus and Crete in pawn to England to negotiate peace with Muhammad Ali,[58] but Britain declined to intervene. Russia did not, forcing Muhammad Ali to abandon his claims to Cyprus, though he kept Crete. Engel believed that Cyprus 'might have suited him better'.[59] Whitehall may not have been so unwilling to intervene had it known that the Ottomans would turn to Russia. In the 1830s, London tried to overturn the Russo-Ottoman alliance of Unkiar Skelessi. The chance came in 1839 when Britain joined Russia to aid the Sultan against Muhammad Ali. The British seized Acre and Syria, using Malta and Cyprus as bases.[60]

In 1924 the Foreign Office clerk and historian, Sir James Headlam-Morley, wrote that there was a 'curious proposal' for Britain to annex Cyprus and Acre in 1840–41 as payment for helping defeat

Muhammad Ali, which 'met with wide approval in England'.[61] Few historians mention this,[62] and none has explored it. A British journal advocated Cyprus' occupation,[63] irritating a French counterpart. Lord Palmerston had isolated France with the Convention of 15 July 1840. In October, Francois-Pierre-Guillaume Guizot, who had warned that France would be isolated if it supported Muhammad Ali, formed a government.[64] In November 1840 *La Presse* published a letter from Beirut claiming that London had obtained a mortgage on Cyprus from the Porte as compensation.[65] *The Times* attacked the French for criticising the British suggestion to retain Acre and Cyprus.[66] The French worried about the British dominating the eastern Mediterranean and consolidating their Indian empire,[67] so Guizot wanted a guarantee from the European Powers for communications between the Mediterranean and the Red Sea.[68]

Ludwig Ross, a German archaeologist who discovered the Parthenon's substructure, corroborated the story. When visiting Cyprus in February 1845, the Muslims feared that the Porte would compensate Britain with Cyprus.[69] The English Consul, Niven Kerr, told him that the rumours originated in 1840 when Rashid Pasha, the Grand Vizier, advised the Sultan to seek a loan from English merchants. The Porte offered its customs dues if Palmerston guaranteed its borders. The bankers thought it unprofitable administering so many custom houses, so the Porte offered Cyprus, Crete and Mytilene. But Whitehall feared that their annexation would alienate the other powers.[70] Nevertheless, Ottoman insecurity remained an issue and Engel thought that

> under the new sun which appears to be rising in the east, Cyprus too will spring to new life and prosper ... It will acquire a substantial influence, not as an independent state, but as a prop of supremacy in the Eastern end of the Mediterranean ... [for] the Egyptian ... a new Asiatic, or to the newly founded Hellenic kingdom – the last alternative, I think, being the most to be desired.[71]

The British architects that selected Cyprus in 1878 believed it would be such a prop to British interests, while Greek nationalists considered it an unredeemed part of Greece.

Greece and the Holy Land

There are perhaps two ways of looking at cultural imperialism: as the practice of promoting and introducing the cultural and social traditions of one people on to another people(s) through formal or informal imperial/colonial domination; and the involvement of imperial powers in the cultural and political making of communities, because of their historical importance to the cultural identity of the imperial power. Eric Hinderaker believed that empire was 'a cultural artefact as well as a geopolitical entity; it belongs to a geography of the mind as well as a geography of power'.[72] Before him, Kathleen Wilson had shown that even before 1775, in Britain, an awareness of empire had penetrated beyond the ruling classes and those involved in colonial trade.[73] Linda Colley argued that the English had viewed their American empire as a cultural, political and religious extension of themselves, but when it was lost, the imperial structure shifted from the West, despite settler colonies in Australia, New Zealand and Canada, to the East. The empire was primarily non-Christian and non-white – Oriental and not Occidental.[74]

In *Orientalism*, Edward Said argued that the corpus of travel writings on the East from the late eighteenth century was a prefabricated construct ('Orientalism') that eroded the Orient into one of the West's 'deepest and most recurring images of the Other'. The Orient signified a system of representations framed by Western political forces that brought it into the Western consciousness and imperial ethos. For Europeans the Orient was the 'Other', the contrasting identity of the West. Orientalism was the Orient's image expressed as an entire system of thought, scholarship and representation.[75] Possession of such a vast and alien empire resulted in the British contrasting themselves with these 'other' people and seeing themselves as special and superior. Whatever their ethnic background, the British united behind its empire and acted the roles of the heroic conqueror, just ruler and civiliser of the native.[76] The dark and mysterious 'Other' was attractive and trying to define it was empowering. Also, Europeans sought reinvigoration by defining and exploring the East.[77]

The Orient had a special place within a Western European – primarily British and French – imperial imagination. With respect to the Near East – the cradle of civilisation – this imagination rested on the area being Europe's spiritual ancestor. Thus it was familiar and not Europe's opposite. The creation of a unitary ideal of ancient Greece during the Enlightenment and the relationship with the Holy Land, the Bible and the crusading legacy evolved during the Romantic period, form the essentials of British identity.[78] Trade had brought travellers to the Near East for many centuries, but interest in the region grew further when France and Britain fought over the eastern Mediterranean in the 1790s. In the early nineteenth century, the 'Grand Tour', which young, educated upper-class males had been making to the Near East since the middle of the seventeenth century in order to see at first hand the cultural artefacts of antiquity, began to take on a more spiritual meaning.[79] Bernard Wasserstein claimed that the diplomatic intrigues between the French, Germans, English, Greeks and Russians from the sixteenth to the nineteenth century were intended to achieve 'spiritual imperialism' or religious primacy over a city that was holy to all of the monotheistic faiths.[80] Changed attitudes towards Islam during the Enlightenment also attracted European interest in the region.[81] Spiritual imperialism should not, however, be associated only with religion, but also with classical spiritualism and the appropriation of ancient Greece to European identity. Thus, the Orientalist framework rests not only the study of the Orient, but also the imperialism and cultural identity of Europe. So, as Bar-Yosef observed, Orientalism can narrativise something that is 'outside' as being unequivocally 'inside'.[82]

Where the Orient begins and the Occident ends is vital to the situating of the Near East in the Orientalist framework, and for Cyprus this is interesting because it resists any clear-cut division between Orient and Occident, belonging to both and yet to neither. The British associated Cyprus with two traditions essential to British identity and, as shown, these were incompatible. The first was the Holy Land or Crusader imagination, which was spiritual and strategic in its imperial manifestation; the second was the Hellenic, which was intellectual and cultural as well as political, since during the Enlightenment, Europe appropriated ancient Greece into Europe's forerunner. Cyprus' Ottoman legacy was suppressed as alien to the imagination of the island.

Thus, for most, the 'Other' in the case of the Near East was 'familiar'. In the late eighteenth century Ottoman-ruled Greece attracted many European visitors, including Frederick North, the son of Lord North – one of the longest serving British prime ministers (1770–82). North became a Philhellene during his tour of the Ionian Islands (then under Venetian rule) and Greece from 1791 to 1792. While living in Ithaca, visions of scenes from Homer's *Odyssey* stirred his imagination. In January 1792, he was secretly received into the Orthodox Church. This meant that when he entered Parliament upon his father's death later that year he was the first Orthodox Christian to do so. North left Parliament two years later and became the first governor of Ceylon, until 1805 when Sir Thomas Maitland relieved him due to ill-health.

Returning to Europe, his mission became to spread Western education to 'Greece'. In 1814 he was elected president of the Philomousis Society of Athens and in his acceptance address in Attic Greek he called himself 'an Athenian citizen'. In 1820 he became the Director of Education in the Ionian Islands, now under British protection, and he established the Ionian Academy, despite opposition from Maitland, the Lord High Commissioner.[83] Lord Guilford, as North became, was one of the first of many Philhellenes who recreated a modern Greece on the back of the unitary ideal of ancient Greece. In 1810 he met Lord Byron in Patras, who was to become one of the greatest Philhellenes of all. Byron visited the Near East during 1809–11, and in 1815, and his poetry expressed an idealised view of the nation through dispossessed Greeks and Jews (also Armenians), whose ancestors had formed the Hellenic and Hebrew pillars of civilisation, to which Europe, he thought, must turn for regeneration.[84]

So who really discovered 'Greece'? The West did. In the 1820s the 'Greek War of Independence' against the Ottoman Turk captured the imagination of many in London and Paris. The people of future Greece were multi-ethnic, multi-religious and multi-lingual, bearing the name of Greeks to Europeans because they adhered to the Orthodox Church, which had preserved the Greek language. Aside from the language, the rest was in the West's imagination. During the Enlightenment, when the West turned to ancient Greece (and Rome) for inspiration, Orthodox Christians educated in the West suddenly became Greeks and began to ask: 'if Greece was the cradle of modern civilisation, how could the West allow it to be ruled by its opposite, the oriental Turk'? Philhellenes and westernised Greeks first called for Greece's creation. Thus, it is wrong to assert that Greeks – aside from those 'enlightened' by Western thought – fought for a Greek nation.[85]

Greece is not an example of spiritual imperialism in the religious sense, but in a classical sense. Europe created a unitary ideal of an ancient Greece that came to represent the cradle of modern intellectual and political cultural identity. It then created a unitary ideal of a modern Greece. Napoleon planned to create 'natural' borders for France and to this end planned a number of 'satellite' republics – the Bavarian, Illyrian, Neapolitan, the Hellenic and others. His defeat ended these plans, but not the idea of a dependent Greece. Although at first British politicians did not want a Greek state, the increase in Russian influence in the Balkans after 1815 and Russian talk of recreating a Byzantine Empire required the propagation of an alternative concept, like the renaissance of classical Greece. The intellectual climate in Western Europe was favourable to such a project. The Russian intervention against the Ottomans in 1827, while the Greek revolt raged, drew London and Paris into bringing the scheme to birth.[86] Modern Greece became one of the prime examples of the fall motif – a reincarnation of the fallen ancient Greece – and a model of Europe, which had 'rediscovered' it.[87] Byron's death at Messolonghi was formed into a cardinal point on the script of the Greek nation. The European creation of a modern Greece presents a case of spiritual imperialism, but, as shown in Chapter 6, it also presents the most striking example of the problem of the dichotomy that is the 'Orient' and the 'Occident', because it denies the Ottoman influence on the modern Greeks.[88] In its imperial manifestation this imagination seeks to unearth a classical European past beneath the Muslim reality.

The British situated Cyprus within this classical Greek imagination. Indeed as early as the 1820s Byron associated Cyprus with ancient Greece. In *Don Juan: Canto the Fifth* verse XCVI he speaks of a Venus rising from the waves with Paphian eyes, in reference to Venus or Aphrodite rising from the waves off Paphos, while in *Canto the Eleventh* verse XXX he writes of 'pedestrian Paphians' (female street entertainers or prostitutes) in reference to the attendants of Aphrodite.

The second stream in the European imagination of spiritual imperialism, the Holy Land, held more possessive undertones through the Christian and biblical tradition, and because of the place of the Crusades, a failed imperial venture, in British identity. Undoubtedly, the Holy Land is the region most associated with Holy scripture, but Cyprus also has significant connections to the Bible and early Christian history. The Apostle St Barnabas (who was a Hellenised Jew of Cyprus) and Saul converted the Roman proconsul, Sergius Paulus, to Christianity; and thereafter Saul took the name of Paul. St Barnabas' remains were subsequently found in Cyprus, allowing the Church of Cyprus to become independent, while he is a popular saint in the Anglican Church, with sixteen churches dedicated to him in London, and hundreds more across the country.[89]

Colley has shown that Protestant culture and the conviction that Britain was God's favoured nation – the New Israel – shaped the construction of Britain's imperial culture.[90] More recently, Bar-Yosef argued that in the late eighteenth and early nineteenth centuries the biblical imagery fell back on the geographical space from which it originated because of the increase in trade, travel and war. The Holy Land suddenly had a new place within a British imperial vision.[91] This owed a great deal to the persistence of English millenarianism throughout the eighteenth century and its ascendancy with the French Revolution and the Napoleonic Wars.[92] Converting Jews to Christianity and relocating them to the Holy Land were the vital elements in this apocalyptic design.[93] There were many self-styled prophets, who were convinced of their duty to lead the children of Israel in rebuilding Jerusalem. With the war in the eastern Mediterranean, Palestine's strategic importance as the eastern terminus of a land passage to India became central to millenarian calculations and it was expected that the Jews would remain indebted to the British for restoring them to Jerusalem.[94] Although there were few Jews in Cyprus, its location to Jerusalem dictated its strategic appeal and it was a usual stop before a traveller reached the Holy Land.[95]

One traveller to the Near East in the 1830s, who projected the spiritual imperialism about Cyprus through the Holy Land context, was Benjamin Disraeli. Romanticism and Byron had influenced Disraeli; in the 1820s, he started wearing eye-catching dress, with ruffled shirts, velvet trousers, coloured waistcoats, jewellery, and his hair in cascades of ringlets.[96] A Christianised Jew with an aristocratic Sephardic (Jews who had prospered in Muslim Spain and Portugal) heritage, Disraeli had an ambiguous status in British society. The Orient fascinated him, perhaps because he was, in his eyes and in those of most others, an Oriental. Disraeli, although inconsistent with many of his principles, consistently expressed pride in belonging to the Jewish race, which he understood to be Oriental.[97]

Recently, Ivan Davidson Kalmar has argued that Disraeli's vision of the Orient informed not only his personal identity and his fiction, but also his policies as a politician.[98] Cyprus did not figure much in Kalmar's analysis and yet it constitutes a very significant component of his thesis.

In 1830, Disraeli's Grand Tour to the Near East was an attempt to resolve the contradictions in his identity – his Jewish and Anglican/ English identities.[99] He marvelled at the grandeur of Ali Pasha's court in Ioannina and life in Constantinople, which was 'an Oriental tale of enchantment'.[100] Yet, it was not the Orient that he was discovering that excited him, but the imagined Orient he brought with him that produced a sense of belonging. This was reflected in his statements on Cyprus, where he spent a day: it is a 'land famous in all ages, but more delightful to me as the residence of Fortunatus, than as the rosy realm of Venus, or the romantic Kingdom of the Crusaders.'[101] The two contrasting imaginations, the pagan Grecian and the Christian Crusader, were acknowledged despite the lesser-known German story delighting Disraeli more.

Disraeli's tour informed most of his novels, which the 'educated' classes, including the Queen, widely read, although there were no best-sellers.[102] Disraeli drew on Near East themes to ideologically position himself on prominent political issues of the 1840s.[103] In *Contarini Fleming* (1832) the protagonist wants Oriental languages to replace Greek – Latin being the language students mostly favoured and found easier to learn. In *The Wondrous Tale of Alroy* (1833) a twelfth-century Middle East Jew faced the dilemma of establishing a purely Jewish regime or a larger multi-religious empire. But it was in *Tancred: or, The New Crusade* (1847), which sold 2,250 copies,[104] where he outlined the role of the region in his imperial ideology. *Tancred* was the last part of a trilogy after *Coningsby* and *Sybil*, which linked domestic, social and political reform with a fantastically grand imperial synthesis.[105]

In *Tancred* Disraeli's imperial vision in the Near East harked back to the Crusades. The book's title refers to a 'new crusade' and the name Tancred connects it to two figures linked to the Crusades: Tancred of Tauteville (1072–1112), who started the crusades in the eleventh century and later became regent of the Principality of Antioch and Prince of Galilee; and Tancred, the King of Sicily, who was forced to support the Third Crusade.[106] It is not clear which figure Disraeli had in mind, but he connects his story to the Third Crusade. *Tancred's* protagonist, Tancred Montacute, a young English aristocrat, had an ancestor, Tancred de Montacute, who participated in Richard's crusade, and had saved Richard's life at the siege of Ascalon. His namesake, six centuries later, wishes to repeat the moment when he visits the Holy Land and experiences a 'direct' connection with God.

Disraeli's desire to bring the Near East into the British imperial structure was a 'new crusade'. Tancred Montacute sets out on a mystical quest through the Holy Land (like Disraeli) to acquire spiritual sustenance from the Semites. Disraeli identifies the quest with the salvation of the West/Europe from materialism, which he thought could come only through the aristocracy rediscovering the Oriental (Semitic) knowledge to which the West/Europe owed its foundation. The novel proposes, through a Syrian prince, the creation of a greater Syria of Arabs, Assyrians and Jews, because they have a common Jewish past, under the Empress of India, Queen Victoria.[107] The Near East's linking to India would provide economic advantages for the middle class and work for the working class. Disraeli was advocating expansion as an inevitable extension of the British governing structures.[108] In *Tancred*, Disraeli proposed to solve British societal tensions by placing them in an imperial framework,[109] more specifically, a cultural and spiritual framework, by uniting England with Asia. In the fifth edition of *Tancred* (1849), Disraeli attached a preface which discusses Asia's importance to Europe in terms of Christianity's Jewish origins. Disraeli was clarifying to those readers that may not have understood the meaning of *Tancred*, namely that Judaism was the seed of European civilisation.[110] So Disraeli was not talking about making the Holy Land more Christian or Occidental, but Christianity and the Occident more Oriental. As Kalmar asserted, Disraeli offered a union of the Chosen People of the Bible with the modern chosen people of England.[111] Daniel Bivona claimed that Disraeli located orientalist fantasy in something resembling a Near East whose politics, society and culture he appropriated to English political categories.[112] Said thought that *Tancred* was not 'merely an orientalist lark but an exercise in the astute political management of actual forces on actual territories'.[113] These regions, as Bivona claims, were mired in a peculiar Disraelian vision of them.[114]

Bar-Yosef argued that by the 1870s *Tancred* was no longer judged aesthetically but merely as an extension of Disraeli's foreign policy.[115] This much quoted, yet never contextualised, statement of a Disraeli character in *Tancred*, can now be understood as his conception of Cyprus within this imperial framework: '. . . the British want Cyprus, and they will get it . . . [they] will not do the business of the Turks again for nothing'.[116] To be sure, Disraeli, by 1847 a Tory MP, was also reflecting the political reality of the 1840 Syrian campaign in these words. Headlam-Morley too was right when asserting that the arguments that Disraeli and Salisbury made in support of taking Cyprus in 1878 'bear a significant resemblance to those of 1840–41' and 'in shaping their policy in 1878 [they] drew upon the proposals of 1840–41'.[117] It seems that Disraeli's vision for the Near East was drawn from his fiction, because, as prime minister, he not only occupied Cyprus in order to create an empire in the Levant, but he also made Queen Victoria Empress of India. Disraeli knew *Tancred* well, not simply because he wrote it, but also because he preferred it to his other novels.[118] He wanted a Semitic link in the eastern Mediterranean between England and India that would unite the Occident with the Orient. The predictions in 'Il Europe en 1860' entirely reflected Disraeli's vision.

Conclusion

To the British there was an unequalled sense of possession over the Holy Land, which included much of the eastern Mediterranean and especially Cyprus, beginning from the Crusades. This spiritual imperialism was infused with a sense of the romantic because of the place of Richard *Coeur de Lion* in English identity. The imperial imagination remained alive through the medieval period with various royals claiming possession of Cyprus and through the millenarian image of Jerusalem. With the Enlightenment came another imperial imagination – Greece, the origin of Western political and intellectual identity. These two contrasting imaginations – one religious, the other pagan – fell back on the geographical spheres from which they originated when, in the late eighteenth century, Europe began to explore them and increase their commercial and political authority over them. When Ottoman power waned and the cultural, commercial, political and strategic interest of Europe increased in the region, European Powers became drawn into competitive competition over the control and the future of the Near East. Interests soon grew to informal control, which developed into formal territorial acquisition. Cyprus' occupation in 1878 cannot be understood without understanding its place within the British imperial imagination.

Notes

1 S.C. Chew, *The Crescent and the Rose*, Oxford, 1937; Nabil Matar, *Islam in Britain, 1558–1685*, Cambridge, 1998.

2 E. Bar-Yosef, The Holy Land in English Culture, 1799–1917, 255.

3 See generally John M. MacKenzie (ed.), *Imperialism and Popular Culture*, Manchester, 1986.

4 Robert Lang, *Cyprus: Its History, its Present Resources and Future Prospects*, London, 1878, 171–5; George Jeffrey, *Cyprus Under an English King in the Twelfth Century*, Nicosia, 1926; Newman, *Short History of Cyprus*, 97–103; Harry Luke, *Cyprus: A Portrait and an Appreciation*, London, 1957 (revised 1965), 37–40.

5 *The Times*, 24 May 1912.

6 Luke, *A Portrait and an Appreciation*, 37–9; Steven Runciman, *A History of the Crusades*, Cambridge, 1987, 43–4.

7 John Gillingham, *Richard I*, London, 1999, 145, 153–4.

8 P.W. Edbury, The Kingdom of Cyprus and the Crusades, 1191–1374, Cambridge 1991, 5.

9 Gillingham, *Richard I*, 146.

10 Gordon Home, *Cyprus: Then and Now*, London, 1960, 48.

11 Luke, *A Portrait and an Appreciation*, 45.

12 Anthony Luttrell, 'The Hospitallers in Cyprus: 1310–1378', *KS*, 1986, 155–84.

13 Norman Cohn, *The Pursuit of the Millennium*, Oxford, 1957 (rev. edn, 1970), 64–5; Simon Lloyd, *English Society and the Crusade, 1216–1307*, Oxford, 1988, 245.

14 Edbury, *The Kingdom of Cyprus and the Crusades*, 11, 32.

15 Hepworth Dixon, *British Cyprus*, London, 1879, 134, 139.

16 Edbury, *The Kingdom of Cyprus and the Crusades*, 32.

17 Simon Lloyd, 'Edmund, first earl of Lancaster and first earl of Leicester (1245–1296)', *Oxford Dictionary of National Biography* (*ODNB*) (www.oxforddnb.com/view/article/8504, accessed 15 Dec 2005).

18 G.J. Brault (ed.), *Rolls of Arms Edward I (1272–1307)*, I, Suffolk, 1997, 87, 177, 310, 325, 512. The rolls include Herald's roll, Camden roll, Segar's roll, Lord Marshall's roll and Sir William Le Neve's roll.

19 Harry Luke, *Cities and Men*, II, London, 1951, 42; Simon Walker, 'Grey, John, third Baron Grey of Codnor (1305x11?–1392)', *ODNB* (www.oxforddnb.com/view/article/11545, accessed 15 Dec 2005); Timothy Guard, 'Sabraham, Nicholas (b. *c.*1325, d. in or after 1399)', *ODNB* (www.oxforddnb.com/view/article/92452, accessed 15 Dec 2005); Jürgen Sarnowsky, 'Hales, Sir Robert (d. 1381)', *ODNB* (www.oxforddnb.com/view/article/38626, accessed 15 Dec 2005).

20 Home, *Cyprus*, 62.

21 www.quns.cam.ac.uk/Queens/Misc/Elizabeth.html

22 *Punch*, 24 August 1878, 73. Also thanks to Christine Reynolds, the Assistant Keeper of the Monuments, the Library, Westminster Abbey.

23 M.C. Enlart, *L'Art Gothique et la Renaissance en Chypre*, I–II, Paris, 1899; Anna Marangou, *Famagusta: The Story of the City*, Nicosia, 2005, 61–88.

24 Malcolm Kelsall, '"Once Did She Hold the Gorgeous East in Fee . . .": Byron's Venice and Oriental Empire', in Tim Fulford and P.J. Kitson (eds), *Romanticism and Colonialism*, Cambridge, 1998, 255.

25 William Shakespeare, *Othello*, Act 1, Scene III.

26 *ILN*, 16 November 1861.

27 Newman, *Short History of Cyprus*, 172; DE2638/35, Copy of letters patent of Victor Amadeus King of Sardinia, Cyprus and of Jerusalem, Duke of Savoy, of Monserrat and Prince of Piedmont, etc. following petition of Maria Envichetta Malhor, sister of Enrico Shirley and royal patent of 4 June 1773, Additional records of the Shirley family of Staunton Harold, Leicestershire, Earls Ferrers, Leicestershire, Leicester and Rutland Record Office. The House of Savoy still claims the Crowns of Cyprus, Armenia and Jerusalem, passing *de jure* to Princess Maria Beatrice of Savoy, Victor Emmanuel IV's daughter, whom Franz, Duke of Bavaria, represents.

28 Petros Stylianou, 'The Cyprus Revolution of 1607 with Help of the Grand Duke of Toskan', *KL*, XII, 67–8, 1980, 129–30.
29 Petros Stylianou, 'Revolutionary Activities and Suggestions of Sir Antony Sherley for Liberation of Cyprus', *KL*, XII, 1980, 119; Constantinos Nikas, «Μια Προσπάθεια για Απελευθέρωση της Κύπρου στα 1606», *ICCS-1*, I, A, 1987, 23–32.
30 Purcell, *Cyprus*, 197.
31 Macfie, *The Eastern Question*, 7; Karl Roider, *Austria's Eastern Question, 1700–1790*, New Jersey, 1982, 135.
32 Ibid., 137.
33 Marriott, *The Eastern Question*, 155–6.
34 *The Times*, 10 December 1790, 3a.
35 *The Times*, 4 February 3d.
36 Wood, *Levant Company*, 168–9.
37 IOR/H/436, John Taylor, papers, 1790–1792, 67–115.
38 *The Times*, 10 August 1798, 2a.
39 Nelson papers, VI, General Correspondence, V, 1 June–15 October 1798, 34907, Hood to Nelson, 19 September 1798, 272–3; Hood to Nelson, 20 September 1798, 274–5.
40 Ibid., Captain Hope to Nelson, 16 September 1798.
41 Hill, *History of Cyprus*, IV, 101–2.
42 *The Times*, 5 July 1799, 2b.
43 Smith to Nelson, Hill, *A History of Cyprus*, 102; *The Times*, 31 March 1800, 2b.
44 Smith to Bishop Luscombe, Luke, *Cyprus Under the Turks*, 122–5.
45 Hill, *History of Cyprus*, IV, 102.
46 John Barrow, 'Patten's Natural Defence of an Insular Empire', *Quarterly Review (QR)*, IV, 1810, 313–34.
47 J.M.R. Cameron, 'John Barrow: Geographer and Imperialist', unpublished, 1993.
48 John Macdonald Kinneir, *Journey through Asia Minor, Armenia and Koordistan*, 1818, extracts C.D. Cobham, *Excerpta Cypria*, Cambridge 1908 (New York 1986), 412.
49 Captain Henry Light, *Travels in Egypt, Nubia, Holy Land, Mount Libanon, and Cyprus in the Year 1814*, London, 1818, 269.
50 FO78/139, Abstract of papers communicated by M[onsieur] B. de C., 7 October 1825.
51 Ibid.
52 J.A. Koumoulides, 'An Attempt for the Liberation of Cyprus During the Struggle for Greek Independence' *ICCS-1*, III, Part A, 1973, 149–54; Koumoulides, *Cyprus and the War of Greek Independence 1821–1829*, London, 1974, 79–80; Hill, *History of Cyprus*, IV, 137.
53 PRO30/29/8/10, 476, Laisné Villévéque (in Lord Granville's papers), 18 May 1826; 474, Canning to Granville, 1 June 1826.
54 Captain Charles Colville Frankland, *Travels to and from Constantinople in 1827 and 1828 etc . . .*, I, London, 1830.
55 Baron Beaujour, *Voyage Militaire dans l'Empire Ottoman*, 1929, Frederick Burnaby, *On Horseback Through Asia Minor*, London, 1898 (Oxford, 1996), 355.
56 Marsot, Egypt in the Reign of Muhammad Ali, 224, 228.
57 W.H. Engel, *Kypros, Eine Monographie*, I, Berlin, 1841, Cobham's *Excerpta Cypria*, 462.
58 Cobham's *Excerpta*, 462.
59 Ibid.
60 *The Times*, 29 July 1839, 4d; 6 August 1839, 6c; 7 August 1839, 6b, 28 September 1839, 6e; 16 September 1840, 4f; 18 September 1840, 4d; 29 September 1840, 4f; 6 October 1840, 3c; 8 October 1840, 4c; 27 October 1840, 5a; 16 November 1840, 4c; 19 November 1840, 3b.
61 FO371/9897/19108/489, Memorandum, Sir James Headlam-Morley and W.J. Childs, 18 December 1924 (Hereafter Headlam-Morley/Childs Memorandum).

62 Alastos, *Cyprus in History*, 298.
63 *The Times*, 12 December 1840, 4f. This was not *The Times*, although it felt that the proposal was justified.
64 Douglas Johnson, *Guizot: Aspects of French History 1787–1874*, London, 1963, 264–86.
65 *The Times*, 25 November 1840, 4d.
66 Ibid., 2 December 1840, 4f.
67 Ibid., 12 December 1840, 4f.
68 Johnson, *Guizot*, 284.
69 Ludwig Ross, *Reisen nach Kos, Halikarnassos, Rhodos, und der Insel Cypern*, Stuttgart, 1852. C.D. Cobham translated the Cyprus section as A Journey to Cyprus (February and March 1845), Nicosia 1910.
70 Ross, *A Journey to Cyprus*, 66–7.
71 Engel from Cobham, *Excerpta Cypria*, 463.
72 Eric Hinderaker, 'The 'Four Indian Kings' and the Imaginative Construction of the British Empire', *William and Mary Quarterly*, LIII, 3, 1996, 487–526.
73 Kathleen Wilson, 'Empire, Trade and Popular Politics in Mid-Hanoverian Britain: The Case of Admiral Vernon', *Past and Present*, 121, 1988, 74–109.
74 Linda Colley, 'Britishness and Otherness: An Argument', *Journal of British Studies*, XXXI, 4, 1992, 324.
75 Edward Said, *Orientalism*, 1978, 1, 96.
76 Colley, 'Britishness and Otherness', 324.
77 MacKenzie, *Orientalism*.
78 Michael Herzfeld, *Ours Once More: Folklore, Ideology, and the Making of Modern Greece*, Austin, 1982; *Anthropology Through the Looking-Glass*, Cambridge, 1987; Bar-Yosef, *The Holy Land in English Culture*.
79 Linda Osband, *Famous Travellers to the Holy Land*, London, 1989.
80 Wasserstein, *Divided Jerusalem*, 1–44.
81 Norman Daniel, *Islam and the West*, Edinburgh, 1960, 293.
82 Bar-Yosef, *The Holy Land in English Culture*, 33.
83 M.C. Curthoys, 'North, Frederick, fifth earl of Guilford (1766–1827)', *ODNB* (www.oxforddnb.com/view/article/20305, accessed 10 April 2006).
84 Caroline Franklin, ' "Some Samples of the Finest Orientalism": Byronic Philhellenism and Proto-Zionism at the Time of the Congress of Vienna', *Romanticism and Colonialism*, 221–42.
85 See Emmanuel Sarides, 'Byron and Greek History', *History Journal Workshop*, XV, 1983, 126–30 and Yiannis Papadakis, *Echoes From the Dead Zone: Across the Cyprus Divide*, London, 2005, 62–4.
86 Sarides, 'Byron and Greek History', 128.
87 Michael Herzfeld, *Anthropology Through the Looking-Glass*, Cambridge, 1987.
88 Ibid.
89 From a search on the Church of England website.
90 Linda Colley, *Britons: Forging the Nation, 1707–1837*, New Haven, 1992, 28.
91 Eitan Bar-Yosef, '"Green and Pleasant Lands": England and the Holy Land in Plebian Millenarian Culture, c.1790–1820', in Kathleen Wilson (ed.), *A New Imperial History: Culture, Identity, and Modernity in Britain and the Empire, 1660–1840*, Cambridge, 2004, 155–75.
92 Iain McCalman, 'New Jerusalems: Prophecy, Dissent and Radical Culture in England, 1786–1830', in Knud Haakonssen (ed.), *Enlightenment and Religion: Rational Dissent in Eighteenth-Century Britain*, Cambridge, 1996, 312–35.
93 Mayir Verete, 'The Restoration of the Jews in English Protestant Thought 1790–1840', *Middle East Studies (MES)*, VIII, 1972, 3–50.
94 Bar-Yosef, '"Green and Pleasant Land"', 157.
95 Michael Jacobs, *The Painted Voyage: Art, Travel and Exploration 1564–1875*, London, 1995, 19.
96 Jonathan Parry, 'Disraeli, Benjamin, earl of Beaconsfield (1804–1881)', *ODNB* (www.oxforddnb.com/view/article/7689, accessed 5 Oct 2005).

97 Ivan Davidson Kalmar, 'Benjamin Disraeli, Romantic Orientalist', *Comparative Studies of Society and History*, XLVII, 2, 2005, 352.
98 Ibid.
99 Robert Blake, *Disraeli's Grand Tour*, London, 1982, 125–9.
100 Disraeli to Austen, Monypenny and Buckle, *The Life of Benjamin Disraeli*, I, London, 1929, 162, 174.
101 Disraeli to Sarah Disraeli, Alexandria, 20 March 1831, *Benjamin Disraeli Letters*, II (ed.) J.A.W. Gunn, Toronto, 1997, 186.
102 Blake, *Disraeli*, 59, 192; Kalmar, 'Benjamin Disraeli, Romantic Orientalist', 359.
103 Daniel Bivona, 'Disraeli's Political Trilogy and the Antinomic Structure of Imperial Desire', *NOVEL: A Forum on Fiction*, XXII, 3, 1989, 305–25, 305.
104 Blake, *Disraeli*, 193.
105 Daniel Bivona, *Desire and Contradiction*, Manchester, 1990, 2, 18–25.
106 George Jeffrey, *Cyprus Under an English King in the Twelfth Century*, Nicosia, 1926, 39.
107 Jews and Arabs were members of the 'sacred race' to which Israelites and Ishmaelites belonged.
108 Bivona, 'Disraeli's Political Trilogy', 306.
109 Mary Roussou-Sinclair, *Victorian Travellers in Cyprus*, Nicosia, 2002, 66–8.
110 Bivona, 'Disraeli's Political Trilogy', 308–9.
111 Kalmar, 'Benjamin Disraeli, Romantic Orientalist', 357–8.
112 Bivona, 'Disraeli's Political Trilogy', 323.
113 Said, *Orientalism*, 169.
114 Bivona, 'Disraeli's Political Trilogy', 323.
115 Bar-Yosef, The Holy Land in English Culture, 222.
116 Benjamin Disraeli, *Tancred: or, The New Crusade*, 1847, 280–2.
117 Headlam-Morley/Childs memorandum.
118 Monypenny and Buckle, *Beaconsfield*, I, 864.

CHAPTER 3

Justifying the occupation of Cyprus, 1876–78: 'the key of Western Asia'

A country, and especially a maritime country, must get possession of the strong places of the world if it wishes to contribute to its power. (Benjamin Disraeli, February 1863)

Men are much more readily persuaded by acts than by words, and therefore we occupied . . . Cyprus to show our intention of maintaining our hold in those parts . . . When the interest of Europe was centred in the conflicts that were waged in Spain, England occupied Gibraltar. When the interest of Europe was centred in the conflicts that were being waged in Italy, England occupied Malta; and now that there is a chance that the interest of Europe will be centred in Asia Minor or in Egypt, England has occupied Cyprus. (Lord Salisbury at Manchester Free Trade Hall, 18 October 1879)

George Georghallides argued that Britain's occupation of Cyprus 'was a subordinate and secondary consequence of British Near Eastern policy', which had focused on preserving the 'decadent Ottoman Empire' from Russia.[1] On both counts he was only partly right. In fact, British policy was primarily concerned with securing its financial and strategic interests from Ottoman financial and military collapse. Cyprus was to serve as the military and commercial base, and from which to extend imperial interests in the Near East. Thus, Lord Beaconsfield's Cabinet had vested Cyprus with far greater importance than Georghallides had implied. The responsibility for the choice rested with them and not, as traditionally argued, with Colonel Robert Home of the Intelligence Branch of the War Office.[2] Beaconsfield and Lord Salisbury, the Foreign Secretary, thought Cyprus would strengthen British power. Disraeli had sharply criticised the ceding of the Ionian Islands to Greece in 1864 because he believed it weakened British power. The fate of the Ionian Islands stands as a precursor to the larger drama over Cyprus. The reasons for holding it and, eventually, abandoning it throw the Cyprus question into a clear relief.

[65]

The Ionian Islands and Gladstone and Disraeli: the precedent

When Palmerston's Liberal government ceded the Ionian Islands to Greece, Disraeli protested that it weakened the British Empire. The British occupied Malta and the Ionian Islands during the Napoleonic wars and they were both perceived as strategic prizes. But only Malta became valuable. The Ionian Islands, as with Cyprus, did not prove important. Unlike Cyprus, the British succeeded in relinquishing them, despite Disraeli's opposition.

The Ionian Islands comprise Corfu (Kerkira), Paxos, Leukas (Santa Maura), Ithaca, Cephalonia, Zakynthos (Zante) and Kythera (which is geographically detached from the others, being thirty-five miles south of Peloponnesus). Centrally located between the Balkan and Italian peninsulas, they commanded the entrance to the Adriatic.

Venice ruled them from 1402 to 1797 (wholly or partly) – far longer than Cyprus. In 1797 Napoleon asserted that

> Corfu, Zante, and Cephalonia seem of more importance to us than all of Italy. The Turkish Empire is decaying; the possession of the islands would enable us to support it if that were possible, or to take our share.[3]

The statement resembles those made when Cyprus was occupied and was typical of the 'El Dorado' explanation for imperialism, where value was ascribed to places without proof.[4]

In any event, the idea took hold and the Islands changed hands four times over the next twelve years. The French held them only until 1799, when a Russo-Ottoman force seized them and established a republic on the Ragusa model, but the French took them back in 1807. On this, Napoleon told his brother Joseph, King of Naples:

> Corfu is so important to me that its loss would deal a fatal blow to my plans. The Adriatic would be closed, and your kingdom would have on its left flank a port where the enemy could assemble to attack you. You must regard it as more valuable than Sicily. Mark my words; in the current situation in Europe the worst misfortune that can happen to me is to lose Corfu.[5]

Finally, in 1809 the British decided to seize them, exemplifying their supposed strategic value. The British succeeded, except with Corfu, which the French held until Napoleon abdicated in 1814. In November 1815 the Ionian Islands were elevated to the status of 'a single, free and independent state' under British protection.[6] Their first High Commissioner, Sir Thomas Maitland (1815–23), held the position as well as that of High Commissioner of Malta, but spent more time in the

Ionian Islands, showing that the British viewed them as strategically more important than Malta.[7]

Maitland's policy in the Ionian Islands hardly reflected their supposed strategic value: instead of maintaining Corfu's forts, he built a palace at the northern end of the esplanade that blocked the guns of the citadel.[8] During the Greek revolt the mistake became obvious. Reports made for the Duke of Wellington, the Master General of Ordnance, recommended preservation and extension of the forts and the fortification of Vido Island to protect the port. Wellington agreed and sent Lieutenant-Colonels Sir John Jones and George Whitmore to make plans.[9] Implementation cost £182,000, which the Ionians had to pay.

Not surprisingly this infuriated them. They were already displeased with the unrepresentative constitution and Maitland's autocratic rule. The constitution allowed local representation, but gave the Lord High Commissioner 'pretty nearly all the real power',[10] as it did later in Cyprus. Maitland was an autocrat whose staff nicknamed him 'King Tom' and he enjoyed veto power over laws, decrees and most appointments, judicial power over the police force and the ability to detain, imprison and exile anyone without trial.[11]

Strategists like John Barrow, Maitland, Jones, Sir John Oswald, who had conquered and nominally ruled the islands until 1815, Lord Bathurst, the Colonial Secretary in 1815, and Lieutenant-Colonel Charles Napier, believed in the strategic importance of the islands and that it was 'impolitic' to abandon them.[12] Napier was the most vocal. A passionate Philhellene, he dreamt of leading the Greeks in a war against the Turks. In England in 1821 he published *The War in Greece*, which denounced Ottoman rule and argued for European intervention on the Greek side. In Cephalonia he befriended Lord Byron and they schemed to liberate Greece, with Napier leading the Greek army. In 1824 he sought financial aid in London, but the Greek Committee balked at the cost.[13] Napier was a Byronic Philhellene, but unlike Byron – whose romantic nationalism was a reaction to imperialism – Napier wanted the Ionian Islands to remain British. In 1819 he was appointed an inspecting field officer in the Ionian Islands and in March 1822 he became military resident in Cephalonia and started a massive public works programme: roads, prisons, markets and a lighthouse were constructed and marshes and slums cleared.

The pace had slowed when he went on leave to England in 1825 and when he returned, he swiftly remedied the situation. This annoyed his rival, Major-General Sir Frederick Adams, who had succeeded Maitland (1823–32). Jealous of Napier's work, Adams removed public works from his authority in July 1828.[14] Napier argued that the Ionian

Islands were vital for British commercial and political power because they were two-thirds of the way to the Red Sea; half way between England and the Persian Gulf; near the Levant; and could block the Adriatic. They were centrally located to Constantinople, Smyrna, Tripoli, Alexandria, Tunis, Malta, Naples, Venice and Trieste,[15] and protected British commerce in the Levant, and even India. In war they could provide a 30,000-strong militia; possibly raise 10,000 auxiliaries; a large body of sailors; and a number of small vessels. Napier believed that they were 'of vast *political importance to Great Britain*'.[16] Enthusiasts for Cyprus would say much the same.

As in Cyprus there were naysayers too. The report by Colonels Jones and Whitmore, although recommending expensive fortifications, questioned the strategic value of the Islands. They wanted Corfu Town opened; the British troops to hold positions only at two forts; and a reduction in the garrison at Vido. Both believed that Corfu would fall in a sustained attack. Adams' replacement, Lord Nugent (1832–35), had no interest in fortifications and thought the navy could protect Corfu. His successor, Sir Howard Douglas (1835–40) agreed: his support for demolition was accepted and work began in 1839. Within a decade, Lord John Russell, the Colonial Secretary, indicated that the Ionian Islands were useless to Britain and should be transferred to Austria so it could secure Trieste.[17]

Still, the British hung on. Palmerston, the Prime Minister, declared: 'I consider Corfu as a very important position for Mediterranean interests.'[18] In 1858 the Inspector-General of Fortifications, General Sir J.F. Burgoyne, an old Mediterranean hand, argued that none of the fortifications should have been destroyed and that a new line of detached works was needed.[19] First they wanted to build forts; then pull them down, and then, once more, they proposed to build them. There were three options: to maintain the current fortifications, which Burgoyne's report claimed were inadequate; to start a new defence plan, which would cost £200,000, something the Exchequer would not like; or to spend £40,000 as an instalment of the new plan without prejudice to its completion. The last option was adopted and engineers implemented it over the following ten years.[20]

By 1859 the Ionians were demanding to join Greece. In November 1858 Lord Derby's Conservative government decided to send them a young Peelite, William E. Gladstone, as Lord High Commissioner extraordinary. As Gladstone left for Corfu, a despatch from the outgoing Lord High Commissioner (Sir John Young) to the Colonial Secretary was published in the *Daily News*. It advised ceding all of the islands, or all except Corfu and Paxos, to Greece. Gladstone's mission was seen as a step in this direction despite official denials.[21] He blamed *énosis* on the draconian constitution and government and decided on a liberal alternative, but the Corfiotes only wanted *énosis*.[22]

Gradually, Palmerston's government realised that their strategic value had reduced with Malta's naval development.[23] The Colonial and Foreign Offices discussed three options: expanding the British military forces and implementing a restrictive constitution; keeping Corfu and giving the rest to Greece; or ceding the lot. Option one was rejected because the costs outweighed the strategic value. The second option was discarded for fear the Corfiotes would revolt.[24] So in December 1862 the Cabinet agreed to hand them to Greece. The Ionian venture had failed.[25] In a final move of self-destruction, the British destroyed most of the sea batteries and defensive works.

The decision reflected the trend of British imperial contraction. In 1859, London ceded to Honduras the Mosquito Protectorate, a strip of coast in present-day Honduras and Nicaragua, and two years later the Bay Islands in the Western Caribbean.[26] Goldwin Smith, the Regius Professor of Modern History at Oxford, even wanted Gibraltar ceded to Spain.[27] All this provoked vociferous opposition, especially from Disraeli. In February 1863 he lashed out in the Commons against Smith and others.

> Within the last twenty-five years the route to our Indian possessions has been changed; and, whatever the intention of the treaties of 1815, the country has been constantly congratulated on having a chain of Mediterranean garrisons, which secured our Indian Empire. I am perfectly aware that there is a school of politicians – I do not believe they are rising politicians – who are hostile to the very principle of a British Empire . . . Professors and rhetoricians find a system for every contingency and a principle for every chance; but you are not going . . . to leave the destinies of the British Empire to prigs and pedants. The statesmen who construct, and the warriors who achieve, are only influenced by the instinct of power, and animated by the love of country. Those are the feelings and those are the methods which form empires . . . [because] the best mode of preserving wealth is power. A country, and especially a maritime country, must get possession of the strong places of the world if it wishes to contribute to its power.[28]

British interests and approaches to the Near East crisis

Disraeli's fears were not realised. Despite the abandonment of the Ionian Islands, British interests in the Near East increased after the 1860s. They now centred on the strategic and economic importance of the Ottoman Empire and Egypt.

The British priority was to protect investments in the Ottoman Empire.[29] After the Napoleonic Wars, Europe increased trade with the

Ottoman Empire. The collapse of the Levant Company in 1825 opened commerce to merchants and transferred consular appointments to the Foreign Office. Steam and rail encouraged European commercial growth. Successive British governments backed investment and when problems between investors and the Ottomans arose, local consuls and Whitehall often intervened.[30] London and Paris guaranteed the Porte's first loan to fight the Crimean War and European banks in the Near East raised loans – like the Ottoman Bank, which formed in 1856. But the Porte could not repay them and amassed a debt of over £200 million in debt to British and French credit institutions. Its financial ruin risked British informal interests in the Ottoman Empire.[31]

British strategic interests in the Ottoman Empire centred on geography: controlling the sea prevented Russia from dominating the Mediterranean, while a threat emerged to Armenia, Kurdistan, Persia and Afghanistan, which stood between Russia and India. A weak Ottoman Empire could not stop Russia. Accordingly, British governments insisted on concessions to Ottoman Christian subjects to minimise the effects of internal revolts and to prevent Russian and French control in the Levant as the sponsors of the Orthodox and Maronite Christians, respectively. The British also wanted to prevent the establishment of new local powers. So Britain helped establish only a small Greece, prevented the almost perennial rebellious Crete from joining it, and reigned in Muhammad Ali's greater Egypt.[32]

Russian expansion at the expense of a weak Ottoman state threatened British interests. Events came to a head in January 1871, when the Russian Chancellor and Foreign Minister, Aleksandr Gorchachov, unilaterally ended the limitations the Treaty of Paris imposed on Russia's Black Sea fleet and tried to negotiate with the Porte over access through the Straits.[33] This risked an extension of Russian naval power into the eastern Mediterranean, which London did not want. In July 1875, St Petersburg backed the Christian revolt in the Balkans against Ottoman rule, which threatened to increase Russian hegemony on land – a development which London did not want either.

British politicians were divided over the threat. To Gladstone, who had served as prime minister from 1868 to 1874, it was a moral issue: he backed the Russian right to protect Ottoman Christians and believed that British naval power and the Treaty of Paris secured British interests from Russia. To Disraeli, who had briefly served as prime minister in 1868 and defeated Gladstone in the 1874 election, it was a strategic issue: the Ottoman Empire was a buffer against Russian moves into the Mediterranean and Asia and he was willing to sidestep the Treaty of Paris to secure British interests.[34]

Yet there were divisions among Disraeli's ministers. Lord Salisbury, the India Secretary, criticised Disraeli and had joined the Cabinet only to contain him. He thought the only way to protect British interests was to partition the Ottoman Empire with Russia, thus expanding the Empire east of Malta.[35] In contrast, Lord Derby, the Foreign Secretary, did not wish to embroil Britain in a war against Russia to aid the Ottomans or for Britain to take territory.[36] Divisions meant indecisiveness and delay.

At first Conservatives and Liberals agreed that the Ottoman demise in Europe was certain.[37] Even Turcophiles, like H.A. Butler-Johnstone, a former Tory MP who became an independent,[38] argued in the Tory organ,[39] the *Pall Mall Gazette*: 'notorious, palpable, flagrant, ruinous misgovernment must . . . involve in ruin a country with even greater resources and capacities than Turkey.'[40] In August and September 1875 *The Times* (which was publicly committed to no party),[41] the Tory[42] *John Bull* and the *Pall Mall Gazette* and the Gladstonian[43] *Daily News* backed or accepted Christian autonomy in Ottoman Europe.[44] When the Porte asked for a reduction in its debt payments on 6 October, it virtually conceded bankruptcy.[45] This jolted Whitehall and British investors, who had poured over £1 million into Ottoman bonds. *John Bull* declared: 'Turkish rule in Europe is hastening to a speedy end.'[46]

Even though British interests were threatened, the Cabinet wavered. Disraeli had been Prime Minister for little more than a year and even some of his colleagues had no confidence in him.[47] He blamed Ottoman weakness on the intrigues of Russia, Austria-Hungary and Germany, which had formed the Three Emperors' League in 1872.[48] But on 9 November Disraeli declared at the Mansion House that British interests in the Near East were as 'considerable' as those of the League and he would 'guard and maintain' them.[49]

Disraeli then seized the first chance to secure British interests against French competition in Egypt. The Suez Canal, which opened in 1869, further linked British imperial defence, finance and the Mediterranean. The Khedive's industrialisation had failed; debts grew from his involvement in building the Suez Canal and, like the Porte, from failure to repay foreign loans.[50] On 3 November, six days before Disraeli's Mansion House speech, the *Pall Mall Gazette* had called for 'Egypt for the English' and was echoed in editorials in the *Standard, Economist* and *Daily News*.[51] Only control of Egypt could protect British interests in the Near East and India. When Frederick Greenwood, the editor of the *Pall Mall Gazette*, learned that the Khedive was negotiating with French syndicates to sell his 44 per cent share in the Suez Canal Company,[52] he pressed Derby for London to buy them. Derby refused. But Disraeli insisted and persuaded the Cabinet, over the opposition of Derby, Lord Cairns (the Lord Chancellor) and Sir Stafford Northcote (the Chancellor of the Exchequer), to buy the shares.[53] Disraeli, the 'modern sphinx', alone held the 'key to India'.

The rivalry between London and Paris for Egypt's informal control resulted in dual control in late 1876. Disraeli thought this was enough.[54] Salisbury and Lord Carnarvon, the Colonial Secretary, proposed to occupy Egypt and partition the Ottoman Empire.[55] But Disraeli was satisfied with the informal control and the reassertion of British authority in Europe, by opposing the schemes of the Three Emperors' League and backing the Porte.[56]

Disraeli's policy was undermined, however, when Circassian irregulars (*Bashi-Bazouks*) quashed another Balkan revolt. Abdul Aziz was deposed and Midhat Pasha, a liberal, formed a ministry. But the *Daily News* still reported massacres. A Russo-Ottoman war loomed. Disraeli denied the massacres in one of his last speeches in the Commons before Queen Victoria, whom he had made Empress of India, in another achievement from *Tancred*, made him the Earl of Beaconsfield.[57]

In September 1876, Gladstone began his campaign to free the Christians with a pamphlet *Bulgarian Horrors and the Question of the East*, which sold 200,000 copies in a month. It advocated, in the Shakespearean phrase, for the 'bag and baggage' removal of Ottoman rule from Europe.[58] The campaign made it impossible for Beaconsfield to support the Ottomans with British troops, but he could not give the Tsar a free hand.

Bismarck suggested partitioning the Ottoman Empire as the solution: Britain would get Egypt; Austria-Hungary, Bosnia and Herzegovina; France, Tunisia; Italy, Albania; and Russia would dominate the eastern Balkans. Territorial compensations designed to check the influence of one power now justified imperial expansion.[59] But Beaconsfield had no wish to cripple the Ottoman Empire: Russian control of the eastern Balkans and its consequent naval expansion into the Mediterranean would weaken British naval supremacy. British control of Egypt would not prevent that and he thought Paris would object anyway. In December the two powers imposed dual control of Egyptian finances.

In late October Derby brokered an armistice between the Slavic insurgents and the Porte. That prepared the way for the Conference of Constantinople in December at which Salisbury, the Secretary for India, represented the British government. Salisbury had long loathed Ottoman rule and during 1876 decided that peace would prevail only if Britain and Russia joined hands. So Gladstone thought his appointment was 'the best thing that the Government have yet done in the Eastern Question'.[60] Beaconsfield preferred a Cabinet minister to a diplomat and reasoned that the India Secretary would realise the need to check Russia.

The solution: the new crusade

Meanwhile, Beaconsfield proposed a radical idea to tackle the Russians. The War Secretary, Gathorne Gathorne-Hardy revealed that Beaconsfield wanted another 'Malta and Gibraltar . . . [to] prevent the Black Sea being a constant threat' to British Mediterranean maritime power.[61] This does not imply that Gibraltar or Malta were deficient, but that a similar stronghold in the eastern Mediterranean was perceived as necessary.

The proposal coincided with the linking of coaling stations to imperial defence. In the late 1860s John Colomb, a naval officer, argued that the navy could not protect its bases and commerce in peacetime and fight enemy navies in war.[62] In 1874 the First Naval Lord, Admiral Alexander Milne, took the thrust of this argument and asked the War Office to aid in defending coaling stations.[63] Colonel Sir William Drummond Jervois of the Royal Engineers, investigated. He had been the assistant inspector general of fortifications (1856–62) and since 1857 the secretary to the Defence Committee, a permanent War Office body chaired by the Duke of Cambridge. From September 1862 to March 1875 he was the deputy Director of Works of Fortification and reported on the defences of Canada, Nova Scotia, New Brunswick and Bermuda, sites in America during the civil war, Halifax, Gibraltar, Malta, Aden, Perim and other places.[64] Jervois, clearly an expert, reported that it was vital to develop a chain of logistical bases so that the fleet could protect trade in peace and fight the enemy in war. The cost of securing eleven coaling stations equalled that of constructing two ironclads.[65] So a new base was a cheap solution to the current crisis.

Beaconsfield ordered John Simmons, the Inspector-General of Fortifications, to find one to defend Constantinople. Colonel Robert Home, the assistant quartermaster-general of the intelligence branch, investigated. During the Crimean War the resourceful Home had obtained a commission in the Royal Engineers and later worked on the new defences at Portland. He then reported on the defence of the Canadian frontier and in 1865 he became the deputy assistant quartermaster-general at Aldershot. In 1871 he went to the War Office topographical and statistical department and helped transform it into the intelligence branch in 1873. Sir Garnet Wolseley selected him to command the engineers in the Asante War and he became a member of the Wolseley 'ring'. On 1 April 1876 he was promoted to his current role[66] and within months he was investigating whether Bourghaz Bay had potential as a base.[67]

There were many views on the place to seize. On 20 October, the anonymous author of a pamphlet, *The Dardanelles for England: The True Solution of the Eastern Question*, asked: 'having a sheepfold to guard, ought she (Britain) to allow eagles (Russians) to fix their nest on the nearest crag?' British military and commercial interests would be endangered if another power possessed any station in the eastern Mediterranean. Britain had to 'fulfil the functions of an International Turncock, and control the exit of the Dardanelles . . . [and] maintain her line of communication through Egypt with India . . . [by] practically possess[ing] Egypt'.[68] Home believed that there was support in Whitehall and the diplomatic service in the Near East for seizing Constantinople, including Sir William White, the British consul-general to Serbia (later ambassador to Constantinople, 1886–91).[69] But an attack on Constantinople was fraught with military and political dangers.

A position on the periphery was less dangerous, politically and militarily, and Cyprus figured in considerations from the start. On 23 October 1876, three days after the 'Dardanelles for England' pamphlet appeared, the War Office stamped the map of Cyprus published in 1862 by Louis de Mas Latrie, the head of the Imperial Archives in Paris. In 1879 Horatio (later Lord) Kitchener thought this was when Cyprus was first considered, but no historian has referred to the map.[70] Maps are vital for conceptualising the geo-strategic value of territory and it cannot be denied that Cyprus was centrally located at the crossroads of the Balkans, Asia Minor, the Levant and Egypt.

On 20 December Home suggested to Simmons that Britain 'seize Crete, Egypt, or Rhodes, or all of these', but he preferred Rhodes.[71] Six days later he warned against fighting on the Ottoman side, because the 'time has come to cut it up' and take a share of it.[72] Salisbury agreed. Three days before the Porte rejected the European proposals (18 January) at the Conference,[73] he asked Home to visit and report on Rhodes and Cyprus.[74] Salisbury thought spilling British blood to protect the Ottomans was unjustified and wanted another way to secure the road to India,[75] such as partitioning the Ottoman Empire with Russia, and building a base in the eastern Mediterranean.

But Home did not visit Cyprus or Rhodes; instead he reported on the policy options. He argued that to fight Russia meant the 'expenditure of enormous treasure and blood'. Another option was to abandon the Ottoman Empire and seize 'the Dardanelles and Cyprus'. Home believed that fighting the Russians with a divided nation would fail and advised establishing a protectorate over Ottoman Asia[76] – a new

Figure 4 The War Office Stamp on 23 October 1876 on map in
Louis de Mas Latrie book
Source: MFQ 1/724.

crusade along the lines of *Tancred*. As a base to accomplish this, he
preferred Cyprus to Crete and Rhodes.

An old threat over new terrain

Traditionally Russia threatened an advance over sea (through the
Straits) or over land (through the Balkans): now it was over land through
Asia to India. Home upturned imperial strategy. If the Russians
moved into Armenia, they could threaten the Persian Gulf or India.
Home referred to a pamphlet by Baron Kuhn von Kuhnenfeld, a former
Austrian War Minister, who claimed that Russia wanted Mesopotamia
and the Persian Gulf.[77] The threat increased as Armenians called upon
the Russians to save them from Ottoman tyranny.[78]

Simmons agreed with Home. He knew Asia Minor well, having
traversed the frontier from Ararat to the Black Sea as the British
commissioner for the delimitation of the Russo-Ottoman boundary
under the Treaty of Paris. In 1870 he became the governor of the Royal

Military Academy, until he became inspector-general of fortifications.[79] Amongst his correspondence with Home was the July 1872 select committee report on a railway from the Mediterranean to the Persian Gulf, which would secure British ships access to transmit troops, passengers and mail to India. Opinion was divided on whether the costs justified the advantages. Viscount Stratford de Redcliffe, a former ambassador to the Porte, and Lord Strathnairn, a former Commander-in-Chief in India, who had served as consul-general in Syria and in the Constantinople embassy (1841–54), supported the venture. Lord Sandhurst, another former Commander-in-Chief in India, who also had served at Constantinople (1855), disagreed.[80] In April 1877 Simmons warned that if Russia were to dominate Armenia there were 'no obstacles' to it marching on the Bosphorus, the Euphrates and Tigris valleys and, potentially, the Persian Gulf and India.[81]

After the Constantinople Conference collapsed, Austen Henry Layard became ambassador to the Porte. He had travelled the Near East in 1839 and did consular and archaeological work for de Redcliffe. This brought him fame after he discovered ancient Assyrian artefacts that were later enshrined in the British museum, and his book *Nineveh and its Remains* sold 5,250 copies between December 1848 and June 1949.[82] This allowed him to pursue a political career, serving as Palmerston's under-secretary at the Foreign Office and Gladstone's Commissioner of Works. In 1868 he became ambassador to Spain.[83] Layard, a founder of the Ottoman Bank, fought with Gladstone in the 1850s because of his pro-Turkish proclivities.[84] The differences resurfaced when Layard, in London in 1876, read the proofs of *Bulgarian Horrors*.[85] Back in Madrid, alarmed by talk in Parliament of splitting the Ottoman Empire, because he thought Germany and Russia would control the Near East,[86] Layard secretly published an article in the January issue of the *Quarterly Review*.[87] He chided Gladstone, but called for Ottoman reforms in the provinces and rejected a war with Russia and the occupation of Besika Bay, Cyprus or Crete. Only British informal control of the Levant would secure financial and strategic interests and the Ottoman system, and prevent Russia from dominating Mesopotamia.[88]

The Russian threat materialised when Europe failed to convince or coerce the Sultan to support its solution and Russia declared war on 24 April 1877. Beaconsfield's fears had been realised as alarm that Constantinople would fall to the Russians gripped Britain.

The Cabinet still remained divided. Derby suspected that Beaconsfield wanted a war and aimed to check this. Salisbury and Carnarvon rejected intervention to protect the Porte, favouring partition.[89] Beaconsfield, Gathorne-Hardy, Cairns and Lord John Manners, the Postmaster-General, wanted Constantinople defended, and Gathorne-Hardy and Cairns called for Gallipoli's seizure. On 21 April the Beaconsfield faction proposed occupying a position on the Dardanelles. Derby objected. If Britain had the Porte's permission, it would lead to war with Russia; without permission, Britain was 'committing an act of mere buccaneering'. Either way Derby warned that Britain would be 'giving the signal for a general scramble'.[90]

They compromised. On 2 May the Cabinet told the Tsar to respect British interests: Egypt and the Suez Canal; Constantinople and the straits; and the Persian Gulf.[91] The last inclusion shows Armenia's importance. When St Petersburg did not discount Constantinople's temporary occupation,[92] and by the end of May Russian forces captured Ardahan in Armenia, the view spread across Britain that Constantinople's seizure seemed imminent. This seemed to be proved when Derby received the peace terms on 8 June. Bulgaria would be autonomous, Serbia and Montenegro enlarged, Russia compensated with Bessarabia and Batum and Austria-Hungary would receive Bosnia and Herzegovina. Bismarck again invited Britain to occupy Egypt.[93] The French Foreign Minister suggested that London and Paris formally occupy Egypt and use Cyprus to seize Syria.[94] But only Salisbury and Carnarvon supported imperial expansion at Ottoman expense.[95] Beaconsfield rejected partition again. On 16 June he convinced the Cabinet, except Salisbury and Carnarvon, who favoured seizing Egypt, to go to war if Constantinople was threatened.[96] Derby's intervention prevented a schism and the Cabinet agreed to submit to the Commons a vote of credit for £2 million to prepare for a possible expedition.[97]

In June there was fear in Britain lest Russia seize Armenia,[98] although Salisbury successfully led the anti-alarmist debate, as some doubted Russia could succeed.[99] In July the Belgian liberal economist Émile de Laveleye claimed that Russia could not hold Constantinople given Austrian and German interests. He believed that British interests were at threat in Asia, as no other power would help against Russia dominating there. Syria and Egypt were at risk, not India, from a land attack against which the British fleet would be powerless. Laveleye urged London to take Egypt and Cyprus if Russia took Armenia.[100]

> I say Cyprus and not Crete. Crete ought to go to Greece, because the national sentiment there is too much awake to be restrained. In Cyprus this is not the case, and moreover this island, transformed into a Gibraltar, will be a better and nearer commanding-point for the shores of Syria and the entrance to the Suez Canal.[101]

Local nationalism was influencing imperial expansion.

Laveleye believed that a British Cyprus could protect the area between Syria and the Canal, but the island was the third largest island in the Mediterranean, not a mere rock, like Gibraltar. If the responsibilities entailed in occupying Cyprus were not enough, Laveleye wanted Britain to establish Egypt as a second India. Laveleye, who believed that colonies were a source of weakness and the cession of the Ionian Islands to Greece was wise, justified occupying Egypt and Cyprus on economic, humanitarian and strategic grounds.[102]

The Cabinet's indecisiveness did not stop Beaconsfield searching for a base. On 1 April the Director of Works of Fortification and the secretary of Cambridge's Defence Committee, Colonel C.H. Nugent, argued that the defence of coaling stations depended on commerce, the naval station and the theatre of war.[103] The theatre was now the eastern Mediterranean. Three days after the Russo-Ottoman hostilities started, Simmons received a report on finding a coaling station in case of war so vessels did not return to Malta. A small force would defend it in the fleet's absence and it had to be enclosed unlike Gibraltar. After examining the charts of Cyprus and Rhodes, Simmons thought neither had suitable ports. Crete was too long, needed harbour fortifications and the agitation for union to Greece would make governing unviable. Simmons liked Tristoma on Karpathos, between Crete and Rhodes,[104] but after the report of Lieutenant-Colonel J.B. Edwards, RE, and Commander Frederick Egerton, RN,[105] Simmons recommended Vathy in Stampalia (Astropalia), another of the Dodecanese. It was capacious, capable of berthing warships, and could be ready in six weeks after some minor dredging.[106]

Frederick Evans, the Hydrographer to the Admiralty, disagreed. He argued that even after the entrance was dredged (a time-consuming and costly enterprise) it would admit only two vessels passing simultaneously and large ships would need to moor head and stern; thus it was not capacious. Evans preferred Port Maltezana, also on Stampalia, which had a greater capacity, depth of water, and facility of ingress and egress. It was land-locked, so it was easier to defend, and ready.[107] Admiral Arthur Hood, Second Naval Lord, and Admiral Sir Hastings Yelverton, the First Sea Lord, agreed.[108] Although the two services were divided over the harbour, they agreed on the island.[109]

Accordingly, Lord Cairns proposed in the Cabinet, on 4 July 1877, that Stampalia be seized. But this was rejected.[110] Beaconsfield wanted to gauge the Cabinet reaction and did not mind the outcome because, as he told the Queen, the Porte had offered to sell Egypt, Crete and Cyprus.[111]

Cabinet divisions meant that action was hamstrung. Although on 21 July the Cabinet reiterated that if Russia seized Constantinople there would be war,[112] when the Ottomans repulsed the Russians at Plevna, showing that the 'sick man' was not so sick, the Cabinet did not take the initiative. When the Russian forces took Kars in November, the formerly Gladstonian, and now Disraelian, *Daily Telegraph*[113] claimed that

> Russia has now virtually conquered Armenia; Persia falls under her domination; the way to the East, West, and South are open; India will thrill with a suppressed excitement . . . the Czar is on the road to the Dardanelles, and the England of Nelson and Pitt sits quietly watching the drama in a state of sentimental indecision.[114]

Then, when Plevna fell on 10 December, the famous music hall song 'Jingo' exemplified the vociferousness of the 'scare press'.[115]

The Liberals rejected the idea that India and Egypt would be threatened if Russia took Armenia.[116] Samuel Laing, a Liberal MP, believed that British interests were at risk if Russia took Constantinople, because it could fortify the Dardanelles and its ships could roam the Mediterranean. Laing and other Liberals, such as Goldwin Smith, reflecting their Byronic nationalism, thought a Greater Greece with Constantinople as the capital would counterpoise Russia.[117]

The Conservatives saw the issue differently. After Kars fell, Beaconsfield told Musurus Pasha (the Ottoman ambassador at London) and Layard, that London would financially aid the Porte in exchange for territory.[118] The Ottoman Foreign Minister, Safvet Pasha, thought it unlikely that the Sultan would agree. Layard thought that Cyprus was less valuable than Crete, which at least had Suda Harbour. He emphasised Armenia and Mesopotamia's importance, yet did not favour Cyprus, as Laveleye did, but agreed with Simmons and Evans on Stampalia.[119]

Layard reiterated that control of the Euphrates and Tigris valleys and the construction of a railway,[120] which Home had emphasised to Simmons earlier in 1877, would protect British interests. Captain Bedford Pim, a Conservative MP (1874–80) and naval officer famous for his canal project through Nicaragua, thought the railway would relieve the Porte of financial difficulties.[121] The Liberal Edward Cazalet, an industrialist with financial links in Russia, argued that England should establish informal control over Syria and build the Euphrates Valley Railway to undercut Russian expansion.[122] Layard and Algernon Borthwick, owner of the Disraelian *Morning Post*,[123] believed the railway would open up Ottoman Asia's resources. All emphasised the railway's strategic value as an overland route to India and a buffer against Russia.[124] Layard thought that Mohammorah in Persia commanded the eastern terminus of any railway. The political agent in Arabia and the chargé d'affaires in Tehran agreed.[125] Layard told Beaconsfield that the project was 'gigantic', but a good statesman could foresee the future.[126] He was challenging Beaconsfield to forge an informal empire from the eastern Mediterranean to Persia.

Another group wanted Egypt's formal control. Edward Dicey, who since 1870 had been editor of *The Observer*, was a leading voice.[127] Attitudes to this question cut across party lines. Gladstone criticised Dicey; Charles Dilke (another leading Liberal) agreed with Dicey.[128] Wolseley, while on his way to Cyprus to act as its first high commissioner, recalled in his journal (intended for his wife) that

> Dizzy never liked the idea of Egypt, why I know not: perhaps the dreamy Judaism which shows itself thoroughly in some of his books influenced his policy and turned his attention to the Holy Land.[129]

Beaconsfield told his Cabinet on 22 May 1878 that he had rejected occupying Egypt in deference to French feeling, but favoured 'taking civil possession' of it by 'filling all the offices'.[130] That was exactly what happened.

Paving the way

By May 1878 the Cabinet had undergone great upheaval to unite behind a forward policy, which at its heart was the acquisition of Cyprus.

When the Ottomans surrendered on 9 January, Whitehall could ill-afford to procrastinate. It sent the fleet to the Dardanelles on 23 January under Vice-Admiral Sir Geoffrey Phipps Hornby, the Commander-in-Chief Mediterranean station, to warn the Russians against imposing harsh terms. The result was that the Russians advanced to Bourgas on 28 January. The next day, Derby told Russia that the Powers would have to sanction any agreement. When British intelligence reported that an armistice had been signed at Adrianople on 31 January, the British fleet withdrew. But on 6 February, the Russians occupied Tchataldja and the next day the peace terms became known, exciting the 'scare press', and Hornby was ordered back to Constantinople. An Anglo-Russian war loomed.

Now Beaconsfield turned to occupying a base in the eastern Mediterranean. The territory had to pay for the Porte's February default on the loan of 1855, which made the British and French treasuries liable to the bondholders for £40,872 annually.[131] On 2 March Gathorne-Hardy asked Simmons about Alexandretta's strategic potential. Later that day Cambridge and Lord Napier of Magdala, Gibraltar's governor, who was to command an expeditionary force with Wolseley as his chief of staff, told Simmons that Beaconsfield had asked

Gathorne-Hardy to find a place that guaranteed sufficient revenue to pay the Ottoman debt.[132] Simmons discounted Alexandretta and repeated his preference for Stampalia. But Cambridge and Napier were only interested in whether the place had sufficient revenue.[133]

The next day Constantinople and St Petersburg signed the Treaty of San Stefano; so, contrary to the claims of historians, the treaty had not triggered the decision on a base.[134] San Stefano would have created a Bulgaria stretching to the Aegean and it would have given Russia Kars, Batum and Ardahan in Asia, thus tilting the balance of power in Europe and Asia to Russia's advantage. The British objected and Russia agreed to a European power congress at Berlin.

London received Austro-Hungarian cooperation to resolve the European aspect of the problem and Bulgaria was reduced, and for its trouble the Hapsburg's received Bosnia and Herzegovina. As Laveleye had predicted in July 1877, however, London was alone in the matter of resolving the Asian aspect of the crisis.

Beaconsfield's Cabinet was so sure about the base it wanted that it did not consult its military departments, although the War and Colonial Offices and the Admiralty had formed an interdepartmental committee to coordinate imperial defence in case of war with Russia, first meeting on 5 March 1878, two days after the Treaty of San Stefano was signed.[135] The Cabinet relied on the Intelligence Department. During the 1930s historians argued that Cyprus' occupation was decided in haste between 18 April and 10 May on the advice of Colonel Home,[136] who subsequently wrote a memorandum justifying Cyprus' selection over other places investigated.[137] Although it is impossible to put an exact date on when the island was selected it is wrong to attribute its choice to Home.

Vital to the success of the policy was a unified Cabinet. On 21 March Salisbury told Beaconsfield that Britain should occupy two naval stations, Lemnos and Cyprus, and temporarily Alexandretta, in exchange for not opposing the Russian acquisitions in Asia.[138] According to Derby's diary, Beaconsfield addressed the Cabinet on 27 March:

> that we must now decide our policy, that our objects have been the maintenance of the empire, and of peace: that peace is not to be secured by 'drifting': that our attempts to be moderate and neutral have only lessened our influence, and caused our power not to be believed in . . . An emergency had arisen: every state must now look to its own resources: the balance of power in the Mediterranean was destroyed. He proposed to issue a proclamation declaring emergency, to put a force in the field and simultaneously to send an expedition from India to occupy Cyprus and Scanderoon (Alexandretta). Thus the effects of the Armenian conquest would be neutralised, the influence of England in the Persian

Gulf would be maintained, and we should hold posts which are the keys of Asia. Cairns and Salisbury both supported the Premier, showing clearly by their language, that they were aware of the plan . . . others supported more vaguely: I declared my dissent . . .[139]

Clearly, between 21 and 27 March, Beaconsfield and Salisbury had agreed on territorial expansion – Cyprus and Alexandretta's forcible seizure from the Ottoman Empire – to nullify Russian gains in Armenia. This aggressive act against their ally showed that protecting the Ottoman Empire was incidental to preserving their own interests. Immediately, 7,000 Indian troops were summoned to Malta, the reserves mobilised and Parliament sanctioned a special vote of credit for £6 million to seize a place of arms. A horrified Derby resigned and Salisbury became Foreign Secretary.[140] Derby's brother, F.A. Stanley, replaced him in the Cabinet. It was a telling move. As the new War Secretary (Gathorne-Hardy replaced Salisbury at the India Office) he convinced his colleagues that seizing Alexandretta was unlikely to succeed because an expedition to Aleppo needed 70,000 men.[141] This contradicted the report on Alexandretta by Captain G.E. Grover, who had worked with Home at Constantinople from 1876 to 1877.[142] As Wolseley headed to Cyprus he wrote to his wife that the island was 'selected because there was no good position that would suit on the mainland, Alexandretta . . . being so unhealthy owing to undrained marshes'.[143] More indicative of the preference for Cyprus was the appointment of Viscount Sandon as President of the Board of Trade and his inclusion in the Cabinet. His predecessor, Charles Adderley, who had resigned when a peerage was offered, had been outside the Cabinet.[144] Sandon had been a strong performer on education, but had also started carrying a chart of Cyprus in February, having set his 'heart on that island for England, as the key of the East' because it 'was free from all the complications of Egypt and Crete'.[145]

Cyprus realities

Although the Cabinet had not decided to seize Cyprus by March, Beaconsfield and Salisbury clearly favoured Cyprus over Lemnos or any other place. But what was Cyprus like and on what basis was it selected?

There are a number of prerequisites needed to establish a strategic and economic base: healthiness, so troops could encamp; a harbour for war and merchant ships; a docile and sizeable population; and fertility.

Travellers to Cyprus throughout the nineteenth century wrote about its dangerous climate and insalubrity. In 1800 three Englishmen visited

Cyprus and reported negatively about its sanitation and climate: Dr William Whitman of the Royal Artillery, who joined the Ottoman Army en route to Egypt as part of the British military team;[146] Reverend E.D. Clarke, a professor of mineralogy;[147] and Dr J.R. Hume, the Duke of Wellington's physician, who visited Cyprus 'under considerable apprehensions' about its unhealthiness.[148] In September 1814 John Bramsen encountered the same trying conditions. Vondiziano, the British consul, warned him that 'malignant fever was raging . . . with such violence that hardly a house was exempted from its destructive influences'.[149] Bramsen was told that most crews of European vessels were sick and Cyprus' ports were 'highly dangerous to the European, who is very likely to find his grave there'.[150] In the same year, Captain Light spent three weeks in Larnaca at Vondiziano's home and although he advocated that Britain seize Cyprus (Chapter 2), a violent fever raged.[151] Light was comfortable reconciling the contradictions between the unhealthiness and trying climate with the potential value – something that happened in 1878. Similar observations were made in 1828 by Captain Charles Frankland,[152] in 1850 by Frederick Neale, an employee of the British Consulate in Syria,[153] and by a traveller to Larnaca and Nicosia in autumn 1856, who had been 'cautioned against the malaria of Larnaca and its vicinity'.[154]

From 1863 to 1867 the Scottish Meteorological Society established climatological stations at Jerusalem, Beirut, Damascus and Larnaca, to determine their suitability as sanatoriums. Thomas Sandwith, the English Vice-Consul in Cyprus, started the observations in October 1866 and ended them four years later. The results were published in the society's journal. In summer (June to September),the observations were made at Alethriko, three miles from the sea and five miles west of Larnaca, and during the other months at Larnaca. The society's secretary, Alexander Buchan, the first person to use a weather map, analysed the data after Cyprus was occupied. It was exceedingly hot in summer, the transition from the cooler to the hotter months was dramatic, the mountain ranges afforded 'admirable facilities for the establishment of summer sanataria [sic] . . . just as has been done in India' and Cyprus had low precipitation.[155]

Information on Cyprus' harbours was also readily available. Bramsen described Larnaca as unsafe because vessels were exposed to heavy gales.

It is now about a fortnight since we anchored in this port, during which time only three days have been exempted from the violent gales. On more than one occasion we have seen vessels drifting from their moorings, and running foul of other ships . . .[156]

They waited until the end of September to move with the land breeze, but they had 'scarcely cleared the channel when it began to blow directly contrary'. The captain tried to return to port, but the sea ran very high and the ship laboured hard before it could.[157]

In 1844 Niven Kerr claimed that, excepting Alexandretta, there was no better roadstead than Larnaca. Also, with a small expense Famagusta could be made safe for warships.[158] But Famagusta harbour was in a state of neglect, being badly silted and having only twelve feet of depth.[159] English trade in the eastern Mediterranean needed a nautical survey of Famagusta. Accordingly, the Admiralty had Captain Thomas Graves survey Cyprus (after Crete) in May 1849.[160] A decade later Sandwith repeated Kerr's contradictions[161] and 1863 the Vice-Consul Horace Philips White reported that 'should Cyprus fall into the hands of any European power, Famagusta would once more become a place of great importance'.[162]

The consuls agreed on the population's size (about 200,000), potential size (five to ten times that) and character ('political agitation or opposition . . . to the constituted authority . . . [was] unknown').[163]

Niven Kerr to Lord Aberdeen, the Foreign Secretary, in 1844, best reflects the perceived value.

> I have no hesitation in stating my strong conviction that with but little attention and perseverance Cyprus might soon be restored to its former richness, and become one of the most fertile and valuable islands of the Sultans dominions.[164]

Captain Edwin Collen, of the Intelligence Department, wrote a report on Cyprus, which historians have not mentioned. Published on 18 May, it used the consular reports and reflected their contradictions and optimism.[165] But Cyprus was chosen by 2 May, so Collen's report was ready by then or was produced to justify a decision already made.

The policy applied

Despite appearances, it was Derby's policy of negotiation with Russia and peace that prevailed. On 2 May Salisbury told Layard that he dreaded Russia dominating Western Asia and Britain had to enter into a defensive alliance with the Porte to prevent this. To strengthen the commitment a port in the Levant was 'an absolute necessity'. Two days later, Salisbury proposed to the Cabinet the defensive alliance and Cyprus as the port.[166] Although no definite decision was made, the next day Beaconsfield wrote to Victoria:

> If Cyprus be conceded to your Majesty by the Porte, and England . . . enters into a defensive alliance with Turkey, guaranteeing Asiatic Turkey

from Russian invasion, the power of England in the Mediterranean will be absolutely increased in that region, and your Majesty's Indian Empire immensely strengthened.

Cyprus is the Key of Western Asia . . .

If this policy be carried into effect, and it must be carried, your Majesty need fear no coalition of Emperors. It will weld together your Majesty's Indian Empire and Great Britain.[167]

Cyprus' attraction was clearly within *Tancred*'s Oriental reality. On 11 May, Salisbury told the Cabinet that there was no obstacle to the occupation: Berlin, Vienna and Athens would not object; St Petersburg agreed to Britain having 'the key of some part of Turkey', so long as it was not near the Dardanelles; Italy could be ignored; France offered Tunis, if necessary, and Abdul Hamid accepted the proposal, although Cyprus was not mentioned. The Cabinet agreed to demand Cyprus if Russia insisted on keeping Batum, Kars and Ardahan, 'thus a very important decision [was] taken',[168] but really Beaconsfield and Salisbury had taken it on 2 May or earlier. Beaconsfield 'was convinced that the virtual administration of the East by England was the only hope for the prosperity of those countries and peoples'.[169] *Tancred*'s fiction was being put into fact. Indeed it was by no means a joke when on 13 July *The Spectator* wrote: 'When someone quoted *Tancred* two or three months ago in Lord Beaconsfield's presence, the Prime Minister remarked "Ah! I perceive you have been reading *Tancred*. That is a work to which I refer more and more every year, not for amusement, but for instrument."' This led *The Spectator* to claim that 'for the last eight months at least, our policy has evidently been borrowed from *Tancred*'.[170]

Geography played a big part in Cyprus' selection. On 16 May Salisbury told Layard that Cyprus was chosen because it had the 'double advantage of vicinity both to Asia Minor and Syria . . . to enable us . . . to accumulate material of war and, if requisite, the troops necessary for operations in Asia Minor or Syria'.[171] On 24 May he telegraphed Layard to give the Sultan forty-eight hours to agree.[172] Layard could not challenge the selection. He favoured Mytilene as late as 15 May,[173] but Salisbury did not tell the Cabinet. On 31 May Layard told Salisbury that he thought of Cyprus, but believed 'that the absence of a port would be an insuperable objection'.[174]

On 27 May Salisbury told the Cabinet that the Sultan had agreed to the conditions and W.H. Smith, the First Lord of the Admiralty, ordered ships to Crete (where the presence of French ships masked their purpose) in readiness.[175] The Convention was signed on 4 June. Article I stated:

If Batum, Ardahan, Kars or any of them, shall be retained by Russia, and if any attempt shall be made at any future time by Russia to take possession of further territories of . . . the Sultan in Asia . . . England engages to join . . . the Sultan in defending them by force of arms.

In return . . . the Sultan promises to England to introduce necessary reforms, to be agreed upon later between the two Powers, into the Government and for the protection of the Christian and other subjects of the Porte in those territories. And in order to enable England to make necessary provision for executing her engagements . . . the Sultan further consents to assign the Island of Cyprus to be occupied and administered by England.

The Convention embodied all the entangled aims and interests of its authors: Salisbury and Beaconsfield and to a lesser extent Home and Layard.

Home's memorandum and the conclusion

Home's memorandum was an eloquent summary of the justifications for selecting Cyprus, and was written on 8 June 1878, four days after the Convention was signed, and so after the fact for the officials going to Berlin. Simmons wrote in the margin that Home gave it to him to take to Berlin and that it was the reason for selecting Cyprus.[176] Lee believed that it was a clerk's copy transcribed for the Congress, while Temperley thought it based on an earlier document.[177] But a copy would not have carried a later date.

Using the Collen report, Home dismissed numerous places, including Alexandretta and Stampalia, in such a way that it indicates that the memorandum was written after Cyprus was selected. He recognised that Stampalia was well located to protect interests in the Near East and India and that it had two harbours, but rejected it because it offered only a coaling station and water was scarce. Home claimed that Famagusta had the facilities for becoming a harbour 'far superior to any other in the Levant'; meaning that a harbour still needed making. The claim about the water supply was also misleading. Home selectively used the Edwards and Egerton memorandum, failing to state that tanks would solve the problem. The British found Cyprus no better, so obviously there was no investigation into water there. Clearly Home was too eager to justify the choice of Cyprus.

Home claimed that Cyprus 'appears to offer very great advantages': political, military, naval and commercial.[178] The political element was the kernel of the Eastern Question: the difficulty of making people of different races, religion and language live harmoniously. Thus, the place acquired should be 'sufficiently large, possessed of sufficient material resources and inhabited by such races of people . . . to allow the experiment of what good government will do'. Cyprus' Orthodox and Muslims were the perfect guinea pigs. Room for an army to assemble and encamp in healthy surrounds was pivotal and the place had to feed an army and provide mules, oxen and horses. Home reflected the contradictory accounts that Famagusta harbour could be made into an important naval and coaling station. Commercially, Cyprus was 'admirably adapted for becoming a depot for English manufacturers and trade into Syria and Asia Minor'.[179] There was, of course, no investigation into whether such markets existed.

Conclusion

Cyprus was occupied through diplomatic means to act as the headquarters of a new empire stretching from Asia Minor to Persia and to protect British interests in the Near East and India. This was a departure in policy; all other Mediterranean possessions had been occupied during wartime. The move was ambitious, but it appealed and fitted the romantic imagination of the British prime minister, having expressed in his novels his desire for Britain to establish a multi-religious empire under Queen Victoria and, in his politics, the idea that power could only be projected through occupying the strong places in the world. A select few chose Cyprus without scientific evidence, but based on the reports of men who were on the spot some decades earlier who spoke glowingly about potential rather than actual value. The selection was not ad hoc; on the contrary, it was made in advance of any investigation into Cyprus – that is how confident the architects of the decision were.

Notes

1 Georghallides, *A Political and Administrative History of Cyprus*, 3.
2 Temperley, 'Disraeli and Cyprus', 277; H. Temperley, 'Further Evidence on Disraeli and Cyprus', *EHR*, XLVI, 1931, 457–60; D.E. Lee, 'A Memorandum Concerning Cyprus', *Journal of Modern History (JMH)*, 1931, 235–41; Lee, *Great Britain and the Cyprus Convention Policy*, 77; W.N. Medlicott, *The Congress of Berlin and After*, London 1938, 19; Georghallides, *A Political and Administrative History of Cyprus*, 5; M.S. George, *The Cyprus Convention Policy*, London, 2000, 36.
3 Napoleon to the Directory, summer 1797, Michael Pratt, *Britain's Greek Empire*, London, 1978, 61.
4 Kanya-Forstner, 'French Expansion in Africa: The Mythical Theory'; R.F. Betts, *Tricouleur*, London, 1978.
5 Napoleon quoted, Pratt, *Britain's Greek Empire*, 61.
6 C.W. Crawley, 'John Capodistrias and the Greeks Before 1821', *Cambridge Historical Journal (CHJ)*, XIII, 2, 1957, 172; Pratt, *Britain's Greek Empire*, 102; Clogg, *A Short History of Modern Greece*, 46–7.

7 H.M. Chichester, 'Maitland, Sir Thomas (1760–1824)', rev. Roger T. Stearn, *ODNB* (www.oxforddnb.com/view/article/17835, accessed 15 May 2005).

8 WO33/7, Report, Colonels Lefroy and Owen, 1859.

9 Hughes, *Britain in the Mediterranean*, 105; R.H. Vetch, 'Jones, Sir John Thomas, first baronet (1783–1843)', rev. Roger T. Stearn, *ODNB* (www.oxforddnb.com/view/article/15054, accessed 15 May 2005).

10 CO136/300, Maitland to Bunbury, 3 May 1816.

11 Gallant, *Experiencing Dominion*, 8–9.

12 John Barrow, 'Ionian Islands', *QR*, XXIX, 1823, 86–116; Colonel Charles James Napier, *The Colonies: Treating of their Value – Of the Ionian Islands in Particular*, London, 1833; C.K. Webster, *The Foreign Policy of Castlereagh, 1815–1915*, London, 1925, 410–11; H.M. Chichester, 'Oswald, Sir John (1771–1840)', rev. John Sweetman, *ODNB* (www.oxforddnb.com/view/article/20923, accessed 15 May 2005).

13 Douglas Dakin, *The Greek Struggle for Independence 1821–1833*, London, 1973, 50–1, 108, 112, 118, 166–7.

14 Pratt, *Britain's Greek Empire*, 112, 112–14.

15 Napier, *The Colonies*, 8.

16 Ibid., 13, 16–17. Emphasis is Napier's.

17 Lord John Russell Memorandum, 1 May 1848, Spencer Walpole, *Life of Lord John Russell*, II, London 1889, 41.

18 Palmerston to Sir Henry Wood, private, 21 December 1850, Evelyn Ashley, *Life of Henry John Temple, Viscount Palmerston, 1846–1865*, I, London, 1876, 266.

19 *Collected Papers and Memoranda on Defences*, WO, 1 December 1859, containing Memorandum on the Proposed Defences at Corfu, General Sir J.F. Burgoyne, 12 July 1858.

20 Hughes, *Britain in the Mediterranean*, 113.

21 *The Times*, 29 November 1858, 6c, 6e, 10b.

22 Ibid., 15 February 1859, 9c; 26 February 1859, 9a.

23 Pratt, *Britain's Greek Empire*, 151–2; Hughes, *Britain in the Mediterranean*, 116.

24 Gallant, *Experiencing Dominion*, 13–14.

25 Morley, *Gladstone*, I, 620; Pratt, *Britain's Greek Empire*, 153; Bruce Knox, 'British Policy and the Ionian Islands, 1847–1864: Nationalism and Imperial Administration', *EHR*, XCIX, 392, 1984, 503–29.

26 David Waddell, 'Great Britain and the Bay Islands, 1821–1861', *HJ*, II, 1, 1959, 59–77.

27 R.L. Schuyler, 'The Climax of Anti-Imperialism in England', *Political Science Quarterly (PSQ)*, XXXVI, 4, 1921, 539–41; Christopher A. Kent, 'Smith, Goldwin (1823–1910)', *ODNB* (www.oxforddnb.com/view/article/36142, accessed 22 June 2005).

28 *Hansard* (Commons), III, 169, 95–6.

29 Owen, *The Middle East in the World Economy*, 100–21; Pamuk, *The Ottoman Empire and European Capitalism*, 55–81.

30 Owen, *The Middle East in the World Economy*, 89–90.

31 Ibid., 101–2; Pamuk, *The Ottoman Empire and European Capitalism*, 59. The Ottoman Bank became the Imperial Ottoman Bank in 1863.

32 K. Bourne, 'Great Britain and the Cretan Revolt, 1866–69', *Slavonic and East European Review (SEER)*, XXXV, 1956, 74–94.

33 W.E. Mosse, 'The End of the Crimean System: England, Russia and the Neutrality of the Black Sea, 1870–71', *HJ*, IV, 2, 1961, 164–90.

34 R. Blake, *Disraeli and Gladstone*, London, 1969; Clayton, *Britain and the Eastern Question*, 155; M. Willis, *Gladstone and Disraeli*, Cambridge, 1989, 5–7.

35 D. Steele, *Lord Salisbury: A Political Biography*, London, 1999, 126–9; A. Roberts, *Salisbury: Victorian Titan*, London, 1999, 149–50, 153–4, 170, 173–4; John Charmley, *Splendid Isolation?*, London, 1999, 15.

36 T.W. Reid 'Lord Derby at the Foreign Office, 1876–1878', *Macmillan's Magazine (MM)*, XL, 1879, 180–92; P.J.V. Rolo, 'Derby', in K.M. Wilson (ed.), *British Foreign Secretaries and Foreign Policy*, London, 1987, 102–18; Charmley, *Splendid Isolation?*, 14–25. D. Steele, 'Stanley, Edward Henry, fifteenth earl of Derby

(1826–1893)', *ODNB* (www.oxforddnb.com/view/article/26266, accessed 17 June 2005).

37 Roberts, *Salisbury*, 149.
38 R. McWilliam, 'Johnstone, Henry Alexander Butler- (1837–1902)', *ODNB* (www.oxforddnb.com/view/article/42333, accessed 20 Nov 2004).
39 S. Koss, *The Rise and Fall of the Political Press in Britain*, I, London, 1981, 211.
40 *Pall Mall Gazette*, 15 July 1875, 10.
41 Koss, *Political Press in Britain*, 211.
42 Ibid., 48, 150.
43 Ibid., 53, 95, 99, 175, 185–6.
44 *John Bull*, 21 August 1875, 568, 4 September 1875, 601; *The Times*, 23 August 1875, 7; *Pall Mall Gazette*, 10, 17, and 24 September 1875; *Daily News*, 6 September 1875, 4.
45 D.C. Blaisdell, *European Financial Control in the Ottoman Empire*, New York, 1929, 80–4.
46 *John Bull*, 6 November 1875.
47 Lady Gwendolyn Cecil, *Life of Robert Marquis of Salisbury*, II, London, 1922, 43–51.
48 *Pall Mall Gazette*, 22 July 1875, 11; 23 August 1875, 8; 24 August 1875, 1.
49 *The Times*, 10 November 1875, 10a.
50 Owen, *The Middle East in the World Economy*, 122–48; G. Fede and R. Just, 'Debt Crisis in an Increasingly Pessimistic International Market: The Case of Egyptian Credit, 1862–1876', *Economic Journal*, XCIV, 374, 1984, 340–56.
51 *Pall Mall Gazette*, 3 November 1875, 1–2; *Standard*, 4 November 1875, 4; *Economist*, 20 November 1875; *Daily News*, 22 November 1875, 4.
52 Koss, *Political Press in Britain*, 222.
53 Blake, *Disraeli*, 582–3.
54 Robinson and Gallagher, *Africa and the Victorians*.
55 Cecil, *Salisbury*, II, 79–80; A. Hardinge, *The Life of Henry Howard Mylyneux Herbert, Fourth Earl of Carnarvon, 1831–1890*, Oxford, 1925, II, 92.
56 Monypenny and Buckle, *Beaconsfield*, II, 890–2, 896–8; Blake, *Disraeli*, 587–8.
57 *Hansard* (Commons), 10 July 1876, CCXXX, 1181–2.
58 W.E. Gladstone, *Bulgarian Horrors and the Question of the East*, London, 1876; Blake, *Disraeli*, 597–8.
59 Baumgart, *Imperialism*, 36.
60 Roberts, *Salisbury*, 152–6.
61 A.E. Gathorne-Hardy (ed.), *Gathorne Hardy, First Earl of Cranbrook, a Memoir with Extracts from His Diary and Correspondence*, II, London, 1910, 372–7.
62 Schurman, *Imperial Defence*, 26–8.
63 Ibid., 31–2.
64 J.S. Kinross, 'Jervois, Sir William Francis Drummond (1821–1897)', *ODNB* (www.oxforddnb.com/view/article/14800, accessed 22 Dec 2004).
65 Schurman, *Imperial Defence*, 32, 34, 48.
66 T. Ferguson, *British Military Intelligence 1870–1914*, Maryland, 1984, 52, 68–9, 77; R.H. Vetch, 'Home, Robert (1837–1879)', rev. R.T. Stearn, *ODNB* (www.oxforddnb.com/view/article/13648, accessed 23 Feb 2005).
67 FO358/1, Simmons to Home, 3 June 1876.
68 *The Dardanelles for England: The True Solution of the Eastern Question*, London, 1876, 5, 8.
69 FO358/1, Home to Simmons, 20 December 1876.
70 Captain H.H. Kitchener, 'Notes on Cyprus', *Blackwood's Edinburgh Review*, August 1879, 157. Kitchener had studied the map in preparation to survey Cyprus.
71 FO358/1, Home to Simmons, 20 December 1876.
72 FO358/1, Home to Simmons, 26 December 1876.
73 W.L. Langer, *European Alliances and Alignments, 1871–1890*, New York, 1931 (1950), 105–9.
74 FO358/3, Salisbury Memorandum, 15 January 1877.
75 Cecil, *Salisbury*, II, 122.

76 FO358/1, Home Memorandum, 8 February 1877.
77 Home Memorandum on the Dardanelles, 3 February 1877, extract *Reports and Memoranda*, 0631, WO, 1877, 130–1.
78 *The Times*, 3 January 1877, 10b, 6 January 1877, 6e, 2 February 1877, 8a, 4 April 1877, 10c.
79 R.H. Vetch, 'Simmons, Sir John Lintorn Arabin (1821–1903)', rev. James Lunt, *ODNB* (www.oxforddnb.com/view/article/36094, accessed 23 Dec 2004).
80 FO358/3, Select committee report on the Euphrates Valley Railway; with the proceedings, 22 July 1872.
81 FO358/2, Simmons Memorandum, 17 April 1877.
82 G. Waterfield, *Layard of Nineveh*, London, 1963, 190–2; Bar-Yosef, *The Holy Land in English Culture*, 98. Nineveh is near Mosul.
83 Waterfield, *Layard of Nineveh*, 511–12.
84 Ibid., 237–47.
85 Ibid., 352.
86 Ibid., 353.
87 R.W. Seton-Watson, *Disraeli, Gladstone and the Eastern Question*, London, 1935, 204.
88 Anonymous, 'The Eastern Question and the Conference', *QR*, CXLIII, January 1877, 276–320.
89 FO358/2, Memoranda, Simmons, 19 April, 2 and 11 May 1877.
90 Lord Derby, diary, 21 April 1877, 392, (ed.) J. Vincent, *The Diaries of Edward Henry Stanley, 15th Earl of Derby (1826–93), Between September 1869 and March 1878*, London, 1994. Hereafter Derby diary.
91 Ibid., 1 and 2 May 1877, 397; C.1770, Derby to Shuvalov, 6 May 1877.
92 Derby diary, 8 June 1877, 406–7.
93 FO64/878, 211 and 221, Russell, Berlin, to Derby, 19 and 27 May 1877.
94 FO22/2239, 474 and 476, Lord Lyons, Paris, to Derby, 7 June 1877.
95 Derby diary, 16 June 1877, 409–10.
96 Ibid.
97 Ibid., 17, 18, 20 June 1877, 410–11.
98 *The Times*, 28 June 1877, 9a, 30 June 1877, 13a, 5 July 1877, 9a, 10 July 1877, 5c, 13 July 1877, 10a.
99 Ibid., 5 June, 1877, 5a, 8a, 15 June 1877, 8a, 9c, 16 June 1877, 12b.
100 Emile de Laveleye, 'British Interests in the Present Crisis', *Fortnightly Review (FR)*, XXII, July 1877, 25–34.
101 Ibid.
102 Ibid.; Emile de Laveleye, 'England and the War', *FR*, XXIII, February 1878, 153–66, 163–6.
103 Schurman, *Imperial Defence*, 50–1.
104 FO358/3, Simmons Memorandum, 27 April 1877.
105 FO358/3, Report, Lieutenant-Colonel J.B. Edwards, RE and Commander Fred Egerton, Commander of *Salamis*, 9 June 1877.
106 FO358/3, Simmons Memorandum forwarding Edwards and Egerton report, 26 June 1877.
107 FO358/3, Observations on the Proposed Coaling Station at the East End of the Mediterranean, in reference to a WO Confidential Letter of 27 June 1877 (for Yelverton) by Evans, 30 June 1877.
108 FO358/3, minute, signed, A.H. 31 June 1877; FO358/3, minute, signed, H.Y. 3 July 1877.
109 FO358/3, Simmons Memorandum 10 July 1877; FO358/3, Memorandum on the Observations of the Hydrographer and Lords of the Admiralty, Lieutenant-Colonel J.B. Edwards, 5 July 1877; FO358/3, Memorandum, Lords of the Admiralty, 2 August 1877.
110 Derby, diary, 4 July 1877, 415.
111 Seton-Watson, *Disraeli, Gladstone and the Eastern Question*, 225.
112 Gathorne-Hardy, *Memoir*, II, 25–6; Monypenny and Buckle, *Beaconsfield*, II, 1026–30.

113 Koss, *Political Press in Britain*, 200–1.
114 *Daily Telegraph*, quoted in *Pall Mall Gazette*, 20 November 1877, 2.
115 D.C. Somervell, *Disraeli & Gladstone*, London, 1925, 193.
116 W.E. Gladstone, 'Aggression on Egypt and Freedom in the East', *NC*, II, August 1877, 149–66; W.E. Gladstone, 'The Peace to Come', *NC*, III, February 1878, 207–26.
117 Samuel Laing, 'A Plain View of British Interests', *FR*, XXIII, January 1878, 335–48; Goldwin Smith, 'The Eastern Crisis', *FR*, XXIII, May 1878, 647–61.
118 Monypenny and Buckle, *Beaconsfield*, II, 1123–4.
119 Layard to Beaconsfield, secret, 12 December 1877, Lee, *Great Britain and the Cyprus Convention Policy*, 185–90.
120 Ibid.
121 Captain Bedford Pim, *The Eastern Question, Past, Present and Future*, 3rd edition, London, 1877, 36–7.
122 Edward Cazalet, *The Eastern Question an Address to Working Men*, London, 1877; *The Berlin Congress and the Anglo-Turkish Convention*, London, 1878; A.C. Howe, 'Cazalet, Edward (1827–1883)', *ODNB* (www.oxforddnb.com/view/article/40812, accessed 1 Feb 2005).
123 Koss, *Political Press in Britain*, 81, 199.
124 Layard, 'The Eastern Question and the Conference', 302–3; *Pall Mall Gazette*, 26 November 1877, 2–3; 27 November 1877, 1; 3 December 1877, 3; A. Borthwick, *An Address on the Eastern Question*, London, 1878, 5–6, 17–18.
125 S. Mahajan, *British Foreign Policy 1874–1914: The Role of India*, London, 2002, 47; Layard to Beaconsfield, secret, 12 December 1877, Lee, *Great Britain and the Cyprus Convention Policy*, 185–90.
126 Ibid.
127 Edward Dicey, 'The Future of Egypt', *NC*, II, 4, August 1877, 3–14; 'Mr. Gladstone and Our Empire', *NC*, II, 7, September 1877, 292–308; 'Egypt and the Khedive', *NC*, II, 10, December 1877, 854–67. Dicey had worked for the *Daily Telegraph* and *Daily News*.
128 Gladstone, 'Aggression on Egypt and Freedom in the East', 149–66; Charles Dilke speech at Chelsea quoted, Laveleye, 'England and the War', 165.
129 Wolseley journal, 19 July 1878, 6.
130 Sandon journal, 22 May 1878, 7.
131 FO78/2767, Derby to Layard, 18 February 1878; *Hansard* (Commons), CCCXXIII, 8 March 1888, 569.
132 FO358/1, Simmons Memorandum of meeting with Gathorne-Hardy, 2 March 1878.
133 Ibid.
134 Georghallides, *A Political and Administrative History of Cyprus*, 5.
135 Schurman, *Imperial Defence*, 61–4.
136 Temperley, 'Disraeli and Cyprus', 277; Temperley, 'Further Evidence on Disraeli and Cyprus', 457–60; Lee, 'A Memorandum Concerning Cyprus', 235–41; Lee, *Great Britain and the Cyprus Convention Policy*, 77; Medlicott, *The Congress of Berlin and After*, 19; Georghallides, *A Political and Administrative History of Cyprus*, 5; George, *The Cyprus Convention Policy*, 36.
137 FO358/1 Home Memorandum, 8 June 1878.
138 Salisbury to Disraeli, 21 March 1878, Cecil, *Salisbury*, II, 213–14.
139 Derby, diary, 27 March 1878, 532.
140 Derby made it clear that he had resigned over the proposal to seize Cyprus. Viscount Sandon's journal reveals that W.H. Smith told him that Derby resigned over Cyprus. Viscount Sandon, *The Cabinet Journal of Dudley Ryder, Viscount Sandon*, eds C. Howard and P. Gordon, London, 1974, 11 May 1878, 1. Hereafter, Sandon journal.
141 Ibid., 15 May 1878, 5.
142 FO358/5, Captain G.E. Grover, *Iskenderun*, London, 8 April 1878.
143 Wolseley journal, 19 July 1878, 6.
144 Blake, Disraeli, 557.

145 Sandon journal, 11 May 1878, 4–5.
146 William Wittman, *Travels in Turkey, Asia Minor, Syria and across the Desert into Egypt during the years 1799, 1800, and 1801 . . .* , London, 1803, 115.
147 Rev. E.D. Clarke, *Travels in Various Countries of Europe, Asia and Africa*, II, Cambridge, 1810–1823, 309–11.
148 Robert Walpole, *Travels in Various Countries in the East*, London, 1818, 246–7. Walpole used Hume's journal.
149 John Bramsen, *Travels in Egypt, Syria, Cyprus*, London, 1820, 300.
150 Ibid., 301, 304.
151 Light, *Travels*, 240, 242.
152 Frankland, *Travels*.
153 Frederick Neale, *Eight Years in Syria, Palestine, and Asia Minor from 1842 to 1850*, London, 1850, 282–97.
154 Anon., 'Island of Cyprus and its Inhabitants', *Dublin University Magazine*, XXXXVIII, 1856, 179.
155 Alexander Buchan, 'The Climate of Cyprus', *Journal of the Scottish Meteorological Society*, 1880, 189–93.
156 Bramsen, *Travels*, 299–300.
157 Ibid., 312.
158 FO78/580, Niven Kerr to Lord Aberdeen, 31 January 1844.
159 FO78/621, Kerr to C.H. Wellesley, 31 December 1845.
160 FO78/802, 31 May 1849; FO78/802, 21 September 1849.
161 Quoted, Capt. E.H.H. Collen, *Report on Cyprus, based on information obtained chiefly from Consular Reports, Foreign Office, 1845–1877*, London, 18 May, 1878, 3.
162 Vice-Consul White quoted, Capt. A.R. Savile, *Cyprus*, London, 1878, 66.
163 *Cyprus. Translation of a Report Forwarded by Mr. Campbell, British Consul at Rhodes, upon the Island of Cyprus, for the Years 1854–8*, London, 1859; *Cyprus. Report. General and Statistical, by Mr. Vice-Consul White*, LXX, London, 1863; *Cyprus. Commercial Report by Vice-Consul White of the Island of Cyprus for the Year 1862*, LXX, London, 1863.
164 FO78/580, Niven Kerr to Lord Aberdeen, 31 January 1844.
165 Collen, *Report on Cyprus*, 1878.
166 Sandon journal, 11 May 1878, 3. Sandon was not present at the Cabinet meeting of 4 May.
167 Disraeli to Victoria, 5 May 1878, Cecil, *Salisbury*, II, 269.
168 Sandon journal, 11 May 1878, 3.
169 Ibid., 5 June 1878, 19.
170 *The Spectator*, 13 July 1878, 883.
171 Salisbury to Layard, 16 May 1878, Cecil, *Salisbury*, II, 269.
172 Sandon journal, 24 May 1878, 9–10.
173 Layard to Salisbury, private, 15 May 1878, Lee, *Great Britain and the Cyprus Convention Policy*, 192–4.
174 Seton-Watson, *Disraeli, Gladstone and the Eastern Question*, 424, fn. 2.
175 Sandon journal, 27 May 1878, 12–13.
176 FO358/1 Home Memorandum, 8 June 1878. Hereafter Home's 8 June 1878 Memorandum.
177 Temperley, 'Further Evidence on Disraeli and Cyprus', 459; Lee, 'A Memorandum Concerning Cyprus', 236.
178 Home's 8 June 1878 Memorandum.
179 Ibid.

CHAPTER 4

The sublime illusions, 1878–80: the Mediterranean 'Eldorado'

Its occupation by us was accompanied by many incidents that cast around it more the *eclat* of warlike conquest than the less demonstrative acquisition of peace or purchase. The popular mind once excited, becomes capable of strange enthusiasms. Cyprus grew in imagination into an earthly paradise. Thus wagged the little tongues of that great Babel called public opinion; and ere a week had passed from the date of the announcement of our Cypriote acquisition, a picture had arisen of our new possession as utterly false to the reality as though some German, deeply read in the Roman History of Britain, had become the purchaser of a property in Sussex, and expected to find existing in full sway upon his estate the manners and customs of Boadicea. (William Francis Butler, *Far Out: Rovings Retold*, 1880, 330–1)

Did the Conservatives achieve their principal aim in occupying Cyprus – its establishment as a place of arms? There was much euphoria over the selection of Cyprus, which Liberal opposition tempered. The ensuing political confrontation and the issue of converting Cyprus into a strategic asset were resolved only when the realities on the ground presented serious problems to the fulfilment of the desired policy.

The 'Eldorado' effect

Euphoric crowds greeted Beaconsfield's declaration of 'peace with honour' as he and Salisbury arrived at Charing Cross. Cyprus was the talk of the town and, as William Butler claimed, 'it possessed associations connected with the earlier ages of our recorded history, which rendered it a familiar name to every schoolboy'.

Daily journals, weekly reviews, monthly magazines, all made it a topic of animated discussion. Forgotten history was searched to find episodes of early English dominion in the island. Political parties made its acquisition (*sic*) matter of grave parliamentary debate and even popular preachers drew pulpit parallels between the record in Holy Writ of Saul and Barnabas sailing for Salamis, and British civilisation in the shape of a brigade of regular infantry and a division of Sepoys landing at Larnaca.[1]

Commentators emphasised the historical continuity from when Richard *Coeur de Lion*[2] trounced Isaac and compared Beaconsfield to the Apostle Barnabas, the patron saint of Cyprus (Appendix I). On 20 July the *Illustrated London News* published the first images of Britain's new gem. The front page sketch of Famagusta glorified 'The Ancient Venetian Port of Cyprus' (Figure 5), while *Punch* celebrated

Figure 5 'Famagusta: The Ancient Venetian Port of Cyprus'
Source: *Illustrated London News*, 20 July 1878.

[94]

Figure 6 'A Blaze of Triumph'
Source: Punch, 27 July 1878.

Beaconsfield's 'blaze of triumph' in carrying the Sultan 'piggy-back' on a tightrope (Figure 6).

Two days after the Convention was announced, an editorial in *The Times* claimed that Cyprus would 'be an admirable naval station, whether for the purpose of protecting the Suez Canal, securing a second road to India, or giving this country the requisite authority in its relations with the Porte'.[3] But the next day, John L. Haddan, formerly an engineer-in-chief in Syria and the author of *Ironclads and Forts* (1872), revealed that Larnaca – where the troops had landed – was unsafe, as vessels had to anchor half a mile from shore (Figure 7).[4] Thus uncertainties over Cyprus' value were evident from the start.

The occupation resulted in many books, pamphlets and articles on its past, present and future as British and Levantine prospectors descended on Cyprus. These men were not all reliable sources. A Constantinople Jew, Zachariah Williamson, later the arms dealer Sir Basil Zaharoff, sent letters to a London newspaper editor claiming that gold was washing down the hills![5] Edward Vizetelly, a journalist and not too reliable a source who related the story, claimed quite rightly that 'every one in England imagined that the island under British rule would have a great future'.[6]

More reliable sources justified the choice for strategic reasons. John Baldwin Hay, formerly the American consul-general at Beirut, asserted that Cyprus was 'admirably adapted for . . . naval and military occupation' and its location meant troops could 'be concentrated upon the coasts of Asia Minor, Syria, and Egypt, without much loss of time'.[7]

Robert Hamilton Lang, the head of the Ottoman Bank at Larnaca and Britain's acting vice-consul intermittently since 1861, unceasingly promoted Cyprus. He thought it would become 'an oasis in the surrounding desert of unenlightened administrations'[8] and a 'glance at any map' showed it was a strategic 'pearl'.[9] All the great civilisations had seized it as the first step on Egypt[10] and 'judged' by the past Cyprus' future was 'full of hope'.[11] Indeed, in a 'few years the people of Cyprus will be the most favoured nation in the world',[12] or, as another commentator put it, the Mediterranean 'El Dorado'.[13]

One anonymous pamphleteer asserted that 'any one skilled in the art of war will at once see how great is the value of this island . . . for arranging an army for conflict, or for landing it to resist the advance of an enemy on the Asiatic Continent'.[14] He quoted, verbatim, *The Times* editorial and argued that with Gibraltar, Malta and Cyprus, Britain now had a 'firm hold over the whole of the Mediterranean'. He exaggerated that Cyprus had accessible ports, excellent coaling depots and docks[15] and that it would soon be 'peopled by a million . . . happy and prosperous souls' as it was during its Venetian days.

> Under the aegis of England those days will come again; once more Cyprus will boast of abundance, healthiness, and happy homes, and the inhabitants will recognise what they have been strangers to for hundreds of years, the wholesomeness of industry, and the security of State promises.[16]

Kyriacos Demetriou was right when he asserted that 'the island had been wrapped in a veil of mythical narratives, its contemporary development being entirely a matter of indifference'.[17] Cyprus was not the first or last place to be built into an Eldorado only to fall flat. The French did it with Western Africa,[18] the Italians with Libya[19] and the

British with Palestine.[20] Unlike Western Africa and Libya, Cyprus did not have the vast tracks of land from which myths of 'new Australias' could be built upon, nor did it have as powerful a place in English culture as the Holy Land. Nevertheless, Cyprus had enough cultural and economic associations from which the architects and supporters of the occupation could manufacture myths in order to justify and build expectations that the island would have a vital place within the British imperial schema.

These expectations obscured Cyprus' potential and actual value, which the Cabinet thought would be realised only by the Foreign and not the Colonial Office, and which under the Liberals would probably give Cyprus a constitution.[21] But the magnitude of the task put off even Salisbury. As William Butler, a friend of the first high commissioner, Sir Garnet Wolseley, put it: 'the Cypriote canticle had . . . been pitched in too high a key, and a collapse was inevitable ere that song had reached its second part'.[22]

The Liberal opposition

The Liberals lost no time in attacking the Beaconsfield government over its acquisition, which produced an apologia from the government. On 11 July, the leader of the Liberal peers, Lord Granville, a former colonial secretary, and in the Commons Sir Julian Goldsmid asked if Cyprus had a harbour. They received virtually identical answers: 'Technically speaking, there is no harbour; but there are three very fair anchorages, from which it is usually easy to land.'[23] This was not a very confident reply. Four days later Goldsmid remarked that Cyprus needed a good harbour not bad roadsteads and that an Austrian Lloyd steamer he was aboard rolled for twenty-four hours at Larnaca waiting to discharge its cargo because 'the surf was so high that . . . [it] was unsafe for boats to put off'. This frequently occurred, he added, making it unsuitable as a naval station.[24]

But not all Liberals agreed to attack the Cyprus policy. The Liberal peer and ornithologist, Lord Lilford, had studied Cyprus' marshes in 1875 and thought after draining a good harbour could be made at Famagusta.[25] The men on the spot agreed. Lang argued that Limassol and Larnaca had 'the very best holding-ground' and, although storms produced violent waves, he had not seen a European vessel damaged. Famagusta harbour was clogged, but once dredged and the vicinity made healthy, it would make a fine military, naval and commercial base.[26] James Lewis Farley, the Ottoman Consul at Bristol (1870–84) in recognition of being the accountant-general of the State Bank of Turkey at Beirut (1856–60) and Constantinople (1860–70) and writing on

Ottoman socio-economic issues, believed that 'Cyprus would possess one of the finest harbours in the Levant' in Famagusta.

Cyprus' potential as a military station was also attacked because of its climate and insalubrity. Haddan warned that Larnaca's heat was 'unbearable' and that an elevated camp was needed.[27] On 15 July, Lord Oranmore and Browne, an Irish peer, claimed that abroad the climate was considered 'deadly' and warned of the fever affecting the troops.[28]

The government, gathering that it was being criticised for imprudence, asserted that Cyprus was a 'splendid garden' that could serve as a 'sanatorium for the invalids of Europe'.[29] It was supported by Staff Commandant D. Farrant RN, whose visits to Cyprus had made his service on the Syrian coast (1856–67) bearable.[30] Then Lilford declared that Cyprus was the healthiest Mediterranean island: 'more healthy than Sardinia or Corsica, and certainly than Sicily'.[31] Lang added that only Larnaca and Famagusta, where marshes infected the air and induced fever and ague, were insalubrious. Through public subscription, he had remedied two marshes at Larnaca, but much needed doing at Famagusta.[32]

Although some Liberals were not hostile to the acquisition[33] and the Tory chief whip, Sir William Hunt Dyke, thought some would 'object to an attack', he believed that Gladstone would 'make an impetuous charge' and carry some with him.[34] Indeed on 21 July at Southwark, Gladstone called the Cyprus Convention an 'insane covenant . . . [a] gross . . . act of duplicity of which every Englishman should be ashamed . . . [and] which has not been surpassed . . . and rarely equalled, in the history of nations'.[35] Two days later Salisbury assured critics that Cyprus would prosper under honest government,[36] a rhetorical theme of imperialism. Granville promptly accused him of adopting 'a system of secrecy' that he had never seen before,[37] which stemmed from no, or poor, research. Granville asked whether Cyprus would be of any use.

> No one can say that it will add to our military or naval strength . . . and I have great doubt . . . whether the Government can quote any opinion which they received previous to the Convention favourable to the Island . . . I do not know a single naval officer . . . who has not pronounced against it as a naval station.[38]

Lord Hammond, formerly the permanent under-secretary at the Foreign Office (1854–73), wondered if paying the tribute would allow for development and the pay of the civil, naval and military establishments. He was baffled at 'how an Island in a remote corner of the Mediterranean could serve as a basis of operation against a Russian invasion . . . of Asiatic Turkey' or to reform Asia Minor.[39]

Figure 7 Landing at Larnaca, 1878
Source: *Illustrated London News*, 17 August 1878.

When we considered, not only the expense incurred by the occupation and administration ... but that we had also undertaken the protection of Asiatic Turkey from encroachment on the part of Russia, and ... the protection of the Turkish subjects in Asia Minor against maladministration ... and when, in return for these onerous engagements, we found ourselves saddled with ... an unhealthy Island, insufficiently supplied with water, without a harbour for our ships, accommodation for our garrison, or establishments for those engaged in civil administration, we could not look without grave apprehension at the prospect before us.[40]

Beaconsfield defended the choice of Cyprus and promised that 'by this time next year' there would be good harbours to accommodate warships.[41] At the lavish Conservative banquet for him and Salisbury at Knightsbridge on 27 July he asked who would enter into an insane convention:

a body of English gentlemen, honoured by the favour of their sovereign and the confidence of their fellow-subjects ... or a sophisticated rhetorician, inebriated with the exuberance of his own verbosity ... [?][42]

Entrepreneurs shared Beaconsfield's plans for Cyprus and Ottoman Asia. The Duke of Sutherland, a former Liberal MP (1852–61) who attended the coronation of Tsar Alexander II (1856) and the opening of the Suez Canal (1869), but called Gladstone a Russian agent after his 'Bulgarian Horrors' pamphlet,[43] formed the 'Asia Minor and Euphrates Railway Association', the day the Cyprus Convention was announced, with W.P. Andrew and Sir John McNeill, two advocates of the railway.[44]

The executive committee included Sir H. Drummond-Wolff, Frederick Greenwood and Algernon Borthwick. The association told Beaconsfield on 17 July that Cyprus gave Britain 'the first strategic position in the world' relative to the railway.[45] Edward Cazalet, a Liberal, agreed and wanted an impregnable depot and a harbour for British troops and stores on Cyprus to command its western terminus.[46] On 26 July, however, Beaconsfield told the Cabinet that it was impossible to give the guarantee Sutherland wanted.[47]

Famagusta harbour attracted entrepreneurs. On 27 July 1878, Hamilton Fulton, an engineer of railways, bridges and canals in England and who proposed to supply water to London through the Wye river,[48] informed Salisbury that he represented a group wanting to build a 350-acre harbour at Famagusta with steam tramways to Nicosia and Larnaca.[49] But nothing came of this proposal.

Punch, which had criticised the acquisition of Cyprus from the start,[50] mocked the idea that Whitehall would build a harbour at Famagusta on 3 August.[51] Five days later an editorial in *The Times* asserted that it was 'not proposed to make Cyprus a fortress, like Malta and Gibraltar, and . . . a very small garrison will ultimately suffice for its occupation'.[52] This came a month to the day after the Convention was announced and no reason was given. The paper also claimed that the troops were 'comfortably and healthily encamped',[53] despite reports of their ill-health that appeared on 3 August in the *Daily News* from its reporter in Cyprus Archibald Forbes.[54]

The realities I: climate, insalubrity and fever

Those sent to administer Cyprus and visitors were appalled by the discrepancy between its appearance and its image created through classical and medieval education. One reason why Beaconsfield's government did not convert Cyprus into a place of arms was that fever gripped the troops. Over 5,000 Indian troops at Malta were sent so 'they might feel they had done something'[55] and over 3,000 British troops, including the famous Black Watch.[56] The hot summer and insalubrity (marshes near major towns and on the plains) induced fever, malaria and sunstroke. On the first day Sergeant Samuel M'Gaw of the Black Watch, the only soldier to win the Victoria Cross at Amoaful during the Asante campaign, died of heat apoplexy while marching to Cheflik Camp near Larnaca.[57] He was the first of many.

By the end of July *The Times* reported that the surgeon Sir Anthony Home and his staff had been ordered to Cyprus. Then on 6 August Wolseley left Nicosia,[58] telling his wife: 'I am very anxious to get out of Nicosia, for I am sure if we remained . . . we should all suffer: it is

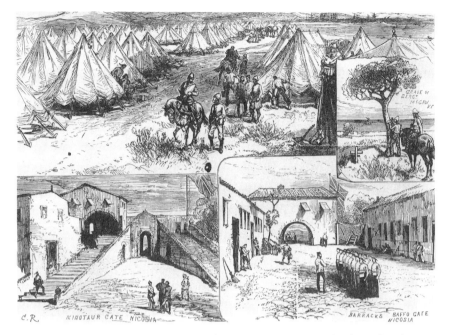

Figure 8 Cheflik Camp, Grave of Sergeant M'Gaw and other Sketches
Source: Illustrated London News, 17 August 1878.

one great cess-pit into which the filth of centuries has been poured.'[59] Wolseley rejected the house selected for him in Nicosia in preference for the Metochi of Kykkos, a mile beyond Nicosia's walls, offered by Archbishop Sophronios.[60] Home later reported that, in the first week of August, the fever began to cut down the troops and on the fifth week the 'sickness was epidemic in amount'.[61]

The Cabinet fumed at Archibald Forbes's reports: it also suspected Wolseley was his source.[62] On 10 August, the *Illustrated London News* claimed that it was 'tolerably clear' that the climate was 'anything but salubrious'[63] and three days later *The Times* admitted that the troops were 'suffering considerably'.[64]

The Liberals tackled the government on 14 August, but Stanley, the War Secretary, quoted a letter from Wolseley two days earlier: 'There is no serious illness among the troops.'[65] In another received on 14 August, Wolseley reiterated that the 'health of the men continues excellent', so there was no cause for alarm, Stanley told Parliament.[66]

But no record of Wolseley's letter to Stanley has survived and Stanley's statements conflicted with Wolseley's letter to Salisbury on 12 August. Wolseley informed Salisbury that the soldiers were feeling the heat and on the day of his letter eleven were taken ill with fever.

Figure 9 Monastery Camp, 1878
Source: Illustrated London News, 17 August 1878.

Nicosia was so bad ('no more than a cess-pit of filth' he also told Salisbury) that he wanted the capital elsewhere.[67] Stanley also knew that Wolseley needed six more doctors.[68] Clearly Stanley was playing down the crisis for political reasons.

The fever altered policy. On the day Stanley addressed Parliament he told Salisbury that he wanted a British regiment withdrawn in September and with the Indian contingent also leaving, only two regiments and a company of engineers would remain.[69] Salisbury agreed.[70] The next day Stanley told Parliament that the fever was not severe[71] and when, on 16 August, a *Daily News* report incited the ˙Liberals, he replied that it was abating.[72]

Punch continued to ridicule the government, implying in a cartoon on 31 August 1878 that Beaconsfield needed a schoolboy to research into the Cyprus question[73] and now Farley, Lang and Archdale Stuart Palmer, the correspondent of *The Times* in Cyprus, joined in.[74] Farley claimed that the island had a 'reputation' as 'one of the healthiest in the Mediterranean' and if the government had any foresight to consult a local firm accommodation could have been ready in time, avoiding 'the fiasco'.[75] Palmer claimed that only 'English stupidity' was to blame for using bell tents to pen the troops to swelter into fever.[76] Lang added:

> Had I obliged my European servant in Cyprus to work like a galley-slave during the heat of the sun, to sleep under canvas, to march with tight-fitting clothes, and . . . heavy boots, under a temperature of 120deg., it might have been very naturally concluded that I wished to make away with him.[77]

[102]

The crisis in Cyprus gave Gladstone the opportunity to launch a more general assault on the nature of imperial expansion and the taking of Cyprus in 'England's Mission'.

> The Government . . . [has] appealed, under the prostituted name of patriotism, to exaggerated fears, to imaginary interests, and to the acquisitiveness of a race which has surpassed every other known to history in the faculty of appropriating to itself vast spaces of the earth, and establishing its supremacy over men of every race and language.[78]

Gladstone believed that the policy to obtain Cyprus was cunningly devised and had nothing to do with the defence of Asia Minor.

> Cyprus has no more of real connection with the defence of the Armenian, than of the Canadian frontier. Neither has it any relation at all to a Protectorate of moral suasion, but only to a Protectorate resting upon force . . .[79]

Above all, Cyprus would not be of value because of its climate and predicted that it

> would be worthless as a military post, even had we already spent the heavy sums necessary to invest it with that character. The harbour at Malta, and its central position . . . render it far preferable . . . Cyprus is . . . a symbol and a counter: negative and valueless for any purpose of ours in itself, but a sign of the vastness of our Empire, and an effectual sign that, in the opinion of our Government, that Empire is not yet vast enough.[80]

Forbes reinforced Gladstone's attack in 'The "Fiasco" of Cyprus'.[81] He accused the Tories of gathering inadequate and fragmentary data and ridiculed the choice of 'this eligibly situated strategic position' that possessed no harbour and was so unhealthy that 25 per cent of the force was officially sick.[82]

> It is from the fever-stricken camp of Chiflick, and the miasmatic 'sanatorium' of Dali, that Lord Beaconsfield, like a modern Canute – *as bit omen!* – says to Russia, 'Thus far and no further'.[83]

This stunning assault excited *Punch* to produce a sardonic poem[84] and gave further ammunition to the opposition, whose MPs started returning from Cyprus.[85]

Nothing Whitehall or the Cyprus government did improved matters. Cheflik was abandoned owing to the fever's severity and the troops were dispersed to all towns, except Famagusta. They were also sent to Dali (ancient Idalium) based on an 'inquiry from persons of local knowledge . . . likely to give responsible advice'.[86] But their health worsened. In the third week at Dali there were 122 admissions with fever.

Dali was abandoned for Mathiati, a slightly elevated village to the west. But the fever did not abate: between twelve and twenty men were hospitalised daily.[87] The government replaced the thin bell tents with huts in September,[88] but Palmer pondered whether they would withstand the elements[89] and Lang thought it was 'a pity to put them up' and that barracks should have been erected.[90]

The troops were demoralised. Esme Scott-Stevenson, whose husband, a Black Watch officer, served in various civil capacities in Kyrenia, claimed that the troops were dejected. Scott-Stevenson socialised with the troops and listened to their complaints of boredom. They all 'got into the same frame of mind – that "hospital" was the only relief from the intolerable monotony . . . [and] thus "going sick" was looked upon as quite the best thing'.[91]

William Butler, Wolseley's close friend, observed that the troops spoke of Cyprus as a place of exile and only humour made life bearable. To quote one:

> The medical fellows never knew the use of the spleen until we got to Cyprus . . . but they've found it now . . . two months sick leave out of this infernal hole . . . The spleen has been what they call a dormant organ of the human body until we took possession of the Island; now its use is clearly understood.[92]

Then at the funeral of a soldier who died from fever one of his 'firing party' shot another in the eye. Hugh McCalmont, Wolseley's aide-de-camp, added acerbically that: 'we are getting on pretty well in our small community'.[93]

The fever's severity was made public with the publication of the names of invalided officers. Limassol and Famagusta lost district commissioners to fever[94] and Captain James Inglis, Famagusta's commissioner, bore the brunt of Liberal taunts as the 'Ghost of Famagusta'.[95] Even the artist of the *Illustrated London News*, Samuel Pasfield Oliver, was 'compelled by an attack of fever to seek refuge in the salubrious highlands of the Lebanon'.[96]

The Tories decided that Cyprus was too hot and unhealthy for troops after it sent Stanley and the First Lord of the Admiralty, W.H. Smith, to investigate in October 1878. Bromley Davenport, a Tory MP, thought the Cypriots would welcome them as Neptune and Mars,[97] while *Punch* compared the visit to Solon going to remodel one of the city states of Cyprus, but this time the visitors were going so they could extract London out of a blunder.[98] Salisbury was also more concerned than his colleague.

> I have really no special point to . . . direct your thoughts beyond the harbours and the barracks . . . If we cannot get an ironclad harbour . . .

Figure 10 Stanley and Smith leaving Nicosia, 1878
Source: *Illustrated London News*, 30 November 1878.

we ought at least to have one in which transports can land & embark troops quickly. A more important matter still is to observe Wolseley's general tone & that of those about him – whether they are really hopeful & cordial in their work or not.[99]

The trip confirmed Cyprus' unsuitability, in its current state, as a military station.[100] Scott-Stevenson revealed that Stanley and Smith were 'horrified at the appearance of the troops'.[101] Smith noted that the 'poor fellows were in a very depressed state, as they had had a good deal of fever and ague, which made them look washed out',[102] and Stanley warned Salisbury that they were 'of little military use in [their] present state'.[103]

Within weeks, only a wing of the 20th Regiment and two companies of Royal Engineers remained.[104] Wolseley revealed that Stanley and Smith, 'in common with the Cabinet', felt that Cyprus did 'not answer the purpose for which it was acquired' and blamed the Intelligence Department for misleading them.[105] Contrary to claims,[106] Wolseley defended Cyprus as a good a place as any for stationing troops.[107] He challenged critics[108] in public too, claiming

> that everything is and has been going on admirably: it pleases the – and –, who write on that side of the question, to make out that Cyprus is a[n] . . . earthly hell, whereas it is far from being so; and all those who have been loudest in abusing it will . . . confess their mistake, and pronounce it as the Mediterranean stations go, by no means a bad one, if not, as I believe . . . the best of any of them.[109]

But Wolseley made decisions detrimental to Cyprus' future as a strategic asset. On 3 September, when the fever was epidemic, he informed Salisbury that a summer station was needed.[110] So while uncertainties over Cyprus' strategic value were unresolved, Wolseley decided on a hill station. Stanley promptly postponed a sanatorium planned for Rhodes and in October sites were identified on the southern mountain range near Troodos, and Kantara on the northern range.[111] But Hugh Sinclair, RE, who arrived in October 1878, found Anthony Home 'very despondent about the fever', joking that it would still be caught in tents pitched on the highest tree at Troodos.[112] The extremes of the summers justified a hill station, but Kantara was the place for it because only at Famagusta could a naval or coaling station be built. But after visiting Famagusta, Wolseley found that: 'There is an air of decay about the place that tells one that it is an apanage of Turkey's Sultan.'[113] Pasfield was amazed that there were no soldiers there and claimed that reports of Famagusta's insalubrity were exaggerated.[114] Surely the solution was to make it healthy?

But Mount Olympus at Troodos was the island's tallest peak and its vast and isolated surrounds offset practical strategic factors.[115] Wolseley chose a site at Troodos in January 1879; in May the wing of the 20th Regiment, the company of Royal Engineers and the married families were camped; a military road from Polymedia, the winter station near Limassol, was started (£13,000)[116] and in September Government Cottage was begun.[117]

Wolseley also decided to replace the British troops with a Muslim force. First he wanted Druze from Lebanon, but Salisbury rebuffed him,[118] so he proposed to raise troops from Asia Minor under Colonel Valentine, who was commanding Turks near the Bosphorus.[119] Stanley, Salisbury and the Treasury approved.[120] After Valentine told Wolseley that 'the services of many thousand most excellent soldiers' was obtainable, Wolseley drafted his plan for the 'Cyprus Regiment of Pioneers', which would function alongside the *zaptieh*. Wolseley estimated the annual cost at £26,582 and urged that it be raised immediately to relieve the British troops.[121]

As a consequence, on 20 March Stanley told Parliament that some of the 20th Regiment would leave.[122] Four days later £26,000 was provided in the Civil Service Estimates for the pioneers. Now the troops could be removed.[123] The proposal was controversial. Whitehall abandoned the idea of a purely military force because Section 4 of the Military Act (41.Vic.c.10) prevented it from serving outside Cyprus and Section 2 of the Army Act (1.Vic.c.29) limited aliens serving in the British army.[124] The radicals George Shaw-Lefevre and Charles Dilke moved a motion to reject the sum because it was semi-military and unjustified.[125] Arthur J. Balfour, who accompanied Salisbury, his uncle, to the Congress of Berlin, defended the government, asserting that the sum was for '*quasi*-military purpose[s]' and would save £70,000 a year on keeping two battalions in Cyprus.[126] Robert Bourke, the undersecretary at the Foreign Office, explained that the amount was intended to defray the extra cost of increasing the *zaptieh* after the troop reduction.[127] Sir William Harcourt condemned the Tories for trying to 'smuggle' a military vote in the Civil Service Estimates and sarcastically asked if it should be in the military or '*quasi*-Military Estimates'.[128] Ultimately, the force was established.[129]

The realities II: Famagusta harbour

The Tories selected Cyprus knowing that the government would have to develop Famagusta harbour which, as the sketch and photograph show, was capacious, but run down, with only a few light craft using it. The government hoped that Stanley's and Smith's trip would result in the harbour's redevelopment. After sailing with Wolseley to Famagusta and anchoring in the outer harbour, joining Admiral Hornby, Smith and Evans (the hydrographer) noted that the reef parallel within the shore constituted a breakwater 'almost as good as Plymouth'.[130] Hornby told Stanley, Smith and Wolseley that Famagusta would make a fine coaling station when dredged and a new pier was built. Wolseley agreed, but only if it were made healthy.[131] Beaconsfield told Queen Victoria that Colonel Edward Hamley – a military strategist and lecturer, who in March 1879 replaced Colonel Home

Figure 11 'The Harbour of Famagusta, Cyprus'
Source: *Illustrated London News*, 1878.

Figure 12 Famagusta Harbour, 1878
Source: John Thomson, *Through Cyprus with the Camera in the Autumn of 1878*, London 1879.

as British commissioner for the delimitation of Bulgaria – was of the opinion that Famagusta would 'turn out a harbour' for ironclads.[132]

During Smith's and Stanley's trip, Captain Harry Rawson (a naval officer who had reported on the Suez canal's defence in 1878 and raised the British flag at Nicosia), and John Millard (a surveying officer from Malta), reported on the anchorages of Cyprus. They proposed to dredge Famagusta's inner harbour to 24 feet and construct a breakwater (with rock from the old quarry) a mile long beyond the reef allowing warships to anchor in 50 feet of water in the outer harbour. The dredged earth would fill the lagoon, which was causing fever. They also proposed a coal depot with a tramway running along the breakwater, so ships could coal. Millard considered that Famagusta had 'very great' natural advantages 'for both a mercantile and imperial harbour'.[133]

Evans and Hornby supported the report. Evans claimed that Famagusta harbour would have an important future:

> The value to Cyprus of an anchorage of such natural capabilities as already exist is great; but in view of the future, when the necessity might arise for ships of a larger draft than 20 to 22 feet to be provided with shelter, the natural reef features of the seaboard offer striking facilities.[134]

This was because the longer the breakwater the larger the anchorage area, meaning that the size of the harbour was endless, unlike at Valetta, which was enclosed. Hornby asserted that the reports proved that a harbour at Famagusta could be made at a 'small expense which would shelter more ironclads than the grand harbour at Malta': in fact, it could accommodate fourteen a cable length apart, unlike at Malta, where similar moorings only fitted nine at three-quarters of a cable.[135]

Sir George Elliot, a Conservative MP (1868–92) working for English firms interested in investing in Cyprus and who had accompanied Stanley and Smith to Cyprus, also had reports made. Elliot, an industrialist, started in mines and his Telegraph Construction and Maintenance Company laid the first permanent transatlantic telegraph (1866).[136] His engineer, Samuel Brown, led the construction of the central section of the Turin–Savona Railway and, from 1870 to 1879, the building of Alexandria's breakwater.[137] Elliot instructed him on 26 November 1878 to survey and report on the lines of railway, the ports of Famagusta, Larnaca and Limassol, the salt lakes and the water supply.[138]

His railway proposals were extensive. Five lines were planned: a main line from Nicosia to Famagusta (36$\frac{1}{4}$ miles); a branch 21$\frac{1}{4}$ miles into that line from Nicosia to Larnaca (14$\frac{3}{4}$ miles); a branch to Kythrea, north-east of Nicosia (4 miles); a line from Nicosia to Karavostasi in Morphou Bay (33$\frac{3}{4}$ miles); and a line from Larnaca to Limassol (42 miles). Famagusta would be revitalised as Brown proposed to level the fortifications on the sea side and make a quay and connect it to the railway. He planned the Larnaca railway to connect with commercial and military needs. The Karavostasi line would aid in exporting Morphou's products and the line from Larnaca to Limassol would complete the network.[139] Salisbury was interested in railways, but the Crown Agents for Overseas Governments and Administrations believed that Cyprus needed roads first.[140]

Brown claimed that Cyprus possessed three harbours 'capable of affording shelter more or less perfect to the larger class of vessels viz. Famagusta, Larnaca and Limassol'. The last two were roadsteads exposed to winds from south and east, but large vessels could anchor 'free from danger', except in bad weather when the surf cut them off from shore, making landing and discharging impracticable.[141] Conversely, Famagusta had 'great natural advantages' and little was required to convert it into 'a port of the first order'.[142] It was sheltered from winds except those blowing from the east. The breakwater constructed during the Middle Ages was intact and both the outer and inner harbours were spacious, with the former being almost equal to Alexandria's grand harbour. He believed that after dredging the inner harbour to 25 feet 'a commodious harbour' for merchant vessels and transports could be formed.[143] From the quay, two jetties, 200 × 40 feet, would accommodate four large vessels, with the smaller craft anchoring by the quay.

He estimated that the works at £50,000.[144] Converting Famagusta into a mercantile and coaling station was relatively inexpensive.

To establish Famagusta as a naval station, a breakwater, extending 1,800 yards from the reef, was needed. Brown believed that more than fourteen ironclads could anchor in the outer harbour if moored head-and-stern as at Alexandria and that such a harbour would provide 'perfect' shelter and 'be second to none in the Mediterranean'.[145]

Wolseley postponed expressing a view on the report until Lieutenant-General Robert Biddulph, Nicosia's District Commissioner, had negotiated the tribute amount in Constantinople. He believed that the Morphou–Nicosia–Famagusta line, with a branch to Larnaca, would be beneficial and that the Famagusta branch should follow the Larnaca section, but only 'if – as I hope may be the case – it is intended for Imperial purposes to improve the harbour'. The Crown agents were asked to verify the estimates[146] and they thought them high.[147] But at £50,000 or less, the cost reasonable for a project of this sort, yet negotiations were not pursued with Elliot.[148]

Furthermore, nothing was done to make Famagusta healthy. In the first six months, only about £150 out of the near £13,000 spent on public works went on Famagusta: the Larnaca–Nicosia road was built at £6,000;[149] Limassol got a new pier, public buildings, store depots, a marketplace and its bridges and roads were repaired;[150] Larnaca got three piers, street drains, public latrines, street lamps, a telegraph office, a slaughter house, hospital huts for the pioneers and a 550-foot quay;[151] barracks were built for the *zaptieh* at Nicosia; and £3,000-worth of eucalyptus trees were planted across the island.[152] Even Kyrenia and Paphos made progress.[153] Famagusta was neglected, except for repairs to some dirt roads, the prison, the Konak and the building of latrines and *zaptieh* accommodation.[154] The only imperial work at Famagusta was the placing of a cast buoy to mark the northern reefs and a new beacon on the shore.[155]

When the Conservatives tabled the Admiralty reports in Parliament, the Duke of Somerset, a former Whig First Lord of the Admiralty (1859–66), asked if the potential would be invested in.[156] Famagusta, Salisbury asserted, was selected to be made 'fit for the purposes of a great Power'. The cost was low and London would pay.[157] Yet

in reference to the expenditure, it happens that the Imperial Government has a good deal to do with its money at present; and they may, there-fore, be willing to put off this particular work until they may have less expense upon their hands. Before proceeding with the construction of the harbour works, some steps must be taken towards making the place more healthy. That is one of the reasons why . . . we should not move too hastily in the matter.[158]

Making Famagusta healthy needed money and as sanitary works were a local matter they would be paid from local revenue, only one-fifth of which was applicable to public works. Also, there were more pressing matters to direct local revenue: roads to the capital, the construction of adequate prisons, post offices and more. Thus, 'possibly' in the next financial year the sanitary works might be tackled.[159] Nevertheless,

> The Government think that the harbour of Famagousta is one of great importance, and that every means to adapt it to our convenience should be used as quickly as is consistent with other circumstances. The work, however, is not pressing . . . The Treaty of Berlin, we hope, will establish permanent peace; but then we know that noble Lords opposite once thought that the Treaty of Paris would do the same; and when such men as Lord Palmerston were deceived, we cannot conceal from ourselves the fact that the time may arrive when England will have to look actively after her interests in that part of the world, and when she would have to give forcible effect to her policy. I hope that time is far distant, and therefore we do not wish to incur any financial extravagance for the purpose of accomplishing works of this kind with unnecessary speed.[160]

Salisbury was back-pedalling. He contradicted himself on more than one occasion: claiming that the cost was low, but that the government would not indulge in financial extravagance; that Famagusta had to be made healthy before the harbour was redeveloped, although the experts had outlined that its dredging would contribute to that and he refused to pay for it with imperial funds. By tying redevelopment to the sanitary works and to possible instability in Ottoman Asia, Cyprus was being held as insurance for when it would be needed. But Salisbury failed to understand that there would be no payout unless funds were invested in it. Until then, Cyprus would play no part in imperial strategy.

Salisbury's comments upheld the Liberal criticism that Cyprus was strategically useless and Granville, realising this, ridiculed Beaconsfield's prediction of July 1878: 'We were told that this year we should have a sufficient harbour . . . but it would seem . . . that we may have to wait 15 or 20 years before the harbour is begun.'[161] Three days later a more heated debate occurred in the Commons that further polarised the sides and seriously questioned the future of Cyprus as a vital cog in imperial strategy.[162]

William Fanshawe Martin

The imperial defence strategist, John Colomb, a Conservative MP who advocated cooperation between the army and navy and imperial and colonial defence interests, maintained in a speech before the Royal

United Service Institution on 28 March 1879 that Cyprus was in the military class of colonies with Fiji, Bermuda, Malta and the Falklands.[163] But the case against Famagusta was boosted by a 'devastatingly critical'[164] attack on it by Admiral William Fanshawe Martin.[165] Martin entered the navy at the age of 11 (1813) and spent much of his career in the Mediterranean, becoming a vice-admiral in 1858 and in the next year the Commander-in-Chief of the Mediterranean Station. He was a pioneer of steam tactics and Admiral Sir Frederick Beauchamp Seymour observed in 1886 that the service owed

> more to him than to any man alive . . . he rescued the Navy, and especially the Mediterranean Station from the slough of despond, he had the courage of his opinion, and he was very nearly being a great man.[166]

Martin retired in 1870. Having published only three pamphlets, this indicates how topical the Cyprus question was.[167]

Martin argued that Famagusta was unsustainable as a *place d'armes* because it was defenceless and did not supplant Malta for operations in the Near East, because it was a long narrow anchorage between a straight shore and its low breakwater exposed it to heavy guns: 'Nothing less than a harbour and an arsenal so encircled as to be a stronghold . . . can properly be deemed a naval station and *"a place of arms"*.'[168] Martin claimed that only with 'prodigious sums might . . . defensive works' make Famagusta a stronghold. Even then, horizontal shell firing from a frigate would endanger ships in it. Thus, Famagusta was 'worthless as a naval station . . . [because] defensive works cannot be placed in such a way as to intervene between it and an enemy'.[169] Martin also claimed that the harbour acreage of Famagusta and Valetta had been misrepresented and a proper representation was necessary if the same money were spent on both.[170] This was a preposterous assertion after the sums already spent on Malta. So was his claim that Malta was sufficient for operations in the eastern Mediterranean because it had been in the 1840 Syrian campaign. That was forty years earlier and then Cyprus had also been used.

Martin believed that whoever commanded the sea controlled the Suez Canal and Cyprus was worthless as the Mediterranean terminus for the Euphrates Valley Railway, because it would be on the Syrian coast. Thus, it would not develop commercially to the heights projected.[171] Martin believed that

> the Ionian Islands were commercially and politically worthless, and . . . as a naval station and 'place of arms' they were still worse than worthless. Accordingly they were wisely assigned to Greece.
>
> But before giving up the Islands it was thought desirable to destroy some fortifications which at the time of their being constructed drew

from the Duke of Wellington the expostulating observation, 'Why you are fortifying Vido with gold!' It would be deplorable if a similar folly were perpetrated in Cyprus, which like Corfu, is commercially and politically useless, and as a naval station and a 'place of arms' worse than worthless.[172]

Published in July 1879, the pamphlet had no bearing on the parliamentary debates, but served as the strongest expert denunciation of Cyprus's strategic value and Gladstone used it during the forthcoming election campaign.[173] Martin sent copies to his colleagues and friends and the response shows their support. George Peter Martin, formerly the secretary to the Commander-in-Chief, Mediterranean Station, who encouraged Martin to publish it, believed 'from the manner in which all talk of it (Cyprus) has died out that the Government begins to see the thing in the same light'.[174] Leading naval and army figures who supported Martin included Admiral Thomas M. Symonds,[175] who had served in the Mediterranean and commanded the channel squadron (1868–70);[176] Admiral Edward Fanshawe, the Commander-in-Chief Portsmouth and a veteran of the Syria campaign;[177] Sir Michael Seymour, formerly the Commander-in-Chief of the China Station;[178] General Sir Henry Dalrymple White;[179] and Admiral Henry Eden, formerly a lord of the Admiralty (1855–58), and who teasingly asked Martin: 'I hope you have sent a copy of your pamphlet to Dizzi.'[180] Only two admirals believed that it might be useful if the Euphrates Valley Railway were built[181] and another justified its occupation in anticipation of a war, but in hindsight 'it has become a poor bargain no doubt'.[182]

Some of Martin's supporters predicted, successfully, Cyprus' future place in British imperial structures. Rear-Admiral George William Preedy believed that Cyprus would 'remain a millstone about our necks',[183] while Admiral Sir James Hope, who had just been advanced to the honorary rank of Admiral of the Fleet, suggested that 'the best thing . . . [to] do is after a few years to hand it over to the Greeks'.[184] Thus, within a year of its occupation, experienced naval figures considered Cyprus expendable.

The 'Modern Major-General'

The British encounter with Cyprus, as in the case of Palestine, came as a huge shock because the appearance of both did not resemble the classical, biblical and medieval vision they had come to know so well.[185] Both places were considered barren. In reality Cyprus, with a population well below 200,000, was more so than Palestine, which was primarily uninhabited in its mountain districts. This desolation was blamed on Ottoman despotism and Oriental backwardness. In Palestine's case, the Eastern desolation helped transform the Oriental landscape into an English one, because for the British there was a sense of being at home.[186] But this was not because the British were identifying physical similarities between Palestine and parts of Britain, but because they were comparing the contemporary Palestine with the biblical geography, that is, with places and features that belonged to their spiritual imagination.[187] So the Oriental features were seen as theirs. Kinglake imagined Palestine as the final frontier of civilisation, an Orient, which is also an Occident.[188] In Cyprus there also was a sense of the physically familiar, but here it was not drawn from a British relationship with biblical features because geographically Cyprus does not have much of a place in the Bible. Rather it was drawn from comparing the isolated wooded mountain areas of Troodos, where the British created a hill station, with English rural/country life and with India.[189] The plains of Cyprus were unfamiliar – worse than the barrenness and heat of India – and thus not for Europeans, who had to go to the hill station for relief.

Cyprus' incredible desolation depressed the British officials sent to govern and prepare it as a strategic base. Wolseley was Britain's pre-eminent soldier when Cyprus was occupied with various music compositions in his honour. However, not all celebrated him; Gilbert and Sullivan had him in mind when creating 'the very model of a modern Major-General' in *The Pirates of Penzance*. But Wolseley took no offence to the show, which premiered in New York while he was in Cyprus; he often sang the part himself to entertain his family![190]

Wolseley was clearly a distinguished soldier, but did not have the ability or character to convert Cyprus into a base. London permitted him to choose his staff and accordingly he selected from his 'Asante (or Wolseley) Ring' of officers for whom he acted as patron because of their loyalty and bravery.[191] Although familiar faces surrounded him, Wolseley became frustrated and apathetic. McCalmont believed that Cyprus would have been no use in an Anglo-Russian war because 'one's first impressions of the island were far from favourable'.[192] They expected a ready base, but it had no roads, water or trees.[193] This perplexed and depressed Wolseley:

> The wells are few, and scarcely a river or rather what is marked on the map as a river, has more than a pool here and there of stagnant water in it. Where are the forests we thought Cyprus was covered with? This is in everyone's mouth, yet no one can give a satisfactory answer. Like everything else that made this country a splendid one in ancient times, the forests have disappeared under the influence, the blighting influence, of the Turk.[194]

In 1889, Wolseley's successor, Sir Robert Biddulph, expanded on why the British thought that Cyprus should have been wooded and why it was not.

> In Old Testament times shipbuilding took place. In Balaam's prophesy it was stated that 'ships shall come from the coast of Chittim', and it was with Cyprus timber that Alexander the Great built the fleet which he launched on the Tigris and Euphrates.[195]

Biddulph blames the Venetians and Muhammad Ali of Egypt for the disappearance of Cyprus' forests.

Wolseley's inglorious exit typified the failure of the Cyprus venture. By early 1879 the respected medical journal *The Lancet* was attacking him and the government. It claimed that it was 'difficult to persuade the public that inefficiency of the heads of the military departments' was not the 'chief cause' of the suffering.[196] *The Lancet* believed that Home's May 1879 report on the fever undermined the home and local government's credibility. Home presented a grim picture, but excused the authorities because the information on the climate and medical history of Cyprus was contradictory.[197] *The Lancet* saw a cover-up and thought that as the former head of the Statistical Branch of the Army Medical Department, Home should have given the tabular statement of hospital admissions, deaths and causes of death, and referred to the Royal Engineers, Royal Artillery and the Indian contingent.[198] Home did not mention his or his staff's fever either, yet the newspapers reported it.[199] *The Lancet* accused Wolseley's introduction to Home's report[200] of ignoring the medical statistics, which were 'inconvenient to the military authorities' for teaching a 'lesson as to the necessity for more foresight in sanitary matters'. 'Could a more severe criticism', it pondered, 'be passed on the manner in which the military occupation of the island actually took place?'[201]

Wolseley was further frustrated by those not in his 'ring'. He told his wife that

> I am sorry to say the 'Black Prince' is here with HRH the Duke of Edinburgh (Prince Alfred, Queen Victoria's second son, who organised the landing) . . . He is fond of 'havering' and has interviews with me on trifling subjects . . . which I want to keep myself aloof from . . . I wish these Royalties would keep out of my way: they retard public business and no one likes this 'Edinburgh'.[202]

Wolseley reserved his greatest revulsion for the man who first occupied Cyprus, Admiral Lord John Hay.

> He is the devil to talk to and talk such nonsense. I thought generals were far from brilliant but they are Solons compared to the pompous ignorance of such men as Admiral Lord John Hay . . .[203]

Wolseley also detested many of his visitors. He thought Dr Stopford, the Bishop of Gibraltar, 'a poor miserable little devil'[204] and called Hepworth Dixon: a 'pompous ass', 'egotistical', 'untruthful', 'dirty', 'repulsive', 'not a gentleman' and 'one of those creatures – I cannot call him a man – whom soldiers feel a longing to kick at'.[205]

Not surprisingly Wolseley grew to hate Cyprus. As a soldier in his prime, he wanted to lead expeditions, not to be stuck in a pestiferous backwater. He could have gone to India as commander of the Bombay army and McCalmont 'knew that he was bitterly disappointed at having been let in for this Cyprus tomfoolery'.[206] When in November the Indian government went to war with Afghanistan's Amir, nobody in Cyprus was 'satisfied with being planted down in this backwater'.[207] Smith noted that 'poor Sir Garnet felt our parting'.[208] Even Dilke admitted that Wolseley 'was eating out his heart upon this modern Elba, when he was greatly wanted elsewhere'.[209] Wolseley told Charles Low, his biographer:

> All our thoughts here are now turned to the Afghan frontier, and I long to be in the saddle leading our men through these passes which former wars have made so familiar to us in history. I like being the Governor of a new place like Cyprus during peace, but when 'the blast of war blows in our ears,' I long to run to the sound.[210]

Scott-Stevenson confirmed that Wolseley's heart was not in his Cyprus mission.

> It was no doubt disappointing to find the country so little advanced in civilisation, and so few traces left of its ancient splendour. Rhodes and Crete are equally backward in many respects, but the remnants of their prosperous days are still to be found, – an inducement to the earnest searcher to remain a few years there. But here the remains of the Middle Ages have been swept away by plunderers, that there is nothing left for the explorer, except in the tombs of ancient Greeks and still more ancient Phoenicians.
>
> It is no wonder that men like Sir Garnet and his staff grew sick of the place. When the Commander-in-Chief saw his ten thousand troops dwindle down to half a battalion, without even band being left him, and his staff one by one going off to scenes of more stirring adventure, it was natural that he, too, should seize the first opportunity to return to England.[211]

Indeed, within months of arriving, Wolseley regretted not going to India because he would have commanded the Afghanistan campaign.[212] As early as September 1878 he informed Colonel George P. Colly that he would leave Cyprus if asked to command the expedition.[213] When news reached him in November that the troops were doing well he exclaimed to his wife: 'How I wish I were with them – alas! alas!'[214]

Wolseley's exit exemplified his lack of interest in his Cyprus mission. He left on 21 May 1879 for London. After the Cabinet asked for his advice on the Zulu War, which had started in January, he was offered the high commissionership of the Transvaal and Natal. The hurried appointment upset the Queen and confused the Liberals.[215] Wolseley left Cyprus in the lurch within a year of his appointment.

The contradictions and the fall

During the April 1880 election campaign, Beaconsfield and Salisbury continued to insist on Cyprus's strategic value. In the face of the attacks on its strategic merits, Admiral Milne's Colonial Defence Committee wrestled with imperial defence planning for an Anglo-Russian war. But the focus was on Australia, New Zealand and Canada, not on Gibraltar, Malta, Bermuda, Halifax, Aden and Cyprus.[216] The committee convinced the authorities to investigate further because Britain had nearly gone to war with Russia unprepared.[217] In July 1879 a Royal Commission was formed, headed by Lord Carnarvon, the former Conservative Colonial Secretary, in order to examine the places to be defended and the armaments, garrison and costs. Although it did not start until September and its reports were not completed until well into the Gladstone ministry, Beaconsfield and Salisbury did not wait for the reports to determine Cyprus' value. Beaconsfield told Robert Greaves, who was administering Cyprus until Wolseley's successor arrived, that:

> Of course you agree as to the value of Cyprus to us as a place of arms . . . for any force required for service in Turkey or Egypt, and as a sanatorium, which could be formed on Mount Olympus. Then there is the harbour of Famagusta, which in old days used to be one of the finest Harbours in the Mediterranean, and could now, with a little dredging, be made available for our fleet.[218]

Greaves disagreed:

> I wrote . . . that I was very sorry I could not agree about the value of the island, as it was a very unhealthy place for British troops, and the sides of Olympus were so steep that a tent could not be pitched on it without digging out a foundation. As to Famagusta, it might have been a harbour for rowing-boats in the old days, but in the opinion of the Engineers it could only be made use of for our ships now by such dredging as would either cover the present island with silt or make another island out at sea![219]

When Robert Biddulph succeeded Wolseley,[220] Salisbury reaffirmed that 'the aim of . . . English policy is in the first instance strategic'.[221]

The island has a considerable military value in the case of any operations directed against the Valley of the Euphrates, and . . . still larger naval
value in case it should ever become necessary to take material precau-
tions for securing English interests on the Suez Canal or on the coasts
of Syria and Egypt.[222]

The 'most important strategical object . . . [was] the restoration of the
harbour of Famagusta', but it was too expensive to complete with funds
from Cyprus 'so long as it is subject to the Turkish Tribute'. Thus,
it would have to wait until the Treasury could pay, but 'as long as
the sanitary condition of the place . . . [was] so bad . . . any works of
restoration would meet with considerable difficulty, and therefore
the sanitary question must . . . take the first rank'. Money prevented
remedying the insalubrity soon, but the work was important and he
wanted economical methods of undertaking the work devised.[223]

Why did Whitehall still want to establish Cyprus as a stronghold?
One explanation was the deterioration in Anglo-Ottoman relations.
In isolation the Anglo-Turkish Convention was a blessing for the Porte:
Cyprus for British protection against Russia; but in conjunction with
the other agreements. Abdul Hamid only saw another power with its
fingers in the pie. He agreed to British consuls supervising reforms in
Armenia, but tried to block their appointment. On 16 September 1879
Salisbury privately expressed fear that Constantinople would not
implement the reforms.[224] A month later he publicly accused it of being
feeble, yet justified Cyprus' occupation (epigraph Chapter 3).[225] The
Sultan's intransigence further threatened British interests. Was
Famagusta the key to protecting them? In October and November
Salisbury ordered reports on the diseases of Famagusta from the Chief
Surgeon Dr C. Irving; on the harbour from Thomas Ormiston, a con-
sulting engineer for the Bombay Port Trust;[226] and on Famagusta's
sanitary condition from the Italian engineer, Davide Bocci.[227]

Irving's report outlined the diseases at Famagusta: smallpox, typhoid,
malarious fever and ague, which was 'exceedingly prevalent' from
October 1878 to July 1879. Few adults died, but hundreds of children
did. All but two English officials suffered from ague and they had not
arrived until winter. The affected area was in the old city, Varosha,
the nearby villages and Lake Paralimni and stemmed from winter rain
forming marshes. The solution was to make small embankments at
the mouth of ravines, thus confining rains to small lakes, to deepen
and fill ditches, clear Lake Paralimni's marshes and plant trees.[228]

Ormiston spent four days at Famagusta (8–12 November) and
focused only on the requirements for a naval station. He recommended
the dredging of a 20-acre section of the outer and inner harbours to
25 feet and estimated the costs (including a dredger) at £70,687. He

also suggested removing the old mole to widen the entrance and adding a 150-foot wharf, bringing the costs to £95,000.[229] The length of the breakwater would determine how many large vessels the outer harbour could accommodate. A 2,200-yard breakwater brought the cost to £272,453 and one 2,900 yards to £354,301 (Appendix VIII), forming a harbour 460 acres and 580 acres, respectively. Ormiston completed his report on 10 January 1880, three months before the election, and Salisbury told him that he 'read [it] with great interest', but did not say if the proposals would be implemented.[230]

Bocci arrived on 22 January to report on the measures to remedy the causes of insalubrity. His request for hydrographic maps, geo-detic surveys and hydrometrical data could not be met and the lakes and marshes were dry, forcing him to undertake planimetrical and altimetrical surveys from which to base his report.[231] Thus the report was not presented until after the election. Many Cyprus government officers thought the island would have become a strategic asset had the Conservatives won the 1880 election, but this was questionable. Bocci's recommendations (Appendix III) amounted to £111,500: a sub-stantial sum, especially when added to the estimates to redevelop the harbour. Imperial funds would be needed for both.

Another explanation for wanting Famagusta harbour redeveloped was political: the Conservatives could not readily admit that Cyprus was a failure. Criticism of the occupation increased and it was a popular joke, as shown by the topical song 'What Shall We Do With Cyprus?' which argued that Cyprus was merely another useless addition to Queen Victoria's vast collection of possessions (Appendix IV).

In impassioned speeches (which he called 'festivals of freedom') to large crowds through Midlothian during the 1880 election campaign, Gladstone assailed Beaconsfield's foreign and imperial policies for being immoral and a financial drain. He told an audience to remember that 'the sanctity of life in the hill villages of Afghanistan' was as 'sacred in the eyes of Almighty God as are your own'.[232] He also continued to slam the Conservatives on Cyprus, which he called, among other things, a 'worthless bribe'.[233]

The Conservative leadership naturally continued its apologia. Stanley and Sir Michael Hicks-Beach, the Colonial Secretary, thought it unfair that Lord Hartington, the Whig leader, had criticised the failure to make Cyprus another Malta and Gibraltar after only one bad summer.[234] There were no actions, however, to back the words.

Instead it was decided to tie Cyprus' finances to the Exchequer. Soon after it was occupied, Abdul Hamid wanted London to obtain a loan of £6,000,000, secured mainly on the island's surplus revenues, to pay the Ottoman public debt.[235] But there was no faith in him using the loan to do so. In December 1879, Salisbury decided that the Ottoman debt would be made a first charge on the Cyprus tribute.[236] The Porte had just agreed to pay its indirect taxes (duties on stamps, spirits, tobacco and salt) and the Cyprus tribute to local creditors.[237] London's decision, made after the breakdown in Anglo-Ottoman relations, meant that the Cypriots would pay the £40,872 annual British obligation to the bondholders of the 1855 Ottoman loan. Since Abdul Hamid refused to implement reforms in Asia Minor, the Conservatives would have been justified in relieving the Cypriots of the tribute. The money could have been used to develop the island. Biddulph had negotiated in 1879 the sum of 23,021,978 piastres as the average surplus of the past five years and proposed to convert it to Turkish lira at the rate of 213 piastres to one Turkish lira – the rate in March 1880. The sum came to £48,000. Salisbury agreed.[238]

Then the military establishment reduced its responsibilities further. In March 1880 Stanley told Salisbury that the Cyprus government had contributed only £2,000 of the £12,680 spent on the Limassol–Platres road connecting Polymedia to Troodos. A further outlay of £1,000 was planned in 1880–81. Stanley wanted the Cyprus government to take over the road or pay towards its keep, especially since he was told that it 'pass[ed] through a very rich wine growing part of the country ... [and was] much used by the residents along and in the neighbourhood of its line'. On 13 April, only days before the Conservatives fell from power, Salisbury asked Biddulph to propose a plan to take over the road.[239]

Conclusion

There was a fantastic disparity between the aims and expectations in occupying Cyprus and the realities and achievements. Cyprus was chosen without reference to what was needed to make it a viable strategic asset. When the realities became plain and the media and Liberals exposed them, Cyprus crashed from a 'gem' to a 'millstone'. The Conservatives reluctantly admitted to certain realities, withdrawing most of the 10,000 garrison and postponed the redevelopment of Famagusta harbour. They still asserted that Cyprus would become a stronghold, but did not act on a report to redevelop Famagusta harbour in early 1879 – which was reasonably priced – nor did they decide on a further report in early 1880. A report on remedying Famagusta's insalubrity arrived after the election campaign and showed that, if undertaken, the decision to use local revenue needed reversing. When the parties went into the April 1880 elections, Beaconsfield and Salisbury still advocated Cyprus' strategic value, but whether they believed it or their stance was political, is unclear. Regardless, misguided perceptions of advantage underlay the imposition of British rule of Cyprus.

Notes

1 William Francis Butler, *Far Out: Rovings Retold*, London, 1880, 281.
2 B.H. Cowper, *Cyprus: Its Past and Present*, London, 1878, 3; Dixon, *British Cyprus*, 280; Edward Vizetelly, *From Cyprus to Zanzibar by the Egyptian Delta*, London, 1901, 2, 40.
3 *The Times*, 10 July 1878, 9.
4 Ibid., 20 January 1873, 4d; 11 July 1878, 6.f.
5 Vizetelly, *From Cyprus to Zanzibar*, 1.
6 Ibid., 2.
7 Anon. (John Baldwin Hay), *The Occupation of Cyprus: Immediate and Probable Effects*, London, 1878, 3–4.
8 Lang, *Cyprus*, 199.
9 Robert Hamilton Lang, 'Cyprus' (Part I), *MM*, XXXVIII, August 1878, 329.
10 Lang, *Cyprus*, 197.
11 Lang, 'Cyprus' (I), 329.
12 Ibid., 335.
13 *The Standard*, 26 July 1878, signed as 'Cyprus'.
14 Anon., *Cyprus: Its Value and Importance to England*, London, 1878, 4.
15 Ibid., 5, 8, 13.
16 Ibid., 5.
17 Kyriacos Demetriou, 'Victorian Cyprus: Society and Institutions in the Aftermath of the Anglo-Turkish Convention, 1878–1891', *BMGS*, 1997, 6.
18 Kanya-Forstner, 'French Expansion in Africa: The Mythical Theory'.
19 Wright, 'Libya', in Joffe and McLachlan (eds), *Social & Economic Development of Libya*, 67–79.
20 Bar-Yosef, *The Holy Land in English Culture*.
21 Sandon Journal, 17 and 31 July 1878, 41, 46.
22 Butler, *Far Out*, 330–1.
23 *Hansard* (Commons), CCXLI, 11 July 1878, 1243, 1225–6; *Hansard* (Lords), CCXLI, 11 July 1878, 1225–6.
24 *The Times*, 15 July 1878, 6.f.
25 Ibid., 19 July 1878, 1949–50.
26 Robert Hamilton Lang, 'Cyprus' (Part II), *MM*, XXXVIII, 1878, 337–47, 343–4.
27 *The Times*, 11 July 1878, 6.f.
28 *Hansard* (Lords), CCXLI, 15 July 1878, 1433–4.
29 Ibid.; Laing M. Meason, 'A Fortnight in Cyprus', *Temple Bar*, LIV, 1878, 48–61.
30 *The Times*, 18 July 1878, 6.f.
31 *Hansard* (Lords), CCXLI, 19 July 1878, 1950.
32 *The Times*, 22 July 1878, 8.b.
33 The Liberal Edward Cazalet supported the occupation. Cazalet, *The Berlin Congress and the Anglo-Turkish Convention*, 29. Hugh Childers, a First Lord of the Admiralty under Gladstone, admitted that Cyprus's acquisition was not a bad move. Childers Diary, 11 July 1878, Lieut-Colonel Spencer Childers, *The Life and Correspondence of the Right Honorary Hugh C.E. Childers*, I, London 1901, 254.
34 CAB41/11/16, Northcote on Cyprus, 10 July 1878.
35 *The Times*, 22 July 1878, 9b, 10c.
36 *Hansard* (Lords), CCXLII, 23 July 1878, 18–21.
37 Ibid., 22.
38 Ibid., 23–4.
39 Ibid., 26.
40 Ibid., 25–6.
41 Ibid., 27–8.

42 *The Times*, 29 July 1878, 10a.
43 Clayton, *Britain and the Eastern Question*, 154.
44 Lee, *Great Britain and the Cyprus Convention Policy*, 133–6. McNeil was formerly British envoy to Persia.
45 FO78/2893, Memorandum on Asia Minor and Euphrates Railway proposal, 17 July 1878.
46 Cazalet, *The Berlin Congress and the Anglo-Turkish Convention*, 27.
47 Sandon Journal, 26 July 1878, 43.
48 *BBA*, 0434; *The Times*, 3 September 1866, 10f.
49 CO67/2, Hamilton H. Fulton to Salisbury, 27 July 1878; Salisbury to Fulton, 30 July 1878; Fulton to Salisbury, 3 August 1878.
50 Andrekos Varnava, '*Punch* and the British Occupation of Cyprus in 1878', *BMGS*, XXIX, 2, 2005.
51 *Punch*, 3 August 1878, 45.
52 *The Times*, 8 August 1878, 7.c.
53 Ibid.
54 Sandon journal, 3 August 1878, 47.
55 Ibid., 7 June 1878, 22.
56 *Cyprus: Report from the Principal Medical Officers in Cyprus, Giving a Medical History of the Troops Stationed in that Island Since July 1878*, War Office, May 1879, 3 (hereafter *Home Report*); *The Times*, 7 August 1878, 5a; Major A.G. Harfield, 'British Military Presence in Cyprus in the 19th Century', *Journal of the Society for Army Historical Research*, 1978, 160–70.
57 William Baird, *General Wauchope*, 4th edition, Edinburgh and London, 1902, 61;
58 *The Times*, 9 August 1878, 5.a.b.d.
59 Wolseley Journal, 31 July 1878, 33.
60 Ibid.
61 *Home Report*, 5–7.
62 Sandon Journal, 3 August 1878, 47. Accordingly, Salisbury censured Wolseley.
63 *ILN*, 10 August 1878, 13.
64 *The Times*, 13 August 1878, 3.d.
65 *Hansard* (Commons), CCXLII, 14 August 1878, 1946.
66 Ibid., 1946–7.
67 Wolseley letters, 41324, British Library, Wolseley to Salisbury, 12 August 1878, 9.
68 CO67/2, immediate, Salisbury to Stanley, 12 August 1878.
69 CO67/2, WO to FO, 14 August 1878.
70 CO67/2, FO to WO, 22 August 1878.
71 *Hansard* (Commons), CCXLII, 15 August 1878, 2023–4.
72 Ibid., 16 August 1878, 2089–90.
73 *Punch*, 31 August 1878.
74 *The Times*, 12 July 1878, 8b; Lang, 'Cyprus – Is it Worth Keeping?' *MM*, XL, 1879, 441–8.
75 Farley, *Egypt, Cyprus and Asiatic Turkey*, 153–4.
76 *The Times*, 2 September 1878, 8.a; Wolseley Journal, 3 August 1878, 39. Palmer was the editor of the *Cyprus Graphic*.
77 Ibid., 15 October 1878, 4e.
78 W.E. Gladstone, 'England's Mission', *NC*, September 1878, 568–9.
79 Ibid., 565.
80 Ibid., 566–7.
81 Archibald Forbes, 'The "Fiasco" of Cyprus', *NC*, IV, October 1878, 609–26. Forbes wrote a book on the Black Watch but did not mention its time in Cyprus.
82 Ibid., 617.
83 Ibid., 615.
84 Varnava, 'Punch and the British Occupation of Cyprus', 177–8.
85 *The Times*, 15 October 1878, 4; ibid., 26 December 1878, 4e.
86 *Home Report*, 8–9.
87 Ibid., 12–13.

88 *The Times*, 25 September 1878, 5b; 29 October 1878, 8bc.

89 Ibid., 24 October 1878, 4c.

90 Ibid., 15 October 1878, 4e.

91 Scott-Stevenson, *Our Home in Cyprus*, 38, 40.

92 Butler, *Far Out*, 355.

93 McCalmont, *Memoirs*, 149.

94 *The Times*, 14 September 1878, 6.b; 21 September 1878, 5.c; 12 October 1878, 4; 5 November 1878, 6.b.

95 Ibid., 4 February 1879, 10.b. Sir William Harcourt called Inglis this in a speech. Ibid., 11 February 1879, 5b.

96 *ILN*, 5 October 1878, 34.

97 Sir Herbert Maxwell, *Life and Times of the Right Hon. William Henry Smith, M.P.*, II, London 1893, 335; Cross papers, 51273, 69.

98 *Punch*, 30 November 1878, 251; Varnava, 'Punch and the British Occupation of Cyprus', 177–8.

99 Salisbury to Smith, 21 October, Viscount Chilston, *W.H. Smith*, London, 1965, 127.

100 *The Times*, 31 October 1878; 2 November 1878, 5.c; 4 November 1878, 5; 5 November 1878, 7. They were accompanied by Admiral George Wellesley, First Naval Lord; Sir Massey Lopes, Civil Lord of the Admiralty; Admiral Sir W. Houston Stewart, Controller of the Navy; Algernon Egerton, First Secretary to the Admiralty; Captain Codrington, Wellesley's private secretary; R. Dalyell, Stanley's private secretary; Captain FitzGeorge, of the Intelligence Department; Lord Colville of Culross; Sir Henry Holland; and Sir George Elliot.

101 Scott-Stevenson, *Our Home in Cyprus*, 64–5.

102 Smith Diary, 4 November 1878, Maxwell, *Life and Times of the Right Hon. William Henry Smith, M.P.*, I, Edinburgh and London, 357.

103 CO67/3, secret, telegram, Stanley to Salisbury, 5 November 1878.

104 Lang, 'Cyprus – Is it Worth Keeping?', 443; Wolseley Journal, 4 November 1878, 123–4.

105 Wolseley Journal, 5 November 1878, 126.

106 Halik Kochanski, *Sir Garnet Wolseley: Victorian Hero*, London, 1999, 93–4.

107 Wolseley Journal, 5 November 1878, 126.

108 *The Times*, 14 September 1878, 9.c.

109 Sir Garnet Wolseley, 'Letter from Cyprus', *MM*, XXXIX, 1878–79, 96.

110 Wolseley letters, Wolseley to Salisbury, 3 September 1878, 19–20.

111 CO67/3, WO to FO, 5 September 1878; *ILN*, 5 October 1878, 34.

112 Hugh Montgomerie Sinclair, *Camp and Society*, London, 1926, 72.

113 Wolseley journal, 24 July 1878, 10.

114 *ILN*, 5 October 1878, 33–4; G.S. Woods, 'Oliver, Samuel Pasfield (1838–1907)', rev. Elizabeth Baigent, *ODNB* (www.oxforddnb.com/view/article/35307, accessed 22 Aug 2005).

115 Andrekos Varnava, 'Maintaining Britishness in a Setting of their Own Design: The Troodos Hill Station in Cyprus during the Early British Occupation', in Kate Darian-Smith, Patricia Grimshaw, Kiera Lindsey and Stuart Macintyre (eds), *Exploring the British World*, Melbourne, 2004, 1102–33; Andrekos Varnava, 'Recreating Rural Britain and Maintaining Britishness in the Mediterranean: The Troodos Hill Station in Early British Cyprus', *The Cyprus Review*, XVII, 2, Autumn 2005, 47–80.

116 *The Lancet*, 20 December 1879, 921; K.W. Schaar, M. Given and G. Theocharous, *Under the Clock*, Nicosia, 1995, 13.

117 SA1:14675 W.2/29/11, Samuel Brown report for March–October 1881.

118 FO226/193, Wolseley, raising a Druze force for Cyprus, 1878; CO67/1, 98, Wolseley to Salisbury, 14 October 1878.

119 Wolseley letters, Wolseley to Salisbury, 20 August 1878, 11; Wolseley to Layard, 22 August 1878, 16.

120 CO67/3, confidential, WO to FO, 20 September 1878; CO67/1, 108, FO to Wolseley, 27 September 1878; CO67/3, FO to T, 30 September 1878; CO67/3, immediate, T to FO, 8 October 1878.

121 *Correspondence Relating to the Island of Cyprus*, confidential, 1878–79, October 1879, 166, Wolseley to Salisbury, 7 November 1878.

122 CO67/6, immediate, Salisbury to WO, 4 March 1879; CO67/4, 97, Wolseley to Salisbury, 18 March 1879; CO67/6, 7690/555, pressing, WO to FO, 27 March 1879; *Hansard* (Commons), CCXLV, 20 March 1879, 1318–19.

123 *Hansard* (Commons), CCXLV, 27 March 1879, 1857; CO67/4, 214, Salisbury to Wolseley, 12 April 1879; CO67/6, immediate, FO to WO, 31 March 1879.

124 CO67/7, 51, Law Officers (LO) to Salisbury, 11 June 1879.

125 *Hansard* (Commons), CCXLVIII, 28 July 1879, 1411–12; 29 July 1879, 1563–8.

126 Ibid., 29 July 1879, 1569–70.

127 Ibid., 1573–4.

128 Ibid., 1574–8.

129 CO67/1, 178, Wolseley to Salisbury, 19 December 1878; Major A.G. Harfield, 'The Cyprus Pioneer Corps and the Cyprus Military Police During 1879–1882', *Bulletin Military Historical Society*, XXVI, 1975, 1–8.

130 Smith Diary, 3 November 1878, Maxwell, *William Henry Smith*, I, 355; Dixon, *British Cyprus*, 280.

131 Wolseley Journal, 3–4 November 1878, 123–4.

132 Beaconsfield to Queen Victoria, secret, 27 November 1878, Monypenny/Buckle, *Disraeli*, 1267.

133 C.2244, Rawson Report on Famagusta, 23 October 1878, 4–5.

134 C.2244, Evans Memorandum on the anchorages of Cyprus, 4 December 1878, 9.

135 C.2244, Hornby to the Secretary of the Admiralty, 20 January 1879, 3.

136 Colin Griffin, 'Elliot, Sir George, first baronet (1814–1893)', rev., *ODNB*, (www.oxforddnb.com/view/article/37393, accessed 28 Jan 2005).

137 *The Times*, 27 November 1891, 6c.

138 Samuel Brown, *Three Months in Cyprus During the Winter of 1878–9*, London 1879. Brown did not mention his Famagusta harbour report.

139 CO67/7/7749, Brown to Elliot, 31 March 1879.

140 CO67/8, Memorandum on Railways, Currie, 10 October 1879.

141 CO67/7/7749, Brown to Elliot, 31 March 1879.

142 Ibid.

143 Ibid.

144 Ibid.

145 Ibid. Falkland Warren, the Commissioner of Limassol, told Brown to examine the possibility of constructing a harbour west of Limassol. Brown found this place too shallow. He also investigated, on Wolseley's suggestion, the Akrotiri Salt Lake, where there were signs of an ancient port. But Brown believed that the passage to the sea was probably used to admit larger amounts of sea water to facilitate salt production and given that there were no historical references to a harbour, it was doubtful that one had existed there.

146 CO67/7/7749, 134, Wolseley to Salisbury, 30 April 1879.

147 CO67/7/7749, CO to FO, 18 June 1879.

148 CO67/6, Salisbury to Elliot, 25 February 1879; CO67/7, CO to FO, 21 August 1879.

149 CO67/5, 39, Biddulph to Salisbury, 28 July 1879. In January 1879 the van of the explorer and engineer Sir Samuel Baker could not traverse it because of the rounded rocks used for the foundation. Baker, *Cyprus as I Saw it in 1879*, 11.

150 *The Times*, 9 October 1878, 6.b; ibid., 1 January 1879, 4.e; Thomas Brassey quoting Colonel Warren, *Hansard* (Commons), CCXLV, 24 March 1879, 1556–7; Baker, *Cyprus as I Saw it in 1879*, 155–6.

151 CO67/5, 39, Biddulph to Salisbury, 28 July 1879; Schaar, Given and Theocharous, *Under the Clock*, 23; Baker, *Cyprus as I Saw it in 1879*, 2.

152 CO67/5, 39, Biddulph to Salisbury, 28 July 1879.

153 Baker, *Cyprus as I Saw it in 1879*, 111; Baird, *General Wauchope*, 63–4; Schaar, Given and Theocharous, *Under the Clock*, 13.

154 CO67/5, 39, Biddulph to Salisbury, 28 July 1879.

155 SA1:2691 H/32/1, Hydrographer Notice 40, Mediterranean Pilot, II, 3, 1880, 9, Notices to Mariners 18, 30 January 1879; 111, 30 July 1879; 138, 19 September 1879.
156 *Hansard* (Lords), CCXLIV, 21 March 1879, 1411.
157 Ibid., 1413.
158 Ibid., 1413–14.
159 Ibid., 1414–15.
160 Ibid., 1416.
161 Ibid., 1417.
162 *Hansard* (Commons), Vol. 244, March 24, 1879, 1510–61.
163 Captain J.C.R. Colomb, *The Defence of Great and Greater Britain*, London, 1880, 160.
164 Lee, *Great Britain and the Cyprus Convention Policy*, 119.
165 Martin, Sir William Fanshawe, 4th Baronet, Admiral; papers, 1816–95, British Library, Manuscript Collections, Reference: Add MSS 41408–62. Hereafter Martin papers.
166 Lord Alcester (Seymour) to John Knox Laughton, 4 November 1886, *Letters and Papers of Professor Sir John Knox Laughton, 1830–1915* (ed.) Andrew Lambert, Ashgate, 2002, 43–4.
167 J.K. Laughton, 'Martin, Sir William Fanshawe, fourth baronet (1801–1895)', rev. Andrew Lambert, *ODNB* (www.oxforddnb.com/view/article/18222, accessed 16 Feb. 2005).
168 Admiral Sir William Fanshawe Martin, *Cyprus as a Naval Station and a Place of Arms*, London, 1879, 4.
169 Martin, *Cyprus as a Naval Station and a Place of Arms*, 4.
170 Ibid., 5.
171 Ibid., 6, 10.
172 Ibid., 12.
173 *The Times*, 25 March 1880, 7f.
174 Martin papers, 185–6, George Peter Martin, paymaster, to Martin, 8 July 1879; 178–9, G.P. Martin to Martin, 10 June 1879.
175 Ibid., 180–1, Symonds to Martin, 6 July 1879.
176 J.K. Laughton, 'Symonds, Sir Thomas Matthew Charles (1813–1894)', rev. Andrew Lambert, *ODNB* (www.oxforddnb.com/view/article/26891, accessed 28 Jan 2005).
177 Martin papers, 193–4, Fanshawe to Martin, 14 July 1879; Fanshawe was a Liberal.
178 Ibid., 203, to Martin, 19 July 1879.
179 Ibid., 233–4, White to Martin, 2 January 1880.
180 Martin papers, 206–7, Eden to Martin, 20 July 1879.
181 Ibid., 189–90, Ewart to Martin, 10 July 1879; 199–201, Admiral Hugh Dunlop to Martin, 16 July 1879.
182 Ibid., 191–2, Littleton to Lady Hatherton, 14 July 1879.
183 Ibid., 187–8, Preedy to Martin, 9 July 1879.
184 Ibid., 204–5, Hope to Martin, 19 July 1879.
185 For Palestine see Bar-Yosef, The Holy Land in English Culture, 81–2.
186 Bar-Yosef, The Holy Land in English Culture, 85–7.
187 Beshara B. Doumani, 'Rediscovering Ottoman Palestine: Writing Palestinians into History', *Journal of Palestinian Studies*, XXI, 2, 1992, 5–28.
188 Bar-Yosef, The Holy Land in English Culture, 85–6.
189 Varnava, 'Maintaining Britishness in a Setting of their Own Design', 1102–33.
190 J.H. Lehmann, *All Sir Garnet*, London, 1964, 282.
191 Halik Kochanski, 'Wolseley ring (act. 1873–1890)', *ODNB* (www.oxforddnb.com/view/article/69913, accessed 24 Jan 2005).
192 McCalmont, *Memoirs*, 146–7.
193 Scott-Stevenson, *Our Home in Cyprus*, 66.
194 Wolseley Journal, 30 July 1878, 22.
195 *The Times*, 13 September 1889, 5d.
196 *The Lancet*, 4 January 1879, 22.
197 *Home Report*.
198 *The Lancet*, 31 May 1879, 776–7.

199 *The Times*, 30 August 1878, 3.f; 7 September 1878, 5.c; 10 September 1878, 3.c.
200 Wolseley to Stanley, 5 March 1879, *Home Report*, 1.
201 *The Lancet*, 24 May 1879.
202 Wolseley Journal 19 July 1878, 9. This was contrary to Pasfield's praise: HRH 'deserves the greatest credit for the way ... all the arrangements for the disembarkation have been carried out'. *ILN*, 17 August 1878.
203 Ibid.
204 Ibid., 13 December 1878, 156.
205 Ibid., 4, 20, 28 October, 5, 10 November 1878, 100, 112, 119, 127, 129.
206 McCalmont, *Memoirs*, 147.
207 Ibid., 148.
208 Smith Diary, 5 November 1878, Maxwell, *William Henry Smith*, I, 359.
209 *Hansard* (Commons), CCXLIV, 24 March 1879, 1510.
210 Charles Rathbone Low, *General Lord Wolseley*, London, 1883, 360.
211 Scott-Stevenson, *Our Home in Cyprus*, 66.
212 Wolseley Journal, 24 September 1878, 90.
213 Ibid., 25 September 1878, 90.
214 Ibid., 26 November 1878, 150.
215 Kochanski, *Sir Garnet Wolseley*, 96; *Hansard* (Commons), CCXLVI, 27 May 1879, 1354–5; ibid., 10 June 1879, 246, 1550; ibid., 20 June 1879, 358–400.
216 Schurman, *Imperial Defence*, 66.
217 Ibid., 74–5, 77.
218 Beaconsfield to Greaves, George Richards Greaves, *Memoirs of General Sir George Richards Greaves*, London, 1924, 137–8.
219 Greaves, *Memoirs*, 138.
220 CO67/7, 13, FO to Biddulph, 3 June 1879.
221 PRO30/29/280, 57, secret, Salisbury to Biddulph, 4 July 1879.
222 Ibid.
223 Ibid.
224 Salisbury to Major Trotter, 16 September 1879, Cecil, *Salisbury*, II, 321–2.
225 *The Times*, 18 October 1879, 9a–b, 10a.
226 CO67/8, immediate, FO to Ormiston, 9 October 1879; R.M. Birse, 'Ormiston, Thomas (1826–1882)', rev. Mike Chrimes, *ODNB* (www.oxforddnb.com/view/article/37826, accessed 7 Feb. 2005).
227 *Report on the Sanitary Condition and Drainage of the District of Famagusta and the Mesaoria in Cyprus*, the Chevalier David Bocci, Chief Engineer, RE, Parma, 5 June 1880, CO, November 1881. Hereafter Bocci Report.
228 CO67/10, General Report on Famagusta District by Civil Surgeon, 20 November 1879.
229 *Report by Mr. Ormiston on Improvements Proposed at the harbour of Famagusta dated January 10, 1880*. C. 2544, London, 1880, 4–5.
230 CO67/14, private, FO to Ormiston, 5 March 1880.
231 Bocci report, 3–6.
232 *The Times*, 27 November 1879, 10a.
233 W.E. Gladstone, *Midlothian Speeches, 1879*, Leicester, 1971, 125–6.
234 *The Times*, 27 October 1879, 10f; 30 October 1879, 10a.
235 C.G.A. Clay, *Gold for the Sultan: Western Bankers and Ottoman Finance 1856–1881*, London, 2000, 394, 401.
236 CO67/11, 56, Biddulph to Salisbury, 2 February 1880.
237 *The Times*, 29 November 1879, 5a; 13 May 1881, 5b.
238 CO67/11, Biddulph to Salisbury, 25 March 1880; CO67/9, 145, Salisbury to Biddulph, 28 March 1880.
239 CO67/14, Cyprus 2/246, WO to FO, 31 March 1880; CO67/10, 164, Salisbury to Biddulph, 13 April 1880.

CHAPTER 5

Financial policy and the development of Cyprus, 1880–1912: The 'mill-stone'

It [Cyprus] has every opportunity to develop. It has even the necessary money, but the British Government seizes it. And hangs this tribute like a mill-stone round the island's neck. (*The Times*, 24 May 1912)

British economic policy in Cyprus was contradictory. Cyprus was occupied to protect and expand imperial interests, yet governments did not spend imperial funds to achieve either. The first imperial funds were spent when Joseph Chamberlain became Colonial Secretary, but the projects did not aim to make Cyprus a strategic asset. Also, Cyprus was perceived as a land of plenty, yet governments subordinated budgets to pay the tribute and still needed a grant-in-aid to do so. Thus, British policy rendered Cyprus economically unviable.

The purchase plan

True to its word, the Gladstone government made swift changes. In May 1880, Charles Dilke, the under-secretary at the Foreign Office, announced Cyprus's future transfer to the Colonial Office,[1] where stringency was the norm. Gladstone also announced sweeping changes to local laws, including forced labour.[2] After a debate in the House of Commons on 1 June, an editorial in *The Times* exulted: 'Gladstone now recognises that our position in the island must be accepted.'[3] The Liberals questioned that assessment however, and were as confused as the Conservatives over what to do with Cyprus.

An unlikely approach from the Sultan presented a solution. Gladstone replaced Layard at Constantinople[4] with George Joachim Goschen, the First Lord of the Admiralty (1871–74) in his first ministry. Goschen knew the region well, having represented the Council of Foreign Bondholders in Egypt. He had opposed Beaconsfieldism as 'un-English' because it had sullied England's standing as 'the most clean-handed member of the European family'.[5] Gladstone wanted the

Porte to cede territory to Greece and execute reforms as agreed in Berlin. When this was refused, Lord Granville (the Foreign Secretary) wanted European coercion.[6] When this was rejected, Goschen warned the Porte that the guarantee against Russia was contingent on reforms.[7] Abdul Hamid did not want reform or the British guarantee, and so proposed, through his ambassador in London, Mursurus Pasha, the annulment of the Anglo-Turkish Convention. He hated the interference of the British military consuls appointed in autumn 1878 and spring 1879 in the internal administration of his Asiatic dominions and would release Britain from guaranteeing Ottoman Asia to remove them. The Sultan did not want Cyprus back, but the tribute commuted to a lump sum. Ottoman economic problems and the failure to pay foreign debt needed arresting.[8] Mursurus left for Constantinople on 20 May having told Granville to expect a proposal on his return.[9]

The Cabinet then defined Cyprus' place within British imperial structure. Granville informed Goschen on 10 June that the Cabinet believed that Cyprus was worthless 'in a military or political sense' (the queen disagreed); its tenure was 'uncertain and anomalous'; its acquisition had blackened England's name; and the Convention presented onerous obligations. The Cabinet, with Victoria's consent, agreed to raise a loan on Cyprus' revenues to buy the island and finance public works.[10]

Admiral Sir Beauchamp Seymour, formerly the Junior Naval Lord under Goschen (1872–74) and now the Commander-in-Chief of the Mediterranean Station, advised purchasing Cyprus. On 30 April, days after the election, Seymour informed Hugh Childers, his former head when he was First Lord of the Admiralty (1868–70) and now the War Secretary, that his visit to Cyprus confirmed his view that it should not have been occupied, but since it had, Britain should buy it because trade was diminishing and money was needed to redevelop Famagusta harbour.[11] Twelve days before the letter to Goschen, Seymour added three more reasons; 'its strategical position with respect to the Suez Canal . . . and the Euphrates railway of the future' and because it would bring investment.[12]

Military advice also pointed to redeveloping Famagusta. Lieutenant-General Sir John Adye, the governor of the Royal Military Academy, thought that the £5,000 earmarked for permanent barracks at Polymedia should be spent at Famagusta, where a coaling and commercial station could be made.[13] After serving in the Crimean War and the Indian Mutiny, Adye supported Cardwell reducing colonial garrisons and minimised the Russian threat in the 1876–78 crisis. Gladstone's government trusted him to give advice that saved money and included the navy in considerations.[14] In 1870, Adye warned against an army-centric approach to planning.[15] He thought that the military and naval stations should be at Famagusta, which was also the outlet for Mesaoria's produce. This was important because 'by selecting the same Port for our Military base the improvements carried out by the merchants would also be available for Military purposes.'[16]

The High Commissioner, Sir Robert Biddulph, formerly Cardwell's private secretary and later his biographer,[17] approved. He advised temporarily housing the troops in semi-permanent huts at Polymedia until Famagusta was ready.[18] Seymour, Adye and Biddulph agreed that Famagusta was the place to develop and the Liberals realised that Cyprus would need to be purchased in order to pay for it.

However, uncertainties persisted. After Granville's letter to Goschen, Ormiston's report was tabled in Parliament.[19] The Duke of Somerset repeated his question to Salisbury about the Admiralty report the previous year. The Colonial Secretary, Lord Kimberley, rejected Ormiston's estimate of £350,000 as it neglected fortifications and sanitary work. To the Liberals, the cost was a further demonstration that the Tories had erred in taking Cyprus. Kimberley stated that 'the whole subject of Cyprus, whether as regarded their tenure or . . . of rendering it useful as a great military or naval station . . . seemed to him to be so difficult' that he would not 'pledge himself to the course which should be taken'.[20]

The interests of the navy, army, Colonial and Foreign offices entangled policy. Edward Fairfield, a Colonial Office clerk since 1866, thought it was a War Office matter where to station the troops, yet Kimberley wanted the Colonial Office to decide whether to redevelop Famagusta.[21] The uncertainties were reflected in Granville's order to Goschen to wait for the Porte, because when there was no Ottoman approach he did nothing.[22]

The tribute: 'A scandal of the British occupation'[23]

Answering a question in Parliament as to whether Famagusta harbour would be redeveloped in the light of French occupation of Tunis in 1881, Gladstone announced that Cyprus would need a substantial grant-in-aid.[24] His stringency meant that imperial funds for Famagusta were unthinkable. This was understandable. When he left office in 1874 there was a £5.5 million surplus, but 1878 opened with a deficit of a similar amount following the Zulu and Kafir wars.[25] But Cyprus could have paid for Famagusta harbour's redevelopment had the Liberals not fixed the tribute at a higher rate.

When the arrangement between the Porte and its local creditors worked, British and French bondholders pressured their governments for a similar deal. Talks started in October 1880. To pay the debt the Porte made available the indirect taxes and the 'tributes' from autonomous Eastern Rumelia, the Bulgarian principality, and Cyprus. But the Liberals did not want the Cyprus revenue going into a general sinking fund devoted to the 1855 guaranteed loan. They wanted it to pay the £82,000 per annum liability (of London and Paris) to the bondholders. In December, the Porte agreed to this, if the exchange rate were 120 piastres (the rate when Cyprus was occupied) and not 213 piastres as Biddulph had wanted. Thus, there was enough to pay the British and French obligation, so in February 1881 the Treasury decided that Biddulph's rate was 'scarcely compatible with good faith'. When the Administration of the Ottoman Public Debt was created in December 1881, the Porte insisted on 100 piastres and in February 1882 the Colonial Office agreed on 108 piastres and 10 paras, making a total of £92,686.[26]

In 1886 the short-lived Liberal government was asked about the tribute and the under-secretary of state at the Colonial Office, George Osborne Morgan, claimed that London retained the money because, once it was paid, it became Ottoman revenue. Since the Porte had defaulted on the 1855 loan, which London and Paris guaranteed, the money was deposited into a 'special account' in the Bank of England and applied to pay the Ottoman default. Morgan justified the tribute relieving French liabilities because it was 'one of the first rules of equity' that when a guarantor obtained the assets of the defaulted party it must be shared with any co-guarantor.[27] In November 1888, Goschen, now Chancellor of the Exchequer in Salisbury's government, explained that £82,000 was needed to pay London and Paris's liability and the £10,000 was kept for the loan's one per cent sinking fund.[28] But, within a year, he explained the arrangements differently. The £10,000 excess had paid the ransoms of Captain Henry Synge and Harry Suter, captured by brigands in Macedonia in 1882.[29] The Liberals had directed £24,803 of the tribute to that end,[30] but on what authority? And the rest? Goschen explained that it went to building a sinking fund for the defaulted sinking fund of 1855.[31]

The tribute crippled finances. As early as June 1880, Biddulph had claimed that revenue could cover Cyprus' administration and development, but not the tribute too.[32] Revenue reached £200,000 only three times in the nineteenth century: in 1891–92, 1898–99 and 1899–1900, with lows of £145,443 in 1887–88, £149,363 in 1888–89 and £160,112 in 1902–3, owing to drought and bad harvests.[33] If the extra £45,000 had not been taken, Famagusta's sanitation and the harbour that Samuel Brown proposed (he became head of the Government Engineer's Department in summer 1880)[34] could have been built.

[130]

Fairfield, who backed Biddulph's lower figure,[35] rightly stated that London rejected buying Cyprus because it was 'more profitable' to give 'Cyprus moderate annual aid . . . retaining the Tribute towards recouping' the Ottoman loan.[36] In October 1883, a year before the Ottoman contract of Messrs Collas and Michel on Cyprus' lighthouses expired, Biddulph wanted to plan for their takeover,[37] but the first thing Kimberly thought of was to add another £113 11s 3d to the total, as the Anglo-Turkish Convention allowed, bringing it to £92,799 11s 3d.[38] The tribute came first in all matters pertaining to finance. It reduced funds available for local use and became a grievance for Orthodox and Muslim Cypriots (see Chapter 6), with every high commissioner wanting it commuted.[39]

There were suggestions to commute the tribute, but the Exchequer did not look to do so. In 1894, Charles Christian, formerly the manager of the Cyprus branch of the Imperial Ottoman Bank, proposed to commute it, but Fairfield rejected it.[40] In 1895, Sir Edward Hamilton, a respected Treasury officer, proposed to redeem the Ottoman Guaranteed Loan and commute the tribute simultaneously. Salisbury liked the scheme but thought that France would object.[41] The Porte agreed to the commutation for between £300,000 and £400,000. 'But', Hamilton wrote in his diary in March 1896: 'the Government must be prepared to couple with the commutation the redemption of the whole of the Turkish Guaranteed Loan of 1855, and to face difficulties on the part of France.'[42] In June 1896 he drafted a letter to Paris which Salisbury approved.[43] In December 1896, however, the Ottoman ambassador, an Orthodox Christian, told Hamilton that the Porte should share the benefits of the commutation with Cyprus.[44] A year later the Ottoman position was clearer: it would not agree to the full commutation. Hamilton adapted his scheme, thus: reduce the tribute to about £30,000 a year; London to raise a new loan on the security of the reduced tribute and the Egyptian tribute; and the amount raised not needed for the old loan's redemption would go to the Porte.[45] But Hicks-Beach back-tracked in June 1898.[46] A year later, Hamilton put Hicks-Beach's objections down to 'pure "cussed-ness" on his part'.[47] Years later Hamilton claimed that had Salisbury or Hicks-Beach shown 'any real anxiety about carrying the Agreement through' the tribute would have been reduced and the grant-in-aid ended.[48] When he made that statement (1904 or 1905) the Cypriots had paid nearly £2.2 million in tribute.[49]

In 1905, owing to the three-year drought, the Colonial Office asked the Treasury to increase and fix the grant-in-aid to alleviate the tribute's burden. Sir Montagu F. Ommaney, the permanent under-secretary at the Colonial Office, asserted that 'Cyprus cannot be administered in a proper manner if she continues to pay to this country more than, say, 20 per cent of her annual revenue'.[50] After the High Commissioner Charles King-Harman met with Treasury and Colonial Office officials, the grant-in-aid was fixed at £50,000, but the tribute's effects can be seen in the figures. Ommaney was gravely incorrect. Cyprus forfeited nearly 43 per cent of its revenue. Had there been no tribute (or grant) the local revenue would have paid for the British administration and left nearly £2.3 million in surplus (Appendix V).

The figures show that the tribute made Cyprus' development unviable. For that the British had themselves to blame.

Famagusta harbour, 1880–82

On 1 January 1881, Robert Hall, the secretary of the Admiralty, advised Kimberley that it was not worth redeveloping Famagusta harbour until its environs were made healthy.[51] Hall was Somerset's private secretary when he was the First Lord of the Admiralty and Goschen had made him the Admiralty secretary in 1872. Although his view on Famagusta harbour reflected Kimberley's, Hall thought it could be important to imperial defence.

> The possession of a secure coaling station at the nearest point to Port Said might . . . be of great value in time of war providing that it is sufficiently fortified and defended by a garrison large enough to protect it from Naval attack.[52]

Hall advised that the War Office should investigate the costs of transferring the military station to Famagusta, but existing coaling stations took precedence.

The Colonial Office was worried. Fairfield argued that if a naval station at Famagusta was wanted, Cyprus would have to pay for the sanitary works.[53] The indecision baffled him:

> this question of making Cyprus a great place of arms appears to be not yet ripe for decision and to be one with which the various departments concerned seem inclined to play battle-don and shuttlecock for an indefinite time.[54]

In 1881 an editorial in *The Times* mocked Cyprus's strategic value,[55] but men on the spot countered. H.H.K. (Kitchener) replied that only drainage was needed to restore Famagusta to 'its pristine salubrity when it was the mart of the East'.[56]

The Colonial Office was opposed to improving Famagusta, although investors were interested. In October 1881, George Goussio, the manager of the Anglo-Egyptian Bank in Cyprus, requested a concession to build a harbour for four warships at £50,000. Goussio, who Edward

Vizetelly thought was 'a remarkable man',[57] wanted London to pay the excess and guarantee the bank £3,800 annually to pay the interest and sinking fund. Biddulph advised against the terms because he thought he could get a cheaper estimate.[58]

As with other possessions,[59] the Colonial Office rejected concessionaries in Cyprus preferring to use the Crown Agents, the commercial agents of British overseas possessions. The Crown Agents claimed that they served the colonies cheaply,[60] but they owed their existence to the Colonial Office refusal to assign projects to colonies, and in reality their services were expensive.[61] Brown thought he could do the work more cheaply. He took ten months to reply to the request for an estimate on Famagusta harbour because he was delayed building piers at Limassol and Larnaca after the Crown Agents overruled his lower estimates.[62]

Brown found that the depth of water on the breakwater line, a vital element in costs, favoured Famagusta over Alexandria. The area was the same and the sea's force was less, so the twenty-ton blocks Ormiston advised were unnecessary and there was good stone at the quarry. Thus, Brown's scheme was cheaper. His first plan was similar to that of 1879, excluding the two jetties, and cost £49,195. It was enough for military and commercial aims. But if a 1,500-yard breakwater was built and part of the outer harbour dredged, bringing the total to £136,781, twenty-four large ships could moor head and stern, giving Famagusta an outer and an inner harbour.[63]

Biddulph told Kimberley that the £50,000 plan was worth adopting with further extensions left to the future,[64] but the assistant undersecretary at the Colonial Office, Robert Meade, thought Cyprus did not have the funds.[65] Kimberley wanted Fairfield's view.[66] Fairfield was an important Colonial Office official, who R.B. Pugh was to describe as 'charming, popular, humane, slightly flippant, [and] slightly dissipated'.[67] He was rare in the Colonial Office, being interested in Africa and Cyprus. Fairfield investigated the island's finances from 6 November to 8 January 1882 and told Kimberley that Famagusta would not attract Limassol and Larnaca's trade and that a naval station would mean Cyprus paying for sanitary works.[68]

This was enough. On 19 February, three days after the tribute was fixed at the higher rate, Kimberley minuted: 'If ever Cyprus has £50,000 to spare, it might be worthwhile to institute this scheme [but] at present I don't see where the money is to come from.'[69] He told Biddulph that taxpayers already bore a heavy annual charge in aid of the revenue.[70]

London certainly provided a grant-in-aid, but it was so that Cyprus could pay the tribute. £78,000 was needed in 1881–82, increasing in

1882–83 to £90,000; almost covering the full amount. The grant, how-ever, decreased to £20,000 and less, for the next four years. Salisbury was right in claiming in July 1882 that Cyprus was not as bad a finan-cial bargain as it had been portrayed.[71]

Edward Fairfield's memorandum

Having set the tribute at a higher rate, the Liberals justified referring to Cyprus as a drain and cutting costs. In June 1881 an English resident of Cyprus claimed that public works spending would need to be slashed in order to pay the tribute.[72] Robert Hamilton Lang, who in 1882 served as a director of the Ottoman Public Debt, and in 1883 became the director of the *Regie des Tabacs Ottomane*, advised £12,000 in cuts.[73]

Fairfield's trip to Cyprus aimed to produce a budget so Cyprus could pay the tribute with a minimal grant-in-aid.[74] He proposed to slash the salaries of officials and hit Brown's department hard.[75] The sum of £50,000 went to public works from 1878 to 1881, excluding items the Cyprus government was not charged for: the prefabricated Gov-ernment House, which the War Office provided (£5,150)[76] and the pioneers' barracks used as government offices in Nicosia (£6,107). In 1881–82 the public works budget was over £30,000 and in 1882–83 was estimated at £24,268. Thus, £120,000 would be spent in five years.[77] Fairfield advised fixing expenditure and – since roads connecting the towns and principal villages and the improved facilities at the ports of Limassol and Larnaca would be soon done[78] – £13,000 a year was 'reasonable', comprising: staff £2,500; maintenance, £2,000; miscellan-eous works, £2,500; roads and bridges, £5,000; and stores, £1,000.[79]

Biddulph thought it was staggeringly low: 'I fear this would be alto-gether inadequate, if it is deemed necessary to improve the material condition of the Island to any appreciable extent.'[80] Brown and his men had done more work than Fairfield had credited them with. He neglected their superintendence of Municipal and *Evkaf* works and locust destruction.[81] All were demanding, but the last was dangerous and vital for a country reliant on consistent harvests. In summer 1880, the locusts, which had been eradicated during the last decade of Ottoman rule, returned. Biddulph had instituted compulsory egg collection, resulting in an increase from 29,933 okes collected in 1879 to 189,000 in 1880. Yet they returned in 1881. From July 1881 to February 1882, a staggering 1,063,555 okes (about 1,330 tons) of eggs were destroyed. The Cypriots collected the eggs, but Brown's depart-ment had to destroy them and the live insects by building thousands of locust traps and cloth screens. The amount spent on their destruc-tion in 1882–83 was £32,000.[82]

Biddulph was also aghast at Fairfield's claim that few public works were needed. He warned that, apart from the Nicosia–Larnaca road, only networks had been marked, and were still unsafe for carts.[83] Communications were so bad that in September 1880 the people of the Karpass offered to construct bridges if the British would provide a mason and cut stone.[84] Biddulph asked for £60,000 over five years.[85] He also revealed that improvements and new government officers were needed in Famagusta, Paphos and Nicosia. Limassol pier also needed extending so steamers and transports could dock.[86] He warned Kimberley: 'It is not difficult to effect a reduction of expenditure by stopping public works, and we need only go back to Turkish times to see the results of that principle.[87]

But in May 1883, the Colonial Office and the Treasury agreed to Fairfield's budget. The new Colonial Secretary, Lord Derby, the former Conservative Foreign Secretary, added:

> it should be announced, once and for all, that there is no thought and no prospect of Cyprus being developed by the bounty of Parliament, but that . . . the inhabitants must work out their development at their own cost and by their own labour.[88]

Accordingly, the total expenditure, including the tribute, was fixed at £205,000 for 1883–84. The decision was a major setback to Cyprus' development, and for the next twelve years budgets were based on this policy.

The policy in action

Kyriacos Demetriou was right when he claimed that the British were not concerned about improving the local economy, but he was wrong in thinking that the reason was Cyprus' strategic importance (Chapter 8).[89] The real reason was that the Colonial Office feared that naval interest in Famagusta would require Cyprus to fund sanitary works, thus threatening payment of the tribute.[90]

There was money to improve Famagusta, but it was channelled elsewhere. In 1880 Salisbury had rejected moving the central gaol to Famagusta on the advice of its commissioner, Captain Inglis, because the marshes caused fever.[91] Instead of draining them, as proposed, it was thought cheaper to fill them. This was completed in July 1881,[92] but it did not halt the fever. From June 1883 to May 1884, Biddulph, Brown, and Arthur Young, Famagusta's commissioner, discussed draining the marshes. In May, Biddulph claimed that it 'must stand over for the present' because of insufficient funds.[93] In December 1884, however, Biddulph proposed redeveloping Kyrenia harbour.

Biddulph proposed relocating the long-sentence prisoners from Nicosia to Kyrenia and arranging for them to be employed by working on the harbour. Biddulph, knowing that the harbour was small and shallow, appealed to Fairfield: 'I don't see why we are to sit still and do nothing because we can't make Famagusta Harbour.'[94]

But Falkland Warren and the Receiver General, J.A. Swettenham, opposed the proposal. They wanted Famagusta substituted for Kyrenia.[95] Swettenham believed that Larnaca best served Nicosia's trade and Kyrenia was out of the way.[96] Kyrenia's trade since the British arrival remained miniscule, peaking at £27,500.[97] Warren expressed his 'strong dissent' because the £4,000 estimate was too much to take from the public works budget for a scheme benefiting 1,192 people. Kyrenia harbour was too small (Figures 13) and not a natural trade outlet. Trade with Karamania would improve, but Warren warned that more goats would arrive, which would further destroy what was left of the forests. 'If it is necessary', he wrote to Biddulph, 'to improve a seaport for commercial purposes then local knowledge points plainly and unquestionable to . . . Famagusta.' Warren warned Biddulph that the Cypriots would view 'with great disfavour' the spending of £4,000 on Kyrenia harbour, and especially if they realised it would amount to £8,000 without the convicts.[98]

Figure 13 Kyrenia Harbour in 1879
Source: John Thomson, *Through Cyprus with the Camera in the Autumn of 1878*, London 1879.

Biddulph checked this dissent, telling Derby on 12 January that Kyrenia commanded the Karamania trade. He had 'no desire to press the question . . . to the detriment of commencing work at Famagusta' and would drop it if work started at Famagusta in 1886.[99] But Biddulph knew that was ambitious and the day after he wrote to Derby, he had Brown include £2,500 in the 1885–86 budget for the Kyrenia project.[100]

Fairfield endorsed Biddulph's proposal by claiming that Kyrenia was closer to 'civilisation' than Famagusta, which he claimed was too far from Nicosia and off the Egyptian route.[101] This was nonsense because Kyrenia was nowhere near Egypt.

Before a decision was made, a heavy gale on 20 January smashed the *Lady Franklin*, an English ship anchored in Kyrenia harbour. Biddulph told Derby that the people of Kyrenia had complained about the unsafe harbour in 1882 and Edward Kenyon, the commissioner, blamed the harbour's contours.[102] Meade now supported the scheme. He thought that spending £4,000 at Kyrenia would not affect Famagusta.[103] Derby told Biddulph to 'warn [the] Council [that] prospects of works at Famagusta [were] remote'.[104] Salisbury's government sanctioned the scheme, which would take three years and cost £7,284,[105] showing the continuity in the agenda of the Colonial Office and the power of its junior clerks.

But the project proved a disaster. From the £10,000 public works budget, £3,000 was allocated in 1886–87.[106] A lack of convict labour, however, restricted progress in 1886[107] and, in 1887, storms damaged the quays. Brown reported in November 1887 that the masonry work would be delayed for another year unless the foundations were completed before the rain.[108] Henry Bulwer, Biddulph's successor, complained in March 1887 to the Colonial Secretary, Sir Henry Holland, that the Cyprus government had embarked on the 'expensive work of harbour improvement at Kyrenia' at the expense of pressing work. The sum of £5,000 from the £10,000 public works budget went to public buildings, from which £2,000 would be taken in 1887–88 for Kyrenia harbour. This left nothing for building the lighthouses at Paphos and Cape Greco, which Derby had sanctioned in 1885. Brown's idea to use the light dues was rejected,[109] although the Austrian Lloyds Company demanded a lighthouse at Paphos and the Executive Council wanted it built in 1887.[110]

To find more money, Bulwer wanted Brown to reduce his staff,[111] but his refusal[112] displeased Bulwer: 'You have been given every opportunity of doing so and there is nothing now left but for the government to take the matter into its own hands.'[113] Fairfield and Holland were pleased that Bulwer had enforced what the Colonial Office had wanted during Biddulph's time and after more cuts Fairfield declared Brown's 'Alexandria Ring' defeated,[114] implying that, like Wolseley, he surrounded himself with his cronies.

Instead of being finished in February 1889, Bulwer was told that the Kyrenia harbour works needed another year.[115] Then a storm caused £350 of damage to the western mole. Brown had warned about the north-east wind and had planned for a longer eastern breakwater to deflect it.[116] But Brown had left for Hong Kong in 1889 after the tragic death of his wife in Nicosia[117] and his replacement, Jason Cunningham,[118] while admitting that a longer eastern breakwater would have sheltered the harbour,[119] had extended the western breakwater further than planned and now favoured extending it even more because the water was shallower. Regardless of which breakwater was extended, it would require another year.[120] In late 1889 Lord Knutsford (Holland) was told that more work and money was needed. Aside from the £350 repairs, £240 was spent on a road around the quay where the rails from the quarry were laid, now another £550 was needed to enlarge the quay and the inner slope of the western breakwater and another £50 to repair the eastern breakwater, which was damaged in another storm in October 1889.[121] By summer 1890, Bulwer was impatient and asked Kyrenia's commissioner to keep his eye on proceedings.[122]

The works thwarted Bulwer's aim to improve sea communications, but even when he did manage to undertake projects the Crown Agents, and often disasters, frustrated him. The lighthouse at Paphos was postponed from 1887 to June 1888 and then to spring 1889 because the Crown Agents could not send the light until December. When it was completed, the lamp caught fire when lit, requiring £349 to replace the damaged parts.[123]

Famagusta's neglect was exemplified by the failure to remove stones impeding ships from entering the inner harbour. In August 1886, Claude Cobham, Larnaca's commissioner and the acting Chief Collector of Customs, told Warren that the deputy harbourmaster could clear them for £30.[124] Brown told Warren that the entrance was narrow and uneven in depth, but vessels could be guided around the stones.[125] The matter was forgotten until February 1888 when Warren revived it, but there was nobody to carry out the task, and the cost had gone up.[126] In March, Young suggested that traders from Beirut could do it and a year later Cunningham suggested using the crane used to build Limassol's jetty.[127] In July 1889, Bulwer stated that on financial grounds 'we had better wait till the harbour works at Kyrenia are finished when some of the plant we have there could be transferred to Famagusta'.[128]

In August 1890, Bulwer proposed to upgrade the existing lighthouses and harbour lights and build new lighthouses at Cape Greco and

Cape Andreas.[129] He managed to pay for the upgrade,[130] but Knutsford rejected the lighthouse project at Cape Greco because it was too expensive. Bulwer's persistence resulted in the Admiralty and Board of Trade producing an affordable estimate and, in June 1891, the project was sanctioned.[131] Nevertheless, Bulwer still criticised the Kyrenia harbour project, which was completed as the Cape Greco lighthouse was authorised: 'Whether the work will be as beneficial as was anticipated remains to be seen, but a great deal of time, money and labour has been expended on it.'[132] The work took three years longer than planned and cost £9,356 – over £2,000 more than estimated.[133] Although this sum would not have been enough to redevelop Famagusta harbour, Andrew Provand, a Liberal MP, thought it would have gone a long way towards dredging the inner basin and remedying Famagusta's insalubrity.[134] Indeed, when Bulwer proposed dredging Famagusta's inner harbour, in July 1891, the estimate was £6,200.[135]

The new Kyrenia harbour did not resolve the issue of ships safely lying in its basin and trade did not dramatically increase (Appendix VI). Ships were still wrecked: in 1890 the *Annina B* and in 1892 the *Empress*.[136] When in 1904 Larnaca's mayor, Nicholaos Rossos, called it 'an object of derision for everybody', Adrian Fiddian, a Colonial Office clerk, agreed.[137] Three years later, the inhabitants of Kyrenia passed a resolution and deputed a committee of shipowners calling on a £10,000 redevelopment.[138] In 1925 Coode, Fitzmaurice, Wilson and Mitchell estimated that at least £12,000 was needed to make the harbour safe for small craft in northerly gales.[139]

With the limited funds it was a credit to the engineers in Cyprus, especially Samuel Brown, that Cyprus had been given a fine road network (Figures 14 and 15). The fact that in 1904, the Larnaca–Famagusta road was incomplete exemplified Famagusta's neglect.

A man on a mission

The continuity between Liberals and Conservatives on financial policy, shown by the retention of Fairfield's budget and the Tory sanctioning of the Kyrenia harbour project, was furthered when Knutsford reduced the public works vote from £10,500 to £8,000 because of the drought in the Karpass in winter 1886–87. The crisis was so serious that Bulwer requested £50,000. Holland was stunned. Bulwer visited the Karpass and used a map to make his point (Figure 16).[140]

The Treasury sanctioned £9,650,[141] but the drought resulted in a drastic decrease in revenue, which meant that the grant-in-aid went from £18,000 (1886–87) to £55,000 (1887–88) and only with cuts to

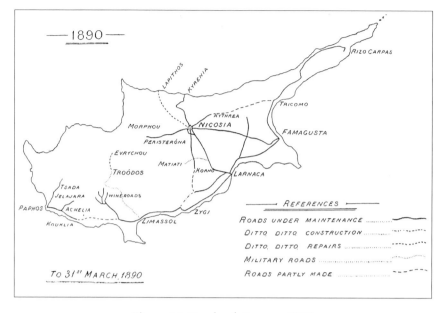

Figure 14 Roads of Cyprus, 1890
Source: C.V. Bellamy, *The Main Roads of Cyprus*, Nicosia, 1903.

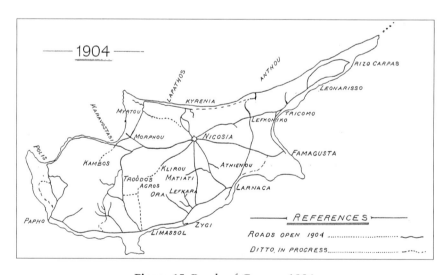

Figure 15 Roads of Cyprus, 1904
Source: C.V. Bellamy, *The Main Roads of Cyprus*, Nicosia, 1903.

[140]

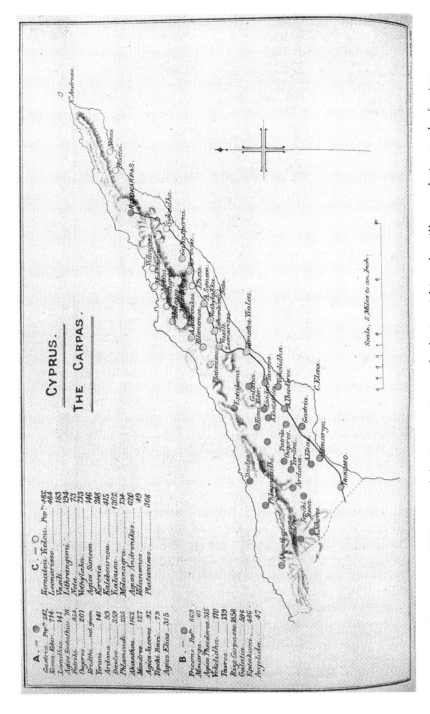

Figure 16 An 1888 map of the Karpass Peninsula distinguishing the villages relative to the famine
Source: C.5523.

public works (£6,940, £7,705, £8,164, were spent in 1888–9, 1889–90, 1890–1) was the grant reduced to £45,000 in 1888–89.[142]

Joseph Chamberlain, who became Colonial Secretary in 1895, was the first to improve conditions. Chamberlain, a Radical, split with Gladstone in March 1886 over Irish home rule and carved a niche in British politics advocating a stronger imperial government and the vigorous development of colonies. His focus was on the new gold reserves in South Africa, which he feared threatened to move power from London to the Boer republics. In Natal, for example, there was considerable exploitation of natural resources.[143] Chamberlain also promoted railway investment.[144] When Salisbury won office Chamberlain was invited to choose a ministry. He selected the Colonial Office and promised capital and credit for railways, harbours and irrigation works in tropical Africa and Cyprus and tariff reform to support Caribbean sugar islands. The works were unparalleled.[145]

Walter Sendall, the high commissioner, told Chamberlain that Cyprus needed irrigation and communication networks.[146] Chamberlain informed Hicks-Beach, the Chancellor of the Exchequer, that London's financial treatment of Cyprus was unacceptable and wanted a fixed £40,000 grant-in-aid for five years and the tribute's eventual commutation. Chamberlain wanted education (especially of the clergy), public works and agriculture addressed and advocated railway and irrigation works across the Mesaoria, telling Hicks-Beach that spending £300,000 on either was justified.[147] Hicks-Beach recognised that Cyprus had been disadvantaged and that the grants-in-aid were furnished to enable payment of the tribute, but he was as parsimonious with taxpayers' hard-earned as Chamberlain was lavish.[148] Chamberlain persisted, however, and asked Hicks-Beach to double the public works vote. He referred to Fairfield's 1882 budget of £10,500. Fairfield replied that the average expenditure since 1883 was £9,600 and Chamberlain argued that a thirteen-year report was irrelevant when the population was 13 per cent higher. Hicks-Beach relented.[149] Chamberlain had already begun to develop sericulture, thanks to the investigations of Thomas Wardle, a leading silk manufacturer and the president of the Silk Association;[150] and agriculture, thanks to M.P.G. Gennadius, the former Agriculture Minister of Greece, whose appointment as Director of Agriculture was a coup for the Cyprus government.[151]

Irrigation was also tackled. J.H. Medlicott, an irrigation engineer in Madras, reported on engineering aspects and the Receiver-General, Alexander Ashmore, who had experience of irrigation schemes in Ceylon, reported on the financial. They found that 245 square miles could be irrigated at £2.15 per acre with a return of 7–11 per cent on the outlay. Thus, about £500,000 was needed.[152]

The Exchequer agreed to an experiment to irrigate 22,000 acres at £60,000[153] because the increase in revenue would decrease the grant-in-aid. The loan was chargeable as regards principal, interest (3 per cent) and sinking fund (1 per cent) on the works and the general revenue. If the revenue met all costs the Exchequer would take half the excess.[154]

Chamberlain also wanted railways. Cyprus had opportunities, starting with Brown's survey for Sir George Elliot and the proposals of a Gladstonian Liberal MP and a supporter of the Canadian Chignecto Railway, Andrew Provand, in 1891,[155] 1894[156] and 1897.[157] His schemes encompassed a railway connecting Nicosia and Larnaca and a branch to Kythrea for £120,000, but were rejected because of his terms.[158] In July 1897, Sendall reported that he could build a line from Nicosia to Larnaca for £70,000, but Chamberlain wanted Famagusta harbour redeveloped first and asked if Brown's £50,000 estimate still applied. The director of public works, Frank Cartwright, thought it did[159] and in February 1898 Chamberlain asked the Treasury for a £150,000 loan.[160]

On 31 May 1898, an Order-in-Council authorised the part payment of the interest and the sinking fund of the projects.[161] Hicks-Beach agreed to the loan but emphasised Famagusta harbour's priority.[162] The Cyprus government forwarded three plans, all similar to Brown's first plan.[163] John Coode thought them inadequate and requested £1,000 to investigate. His estimate of £124,000 was 'so far in excess of previous estimates' that Chamberlain feared that it was 'out of the question . . . to proceed'. Like Brown's £50,000 plan, only the inner harbour would be touched. Coode planned a 300-yard quay instead of Brown's 200-yard, and added a 400-foot jetty and two spurs at the inner harbour's entrance.[164] This shows how expensive harbour construction had become in fifteen years.

The railway had also been undervalued. H.L. Pritchard of the Royal Engineers followed Brown's 1879 survey, but his estimate was £177,000.[165] Chamberlain fumed, largely because the new high commissioner, William Haynes Smith, told him to forget Cartwright's £100,000 estimate because he had found a minute by him stating £150,000.[166]

The estimates exceeded those given to the Treasury, but Chamberlain got a £314,000 loan under the 1899 Colonial Loans Act: £60,000 for irrigation in the Mesaoria; £124,000 for the harbour; and £130,000 for the railway, excluding the Larnaca branch.[167]

Three years of drought passed before the works were started. In 1901, the harvest failed in the Karpass, Tylliria and Paphos. By February 1902 some rain had fallen in these areas, but none in the Mesaoria. Haynes Smith feared a famine.[168] Only 6.17 inches of rain fell from June 1902

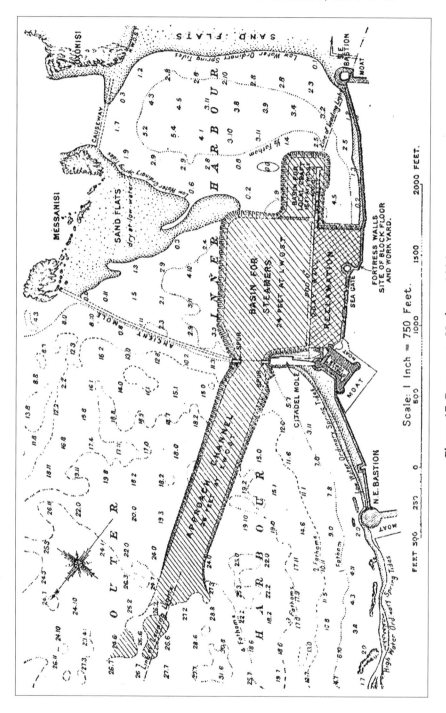

Figure 17 Famagusta Harbour, 1906

Source: George Hobbs, 'Famagusta Harbour, Cyprus', *Minutes of the Proceedings of the Institute of Civil Engineers*, CLXXVI, 3, 1908–09.

to June 1903 in the Mesaoria. Haynes Smith did well in coordinating relief work, and the home Exchequer provided seed corn 'in order to enable the Island to meet the Tribute payment due in January'.[169]

It was hoped that the irrigation works would solve such a problem, but they mostly failed. In 1907, Medlicott reported that the revenue from the works was expanding, but the irrigation works had failed and only reclamation had succeeded. He argued that the financial success of Famagusta harbour and the railway depended on agriculture and it depended on more irrigation and reclamation works. Cyprus' director of public works went further, asserting that they would 'never be a complete financial success' and rejected more reclamation works because the people had more land than they could cultivate. The Liberal Colonial Secretary, Lord Elgin, decided that until the success of the scheme was clear there would be no more money for such works.[170] In 1909 a commission appointed to investigate the irrigation works found that the inhabitants of Aheritou, Kalopsida, Kouklia, Lyssi, Vatili, Engomi, Stylli, Gaidoura, Prastio, Agios Georgios, Arnadi, Spatheriko, Syngrasi and Trikomo were complaining about the lack of economic benefits, and those of Aheritou, Kalopsida, Kouklia, Engomi, Gaidoura, Prastio and parts of Varosha were suffering from malaria owing to the presence of mosquitos in the reservoirs.[171]

The Famagusta harbour works began in November 1903 and were completed in June 1906.[172] Figure 17 shows that the focus was on the inner harbour.

Appendix VI shows the increase in trade after Famagusta harbour's redevelopment. It was moderate at first, increasing during construction, and five years after its completion there was a dramatic increase in imports and exports from the last year before it was opened. But it was not until the First World War that activity dramatically increased.

Work on the railway was started in May 1904, and it was launched with much fanfare in October 1905.[173] To observers it appeared to offer one solution to Cyprus' obscurity in British imperial calculations. One such observer, an anonymous reporter in *The Bystander*, believed it would greatly develop trade in the island.[174] The railway, however, proved a financial failure. By 1913 it had lost nearly £37,000 and although it made a profit over its first twenty-five years it was well short of the loan interest and the sinking fund charges.[175]

Conclusion

The payment of the tribute at the rate fixed by the Liberals in 1881, and the implementation of a tight budget in 1882, so Cyprus could meet it, stunted the progress that Beaconsfield's government had envisaged for Cyprus when it was occupied. For this same reason, the Colonial Office discouraged improving Famagusta for fear that the defence authorities would want to build a naval base there and thus require Cyprus funds to make it healthy. In enforcing the tribute – although the Ottoman government had broken the Anglo-Turkish Convention by refusing to undertake reforms in Asia Minor – it was the Cypriot people who suffered, and it also quashed the development of the island from local funds. There was a clear disparity between the expectations of economic profit at the time of the occupation and the reality. When the tribute and the grants-in-aid are removed from the books, the wealth, albeit to a lesser extent, which Beaconsfield's government projected becomes visible. Not even when imperial funds were spent were the British able to make Cyprus an economic asset or the people content.

Notes

1 *Hansard* (Commons), CCLII, 21 May 1880, 233; C.2930, FO to CO, 6 December 1880.
2 *Hansard* (Commons), CCLII, 1 June 1880, 897, 919–26.
3 *The Times*, 2 June 1880, 11b; D. Nichols, *The Lost Prime Minister: A Life of Sir Charles Dilke*, London, 1995, 94.
4 Gladstone criticised him while campaigning. *The Times*, 26 November 1879, 10a; Waterfield, *Layard*, 443–63.
5 *Ripon Gazette*, 20 March 1880.
6 FO65/1076, Granville to embassys in Paris, Rome, Berlin, St. Petersburg and Vienna, 4 May 1880.
7 Thomas Spinner Jr, *George Joachim Goschen*, London, 1973, 64, 68, 72.
8 Mustafa Aydin, 'Determinants of Turkish foreign policy: Historical framework and traditional inputs', *MES*, XXXIV, 4, 1999, 7–8.
9 FO78/3074, 71, very confidential, Granville to Goschen, 10 June 1880.
10 Ibid.; W.N. Medlicott, 'The Gladstone Government and the Cyprus Convention, 1880–85', *JMH*, 1940, 190–2.
11 Seymour to Childers, 30 April 1880, Childers, *Childers*, I, 284–5.
12 Seymour to Childers, 29 May 1880, ibid., 286–7.
13 CO67/16/11174, Cyprus 2/207, Sir John Adye WO to FO, 24 May 1880.
14 E.M. Lloyd, 'Adye, Sir John Miller (1819–1900)', rev. James Lunt, *ODNB* (www.oxforddnb.com/view/article/176, accessed 21 Feb 2005).
15 Schurman, *Imperial Defence*, 22–3. Schurman misspells Adye's name.
16 CO67/16/11174, Cyprus 2/207, Adye to FO, 24 May 1880.
17 Sir Robert Biddulph, *Lord Cardwell at the War Office*, London, 1904.
18 CO67/16/11174, 278, Biddulph to Granville, 24 June 1880.
19 *The Times*, 24 June 1880.
20 *Hansard* (Lords), CCLIII, 2 July 1880, 1380–3.
21 CO67/16/11174, minute, Fairfield, 24 July 1880.
22 Medlicott argues that the British postponed action on Granville's proposals. Medlicott, 'The Gladstone Government and the Cyprus Convention, 1880–85', 186–208.
23 *The Times*, 24 May 1912.
24 CAB41/15/23, 13 May 1881; *Hansard* (Commons), CCLXI, 24 May 1881, 1212–13.

25 E.A. Benians, 'Finance, Trade and Communications 1870–1895', *CHBE*, 181–229, 187–8.
26 CO67/17/14112, Granville and Kimberley, to Biddulph, 9 October 1880; CO67/17/ 20353, St. John to Granville, 2 December 1880; CO67/23/9665, Goschen to Granville, 10 May 1881; CO67/23/9593, Kimberley to Biddulph, 24 May 1881; CO67/23, CO Memorandum on Cyprus Tribute, 16 February 1882; CO67/23, Cavendish to Tenterden and Meade, 20 March 1882; CO67/28/14111, FO to T, 28 April 1882; CO67/29/20909, Goschen to Granville, 4 May 1882; CO67/29/16351, Kimberley to T, u/d; Blaisdell, *European Financial Control in the Ottoman Empire*, 84–99; Clay, *Gold for the Sultan*, 510–11.
27 *Hansard* (Commons), CCCII, 1 March 1886, 1539–40.
28 Ibid., CCCXXX, 22 November 1888.
29 Ibid., CCCXXXVIII, 22 July 1889, 978.
30 Storrs, *Chronology*, 31; Martin Blinkhorn, 'Liability, Responsibility and Blame: British Ransom Victims in the Mediterranean Periphery, 1860–81', *Australian Journal of Politics and History*, XLVI, 3, 2000, 336–56.
31 *Hansard* (Commons), CCCXXXVIII, 22 July 1889, 978.
32 C.2629, Biddulph to Granville, 7 June 1880.
33 C.5812, Bulwer to Knutsford, 10 June 1889; Lawrence, *The British Administration of Cyprus*, 237.
34 CO67/10, Salisbury to Biddulph, 13 April 1880.
35 CO67/17/4928, Kimberley to Fairfield, 15 March 1881.
36 CO67/24/1754, minute, Fairfield, 5 October 1881.
37 CO67/32/19052, Biddulph to Derby, 25 October 1883.
38 CO67/36/12413, CO to FO, 31 March 1884.
39 C.5812, Bulwer to Knutsford, 10 June 1889; C.3996, Sendall's view, 15; CO67/112/ 16037, confidential, Haynes Smith to Chamberlain, 7 July 1898; Haynes Smith told Rider Haggard: 'We have no money, the Turkish tribute takes all our money.' R.H. Haggard, *A Winter Pilgrimage in Palestine, Italy and Cyprus*, London, 1901, 146.
40 CO67/89/555, Christian to Fairfield, 24 January 1894; Fairfield to Christian, 6 February 1894.
41 Sir E.W. Hamilton, *The Diary of Sir Edward Hamilton 1885–1906*, ed. D.W.R. Bahlman, Hull, 1993, entry 27 September 1895, 311–12. Hereafter Hamilton diary.
42 Hamilton diary, 20 March 1896, 322.
43 Ibid., 1, 19 and 21 June 1896, 325–6.
44 Ibid., 22 December 1896, 333.
45 Ibid., 25 January 1898, 350–1.
46 Ibid., 19 and 22 June, 27 July 1898, 358–9.
47 Ibid., 9 June 1899, 375.
48 CO67/141/32864, Hamilton Memorandum, undated.
49 *The Times*, 5 April 1904, 9f.
50 CO67/141/32864, minute, Ommaney, 25 January 1905.
51 CO67/22/74, Robert Hall, Admiralty, to CO, 1 January 1881.
52 Ibid.
53 CO67/22/74, minute, Fairfield, 4 January 1881.
54 Ibid.
55 *The Times*, 12 August 1881, 7f.
56 Ibid., 26 August 1881.
57 Vizetelly, *From Cyprus to Zanzibar*, 39.
58 CO67/21/19445, 405, Biddulph to Kimberley, 27 October 1881; Goussio to Biddulph, 13 October 1881; Goussio proposal, October 1881.
59 Keith Sinclair, 'Hobson and Lenin and Johore: Colonial Office Policy towards British Concessionaires and Investors, 1878–1907', *Modern Asian Studies (MAS)*, I, 4, 1967, 335–52.
60 A.W. Abbott, *A Short History of the Crown Agents and their Office*, London, 1959; R.M. Kesner, 'Builders of Empire: The Role of the Crown Agents in Imperial Development, 1880–1914', *JICH*, V, 1977, 310–30; L.E. Davis and R.A. Huttenback, *Mammon and the Pursuit of Empire*, Cambridge, 1986, 188.

61 David Sunderland, 'Principles and Agents', *Economic History Review*, LII, 2, 1999, 284–306.
62 The original SA1:15143, 30 November 1881; published, with minor corrections, C.3384, 39–45.
63 Ibid., 39–42. Brown further proposed to extend the breakwater to 2,200 yards, construct an inner basin 30½ acres in area, dredged to a depth of 26 feet, with quays 1,350 yards in length, capable of berthing twelve vessels. These works would bring costs to £340,000, but he did not think these necessary.
64 C.3384, Biddulph to Kimberley, 29 December 1881, 39.
65 CO67/21/521, minute, Meade, 14 January 1882.
66 Ibid., Kimberley, 23 January 1882.
67 R.B. Pugh, 'The Colonial Office, 1801–1925', *CHBE*, III, 745.
68 CO67/21/521, minute, Fairfield, 7 February 1882.
69 Ibid., Kimberley, 19 February 1882.
70 C.3091, Kimberley to Biddulph, 22 February 1882, 74.
71 *Hansard* (Lords), CCLXXIII, 28 July 1882, 17–18.
72 Letter is dated 4 June, *The Times*, 16 June 1881, 8.a.
73 Ibid., 27 August 1880, 4.f; 24 December 1881, 4.f.
74 C.3661, Memorandum on the Finances and Administration of Cyprus, Edward Fairfield, June 1882, 9–84.
75 Ibid., 13–14, 42–4.
76 FO881/3987, Memorandum on Cyprus, 11 October 1879 (confidential).
77 Fairfield Memorandum, 18.
78 Ibid., 18–19.
79 Ibid., 19.
80 C.3661, Biddulph reply to Fairfield Memorandum, 30 November 1882, 85–113.
81 Ibid., 89.
82 G.G. Hake, 'Cyprus Since the British Occupation', *Journal of the Society of Arts*, 1886, 791; Robert Biddulph, 'Cyprus', *Proceedings of the Royal Geographical Society and Monthly Record of Geography*, XI, 1889, 711–13; C.F.G. Cumming, 'The Locust War in Cyprus', *NC*, XIV, 1883, 306, 309–16; Haggard, *A Winter Pilgrimage*, 106–8.
83 Biddulph reply to Fairfield, 89.
84 SA1:15321, People of Karpass petition Inglis, 14 September 1880.
85 Biddulph reply to Fairfield, 90–1.
86 Ibid., 90.
87 Ibid.
88 Meade to T, 11 May 1883, C.3661, 3–8, 4.
89 Demetriou, 'Victorian Cyprus', 22.
90 CO67/21/521, minute, Fairfield, 7 February 1882.
91 SA1:14663, Plans, 13 February 1880; SA1:14575, Inglis to Chief Secretary, 20 January 1880.
92 SA1:14574, E.R. Kenyon, District Engineer, Report, 10 January 1880; SA1:14575, Inglis, 20 January 1880; SA1:14663, 13 February 1880; SA1:14675 W.2/29/11, Samuel Brown report for March–October 1881.
93 SA1:14689/W.2/29/25, Minutes and Correspondence.
94 CO67/37/1920, Biddulph to Fairfield, 29 December 1885.
95 CO67/37/1691, Biddulph to Derby, 12 January 1885.
96 Ibid., Swettenham, to Warren, 26 December 1884.
97 Ibid., Kyrenia trade figures.
98 Ibid., Warren, to Biddulph, 9 January 1885.
99 Ibid., Biddulph to Derby, 12 January 1885.
100 SA1:804/85, Kyrenia harbour estimates approved; SA1:15/85, public works 1885–86, 13 January 1885.
101 CO67/37/1920, minute, Fairfield, 2 February 1885.
102 SA1:1347/85, Shipwreck of *Lady Franklin*; CO67/37/3061, 40, Biddulph to Derby, 7 February 1885; SA1:320/85; SA1:328/85.

103 CO67/37/1920, minute, Meade, 17 February 1885.

104 Ibid., CO to Biddulph, 18 February 1885.

105 CO67/39/17003, Meade to CAOG, 29 September 1885.

106 SA1:185/86, Proposed public works, 1886–87, Samuel Brown.

107 SA1:3218/86 and SA1:3852/86, Convict Labour, Kyrenia harbour.

108 SA1:3082/87, Brown to Warren, 8 November 1887.

109 SA1:185/86, Brown to Biddulph, 1 January 1886.

110 CO67/45/5183, Bulwer to Holland, 5 March 1887; Pascotini to Bulwer, 22 December 1886; Mahoreich, Beirut to Pascotini, 16 December 1886; Brown to Warren, 24 December 1886.

111 CO67/44/2481, Bulwer to Stanhope, 24 January 1887; Brown to Warren, 14 December 1886; Warren to Brown, 10 December 1886.

112 CO67/44/2481, Brown to Warren, 6 January 1887.

113 CO67/44/2481, Warren, to Brown, 15 January 1887.

114 CO67/44/2481, minute, Fairfield, 11 February 1887; Holland to Bulwer, 23 February 1887; CO67/46/11126, minute, Fairfield, 10 June 1887.

115 CO67/58/4393, 37, Bulwer to Knutsford, 11 February 1889; 52, Knutsford to Bulwer, 12 March 1889.

116 CO67/61/14296, 223, Bulwer to Knutsford, 6 July 1889.

117 *The Times*, 5 February 1889, 5f; CO67/58/2575, 35, Knutsford to Bulwer, 13 February 1889.

118 CO67/58/2575, 35, Knutsford to Bulwer, 13 February 1889; CO67/58/4394, 39, Bulwer to Knutsford, 12 February 1889; CO67/59/7504, 95, Bulwer to Knutsford, 30 March 1889; CO67/63/8765, 7501/89, T to CO, 30 April 1889.

119 CO67/61/14296, Cunningham to Warren, 3 April 1889.

120 CO67/61/14296, 223, Bulwer to Knutsford, 6 July 1889; Cunningham to Warren, 1 June 1889; CO67/63/16630, Coode Report on Kyrenia Harbour Works, 19 August 1889; Knutsford to Hackett, 23 August 1889; CO67/63/24978, Cunningham to Warren, 29 October 1889. Coode agreed with Cunningham.

121 CO67/63/24978, 372, Hackett to Knutsford, 11 December 1889.

122 SA1:2184/90, Bulwer; SA1:2417/90, Law, acting Chief Secretary, to Cunningham 22 October 1890; CO67/69/10581, GED estimates 1890–91; SA1:3012/90, Cunningham to Law, 23 October 1890; SA1:2754/91.

123 SA1:72/89, GED estimates 1889–90; SA1:2288/90, Bulwer to Knutsford, 27 May 1891; CO67/53/13435, Bulwer to Knutsford, 21 June 1888; Knutsford to Bulwer, 19 July 1888; CO67/60/9882, 124, Bulwer to Knutsford, 1 May 1889; CO67/62/23848, 354, Hackett to Knutsford, 30 November 1889.

124 SA1:3039/86, Cobham to Warren, 14 August 1886.

125 SA1:3039/86, Warren to Brown, 20 August 1886; Brown to Warren, 22 September 1886; Brown to Warren, 30 November 1886.

126 SA1:3039/86, Brown to Warren, 13 February 1888.

127 SA1:930/88, Brown to Warren, 28 March 1888; Cunningham minute to Warren, 27 June 1889.

128 SA1:930/88, Bulwer minute to Warren, 4 July 1889; also SA1:930/88, Bulwer minute to Warren, 13 July 1889; Bulwer minute to Warren, 22 July 1889.

129 SA1:2288/90, minute, Bulwer, 14 August 1890.

130 CO67/69/12430, 143, Bulwer to Knutsford, 27 May 1891.

131 CO67/69/12430, Cunningham to Chief Secretary, 4 October 1890; Knutsford to ADM and BOT, 29 June 1891; CO67/70/14721, 172, Bulwer to Knutsford, 4 July 1891; CO67/71/19070, 253, Bulwer to Knutsford, 16 September 1891; CO67/71/13874, M.1774, R.D. Awdry, ADM, to CO, 8 July 1891; CO67/71/13626, Knutsford to Bulwer, 31 July 1891; SA1:2288/90.

132 CO67/70/15585, Bulwer to Knutsford, 20 July 1891.

133 CO67/141/25603, Memorandum on improvements in shipping facilities at Larnaca, Famagusta and Kyrenia, Adrian Fiddian, 13 August 1904.

134 CO883/4/25, Mediterranean 42, Memo on Provand's Railway Scheme, F.W. Fuller, 21 March 1894.

135 CO67/70/15585, Bulwer to Fairfield, 20 July 1891.
136 SA1:136/90, Shipwreck *Annina B*; SA1:243/90, Italian Consul criticises Kyrenia's Commissioner; SA1:948/92, Shipwreck, *Empress*.
137 CO67/141/25603, Rossos to Rollit, 4 February 1904; CO67/141/25603, Memorandum on improvements in shipping facilities at Larnaca, Famagusta and Kyrenia, Adrian Fiddian, 13 August 1904.
138 SA1:627/1907/1, Kyrenia harbour improvements, inclosures.
139 SA1:627/1907/1, Coode Fitzmaurice Wilson and Mitchell, 16 September 1925.
140 Scott-Stevenson, *Our Home*, 258; C.5523, Bulwer to Holland, 4 April 1887; Bulwer to Holland, 4 May 1887; Meade to T, 7 May 1887, T to CO, 23 May 1887, Bulwer to Holland, 30 May 1887; Bulwer to Holland, 2 June 1887.
141 C.5523, CO to T, 17 December 1887.
142 CO67/83/12504, 10623/93, T to CO, 25 July 1893; C.5812, Bulwer to Knutsford, 10 June 1889; Lawrence, *The British Administration of Cyprus*, 237.
143 Bill Guest and John M. Sellers (eds), *Enterprise and Exploitation in a Victorian Colony: Aspects of the Economic and Social History of Colonial Natal*, Pietermaritzburg, 1985.
144 Robert Kubicek, 'Joseph Chamberlain, the Treasury and Imperial Development, 1895–1903', *The Canadian Historical Association*, 1965, 105–16; P.T. Marsh, 'Chamberlain, Joseph (1836–1914)', *ODNB* (www.oxforddnb.com/view/article/32350, accessed 12 April 2005).
145 *The Times*, 24 August 1895; Kubicek, 'Joseph Chamberlain', 106.
146 CO8835, Mediterranean 45, 15106, Sendall to CO, 23 August 1895.
147 Ibid., 14362, CO to T, 6 September 1895.
148 Ibid., 220141, CO to T, 10 December 1895.
149 Ibid., Fairfield to T, 15 January 1896; 2273, T to CO, 30 January 1896; Fairfield to T, 17 March 1896; 2278, Fairfield to T, 17 March 1896; 6582, T to CO, 27 March 1896; Fairfield to T, 7 April 1896; 7855, T to CO, 13 April 1896; 11936, telegram, Chamberlain to Sendall, 18 June 1896; 13039, telegram, Sendall to Chamberlain, 20 June 1896; 7855, 85, Chamberlain to Sendall, 3 July 1896; 15739, T to CO, 27 July 1896.
150 Ibid., 15356, Wardle to Chamberlain, 29 August 1895; ibid., CO to Wardle, 5 September 1895; 16070, CO to Sendall, 30 September 1895; 12580, Wardle to CO, 11 June 1896.
151 Ibid., 20981, Young to Chamberlain, 11 November 1895, enclosing Gennadius Report I; 9176, Sendall to Chamberlain, 20 April 1896; 9197, confidential, Sendall to Chamberlain, 20 April 1896; 10866, confidential, Sendall to Chamberlain, 9 May 1896; 11853, 119, Sendall to Chamberlain, 18 May 1896; 9176, Fairfield to T, 4 June 1896; 20735, 224, Sendall to Chamberlain, 18 September 1896, enclosing Gennadius Report II; 26239, Royal Gardens, Kew to CO, 21 December 1896; CO67/106/13269, 145, Sendall to Chamberlain, 11 June 1897, enclosing Gennadius Report III.
152 CO883/5, Mediterranean 45, 14361, CO to IO, 25 September 1895; 19803, IO to CO, 8 November 1895; CO to IO, 16 November 1895; 21167, confidential, Chamberlain to Young, 29 November 1895; confidential, Chamberlain to Young, 13 December 1895; confidential, Chamberlain to Sendall, 16 December 1895; 12848, 144, Sendall to Chamberlain, 8 June 1896; enclosure, Medlicott report; 13299, 147, Sendall to Chamberlain, 13 June 1896, enclosure, Ashmore report on Medlicott proposals, 11 June 1896; 14893, Medlicott to CO, 14 July 1876; 18299, 207, Sendall to Chamberlain, 21 August 1896; enclosure I, Ashmore memorandum on Medlicott letter of 14 July, 2 August 1896.
153 Ibid., Meade to T, 28 November 1896.
154 Ibid., T to CO, 23 December 1896; CO to T, 12 January 1897.
155 CO67/71/3684, Provand to Bulwer, 18 February 1891; CO67/69/11649, 140, Bulwer to Knutsford, 27 May 1891; CO67/69/11649, CO to T, 11 June 1891; CO67/71/12373, 8958/91, T to CO, 18 June 1891; CO67/71/12787, Meade, CO to Provand, 21 September 1891.

156 CO883/4/25, Memorandum on Provand's railway scheme, F.W. Fuller, 21 March 1894.
157 CO67/110/5995, Provand to Chamberlain, 20 March 1897.
158 Michael Radford, *The Railways of Cyprus*, Nicosia, 2003, 36–7.
159 CO883/6/5, 17324, Sendall to Chamberlain, 30 July 1897; Chamberlain to Sendall, 20 August 1897; 542, Sendall to Chamberlain, 30 December 1897.
160 Ibid., 542, Wingfield to T, 17 February 1898.
161 Ibid., 14775, Haynes Smith to Chamberlain, 24 June 1898.
162 Ibid., 4774, T to CO, 2 March 1898.
163 Ibid., 6284, 45, Young to Chamberlain, 10 March 1898.
164 Ibid., 10408, CAOG to CO, 10 May 1898; 13020, T to CO, 9 June 1898; 963, CAOG to CO, 11 January 1899; 963, CO to CAOG, 19 January 1899; 6700, T, to CO, 16 March 1899'.
165 Ibid., 16708, Haynes Smith to Chamberlain, 14 July 1898; 16708, Bertram Cox, to T, 28 July 1898; 17739, T to CO, 6 August 1898; 23589, confidential, Chamberlain to Haynes Smith, 26 October 1898; 4675, secret, Haynes Smith to Chamberlain, 14 February 1899; 7431, Haynes Smith to Chamberlain, 15 March 1899, enclosure, Pritchard Report, 10 March 1899.
166 Ibid., 9882, 76, Haynes Smith to Chamberlain, 12 April 1899; 9890, confidential, Haynes Smith to Chamberlain, 12 April 1899; 9322, confidential, Chamberlain to Haynes Smith, 28 April 1899.
167 Ibid., 13568, CO to T, 28 July 1899; 21047, T to CO, 8 August 1899.
168 C.1434, Haynes Smith to Chamberlain, 17 February 1902.
169 C.1434, T to CO, 19 July 1902; Haynes Smith to Chamberlain, 5 January 1903.
170 CO883/7/1, Mediterranean 63, 26488, Medlicott to Elgin, 24 June 1907; ibid., CO to Medlicott, 13 August 1907; 31410, Medlicott to CO, August 1907; 41271, 186, King-Harman to Elgin, 14 November 1907, enclosure, E.H.D. Nicolls memorandum, 6 November 1907.
171 *Report of the Commission appointed to enquire into the Working of the Irrigation Reservoirs in the Mesaoria*, Nicosia, 1909, 2–10.
172 George Hobbs, 'Famagusta Harbour, Cyprus', *Minutes of the Proceedings of the Institute of Civil Engineers*, CLXXVI, 3, 1908–09, 298–307, 307.
173 CO883/6/4, Mediterranean 56; B.S. Turner, *The Story of the Cyprus Government Railway*, London, 1979.
174 Anon., 'Cyprus and its First Railway: Why not make the Island a British Refuge for the Jews?' *The Bystander*, 22 November 1905, 282–3.
175 Radford, *Railways of Cyprus*, 370–1.

CHAPTER 6

From multiculturalism to multi-nationalism: the 'European' possession

What then is the case of Cyprus? It is the case of an island inhabited by people who had been civilised for centuries when we were barbarians, and nothing but barbarians, and who never lost the essentials of civilisation, except indeed, their form. They had been an oppressed people . . . despotically governed by the Turk. (W.E. Gladstone, speech, *The Times*, 30 December 1879, 9a)

The history of the island is so replete with the story of a chequered race adventure that he would be a bold person who would confidently associate the people with any developed nationality in Europe or Asia Minor. (*The Times*, 24 May 1912)

If Cyprus, unlike Crete, posed no nationalist threat to British rule, its Orthodox Christian and Muslim inhabitants would not have been divided along ethnic lines when the British arrived. If so, why were the British facing a nationalist challenge and inter-communal strife by 1912? The imposition of political modernity replaced the religious, civic and regional identity of the Cypriots with an imagined ethnic identity, making British rule problematic.

Politics and identity in Ottoman Cyprus

Ethnic presuppositions plague studies of identity and, owing to the clash of foreign nationalisms (Greek and Turkish) and imperialisms (British, American, Greek and Turkish), Cyprus, in particular, suffers from this. In short, there are 'Greeks' and 'Turks' and their relations are placed within the wider Greco-Turkish conflict or it is stated that they lived in 'peaceful coexistence'.[1] In 1976 Adamantia Pollis argued that Cyprus' inhabitants had always been 'an admixture of ethnic, tribal, and religious groups', divisions until the twentieth century were along 'lines other than nationality' and under Ottoman rule the village, kinship and religion had determined identity.[2]

Ottoman Cyprus' ruling class comprised Muslim and Orthodox Christian secular and religious elite. Some Orthodox clergy had invited the Ottoman invasion because they wanted to shrug off the power of the Catholic Church, established by the Lusignans and continued by the Venetians, in order to become the all-powerful Christian authority on the island.[3] Thus, many Orthodox Christians assumed administrative roles on the Ottoman occupation.[4] Ottoman socio-political structures differed from European models: the millet system divided inhabitants into religious groups. The Ottomans re-empowered the Church to represent the Orthodox millet and the elite, as in Constantinople, assumed governing roles. But the Cyprus Church was autonomous of the Oecumenical Patriarchate in Constantinople and the Apostolic Patriarchates in Jerusalem, Alexandria and Antioch: thus the archbishop was the political and spiritual leader (the *ethnarch*) of the Cypriot Orthodox population.[5] Since the religious and the secular were combined, the Eastern Orthodox Cypriots not only had a religious identity, but also a civil identity, because they had an attachment to the Ottoman Sultan through their archbishop.

By the nineteenth century the Church had become very powerful. It was an ally against rebellion, which was Muslim or Muslim and Orthodox led,[6] as in other Ottoman lands.[7] When Muslim and Orthodox peasants rioted in Nicosia against taxes in 1804, the dragoman, Hadjigeorgakis Kornesios, supported by the Orthodox and Muslim elite, fled to Constantinople to bring Ottoman troops. In this class struggle, exploited Muslims and Orthodox challenged a Muslim and Orthodox ruling class. The Church paid for the troops, but when more Muslims than Orthodox were killed, some Muslims resented the power of Archimandrite Kyprianos, who had outmanoeuvred Archbishop Chrysanthos and Kornesios. Kyprianos wielded much power after becoming archbishop in 1809. Küçük Mehmed, the new governor in 1819, resented this and so obtained a *firman* from the Sultan to eliminate Kyprianos and 500 other Orthodox elite in 1821.[8]

The bloody event became a cardinal point on the script of the 'Greek nation' of Cyprus; in 1901 a memorial with a statue was erected in Nicosia in honour of the 'ethno-martyr' Kyprianos and this, and his portrait, became popular on postcards in 1906. He was an 'ethno-martyr' because he was killed for supposedly colluding with the Greek rebels to spread the revolt to Cyprus.[9] In 1818, Kyprianos allegedly joined the *Philiki Etairia* (Friendly Society) the secret group trying to liberate 'Greece'.[10] But Kyprianos, like Gregory V (the Oecumenical Patriarch), was no nationalist. Freemasons formed the *Philiki Etairia* in 1811 and four years later Kyprianos excommunicated freemasons in Larnaca. When the Greek revolt began in 1821, Gregory, who had

Figure 18 Portrait of the Ethno-Martyr, Archbishop Kyprianos
Source: Postcard, Toufexis, Series 2, no. 81, 1906: Courtesy of
the Laiki Group Cultural Centre Photographic Archive.

condemned the French revolution,[11] issued an encyclical excommun-
icating the insurgents and convinced the *Şeyhülislam* that only a small
Orthodox Christian rabble was responsible. The *Şeyhülislam* did not
issue the Sultan's order to kill them and only when the rebellion spread
did Mahmud II have the *Şeyhülislam*, and then Gregory, executed.[12]
A month later, Mahmud ordered Kyprianos to demand in an encyclical
that the Orthodox surrender all arms, which he did.[13] However,
Mahmud told Küçük that 'upon examining our archives, we nowhere
find from the date when this island fell under our sway that its Christian
inhabitants have been guilty of any disloyalty to our government,
but on the contrary when the Turks revolted, the Christians have
joined our forces'.[14] Yet Küçük capitalised on the opportune climate
to concoct charges against Kyprianos to remove him. Küçük's recall,
in response to the representations of Cypriot Muslims who went to
Constantinople after the massacres, backs this interpretation.[15]

The tragedy did not precipitate 'Turkish' terror against the 'Greeks'.[16]
In 1837 Orthodox primates visited Constantinople to appeal against

the governor's oppressions and purchased control of the government after paying the Grand Signor the sum (3 million piastres) a Muslim paid for the governorship.[17] But after two years the people were no better off and when the reforms of Sultan Abdul-Mejid were introduced a Muslim governor took over. A Central Council was granted comprising the Mufti, Mula, four elected Muslims, the Archbishop and two elected Orthodox.[18] *Berats*, state charters, were issued on an archbishop's election, giving the church the legal power to collect taxes from the Orthodox for the state and for churches, schools and the clergy's living expenses.[19] In 1870, Archbishop Sophronios led an Orthodox-Muslim deputation to Constantinople to appeal for relief from the drought and was allowed to take seed from the state granaries.[20] Religious difference was no obstacle to political, economic, social or cultural integration.[21]

By the nineteenth century the Orthodox and Muslim Cypriots shared a language, folklore, economic and social hardships, and intermarried.[22] The peasants, smallholders in village units, lived as neighbours from the start of Ottoman rule.[23] In 1764 they successfully revolted against the governor for increasing tax[24] and jointly appealed for aid during locust plagues, earthquakes and droughts, which sometimes, as in 1870, the hierarchy backed.[25]

With religion deciding identity, the Muslims were referred to as Mohammedans and the Orthodox Christians as *Romiee*, a word adopted during the Byzantine period when the Orthodox Church disapproved of Hellene because it denoted paganism.[26] Being an island, Cyprus was isolated. It also lacked communication networks,[27] so modernity and the ideas of the nation did not reach society. This led Rolandos Katsiaounis to claim that the Cypriot *Romiee* had a 'very low level of cultural development' before the British arrived – a view shared by at least one British traveller at the time.[28] But this is mistaken, unless 'cultural development' were to mean only 'Hellenic' culture. A decade before the British arrived, Cyprus' archbishop, the scholarly and pious Sophronios III, started his autobiographical note to the Jerusalem Theological School thus: 'my homeland is Cyprus and my parents are Orthodox Christians of the Eastern dogma'.[29] Neither Greece nor being Greek was mentioned, yet he had studied in Athens for nine years (1853–61) and in Smyrna for six (1847–53).[30] Two years before the British arrived, Greece's vice-consul lamented to Athens that 'the spirit of Hellenism in some places is asleep and in others totally non-existent'.[31]

But the Cypriots were socially and culturally integrated. Countless folk tales, poems and songs from the late Ottoman and early British periods illustrate this. Priests and hodjas jointly call people to work; Orthodox and Muslims mourn together; and numerous love stories are

Figure 19 Archbishop Sophronios III taken in 1878
by Max Ohnefalsch-Richter
Source: Magda Ohnefalsch-Richter, *Greek Customs and Traditions in Cyprus*, 1913:
Courtesy of the Laiki Group Cultural Centre Photographic Archive.

told.[32] Joint social ventures, including missions to Constantinople[33] and the building of hospitals, as in Larnaca in 1835,[34] attest to the fact that improving living standards bound the people. Joint objections to the introduction of foreigners, including Muslims in 1860 and 1878, shows the insular nature of society, but also its protectiveness of the evolved social and cultural integration.[35] The increase in mixed villages proves integration: in 1832 an Ottoman census recorded 172 mixed villages;[36] in 1858 the British consul estimated 239;[37] and in 1891 the number had increased to 346.[38]

Studying of the Cypriot 'dialect' shows that it was an admixture of Greek (from Homeric to medieval), Frankish, Venetian, Latin and Ottoman, with Armenian and Persian traces (Appendix VII).[39] In January 1881, three years after the British arrival, Claude Cobham, the only Greek scholar in Cyprus government, told Edgar Vincent that his Muslim worker knew the Greek of Vincent's *Handbook to Modern Greek* (1879) and had to translate Cobham to the Orthodox peasant.[40] Rebecca Bryant compared the disparity between Cypriot and Greek to that between Spanish and Portuguese. Many Muslims spoke only Cypriot and others a dialect related to Anatolian with Cypriot traces.[41] The Cypriot languages are phonetically and syntactically similar and share the non-Greek/Turkish words.[42] Falkland Warren, the chief secretary (1879–91), observed that 'few Christians . . . cannot understand Turkish [Cypriot] and most Turks understand Greek [Cypriot]'.[43]

The British arrive: co-option and modernity

According to historians a prelate welcomed Wolseley thus: 'we accept the change of Government inasmuch as we trust that Great Britain will help Cyprus, as it did the Ionian Islands, to unite with Mother Greece'. The words, another cardinal feature on the script of Cypriot Hellenism, form the basis of the *énosis* policy that dominated Greek Cypriot political discourse during British rule. But in 1996, Katsiaounis proved that they were not, in fact, said,[44] upsetting the received wisdom of Cyprus government officers,[45] analysts before Katsiaounis[46] and even others after him.[47]

The truth was that local politicians invented the *énosis* declaration in 1903.[48] *The Times* correspondent reported that the Bishop of Kitium, Kyprianos, declared his loyalty to Wolseley at Larnaca.[49] In Nicosia Sophronios (Appendix VIII) verified the British view that the Cypriots were 'peaceful and easy to govern' and would 'be faithful and devoted' to the new 'paternal authority'. He admitted that political factors had restricted Cyprus 'from a material and intellectual point of view' and so he

> Hope[d] that this moment heralds a new life and a new era of prosperity for this land, which will mark a new epoch in its annals; that we will all, Christian or Muslim, learn that the law is sovereign of all . . . that we all have the same rights and the same duties; that, in one word, we will be guided in the way of truth, duty and liberty. When justice reigns in the courts; when notions of honour and humanity inspire those who govern, all institutions feel it, and peoples prosper.[50]

[157]

He wanted equality for Orthodox and Muslims alike and did not mention Greece or *énosis*. Clearly, there was a shift in Cypriot Orthodox identity after the British arrived.

Before that happened, however, Sophronios pushed to maintain the existing political and social structures through continued state support. In February 1879 he and the three metropolitans (Paphos, Kyrenia and Kitium) sent a memorial to Wolseley on behalf of the Christians (not 'Greeks') asking him to preserve church rights; to exempt church land from tax; to protect indebted priests from prison and forced labour; to include the clergy in governing councils; and for a church-state concordat to define relations.[51] The British respected Sophronios. Hugh Sinclair, Biddulph's private secretary, thought him

> wise, large-minded and prudent, anxious to be on good terms with us and perfectly truthful and loyal. But he was hard driven by the restless and intriguing Bishop of Kitium . . . and the agitation for annexation to Greece. As the official head of the Greek Community the Archbishop was bound to countenance . . . agitation and opposition; but he saw its uselessness and did his best to moderate their excesses. In his many private interviews with Sir Robert [Biddulph] he . . . deplored his inability to make his flock see reason. He had a fine presence, great dignity and an imperturbable calm manner.[52]

Sophronios gradually lost his authority over his people, largely because he no longer had the secular authority of the state behind him.

Despite liking Sophronios the British did not co-opt the elite as they did in India, Malaya, Africa and the Ionian Islands.[53] In the last of these, the local government worked to cultivate clerics who were pro-British, but this and the wider co-option of elite failed.[54] This had nothing to do with approaches to Cyprus. Salisbury was clear that in Cyprus 'the clergy have used the weakness of Turkish rule . . . to consolidate a power over their people which is inconsistent with all modern views of civil government.'[55] The Ionian Islands had not been under Ottoman control and the British had learned from their stint in control. Cyprus, unlike most possessions, but like the Ionian Islands, was mainly Christian and had a Greek past, so it was perceived as European and would be ruled within the framework of modernity. This meant separating the church and the state, civil structures and identifying the inhabitants along ethnic lines. Under the British 'the Cypriots, to a large extent, ceased to be Cypriots'.[56]

Imposing Hellenism

Historians of Cyprus attribute the British failure to stop Hellenism to a colonial mentality of ignoring early opposition to British rule.[57]

Recently, two commentators have claimed that uncertainty and a refusal to recognise its seriousness governed British policy towards *énosis* until 1907.[58] But there was no colonial policy of laissez-faire towards opposition to British rule: the British fought numerous wars, in India, Natal, Malaysia and Egypt; removed hostile local leaders, from Malaysia to southern Nigeria, and used co-option almost everywhere. The claims do not show why the British – aside from 'uncertainty' (over what is unclear) – were indifferent to *énosis*.

The British were indifferent to *énosis*: they accepted it as genuine and did nothing to stop the growth of Hellenism because Cyprus was not considered strategically important (Chapter 8) and the British shared the same repertoire of myths as the 'Greeks' of Cyprus. Thus, the British facilitated the imposition of Hellenism, creating artificial identities to replace those existing and halting Orthodox-Muslim integration. Michael Herzfeld argued that since Europe claimed ancient Greece as its spiritual ancestor and created a single ideal of it in place of over 150 city-states, linked only by similar language and religion, it also created a unitary ideal of 'modern Greece'.[59] Within weeks of the British arrival, Edward Linley Sambourne represented Cyprus as Aphrodite in *Punch* (Figure 20) and *The Graphic* followed with a photograph of an alluring Cypriot princess in a Grecian setting.[60] When Smith and Stanley visited Cyprus, Salisbury had instructed them to see if Wolseley was holding 'the balance between Turk and Greek',[61] and in rejecting co-option he implied that Cyprus was set for political modernity. Gladstone called Cyprus 'virtually a European Island',[62] alluded to its 'Greekness' (epigraph), declared it would want to join Greece, like the Ionian Islands,[63] and in 1880 unofficially suggested this. British politicians, imbued with modernity, identified the Cypriot Orthodox as Greeks without checking the reality on the ground.

Those that 'knew' Cyprus 'revealed' the 'reality on the ground'. If those that did not visit Cyprus erased the Cypriots from the Orientalist discourse and made them Europeans, those that lived in Cyprus did the opposite. Hamilton Lang had constant contact with Cypriot peasants because of his antiquarian and farming interests. In the preface to his book *Cyprus: Its History, its Present Resources, and Future Prospects*, dated 28 August 1878 (thus his writing of the book predated the British occupation), he explained the identity of the Cypriots thus:

> The Cypriots are generally classified as Greeks, but from the earliest prehistoric times to this day their characteristics have been essentially distinct from those of the Greeks. They are deficient in their liveliness and nervous activity and they are not infected with monomania of Hellenic aspirations. They are docile in the highest degree, industrious, and sober. Their love of home is remarkable, so strong that on several occasions

"BIEN VENU QUI APPORTE!"

Figure 20 'Wolseley Courts Venus'
Source: *Punch*, 3 August 1878.

I found it very difficult to induce men to leave their native village even for considerable pecuniary advantages.[64]

For Lang, the Cypriots differ socially from Greeks. Cypriots do not identify with the Greek state, but rather with their village. Unlike Greeks and the myth of the 'lazy native',[65] from Lang's experience the Cypriots were industrious. In morals they were not loose, as some have suggested, as the Cypriot peasant compares well to the English and Scottish peasant.[66]

Esme Scott-Stevenson, who wrote that Cyprus had little for the explorer except in Greek and, still more, in Phoenician tombs (Chapter 5), presents a good comparison with Lang.

[160]

one ought not to confuse the Cypriotes with the true Hellenes, for in many characteristics the two people are essentially different, almost, indeed, forming a distinct race. The Cypriotes are dull and lazy, they have no ambition, nor the patriotic longings of the Greeks . . . they are good parents, and devoted to their homes and villages. They are docile and extremely easily governed.[67]

For Scott-Stevenson the Cypriots were a distinct race from the Greeks, only agreeing with Lang that they did not have the nationalist passion of the Greeks and kinship and the village determined their identity. Unlike Lang, Scott-Stevenson adhered to the 'lazy native' motif. Here it is unclear: were the Greeks also lazy? In any event, Scott-Stevenson and Lang were clear; the Cypriots were not Greeks.

Wolseley, as the high commissioner, represented the official view of the 'man on the spot'. He could not hide his distaste for the oriental Eastern Orthodox Christian clergy when he was forced to attend the blessing of the British flag soon after his arrival (Chapter 1). Despite this thoroughly Oriental description, the special artist of the *Illustrated London News*, Samuel Pasfield Oliver, entitled his drawing 'Greek Priests Blessing the British Flag at Nicosia', as if to say that the current priests were somehow related to the priests who presided over similar ceremonies for Aphrodite. Wolseley's mocking of the church ritual was common too of the British in the Ionian Islands.[68]

Short-term visitors make an interesting contrast to those that lived on the island. Butler, Wolseley's friend, was a good example. He claimed that Cyprus' identity was blurred because of the countless numbers of different civilisations that had conquered/settled/influenced it yet refers to the Cypriot Orthodox as 'Greeks' and says that although 'semi-Asiatic' they should be given complete freedom over their affairs like French Canadians.

> But people will say, 'Ah, the Greek is different; he is a semi-Asiatic. We really must train and educate this Greek'. My dear, good Mr Bull, you are in sober truth a mere child to this Greek.[69]

Butler, like Gladstone in the epigraph, claims that the Cypriot Orthodox were descendants of the ancient Greeks from which the British were successors and thus mere modern imitators. The idea that the Cypriots should be treated like French Canadians implies a maturity to govern themselves, which is, in part, exactly what the British did.

A fascinating representation of Cyprus comes from John Thomson, who photographed Cyprus in 1878. He combined his Orientalist images, of scruffy natives in their Middle Eastern dress (fezes, baggy trousers and 'Mongolian' boots) and dark features, with his accompanying text of ancient Greek and Christian imagery, British imperial

Figure 21 'Native Group Nicosia'
Source: John Thomson, *Through Cyprus with the Camera in the Autumn of 1878*, London 1879.

renewal, and references to 'Greeks' and 'Turks'. In a scene (Figure 21) in 'front of the ancient Cathedral (now mosque) of St. Sophia', Thomson attempted to photograph a group of 'Greeks' (the Muslims remained aloof) and two negro boys (sons of former slaves in a Turkish house). A turbaned Turk disturbed the photograph when stopping to observe the proceedings.[70] This thoroughly Orientalist scene could have been taken in any street in North Africa or the Middle East – it is clearly of the East and not the West.[71]

The view of archaeologists also makes for an interesting comparison. In August 1878 Reginald Stuart Poole, the keeper of the department of coins and medals in the British Museum, who had visited Cyprus for a few weeks in 1869, wrote in the *Contemporary Review* that 'ethnologically, the Cypriots are of the old stock of the island, not Hellenic, perhaps, but rather proto-Hellenic' – 'Pelasgic'. Poole, who in 1882 was instrumental in founding the Egypt Exploration Fund, adds that there could be 'a touch of the Phoenician'.[72] Interestingly, the archaeologist, even before the metropolitan and local governments had cause, rejected any Hellenic origin of the Cypriot Orthodox. When it became official policy in the 1920s to discourage Hellenism, the metropolitan and local governments used archaeology to invent the 'Eteo-Cypriots'.[73]

[162]

Before the First World War it was the Hellenic motif that dominated and this had a profound effect on the inhabitants of the island. Hellenism changed Cyprus from a multicultural to a multinational place. Inclusions and exclusions form national identity so, as Benedict Anderson argued, the nation is an 'imagined political community' understood within the entangled dynamics of history, culture, ideology and power.[74] Stathis Gourgouris argued that 'nations exist literally as dreams before they become politically and geographically signified as nations' so the 'initial ideological act is to create institutions' that reinvoke the dream state.[75] After Greece was created in May 1832 a nation needed scripting. The *Romiee* were not homogenous – language, culture and social norms were entangled with other linguistic and religious groups. The non-Hellenic needed extracting: the Turkish, Slavic, Latin, Frankish and even the Romaic,[76] to create a hybrid Helleno-Orthodox identity.

Greek governments attached to the programme the policy to establish a Greater Greece – the 'Great Idea'. Hellenised Orthodox Christians included Cyprus within the topological dream of Hellenism. Nationalists in Greece thought the British occupation postponed *énosis* with the 'mother country'.[77] British representatives in Athens and Corfu warned London that Greeks in Trieste and Athens, where a 'Cypriot Association' was formed, planned to send Greeks to agitate for *énosis*.[78] In February 1879, the Cyprus government passed an ordinance against Hellenist committees[79] and in July Salisbury warned Biddulph that they reminded him of the Ionian Islands.[80] By 1880 there were 600 Greek nationals in Cyprus.[81] Hellenised non-Cypriots, mostly from the Ionian Islands, who were introduced to modernity in Italian universities and transferred it to their co-religionists, had settled in Larnaca and Limassol during the nineteenth century and now began to disseminate the 'dream nation'.[82]

Ottoman Romaic communities established commercial bases throughout the Ottoman empire.[83] In January 1873 merchants formed 'the Greek Brotherhood of the Cypriots of Egypt', yet early presidents of the Alexandria branch were the Grollo brothers, Niokles and Frantziskos, born in Larnaca but to Corfiote parents.[84] The Brotherhood's founding members were Hellenised immigrants to, or Hellenised locals of, Larnaca and Limassol (Appendix IX), thus they had a Hellenic consciousness and, as the title shows, they identified the Cypriots as Greeks. The Cairo branch had deplored the absence of Hellenism from the speeches welcoming Wolseley (more proof that *énosis* was never mentioned);[85] aimed to spread Hellenism through the Levant;[86] and financed schools in Cyprus, such as the Pancyprian Gymnasium in Nicosia (1893) which taught the curricula of Greece.[87]

Cypriots educated in Athens, Trieste and Alexandria were also introduced to the ideas of the nation[88] and many returned home to 'teach' Hellenism before and after the British arrival.[89] George Loukas, born in Omodos, Limassol, was a good example. He studied philosophy and Byzantine music in Athens (1864–69) and taught in the Limassol district for thirty-eight years.[90] In 1874 he published a book on modern Cypriot folklore to prove Cypriot 'Greekness' as a response to Jakob Fallmerayer's earlier controversial work.[91] Newspapers were another tool from which to spread Hellenism. The Cairo Brotherhood sent Theodoulos Constantinides, a Cypriot teacher in the 'Greek' schools of Alexandria, to found a Greek newspaper. In August 1878 he began *Kypros-Cyprus*, a Greek-English weekly in Larnaca, with Archdale Palmer. But it failed to sell and in 1879 Constantinides started *Neon Kition*, which – with *Alithia* in Limassol, run by Aristotle Palaeologos, the son of a Constantinopolian and an Athenian – became the anti-British Hellenist organs.[92]

The rejection of co-option split the Orthodox elite into: a faction under Sophronios, which wanted to work with the British to preserve Church rights, relations with the Muslims and improve economic and social conditions; and Kyprianos, the Bishop of Kitium, the Greek nationals and Hellenised Cypriots, who wanted to impose a new order – *énosis*. In 1879 Kyprianos accused Falkland Warren, then Limassol's commissioner, of abuse when collecting taxes. His real problem, however, was with losing his immunity. The matter ended in court, winning him Hellenist plaudits.[93]

The British application of modernity to Cyprus aided one Hellenist project: the imposition of *Katharevousa*, a language created by purifying the spoken tongue from 'foreign' influences. This artificial language was 'syntactically calqued on foreign prototypes but simultaneously claimed as the restored original of the local tongue'.[94] Schools taught it and newspapers used it. Cypriot could not enter the written medium, as Maltese (morphologically related to North African Arabic, with Sicilian vocabulary, syntax and idioms) did at a similar time.[95] The British recognised *Katharevousa*, tying the Cypriot Orthodox to Greece and forcing them to use scribes in legal and government business.[96]

British Liberal reverence of Greek even scuttled the proposal made in 1880 by Biddulph, Cobham and the Director of Education, Reverend Josiah Spencer, to introduce English to schools. The Society for the Propagation of the Gospel sent Spencer to Cyprus in 1878 to promote Anglican-Orthodox unity. He thought English would help and so founded an English school in Nicosia in February 1881.[97] The London Missionary Society had established Methodist Lancastrian schools in the Ionian Islands to spread literacy and religious education,[98] but London had other ideas for Cyprus. Kimberley thought

> the rich and varied literature of ancient Greece, and the great progress ... modern Greece has made in the work of education, affords ample means not only for an ordinary education but for the attainment of a high degree of mental culture.[99]

Although Kimberly did not wish to force English on Malta, Quebec and the Cape[100] – overseas possessions either on the European periphery or with European settlers – the case of Cyprus clearly had Hellenic cultural associations. The result was cultural engineering and isolation of the Cypriots from their rulers. No wonder Konstantinos Amantos, a headmaster of the Pancyprian Gymnasium (1911–12) from Greece, thought that Kimberley was 'enlightened'.[101]

Introducing English threatened the Hellenist agenda. With Cypriot as the mother-tongue, Greek still needed learning and English might threaten that. In August 1881 Hellenists in Limassol and Larnaca spread rumours that the British would replace the 'language of the people',[102] a slur that Hellenists would repeat perpetually.[103] At the banquet celebrating Limassol's new pier,[104] Biddulph denied this, and stated that he could not support agitation for the cession of territory in his care to another country – the evident aim of the Hellenists.[105] But new winds were blowing in London. An editorial in *The Times* stated: 'it would have been far better ... if he had favoured it to the common injury of both countries'.[106] Kimberley agreed: 'I think the "agitators" are much more nearly in the right than our "military bureaucracy".'[107]

The British even allowed schools to adopt the curricula of those in Greece. The director of Nicosia's Girls' School explained in opening the 1869 school year that Orthodox education aimed to mould leaders with a piety to God and respect for their Orthodox and Muslim neighbour.[108] After 1878, schools, hitherto church run, came under the control of the Egyptian Brotherhood, which insisted on teachers from Greece.[109] In 1881 Spencer warned that these teachers 'spread sedition and discontent amongst the people' to weaken trust in the British government.[110] In 1886 he reported that books from Athens such as *On National Instruction* and *The Heroes of Modern Greece* were replacing religious texts.[111]

In April 1881 an article in *Clio*, a Hellenist organ in Trieste,[112] stated that Cyprus had been offered to Greece.[113] It claimed that the Reform Club, leading Radical peers and Lord Derby the former Foreign Secretary, backed it. Kimberley denied the rumour,[114] but telegrams from Nicosia, Larnaca and Limassol had already thanked Gladstone.[115] Pavlos Valsamakis, whose parents probably originated from Cephalonia, sent the Larnaca telegram.[116] The Limassol telegram was signed 'inhabitants of Limassol' and, like the others, was in French, meaning that an educated person must have penned it. Members of the *Kypriakos Syllogos*, a non-political club formed in 1879, sent the Nicosia telegram.[117] Tellingly, Sophronios sent no message.

Gladstone and Lord Granville, the Foreign Secretary, had contemplated giving Cyprus to Greece (Chapter 9), but Gladstone told Biddulph to announce that while he 'earnestly desire[d] the happiness of Cyprus' it was held under a 'convention with the Porte as a part of the Ottoman Empire'.[118] Gladstone had implied that the Cypriot Orthodox would be happier under Greek rule.

After this, Gladstone put free institutions on the agenda.[119] But Kimberley wanted Biddulph to go first.[120] In October Granville faced a dilemma over Sir Arthur Hamilton Gordon,[121] formerly governor of Trinidad (1866–70), Mauritius (1871–74) and Fiji (1875–80), who was unhappy with his New Zealand post, because his 'gifts' were for 'despotic' not constitutional rule.[122] This was not why Granville thought he 'would do very well for Cyprus'.[123] Gordon was an extreme Philhellene: as Gladstone's private secretary during his Corfu mission he lamented the preclusion of *énosis*. He also hated the 'insane' Cyprus Convention.[124] Gordon would have made an interesting choice, and as Fiji's governor he wanted to preserve local social structures through co-option.[125] Granville pushed Biddulph strongly to accept the governorship of British Guiana – so strongly that he refused it and any other post.[126]

In March 1882 Kimberley told Biddulph that Cyprus would be given a legislative council with a local majority. Eventually, it was decided that it would compose of twelve elected local (split 9–3 based on the 1881 census that had found the Orthodox at 73.9 per cent and the Muslims at 24.5 per cent) and six appointed British members, with the high commissioner's vote deciding a deadlock. Undoubtedly this was a liberal constitution: after more than eighty years under British control Malta received a constitution with an elected majority in 1887 (which would be revoked in 1903).[127] But *The Times* claimed that this was designed so that the three Muslims and the seven British could outvote the nine Orthodox.[128] The Liberals 'modernised' Cypriot politics, but created a political distinction between the Orthodox and Muslims.[129]

Cypriot reactions were mixed.[130] Sophronios thanked Queen Victoria – a gesture that Kimberley welcomed.[131] His rivals were equally pleased – ecclesiastics and foreigners could run, even though it was long-standing policy to ban ecclesiastics from any representative body in Malta.[132] Voting conditions and electoral dynamics suited them. The electorates were grouped into Nicosia-Kyrenia, Larnaca-Famagusta and Limassol-Paphos, so Hellenism was later spread to Paphos and Famagusta from its two centres, Larnaca and Limassol. For the 662 towns and villages there were only twenty-two stations. Also, open voting subordinated voting to indebtedness and clientelism.[133] The Muslim elite, led by Mufti Esseïd Ahmed Assim,[134] opposed the council, fearing that proportionate representation would lead to their domination, and threatened to lead a Muslim exodus.[135] But Kimberley told Biddulph to tell them that their claims were inconsistent with the principle to 'secure equal rights to all classes of the population . . . whatever creed and race' and that they were not losing privileges.[136] Cyprus would be run on a modern basis, which contradicted paternalistic structures.

These modern structures gave rise to politicians. In 1884 Kyprianos refused to attend a Holy Synod to discuss regulating church–state relations and spread rumours that Sophronios and the other bishops were paid British agents. The people refused to pay canonical dues,[137] while Kyprianos collected money with the aid of the Hellenists.[138] But Hellenism was slow to take root. Celebrations to mark the Greek War of Independence were not observed in Nicosia until 1885 and were not repeated the following year.[139] Sophronios was more concerned with his people's spiritual and material welfare. In March 1885 he told Biddulph that the bishops of Kyrenia and Paphos and he had virtually no income. Biddulph agreed that they had suffered financially, but rejected making statutory the state's affairs with the church before consulting the people.[140] In May Sophronios published a draft of a proposed law on the issue in *Salpinx*, the Limassol newspaper of the chanter Stylianos Hourmouzios.[141] Biddulph told London that 'not the slightest notice . . . [was] taken of it' and Sophronios warned him that unless things changed 'he would be obliged to resign'.[142]

Kyprianos died in December 1886,[143] but as Edward Fairfield opined, another firebrand would fill the void eventually.[144] However, his successor, Chrysanthos, was Orthodox-centric.[145] Instead, Nicosia's lawyer-moneylenders, such as Paschales Constantinides, who had built a network of patrons and brokers in Nicosia and Kyrenia, and his protégée, Achilles Liassides, jostled for power with the Hellenists. They criticised the British in coffee-houses during the 1887 drought, but in British quarters retained the façade of copacetic relations.[146] As with other Christian Ottoman elites, they subordinated their politics to what was needed to sustain power.[147]

In November 1887, the archbishopric received letters from the peasantry that complained about high taxation and it organised a meeting, where rural representatives appealed for lasting tax reform, suspension of taxes and measures to aid agriculture. The centralised

British bureaucracy was failing in its paternalistic duties to smallholders, unlike the Ottoman bureaucracy, and had dismantled the paternalistic authority of the Church. British economic policy only sharpened social consciousness. The Hellenists in Limassol and Larnaca, however, insisted on a deputation to London to seek more political rights. Sophronios overcame his initial misgivings because he was convinced that he could achieve a positive outcome over his own grievance.[148] Sophronios ensured Muslim input and it was his friend the Mufti who backed two Muslim delegates.[149] But because they rejected abolishing the tribute – believing it would diminish Ottoman sovereignty – the Muslims later withdrew.[150] Prior to leaving, Sophronios proposed to the local government a church–state concordat:

> It is the duty of the Church, by means of her spiritual resources, to support the Civil Authority in the carrying out of all its just and lawful orders. On the other hand the Civil Power, by means of its material resources, must support and assist the Ecclesiastical Power.[151]

Co-option, however, did not come. It was left to private individuals, who organised themselves into paternalistic and imperialist networks, to help Cyprus. High-church Anglicans formed the 'Cyprus Society' in London in July 1888 to advance health and education in Cyprus. The society planned to establish a cottage hospital at Kyrenia, travelling dispensaries and ambulances and to send nurses. The donor of the land, George Ludovic Houstoun, a Scottish laird, wanted the hospital named after General Gordon. The society planned technical and agricultural schools and to improve religious and secular education. Edward Kenyon, Kyrenia's former commissioner, and G.A.K. Wisely, the designer of Government Cottage at Troodos, were behind it. Princess Christian was the president. It comprised leading high-church Anglicans (see Appendix X), including many bishops; Sir George Bowen, formerly an official in the Ionian Islands; Borthwick, the Tory editor of the *Morning Post* and advocate of the Euphrates Valley railway; Major-General Goldsmid, who had called for Cyprus' seizure on the eve of its occupation; the Tory Stanley Leighton, a critic of the tribute; Lieutenant-General Sir John Stokes, a British Commissioner in Egypt (1875) and representative on the Board of the Suez Canal Company (1876); Athelstan Riley, who wrote dozens of books on the Eastern Orthodox Christians; the Liberal navalist, Lord (Thomas) Brassey; and Lord Randolph Churchill.[152] Lord Nelson, a descendant of the famous naval hero, summarised the calling of the Cyprus Society in 1890.

> The Mahometan inhabitants have a claim upon us, and by improving their social position, caring for them in sickness, and raising the character of their education, we may gain a large influence over them for

good. But the greatest call upon us Churchmen is the fact that in Cyprus we are brought into direct contact with a branch of the Holy Eastern Church. It is our duty to meet them in a spirit of Christian Brotherhood . . . We see here an Orthodox Church, holding the old faith and the old customs, and maintaining their own independence under their own archbishop and bishops; but they have been oppressed for ages. Their poverty is great and the need for better education can hardly be exaggerated. It is clearly our duty as a Christian Church, having the same Creeds, the same Sacraments, the same liturgical system, to hold out to them the right hand of fellowship.[153]

After the Reformation, contact started between Anglicans and Orthodox because of theological interests and their rivalry with the Catholic Church.[154] In 1676 an Orthodox Church was founded in Soho, later an Orthodox college at Oxford[155] and Anglicans conferred honorary degrees to Orthodox clerics. But from the mid-1700s relations suffered because of Anglican proselytising. This ended under the sway of the Oxford Movement in the 1830s. When the high-church party was revived, Anglican-Orthodox contact resumed. In 1868 an Anglican church was consecrated at Constantinople and Patriarch Gregory VI agreed to Orthodox clerics burying Anglicans in Orthodox cemeteries. They came closer on doctrine at the 1874–75 Reunion Conference in Bonn. In 1885 the Archbishop of Canterbury, Edward Benson, detailed in his primary charge ('The Seven Gifts') his initiative for 'missions of maintenance' to strengthen local churches in the Near East.[156] The desire for integration resulted in the Third Lambeth Conference (1888) deciding that a basis for unity existed and that ecclesiastical and theological education should continue, particularly with the Orthodox churches under British rule in Cyprus and Egypt.[157]

Kenyon arranged for a warm reception for the deputation.[158] On 18 June, Sophronios visited the House of Commons and met Queen Victoria at a garden party hosted by the Prince of Wales.[159] On 23 June he attended evensong at St Peters in Oxford and on the following day met the Cyprus Society.[160] Benson said that Britain's mission was to make Cyprus suitable for its multi-religious inhabitants. Sophronios thanked him and the Cyprus Society, which he promised to aid.[161] On 27 June the University of Oxford presented him with the honorary degree of Doctor of Divinity.[162] Five days later he attended the civic banquet hosted by the Lord Mayor at the Mansion House.[163] Before leaving, he thanked Benson again and they started a correspondence that continued with Benson's successor.[164]

The Cyprus Society was at its zenith in 1890 when the Irving Dramatic Club performed *The Tempest* at St George's Hall in aid of its mission,[165] but was wound up by 1893.[166]

The Cyprus Society achieved much to improve health services in Cyprus. In 1890 and 1891 it sent nurses to the new government hospital in Nicosia[167] and in 1891 recognition was sought for the 'Gordon Nurses' from Florence Nightingale.[168] It was hoped that recognition would boost paltry funds, which were low, in spite of its wealthy members. In September 1890, Kenyon wrote to High Commissioner Henry Bulwer that the society intended to hire a house at Kyrenia as a temporary district hospital and to send a nurse there.[169] Kenyon asked if the District Medical Officer could take charge of it, while it would be under the management of a local committee, on which the District Medical Officer and the District Commissioner would serve.[170] He also asked for government drugs.[171] Bulwer replied that he wanted to meet the proposal as far as possible, but noted that it fell short of the initial aims. Bulwer agreed so long as the arrangement did not conflict with the District Medical Officer's job, and it that it would be temporary. Bulwer offered a surgeon, dispenser, free drugs up to a reasonable extent, surgical appliances and superintendence.[172] Kenyon explained that the society lacked funds to proceed: 'it is difficult', he went on, 'to arouse sympathy for Cyprus, still more difficult to raise funds'.[173] Kenyon revealed that the society aimed to 'do real good for Cyprus' rather than focus on one district,[174] but in May 1891 he repeated the society's financial problems to Bulwer, also asking that the two nurses in Nicosia be housed in the same place to save money because 'unfortunately the Society has met with so little encouragement that it is difficult to obtain the requisite funds even for the work already commenced'.[175] In September, Kenyon informed Bulwer that C.E. Newton, a member of the Cyprus Society's Hospital Committee, offered to provide and maintain two nurses at Kyrenia if the society covered the rent of a house and furniture for the first year. Newton and Kenyon, and not the society, would manage the hospital.[176] Bulwer assented and the Gordon Memorial Cottage Hospital was opened in January 1892.[177]

Problems began within months. Fisher, Kyrenia's District Commissioner, had asked to move the government dispensary to the Gordon Hospital, and Bulwer's rejection letter was shown to Miss Newton, the superintendent.[178] Then, within months of the Gordon Hospital opening, Fisher requested money from the Cyprus government because the hospital was being run at great sacrifice.[179] Bulwer was livid, accusing Fisher of not appreciating the government's medical work in Kyrenia and asked Fisher to address his request to the chief secretary: 'The line you have taken and what you have said on the subject have made an impression on me that is not favourable.'[180]

In 1896 an eighteen-bed hospital opened in Kyrenia and a local committee, that included Houstoun, ran it. The Cyprus government only offered medicines and the services of the local medical officer: it did nothing to help when there was a shortfall in money from London, resulting in virtually annual contributions from the Kyrenia municipality and much local fundraising.[181] In 1924 Kenyon, still passionate about Cyprus, expressed sorrow in *The Times* that the Cyprus government, which now virtually controlled the hospital, had fired the assistant nurse and forced the head nurse to retire after thirty years' service.[182]

The Cyprus Society failed to undertake any educational work. In 1890 a garden party was held at Princess Helena's College in Ealing where a centre would be formed to head the work. A former student, Miss Potter, agreed to teach in Cyprus and eventually a college would be established there for the higher education of girls.[183] Unfortunately, Miss Potter did not last long in Cyprus and the college never materialised.[184]

The Cyprus Society was wound up in 1893, and the £140 left in its coffers was handed to the Cyprus government.[185] Kenyon, Wisely and some Anglican clergy conducted further work on an individual basis. Why did the Cyprus Society, with so many prominent public figures as members, fail to garner the support of the British people?

Potential donors were more interested in giving to a cause connected to Cyprus' classical past, while Whitehall thought co-option and paternalistic approaches were the mainstay of the Oriental Ottoman system (and British colonial practice in Asia and Africa as opposed to a European space) and would be dismantled.

The Cyprus Society competed for the hearts, minds and wallets of British donors, and in October 1887 the council of the Society for the Promotion of Hellenic Studies established the Cyprus Exploration Fund. Exploring Cyprus was not as exciting as Greece and Egypt; nevertheless, it was interesting enough. In the 1860s the British were among the first to explore Cyprus' antiquities with Lang, who sold some of his finds to the British Museum, and Thomas Sandwith, who read a paper 'On the Different Styles of Pottery found in Ancient Tombs in the Island of Cyprus' to the Fellows of the Society of Antiquaries of London in 1871.[186] But, as Lang admitted,[187] it was the Italian-American Luigi Palma di Cesnola, the American consul, who put Cyprus archaeology on the map. The Keeper of the Department of Greek and Roman Antiquities in the British Museum, Sir Charles Thomas Newton, had contact with Lang, Sandwith and Cesnola, but Cesnola sold his collection to the newly expanded Metropolitan Museum of Art in New York and became the first director in 1879. Perhaps this was one reason why the Cyprus government disapproved of the activities of Alessandro di Cesnola, his brother, confiscating his collection in 1878. That he was an amateur mattered little – the government gladly allowed employees, such as Sinclair, Kitchener, Cobham and Falkland Warren to carry out excavations.[188] Now, however, there would be professionals working with the government on scientific excavations for scholarship, not profit.

Bernard Cohn argued that the imperial project was more than economics, strategy and politics and that the British in India sought to uncover the history of the ruled (the 'historiographical modality').[189] By discovering knowledge of their past, the British thought they could classify them. To do this, they found, collected and classified ancient objects. Although Cyprus was occupied four years before Egypt, as soon as the latter came under British sway an exploration fund was established. Cyprus was not Greece, no matter how much it was identified with it, and ancient Egypt had a greater pull on the nineteenth-century European mind than Cyprus. In fact, the Egyptian Exploration Fund's founding statement ranked the Greeks second only to the Hebrews as objects for investigation.[190]

The British Museum, the universities of Oxford and Cambridge, and leading archaeological societies were represented on the committee of the Cyprus Exploration Fund, which held joint meetings with the British School at Athens. In 1883 a meeting, chaired by the Prince of Wales, with Gladstone and Lords Salisbury and Roseberry present, resolved to create the British School in Athens and raised about £4,000 in donations toward the cause. Like the Cyprus Society, some very prominent men attended the meetings, including: Lord Lingen (Sir Ralph Robert Wheeler Lingen), a student of classics at Oxford, who also entered the Inns of Court as a Barrister at Lincoln's Inn, but became secretary in the Education Office and then permanent secretary of the treasury; Sidney Colvin, a famous literary and art critic, who from 1874 to 1884 was the director of the Fitzwilliam Museum and from 1884 the keeper of prints and drawings in the British Museum, and was also the vice-president of the Society for the Promotion of Hellenic Studies; Richard Claverhouse Jebb, Professor of Greek at Glasgow (1875–89) and Regius Professor of Greek at Cambridge (1889–1905), and was also Conservative MP for Cambridge University (1891–1900); Sir Frederick Leighton, a famous painter and sculptor of primarily classical (especially Hellenic) and religious subjects and President of the Royal Academy of Arts (1878–96); Edward Maunde Thompson, the director and principal librarian of the British Museum (1888–1909), famous for his *An Introduction to Greek and Latin Palaeography* (1912); Walter Leaf, a famous banker who in 1888 became chairman of Leaf and Company Ltd, later chairman of the Westminster Bank, was one of the founders of the International Chamber of Commerce, and also president of the

Hellenic Society and the Classical Association; and Demetrios Bikelas, a historiographer, translator and benefactor, born on Syros, who lived for twenty years in England (1852–72), thereafter in Paris, and was elected President of the first International Olympic Committee.[191] This network of elites sponsored the pursuit of knowledge of the Hellenic past. Apart from D.G. Hogarth (see below), the only member of the Cyprus Exploration Fund who was also a member of the Cyprus Society was Sir George Bowen, who traced the flaws of the modern Corfiotes to their ancient ancestors.[192] Both groups had different agendas, rooted in two different cultural signifiers. Since ancient Greece had a greater pull on the British elite and educated classes than did the connection between Cyprus' Christian tradition and the Church, and the Anglican tradition and the Church, it comes as no surprise that in a matter of months the Cyprus Exploration Fund had raised through private subscriptions £1,200.[193]

The archaeologists were the means from which to obtain the knowledge. They included Sir Charles Newton, who in 1856–57 had discovered the remains of the mausoleum of Halicarnassus, one of the seven wonders of the ancient world, and who had played a leading part in starting the Society for the Promotion of Hellenic Studies, the British School at Athens and the Egypt Exploration Fund; Arthur Evans, who later discovered the Palace of Knossos in Crete; and, among others, Percy Gardner, Disney Professor of Archaeology at Cambridge (1880–87) and thereafter Professor of Classical Archaeology at Oxford, where he stimulated study of Greek art.[194] The archaeologists involved were trained as archaeologists of the Hellenic past.

Three 'students' under the director of the British School at Athens, Ernest Gardner, Percy's brother, would conduct the work. Gardner had furthered the excavations at the Greek city of Naucratis (Egypt) for the Egypt Exploration Fund (1885–86), begun by Sir Flinders Petrie, which gained him entrance as the first student at the newly established British School at Athens under Francis C. Penrose in 1886. The students going to Cyprus were David G. Hogarth, Craven Fellow at the University of Oxford; Montague R. James, Fellow of King's College and the assistant director of the Fitzwilliam Museum in Cambridge; and Dr Francis H.H. Guillemard, the famous traveller and zoologist, who had conducted zoological work in Cyprus in 1887. The Royal Institute of British Architects selected R. Elsey Smith as the team's architect.

In March 1888, the Cyprus Exploration Fund committee appealed for public support in *The Times*.[195] This appeal was only made to a certain section of British society: 'We (*The Times*) have great satisfaction in recommending this appeal to the learned and wealthy classes of this country.' Clearly, this project would only appeal to those interested in its imperial agenda – the discovery of knowledge of Cyprus – and to those who could fund it.

The editor of *The Times* explained that it was not simply about finding knowledge of Cyprus for the sake of it, but about discovering and writing its past:

> Much has been done for it (Cyprus) in the way of economical regeneration under the provident guidance of English rulers, and though the annexation was heralded with a great flourish of enthusiasm, the island has latterly fulfilled that great test of prosperity which consists in having no history to speak of.[196]

The Times further explained that it was not simply about Cyprus, but about discovering knowledge of modern European civilisation: 'Modern civilisation has its roots in the life and thought of races which once occupied the countries surrounding the Mediterranean.' In this imperial project, the British, despite the Greek antiquities in the British museum, were behind the Germans, who for years searched at Olympia and Troy.

> These excavations have been conducted on soil in which respective nations engaged in them have no more than a historical and archaeological interest. Germany, France, and Austria have merely represented and acknowledged the common heritage of Europe in the remnants of Hellenic antiquity, though in so doing they have manifested a true and genuine sense of the continuity of European civilisation. It surely cannot be supposed that England, which ruled for ten years in Cyprus, is less interested than other European nations in tracing the origins of our common civilisation in the antiquities of the Hellenic world.[197]

The editor of *The Times* clearly situated Cyprus within the unitary ideal of ancient Greece. Cyprus was 'virgin soil' when it comes to systematic archaeological exploration, with the exception of Cesnola's work, and so it was not clear what might be found, however 'we know pretty accurately what we ought to look for'.

> Cyprus occupies a peculiar and unique position in the historical development of Hellenic civilisation. It stands as it were between the East and the West, and is the point at which the multifarious influences of the older Oriental and Egyptian civilisations were first brought to bear upon the nascent civilisation of Greece. This is what gives Cyprus its special importance for the intelligent student of Hellenic antiquity.[198]

Exploring Cyprus' archaeological remains was a chance for the wealthy and learned classes to show how much they really cared to learn about the civilisation that had given birth to modern Europe. The appeal ends, despite its strong Hellenic bent, on a Latin note: '*Spartam nactus es; hanc exorna*' was the exhortation of the Spartan mother to her son. In a similar spirit, the whole civilised world may we say to Englishman, '*Cyprum nactus es, hanc explora*'.[199]

Cyprus, like Greece and Palestine, presents an interesting case when situated within Bernard Cohn's ideas. He observed that 'the exploration of the terrestrial world was being carried out at the same time that Europeans were exploring their own origins in the pagan past of Greece and Rome'.[200] Cohn showed that one way of knowing India was through looking for similarities between the living exotics of India and the classical past of Egypt, Greece and Rome. In Cyprus' case the similarities were so much easier to identify.

Within a month of the appeal the results of the exploration filtered to the public through *The Times*. On 2 April it reported that Ernest Gardner had surveyed the Temple of Aphrodite and found 'it was evidently not built on any Hellenic system'.[201] At the July meeting, Gardner announced that Strabo, the famed Greek historian, geographer and philosopher, had led them to it. He believed that the temple was undoubtedly of Phoenician origin, but despite Astarte, the Phoenician goddess of love, pre-dating the Greek Aphrodite, he continued to refer to the Temple of Aphrodite. Elsey Smith believed that there was a resemblance between the temple at Paphos and the description of Solomon's temple in the Book of Kings, thus linking the pagan temple in Cyprus with the biblical temple in Jerusalem.[202] In September 1888, *The Times* published Gardner and Elsey Smith's full report. The article reconfirmed their report of a few months earlier, but this time they added that there was a strong correlation with Solomon's temple and that there were no buildings on the site resembling Greek temples.[203]

Hogarth published his findings, experiences and observations in *Devia Cypria* in 1889. Between the end of May and the middle of August 1888 he explored the west (Paphos) and east (Karpass) of Cyprus. Hogarth combines his reporting of Cyprus's ancient past, where he discusses its Occidental and Oriental remains, with reporting on its Christian heritage.[204]

The ambiguity archaeologists identified did not interest London. Cyprus, being on Europe's periphery and causing no problems to British rule, was being treated on a modern footing. So the Conservative Colonial Secretary, Lord Knutsford, told Sophronios that placing church and state relations on a statutory basis and regulating the payment of dues was a matter for the local legislature.[205] Thus, the British, as well as the Greeks and Cypriots imbued with modernity, planted the seeds of Hellenism.

The members of the Colonial Office were at the forefront in applying modernity to Cyprus. In December 1888, *Énosis*, a weekly newspaper in Larnaca, changed its subheading from 'abolish the tribute to Turkey so that you may save Cyprus' to 'cede Cyprus to Mother Greece'. Bulwer argued that it was treasonable for Ottoman subjects to publicly call for the abrogation of Ottoman sovereignty and the government could 'not allow' the Cypriots 'to overstep the limits' of what was treasonable. He wanted to ban the paper unless it changed the heading.[206] The Colonial Office was shocked. Fairfield, a Radical in domestic politics,[207] observed that in Canada, the Cape and Australia many advocated separation from England, but they were not called traitors.[208] Knutsford rejected Bulwer's request.[209] Then in November 1891, Rustem Pasha, the Ottoman ambassador in London, told Salisbury that an article in the Cypriot newspaper *Sphyna* advocated ceding Crete to Greece. Salisbury wanted the Cyprus government to repudiate it,[210] but Fairfield thought such views were 'found any day in the year in a Gladstonian paper'.[211]

The British introduction of masonic lodges to Cyprus also aided Hellenism. In 1888, a number of soldiers in the garrison formed St Paul's lodge in Limassol. One of the few Cypriot masons, Dr John Karageorgiades, the medical officer for Limassol district and a member of the Panhellenic lodge in Athens, believed that St Paul's would be the breeding ground for the Greek national awakening in Cyprus. Within two years, enough Cypriots had joined for one of the founders, John Percy White, to ask the Greek Grand Lodge to start a Greek lodge because of the language barrier. In 1893 Karageorgiades founded Zeno.[212] Contrary to one nationalist and anti-mason,[213] Cypriot masons were at the forefront of Cypriot Hellenism.

The British did not realise that they were clearing a space and helping to sow the seeds of Hellenism. One reason for this was the Cypriot Orthodox indifference to it. In February 1891 Bulwer informed Knutsford that a gift was to be sent to Crown Prince Constantine of Greece on his marriage. The 'Cyprus Committee' formed in 1878 in Athens proposed the idea and subscriptions were collected to buy a map (ironically Kitchener's) and encase it in silver. But it took so long to raise the £38 that the gift was presented a year after the nuptials. As Bulwer asserted, the gift did not excite or represent the people, but showed the 'activity of the philhellenic clique'.[214]

In the late 1880s, more foreign agitators arrived in Cyprus and extended activity to Nicosia and Famagusta. In 1892 Philios Zannettos, a Peloponnesian doctor who arrived in 1888, attacked the Greek Consul, Raphael A. Fontana (later British Consul in Macedonia), for not denouncing the Cyprus government and the candidature of Arthur Young, Famagusta's commissioner, for the legislature. He accused

Fontana, a Catholic, of being a religious fanatic.[215] Sotiris Emphiedji, Famagusta's former mayor (1878–79, 1882–88) and a member of the legislature (1886–87),[216] nominated Young, who was popular in the Karpass for his efforts during the 1887–88 drought and for encouraging Orthodox and Muslim landowners to form an agricultural association.[217]

Young's election threatened the Hellenists, who ran Liassides and George Chakalli, a law graduate from Athens and English literature from England.[218] Bishop Kyrillos (Papadopoulos) of Kyrenia led the campaign. Kyrenia's inhabitants had protested when he was made their bishop[219] and Bulwer thought him 'more of a demagogue than a priest'.[220] His election to the legislature for Limassol-Paphos, when his See was Kyrenia, shows this.[221] When Chrysanthos died in 1890, Fairfield called Papadopoulos (a possible replacement) a 'Helleniste Eusagé'.[222] Young lost, but the court voided the result as threats of spiritual and temporal injury had stopped many from voting for him. Contrary to Greek commentators, that the 'Greeks' revolted against Young's candidature,[223] 106 people from Rizokarpasso swore they would have voted for him, but were threatened from doing so. Even Emphiedji feared testifying in court.[224]

Then in 1893 *Phoni tis Kyprou*, edited by George Nikopoulos, a former associate of Theodoulos Constantinides, published letters from Charles Dilke and his colleague Henry Labouchere advising Chakalli to fight for *énosis*. Ali Rifki, the Mufti since 1890, and the Muslim elite, implored Sendall to introduce the Ottoman press law to end the publishing of racially inflammatory material. Sendall and Lord Ripon rejected that, but Ripon decided that mentioning *énosis* in the legislature was inappropriate.[225]

The growth of a middle class, under modernity's influence, inflated the Hellenists.[226] One example was the merchant George Papadopoulos, who in 1893 built a theatre in Nicosia, which mounted numerous ancient Greek plays, such as Theodoulos Constantinides' *Mehmet Kuchuk* (1895), played on the anniversary of the massacres of 1821 (9 July).[227] Classical Greek drama in high schools and the touring theatre companies from Greece brought the revision of Cypriot history into the arts.[228]

In 1895 peasants complained to Nicosia's elite that they could not afford to pay taxes. A committee in Nicosia comprising Sophronios, Gerasimos (the Abbott of Kykko, who had studied in Geneva), Paschales Constantinides, Liassides, Theophanis Theodotou (Sophronios' nephew), and George Papadopoulos, told Sendall that island-wide meetings would be held and memorials presented to him. They claimed that 'if Her Majesty's Government which has created for it this state of things is *tired out* and it is *its desire* that it should withdraw, it is the ardent wish of the said Greek element to be united with Greece'.[229] The Cypriot Orthodox elite, knowing governance only under a foreign master, preferred that master to share their faith.

The subsequent meetings show the differing focus on issues between the leaders in Nicosia and Kyrenia and those in Larnaca, Limassol and Paphos. The Nicosia/Kyrenia memorial wanted relief from heavy taxation; protection from the tribute; and *énosis* 'if England contemplates abandoning the country'. Zannettos, Nicholas Lanitis, an extreme nationalist teacher, and Kyrillos Papadopoulos, who had become the Bishop of Kitium, went straight to the point in the Larnaca memorial: 'the only solution and this at the earliest possible date [was] union with mother Greece'. The Limassol and Paphos memorials followed suit.[230]

But the Colonial Office was unfazed. Fairfield justified the laissez-faire policy because

> the maxim of colonial policy holds good that it is best to ignore words, which it is not attempted to translate into action, and which do not in themselves tend to bring about a breach of the peace.[231]

The Colonial Office must have been stunned in 1897 when Sophronios and Ali Rifki led Nicosia's Orthodox and Muslim elite in signing a memorial pleading for the extension of Sendall's tenure for another six years.[232] The petition stimulated the Orthodox Cypriot peasants, merchants, landowners, clerics and moderate Hellenists. Four months later, 102 residents of Limassol signed a petition, led by Karageorgiades, the mason and mayor; Socrates Frangoudis, a wine and carob merchant, member of the board of the Ottoman Bank in Limassol and the legislature (1885–86, 1886–89, 1891–96, 1896–1901, 1902–5); and his son-in-law, the diehard Hellenist, Aristotle Palaeologos, whose anti-British stance was tempered by his appointment as a judge in Kyrenia in 1897.[233] Petitions followed from villages in the wine-growing area and Pissouri, half-way between Limassol and Paphos.[234] More came from Nicosia, Varosha and Kyrenia. The first had nearly 400 signatures, including Theodotou's.[235] Loukas Georgiou, a merchant and mayor (1886–87, 1905–6, 1910–16) led Famagusta's petition, which had nearly 300 signatures.[236] Gregory Demetriades, a landowner, and George Loizides, a teacher who started practising law in Kyrenia in 1896, led the Kyrenia petition.[237] Clearly, there was unprecedented support for Sendall. His love of the Cypriots was exemplified by his personal funding of a scholarship for Cypriot Orthodox girls, which was named the 'Victoria scholarship' in commemoration of the sixtieth year of Queen Victoria's reign, and which had a medal with the words 'Ever to Excel' from Homer's *Iliad*.[238]

While Sophronios and Ali Rifki were writing their memorial, the Greek government of Theodore Deligiannis attacked the Ottoman empire and the new and old Hellenists in Cyprus aroused over 1,000 Cypriot youths to volunteer.[239] Deligiannis' nationalist party was the thrust behind Cretan, and now Cypriot, *énosis* agitators. In February 1890 a former foreign ministry official from his party attacked the Cyprus government in the Greek chamber and nationalist Athenian newspapers backed him.[240] Nicholas Katalanos was an unknown teacher in Nicosia's Pancyprian Gymnasium until the 1896 Cretan revolt, when he aroused seventy-five Cypriot youths to volunteer.[241] In 1897 Zannettos and two young Athens-educated lawyers and new legislature members, Theophanis Theodotou (his failure to achieve progress with the British had irritated him)[242] and Ioannis Economides, Kyprianos' nephew, joined him in the recruiting drive. All were members of Zeno and Economides was a merciless usurer. Sendall was forced to declare Cyprus neutral.[243]

In December 1898 William Haynes Smith, Sendall's successor, told Chamberlain that Hellenists were declaring that *énosis* was worth Crete's suffering now that the Great Powers had placed it under a high commissioner, Prince George of Greece.[244] The Colonial Office rejected retaining Sendall because at sixty-four he was thought old. Haynes Smith, seven years younger, was a man of action. He suggested to Sophronios to collect dues through the courts[245] and told Chamberlain that they should help the church to do so, so the bishops could focus on spiritual duties.[246] Both suggestions were rejected. Two years later, with Sophronios ill, Hellenism was on the march. Kyrenia's commissioner, Tankerville Chamberlain, warned Young (Chief Secretary from 1895):

> Having watched the march of the Hellenic movement for . . . some thirteen years, I must respectfully submit the opinion that unless Her Majesty's Government intend to favour the annexation of Cyprus to Greece serious trouble will sooner or later [result] if something is not speedily done to check what is going on.[247]

The archiepiscopal dispute and the énosis *movement*

In May 1900, Archbishop Sophronios died after a long illness. The Bishop of Paphos, entrusted with arranging the election, had predeceased him, leaving only those of Kyrenia and Kitium (both named Kyrillos). The ensuing battle over who would succeed Sophronios was more than a battle over political leadership: it was a battle over identity.

The austere Bishop of Kyrenia (Vasilliou) and his faction (*Kyreniakí*), led by Paschales Constantinides, claimed Orthodoxy as the people's true identity. They were pro-British and thought secular leaders should focus on improving living conditions and church leaders on spiritual needs. They charged Papadopoulos and his coterie of free-masonry. Cyprus differed from the Ionian Islands where nationalists had accused the pro-British elite of masonry.[248]

While Sophronios was ill, Papadopoulos and Katalanos started building a network to win the archbishopric – a most sacrilegious venture. Haynes Smith thought it would be tragic if they succeeded,[249] but nothing was done. Papadopoulos and his backers (*Kitiakí*) emphas-ised that the Cypriot Orthodox were Greeks[250] and had no qualms about destroying Orthodox-Muslim integration. As Kyrenia's bishop, he swore at Muslims from a mixed Orthodox-Muslim village outside his See for not saluting him.[251] As to the charge of freemasonry, he threatened to sue a man for libel, but only months after the event to coincide with the 1901 legislature elections.[252]

In August 1900, Papadopoulos won the election – a predictable result given his wide network. When the *Kyreniakí*-dominated Holy Synod objected, the *Kitiakí* appealed to the Patriarchs of Constantinople, Jerusalem and Alexandria, but they proposed barring both bishops from running. Vasilliou agreed; Papadopoulos did not. Ioakim III, the Patriarch of Constantinople, supported Vasilliou, while Photius, the Patriarch of Alexandria, backed Papadopoulos.[253] When the Holy Synod, now composed only of *Kyreniakí*, appealed in December to Haynes Smith to preserve the autocephaly of the Church from foreign patriarchates it was because when 'the hour will come that Cyprus may . . . be annexed to the country with which she is nationally con-nected, Her Majesty's Government may be able to say: "I give her to you, having preserved intact . . . the Privileges of her Church."'[254] The passage was discreetly added at the end of a long letter. Haynes Smith told Chamberlain that the *Kitiakí* 'stimulated public feeling by strongly advocating Union with Greece' and the *Kyreniakí* could not 'resist the popular cry', but say *énosis* could only result with British consent.[255] Haynes Smith added that the

> agitation keeps those who support the English administration under a species of terrorism . . . [because] if they . . . support the British admin-istration even in the most ordinary matters of Government, they are held up as traitors in the Greek press, and their families are subjected to a continued stream of abuse which is not infrequently of a most dirty character.[256]

Papadopoulos' power grew under such conditions. In the October 1901, legislature campaign the *Kitiakí* won easily. A.E. Kershaw, the chief commandant of police, reported that Hellenists misled the people into fearing that Britain would alter their religion and language. A Hellenist told him that success came by spreading fear, blaming the British for poverty and offering *énosis* as the answer, a tactic the Ionian islanders had also employed.[257]

Haynes Smith recognised genuine grievances, especially the tribute. To check Hellenism he suggested more social interaction between the officials and the people; a proper flag – a red St George Cross on a white background with the arms of Richard I; a native Cypriot regiment (Chapter 8); a state-church concordat when an archbishop was elected; and power to stop the discussion of *énosis* in the legislature.[258]

The Colonial Office was divided on what to do. A.E. Collins, a junior clerk, thought it was time to check the agitators from spreading fear through sedition laws, press censorship and control of education.[259] But his more experienced colleague John Anderson believed it was useless 'trying to kill an agitation of this nature . . . with tea or cake or with specially designed flags and banners'.[260] Bertram Cox, the assistant under-secretary, thought the pro-Greek press was not as bad as the pro-Italian press in Malta[261] and Ommanney, the permanent under-secretary, thought Cyprus could have some latitude since it was no fortress like Malta.[262] The failure to convert Cyprus into a strategic asset was determining how to handle the Hellenists. Chamberlain agreed with the experienced Colonial Office members, telling Haynes Smith that all he agreed to was the concordat and flag.[263] So the cheap flag Gladstone's government had given Cyprus was replaced with one displaying the arms of Richard I.[264] Symbols of the British empire had little effect. The Hellenists had their own symbols: the flag of Greece and popular postcards of 'ethno-martyrs' and current politicians. Chamberlain also altered Ripon's order to Sendall that discussing *énosis* in the legislature was *ultra vires*.

In October 1904 the Conservatives chose Charles King-Harman to succeed Haynes Smith. King-Harman knew Cyprus well, having served as Biddulph's private secretary (1879–81) and assistant chief secretary.[265] He returned having served as Governor of Sierra Leone (1900–4). King-Harman, a Philhellene,[266] was given a fixed £50,000 grant-in-aid and was instructed to resolve the archiepiscopal dispute. He did. But by favouring the Hellenists – Katalanos liked him[267] – he destroyed the Orthodox-centric faction and alienated Muslim leaders, who started reacting to Hellenism.

Cypriot Muslim divisions and identity

1900 was also momentous for Cypriot Muslims as modernity imperilled their socio-political structures. Ten years earlier, there had been a dispute over the successor to Mufti Esseïd Ahmed Assim. Nicosia's notables nominated Ali Rifki, a teacher and member of the *ulema*, to the *sheikh-ul-Islam* in Constantinople. Simultaneously, villages inundated Falkland Warren's office with petitions for Mehmet Raif Efendi, the mufti's scribe for thirty years, claiming a popular vote decided the nomination. But the Porte denied this. The idea of a 'democratic' vote possibly arose from the Orthodox electing their archbishop.[268]

Like his predecessor, Ali Rifki defended the Sultan and like Sophronios he wanted local structures and multiculturalism preserved. By the 1890s, classes for the Muslim junior high school were conducted in a house and numbers were falling. Ali Rifki, with Sendall's support, built a senior high school, allowing Muslims to study in Cyprus instead of abroad, where many remained.[269] The curriculum followed the Hamidian model, which aimed to produce obedience to the Government; but it also adapted to local needs, with Greek mandatory.[270]

Cyprus' proximity to Anatolia made it ideal for dissidents to publish newspapers for the mainland. First, there were the Young Ottomans; a political and intellectual group formed in the 1860s against what they perceived was the Porte's pernicious policies and drift away from Islam – the key, in their view, to modernisation.[271] In 1879, a Young Ottoman Armenian, Aleksan Sarrafian, published *Umid* (Hope), the first Ottoman language newspaper in Cyprus, which criticised the Sultan for selling the island, because it had been Ottoman from time immemorial. *Umid* was banned after Abdul Hamid protested,[272] but Young Ottoman ideas lingered and became informed by the ideas of the Young Turks, who fled to Cyprus in the 1890s.[273] The British disliked Cyprus being used as a base to distribute anti-Hamidian newspapers and rejected applications to open newspaper houses to such individuals.[274] Yet, Young Turks established branches of the Committee of Union and Progress in Nicosia and Larnaca.[275]

These ideas challenged the existing structures. Members of the Ottoman Reading House (*Kiraanthane-i Osmani*) helped Tuccarbashi Hadji Dervish establish *Zaman* (Time) in December 1891, which the Ministry of the Interior in Constantinople funded. In 1894, Dervish became Dervish Pasha. But after 1895 he employed writers critical of the Sultan and the Cyprus government. In March 1893 Küfizade Mustafa Asaf Bey founded *Kipris*, which after supporting Abdul Hamid also switched to represent Young Turk views.[276]

In 1897 Mehmed Sadik, the *Evkaf* delegate, allowed Ali Rifki to conduct summer mid-day prayers on the veranda of St Sophia mosque and both earned the wrath of Dervish and the Cadi, Vehid Effendi, who thought it was sacrilegious. Within three years their supporters could not attend mosque together. Vehid and Dervish emulated Papadopoulos in creating a fanatical power base to overturn the pro-British elite. Like Katalanos in *Evagoras* and *Kypriakos Phylax*,[277] Dervish used *Zaman* for hyperbole. He and his friends went through villages discussing issues, spreading rumours and obtaining signatures on petitions that protested against the new school's perceived secular curriculum and the administration of the *Evkaf*. For the first time, Cypriot Muslims were mobilised politically.[278]

The Muslim elite did not shirk from the fight. In 1901 the *ulema* wrote a *mazbata* (official report) to Abdul Hamid accusing Dervish of anti-Hamidian activity and associating with Papadopoulos, even campaigning for him in the Karpass and participating in an anti-government demonstration that almost led to a riot. Both Papadopoulos and Dervish were challenging the political, social and cultural structures of Cypriot society.[279]

By 1907, however, the cry for *énosis* was inciting Cypriot Muslims against the Orthodox and Muslims they perceived were ignoring it. Mehmet Shefket and Mehmet Ziai, a hodja, visited Constantinople to ask for the removal of the Cadi, Osman Nuri Efendi, because he did not act against *énosis*. In June, Mehmet Ferid Pasha, the Grand Vizier, told Harry Lamb, the dragoman at the British embassy, that a Greek teacher (Katalanos)[280] spoke in favour of massacring the Muslims. Nicholas O'Conor, the British ambassador to the Porte, asked Sir Edward Grey, the Foreign Secretary, to protect them.[281] King-Harman then sent a memorial from the Muslim legislature members protesting that *énosis* agitation offended them and wanted measures to preserve peace, but King-Harman did not recommend the petition because Shefket and Ziai led a faction against the Cadi who he claimed was loyal to the administration.[282]

Churchill's visit

In June 1907 Elgin informed King-Harman that Winston Churchill, the under-secretary at the Colonial Office, would visit Cyprus in October.[283] During the Boer War, Churchill had reported for the *Morning Post* and won fame for his role in rescuing an ambushed train and for escaping a Boer prison. He became a Conservative MP, but joined the Liberals in May 1904 because of his rift with Chamberlain on protective tariffs.[284] He soon earned a reputation for radicalism.

On 9 October 1907, Churchill landed at Famagusta for a four-day visit on his way to British East Africa. He was the highest government member to visit since Smith and Stanley. King-Harman was pleased, but told John Clauson, who became the Chief Secretary in

1906, that 'there was no occasion for any decoration'.[285] When Churchill arrived, he found the wharf and streets at Famagusta filled with Greece's colours and the shouts for *énosis* nearly deafened him.[286] King-Harman informed Elgin that

> Greek flags were manufactured by the thousand; school children were organised and drilled to wave the national standard effectively; addresses were prepared in which Mr Churchill's visit to Cyprus was likened to the arrival of Mr. Gladstone in the Ionian Islands and in which he was fervently exhorted to . . . restore Cyprus to her Mother Greece.[287]

This prompted Churchill to cancel all political deputations until his second last day.[288]

Abdul Hamid Bey, a rich tobacco manufacturer[289] and the sole Muslim member of the legislature with the others in Constantinople told Churchill that the Muslims resented the cries of *énosis*.[290] Churchill replied that he had 'not discerned . . . any attack on the honour or dignity' of the Muslims or the British and the cry reflected 'Greek' anxiety, and he could not censure them for expressing their democratic prerogative.[291]

Then Papadopoulos read the Greek memorial.[292] It began with the old myth: that Gladstone had ceded the Ionian Islands to Greece; Churchill, it asserted, should do likewise with Cyprus.[293] The Muslim minority, Papadopoulos asserted, had no right to deny 'national liberation' to the majority. He considered British rule transitory and called for legislature and judicial control.[294] Papadopoulos added that British economic policy had failed and the £1,781,942 in tribute taken would have made Cyprus 'a paradise of the East as promised'.[295] If there was no tribute, Cyprus could have funded the recent projects; instead there was an annual burden of paying interest of £13,000.[296]

Cypriot socio-economic problems would thus be solved in the life after *énosis*. The shared Cypriot economic grievances could not be incorporated into a common Cypriot response because Hellenisation subordinated Orthodox responses to *énosis*.[297]

Churchill expressed joy at the Greek political development, but dismissed changing the constitution to give them more power because the Muslims and British would be shut out. Churchill recognised that it was

> only natural that the Cypriot people, who are of Greek descent, should regard their incorporation with what may be called their mother-country as an ideal to be earnestly, devoutly, and fervently cherished.[298]

Churchill knew that these aspirations were identical to Cretan aspirations and that London did not want to diminish Ottoman sovereignty:

the opinion held by the Moslem population . . . that the British occupation . . . should not lead to the dismemberment of the Ottoman Empire, and that the mission of Great Britain in the Levant should not be to impair the sovereignty of the Sultan, is one which His Majesty's Government are equally bound to regard with respect.[299]

His subtle reply accorded with prior rejections and with policy on Crete.[300]

Before leaving Cyprus, Churchill telegraphed Elgin that it was 'terribly starved by [the] Treasury and bears deep mark[s] in moral and material conditions'.[301] He later wrote a memorandum calling on London to improve Cypriot living standards. It was often recirculated[302] and he worked to remove the tribute, succeeding with Sir Ronald Storrs in 1927.[303] In 1907 he was scathing:

> There is scarcely any spectacle more detestable than the oppression of a small community by a great Power for the purpose of pecuniary profit; and that is . . . the spectacle which our financial treatment of Cyprus . . . indisputably presents. It is . . . unworthy of Great Britain, and altogether out of accordance with the whole principles of our colonial policy in every part of the world, to exact tribute by force from any of the possessions or territories administered under the Crown.[304]

Churchill transferred the Liberal focus on socio-economic inequalities at home to the colonial sphere.[305] He rejected returning Cyprus to Ottoman rule or giving it to Greece, but thought the Greeks were justifiably dissatisfied with British rule and this propelled *énosis*. The Muslims protested because they knew it would ruin them. The solution was to implement successful social and economic structures.

The Colonial Office and the Treasury ridiculed Churchill. Elgin was told that Asquith, the Chancellor of the Exchequer, and other officials in his department were 'vastly amused at the Cyprus memorandum'.[306] Sir George Murray, a Treasury official, called it 'insane'.[307] Churchill had challenged the Treasury's control of Cyprus.

The Greek memorial, Churchill's reply and King-Harman's report were published in Command Paper 3996, causing problems for King-Harman.[308] On 8 May 1908 he complained to Elgin's successor, Lord Crewe, that confidential despatches should not be published verbatim, because he was now compromised with the *Kyreniakí*.[309]

In fact he had achieved that alone. On 3 March, Patriarch Ioakim declared Vasilliou the archbishop, but King-Harman and Papadopoulos objected. The next day *Kitiakí* attacked *Kyreniakí* in Nicosia. King-Harman had the *zaptieh* occupy the archiepiscopal palace and called out the Yorkshire regiment from Polymedia, but a battle was still fought on the night of 9 April, forcing him to proclaim martial law.[310] On 6 May he rushed through the legislature the 'Archiepiscopal Election Law' with the votes of the British and the eight *Kitiakí*. On 11 May the Kyrenia club, *Kypriakos Syllogos*, passed a resolution condemning him for his cynical treatment of *énosis*. King-Harman had implied that *énosis* was non-existent in Kyrenia. *Énosis* had gone full circle: the *Kyreniakí* could not afford the tag of 'traitor'. King-Harman sent the resolution to Crewe,[311] who expressed regret, but 'recognise[d] the reality of the sentiment entertained by the Greek population of Cyprus towards the kingdom of Greece' and did not regard his 'observations as to the genesis of the popular demonstrations . . . as being an insult to Cyprus'.[312]

The crisis of 1912

In April 1909 Papadopoulos was elected archbishop unopposed after the *Kyreniakí* refused to partake in the elections, and in 1910 they accepted the result.[313] King-Harman was relieved,[314] but the Colonial Office was subdued at the prospect of a firebrand ruling the church.[315] It was a justified worry. (Although he was in debt and claimed to be penniless, nearly £5,000 was found hidden in his bedroom on his death in 1916.)[316] The Hellenist triumph in 1910 subordinated the Orthodox to a nationalist political discourse.[317]

The Greek Cypriot leaders united behind an old grievance – the tribute. In 1909, when King-Harman wanted the grant-in-aid fixed at £50,000 for another three years and the Colonial Office sought Treasury approval, the latter argued that since 1906 Cyprus had enjoyed 'remarkable prosperity' and £40,000 was enough.[318] Crewe frankly told the Treasury that it was not. There was now a Cypriot generation unfamiliar with Ottoman rule that saw Ottoman territories become autonomous without having to pay a tribute. Even a fixed grant, Crewe feared, would 'prove insufficient' to outweigh the discontent propelling *énosis* and wanted a £50,000 grant over three years.[319] The Treasury, however, argued that political reasons were not grounds for removing the tribute 'at the expense of the British taxpayer'.[320] On 7 March 1910, the Treasury fixed the grant at £40,000 for 1910–11, but would consider representations for 1911–12.[321]

King-Harman fought back. On 29 March he told the elected members who passed a resolution imploring for reconsideration. He told Crewe that after three years of growth, the tribute was 'more firmly . . . placed upon the shoulders of the people' and that the Orthodox members spoke 'with the deep sense of the great responsibility laid upon them . . . [and] in my concern for the welfare of Cyprus I am bound to be in full sympathy with them'.[322] He warned that the resolution's rejection would produce a constitutional crisis and revive anti-British rhetoric. He predicted that the Greek members would resign or induce a Muslim to absent himself, because they were 'quite unreliable supporters of the Government'.[323] The Colonial Office acted. In May the Treasury called for John Clauson.

Nevertheless, Crewe accused King-Harman of interrupting a speech to prevent an argument between a Christian and a Muslim so the debate could continue 'harmoniously in opposition to the views of His Majesty's Government'. He blamed him for leading the locals to believe that it had been decided to revert to a casual subsidy and censured him for asking the officials to retire so the resolution could pass.[324] King-Harman was stunned. He recognised his duty to fulfil orders, but was bound to identify 'with all matters tending . . . to the welfare and progress of the people' entrusted to him. If he had forced the officials to veto the resolution, he thought the 'consequences would have been so serious' as to necessitate London's intervention in the constitution.[325]

Although the Treasury back-tracked,[326] the Hellenists, such as Theodotou, whom Fiddian called a 'lying Greek',[327] attacked the British. King-Harman's conciliatory approach had failed, so he recommended banning foreigners and ecclesiastics from election to the legislature.[328] Although it was long-standing policy to ban ecclesiastics from any representative body in Malta,[329] the Colonial Office wavered. W.D. Ellis, a clerk dealing with Cyprus since 1908, opined that the government 'machine has worked somehow for 30 years . . . [but] now threatens to break down', yet suggested no remedy.[330]

At this crucial moment Sir Hamilton Goold-Adams succeeded King-Harman. His military service in Bechuanaland (1884–85) against the Matabele (1893), and in the Boer War, appeared to make him a strong choice. Goold-Adams had returned to Bechuanaland as civil commissioner and was the governor of the Orange River Colony (1901–10), but was an authoritarian and unfamiliar with Near East affairs. He was also staunchly pro-Turkish, as his prognosis of a fall-out over the Italo-Ottoman War showed: 'the Turks will give in to Italy and then take it out of Greece and . . . the result will be disturbances between the Greeks and Turks in Cyprus.'[331] Ellis retorted: 'there is no acute antagonism between Greeks and Turks in Cyprus.'[332] Lewis Harcourt, Crewe's successor, opined that Goold-Adams had to 'to try to keep the peace' and if he failed London could only send a warship.[333] The choice was hard to fathom because Arthur Young, who had served for over twenty years in Cyprus, was made governor of the Straits Settlement at the same time.[334]

Goold-Adams's tenure further strained British relations with the Greek leaders. When they told him that they would postpone demands for *énosis* to fight for constitutional reform,[335] he drafted a rejoinder for Harcourt,[336] but before he replied Goold-Adams sent it to Paschales Constantinides. Goold-Adams claimed that the Cyprus Convention barred proportional representation and locals having a say in finances and the judiciary.[337] This was wrong, and his brusque dismissal of *énosis* provoked reaction. Goold-Adams only informed Harcourt of the letter after the Greek leaders replied angrily, who correctly observed that London chose the mode of administration and warned against taking *énosis* for granted.[338] Goold-Adams told Harcourt that the move-ment did 'not merit much attention', but he was giving it plenty. He insisted that if proportional representation were granted the official members should be increased to avoid the government being outvoted.[339] Harcourt agreed.[340] The Orthodox members resigned from the legisla-ture on 17 April,[341] citing that the outright rejection of their proposals showed 'contempt for the people'.[342] Goold-Adams was unfazed, com-plaining of the rudeness of the Greek members for not attending the dinner preceding the legislature's opening, or the 'at homes' given by his wife. He told Harcourt that before touring the Karpass he asked deputations to 'eliminate from their addresses matters of a political nature, and to avoid . . . political flags and emblems'.[343] The Greek leaders ordered that they ignored and Goold-Adams found Greek flags and demands for *énosis* at villages where he was expected, but not elsewhere.[344]

But Goold-Adams had given a false impression to Harcourt for the Greek walk-out. The order, issued by his private secretary, Harry Lukach (later Harry Luke), threatened:

> in case political matters are inclined, or political flags and emblems displayed, tending to give political importance to such addresses or peti-tions, His Excellency will refuse to consider any portion of the subject matter brought before him.[345]

This was blackmail. Also, Goold-Adams did not tell Harcourt that it was published on Orthodox Good Friday (23 March in the Old Calendar). Two days later was Greek Independence Day and the Annunciation of the Virgin Mary, a major Orthodox feast-day, but in 1912 it was also Easter, thus increasing sensitivities. Greek leaders blamed Goold-Adams's conduct in the Karpass, especially his refusal to visit the semi-towns Trikomo, Gialousa and Rizokarpasso for their action.[346] Goold-Adams was set on provoking them. Charles Orr, his chief secretary, wrote to a friend on 8 April that

> Little Cyprus is a centralised nest of bureaucracy, everything conveys on to my office table and I select a small portion to send up to the High Commissioner (Sir Hamilton hates pettifogging details) . . .[347]

Goold-Adams focused on provoking the Hellenists, not on improving living standards.

On 28 April a central committee formed under Kyrillos to agitate for *énosis* and constitutional reform. A month later it petitioned Harcourt for a royal commission to revise the constitution.[348] Goold-Adams reacted swiftly. On 2 May he asked Kitchener, now Consul-General at Cairo, if Egypt could provide customs and treasury clerks if Cypriots resigned. He then told General John Maxwell, the Commander-in-Chief in Egypt, that the Greeks were whinging over his 'Czar-like' actions and requested khaki clothes and Martini-Enfield-Carbines so he could strengthen the *zaptieh*. He presumed that the Egyptian authorities would sympathise with his 'efforts to sit on the Cypriot Greeks'.[349]

On 24 May there were bloody inter-communal clashes. Muslims from Mandres, near Nicosia, attacked students and teachers of the Pancyprian Gymnasium because they were singing anti-Muslim songs while returning from the Monastery of St John Chrysostom.[350] Two days later, Greeks demonstrated in Nicosia on the day they celebrate Noah and the Deluge,[351] and on 27 May at Limassol they incited Muslims over Italian successes against Ottoman forces. The company at Polymedia intervened after a Muslim stabbed two Greeks and a Muslim died in a brawl, while the troops shot dead two Greeks. Altogether, 150 were injured.[352] Goold-Adams requested troops from Egypt and London obliged.[353]

Harcourt rejected calls for a royal commission,[354] relying on two reports by John Bucknill, the Cyprus government's King's Advocate from June 1907.[355] He argued that the Greeks aimed at achieving *énosis* and it was 'useless to hope' for their cooperation or to wean them from their 'Greek-speaking co-religionists'. Cyprus had 'no independent future', he added, and concessions should be made to the Greeks until it was ceded to Greece.[356] After meeting Greek leaders in London in August,[357] Harcourt told Goold-Adams that he could grant proportional representation and allow them to examine the estimates.[358]

Conclusion

This chapter has upturned the received wisdom that all the Cypriot Eastern Orthodox Christians were as one in identifying with Greece and the Greek nation and that they welcomed the British in 1878 with demands to join Greece. Far from this, the majority of Cypriot Orthodox Christians identified themselves as Eastern Orthodox Christians of Cyprus and welcomed the British, not as saviours from tyrannical and oppressive Turkish rulers, but as Europeans who would continue the peaceful multicultural realities of Ottoman Cyprus, but under terms of equality before the law for Christians and Muslims. The traditional leaders of the Cypriot Orthodox Christians wanted the British to co-opt them into the governing structures, as the Ottomans had. But despite this favourable space, the British faced a nationalist and inter-communal crisis by 1912. This was because they had applied political modernity to Cyprus. The Conservatives had been right about the Christian and Muslim inhabitants living harmoniously. The absence of an 'ethnic' identity had resulted in social and cultural integration during the Ottoman period. Also, the British practised co-option in almost all other parts of their empire. But most of the Empire was nowhere near Europe. They rejected applying co-option in Cyprus because, as with the failure of the Cyprus Society's paternalistic agenda, the British decision-makers in London and more generally the elite, situated Cyprus within the unitary ideal of modern Greece. They considered that the Cypriot Orthodox Christians shared the same repertoire of Hellenic myths as themselves, hence the interest in archaeology, even though the majority of Cypriot Orthodox Christians did not feel this way. So when the British applied modernist principles – civil and secular institutions and ethnic and racial identification – the existing structures collapsed. The new modernist structures created the space for Hellenic nationalists to spread the topological dream of Hellenism. Since the British decision-makers saw Cyprus through preconceived Grecian filters, they accepted the introduction of the Hellenist agenda in the island because it was perceived as belonging to modern Greece. Hellenic nationalism, propelled by the failure of British social and economic policies, upturned the multicultural system and challenged the viability of British rule.

Notes

1 Kostas Kyrris, *Peaceful Co-existence in Cyprus under British Rule (1878–1959) and after Independence*, Nicosia, 1977; Paschalis Kitromilides, 'From Coexistence to Confrontation: The Dynamics of Ethnic Conflict in Cyprus', in Michael Attalides (ed.), *Cyprus Reviewed*, Nicosia, 1977, 35–70; A.C. Gazioglu, *The Turks of Cyprus*, London, 1990, 250–69; Niyazi Kizilyurek, 'From Traditionalism to Nationalism and Beyond', *Cyprus Review (CR–2)*, V, 2, 1993, 58–67.

2 Adamantia Pollis, 'International Factors and the Failure of Political Integration in Cyprus', in Stephanie Neuman (ed.), *Small States and Segmented Societies*, New York, 1976, 50.

3 Nicholas Coureas, 'The Cypriot Reaction to the Establishment of the Latin Church: Resistance and Collaboration', *Sources Travaux Historiques*, XXXXIII–IV, 1995, 75–84.

4 Costas P. Kyrris, 'The Role of Greeks in the Ottoman Administration of Cyprus', *Proceedings of the First International Conference on Cypriot Studies (ICCS–1)*, III, A, 1973, 149–79.

 5 D. Margarites, *Περί Κύπρου Διατριβή*, Athens, 1849, 32–4; J. Hackett, *A History of the Orthodox Church of Cyprus*, London 1901; K. Kyrris, 'The Role of Greeks in the Ottoman Administration of Cyprus', *ICCS–1*, III, A, 1973, 149–79; Karpat, *An Inquiry into the Social Foundations of the Ottoman State*, 31–40.
 6 Hill, *A History of Cyprus*, 80–110, 157–66, 355–8; P.M. Kitromilides, 'Repression and Protest in Traditional Society: Cyprus 1764', *Kypriakai Spoudai (KS)*, 1984, 91–101.
 7 R. Clogg, 'Anti-clericalism in Pre-independence Greece', in Derek Baker (ed.), *The Orthodox Churches and the West*, Oxford, 1976.
 8 K. Kyrris, 'Symbiotic Elements in the History of the Two Communities of Cyprus', *Kypriakos Logos (KL)*, VII, 1976, 262.
 9 Turkish Cypriot nationalists also accept the 'attempt to overthrow Turkish rule'. Gazioglu, *The Turks of Cyprus*, 240–9.
10 Hill, *History of Cyprus*, 41–2.
11 R. Clogg, 'The Dhidaskalia Patriki (1798): An Orthodox Reaction to French Revolutionary Propaganda', *MES*, V, 2, 1969, 90.
12 Karpat, *An Inquiry into the Social Foundations of the Ottoman State*, 74.
13 Katsiaounis, *Labour, Society and Politics in Cyprus*, 12–13, 18–19.
14 A. Aimilliandis et al., *Μεγάλης Ελληνικής Εγκυκλοπαιδείας – Κύπρος*, Athens, c.1926.
15 Kyrris, 'Symbiotic Elements', 264.
16 F.N. Fokaidi, *Ο Ελληνισμός της Κύπρου*, Southern Rhodesia, 1962. A. Sophocleous, *Συμβολή στην Ιστορία του Κυπριακού Τύπου*, I, Nicosia, 1995, 253.
17 FO78/497, James Lilburn, Consul, to Lord Aberdeen, Foreign Secretary, 26 May 1842.
18 Ibid.
19 Gazioglu, *The Turks of Cyprus*, Appendix 6.
20 *Report by Consul Lang*, LX, London, 1872; Hill, *A History of Cyprus*, 250; Kyrris, *History of Cyprus*, 296.
21 M.H. Yavuz, 'The Evolution of Ethno-Nationalism in Cyprus under the Ottoman and British Systems', *CR–2*, III, 2, 1991, 57–79.
22 A. Aimilianides, «Η Εξέλιξει του Δίκαιου των Μικτών Γάμων εν Κύπρω», *KS*, II, 1938, 209; Kitromilides, 'From Coexistence to Confrontation', 37–8; P. Sant Cassia, 'Religion, Politics and Ethnicity in Cyprus During the Turkocratia (1571–1878)', *European Studies of Sociology (ESS)*, 1986, 3–28; K. Cicek, 'Living Together: Muslim-Christian Relations in Eighteenth-Century Cyprus as Reflected by the Sharia Court Records', *Islam and Christian-Muslim Relations*, IV, 1, 1993, 36–64.
23 R.C. Jennings, *Christians and Muslims in Ottoman Cyprus and the Mediterranean World, 1571–1640*, NY, 1992, 164.
24 Kitromilides, 'Repression and Protest in Traditional Society', 91–101.
25 Kyrris, *History of Cyprus*, 296.
26 J. Kakridis, 'The Ancient Greeks and the Greeks of the War of Independence', *Balkan Studies (BS)*, IV, 2, 1963, 251–64; V. Roudometof, 'From Rum Millet to Greek Nation: Enlightenment, Secularisation, and National Identity in Ottoman Balkan Society, 1453–1821', *Journal of Modern Greek Studies (JMGS)*, XVI, 1, 1998, 11–48.
27 Ross, *A Journey to Cyprus*, 52–3.
28 Katsiaounis, *Labour, Society and Politics in Cyprus*, 55; Meason, 'A Fortnight in Cyprus', 58.
29 Th. Papadopoullos, «Εθναρχικός Ρόλος της Ορθοδόξου Ιεραρχίας», *KS*, XXXV, 1971, 115.
30 *Biographical Lexicon of Cypriots (Koudounaris)(BLC)*, 362–3.
31 Katsiaounis, *Labour, Society and Politics in Cyprus*, 52, from Greek Foreign Ministry archives.
32 Th. Papadopoullos, *Δημώδη Κυπριακά Άσματα εξ Ανεκδότων Συλλογών του ΙΘ' Αιώνος*, Nicosia, 1975, 47–8, 63, 84–8, 150–9, 213–16, 217–19, 220–5, 239–41, 243–50.
33 Hill, *History of Cyprus*, 229–30, 250, 253.
34 Kyrris, 'Symbiotic Elements', 265.
35 Hill, *History of Cyprus*, 253; FO195/1213, Wadkins to Layard, 5 and 18 March and 29 April 1878.

36 N. Kizilyurek, 'The Turkish Cypriot Upper Class and Question of Identity', *Turkish Cypriot Identity in Literature*, London, 1990, 21.

37 *Cyprus. Translation of a Report Forwarded by Mr. Campbell, British Consul at Rhodes, upon the Island of Cyprus, for the Years 1854–8*, XXX, London, 1859.

38 Patrick, *Political Geography and the Cyprus Conflict*, 12.

39 C.M. Bowra, 'Homeric Words in Cyprus', *Journal of Hellenic Studies (JHS)*, LIV, 1934, 54–74; K. Hatziioannou, Περί των εν τη Μεσαιωνική και Νεωτέρα Κυπριακή Ξένων Γλωσσών Στοιχείων, Athens, 1936; R.M. Dawkins, *The Nature of the Cypriot Chronicle of Leontios Machaeras*, Oxford 1945; G. Horrocks, *Greek: A History of its Language and its Speakers*, London, 1997, 298–333; C. Giakoullis, Θησαυρός Κυπριακής Διαλέκτου, Nicosia, 2002; M. Yashin, 'Introducing Step-Mothertongue', *Step-Mothertongue*, 14–16.

40 D'Abernon Papers, British Library, 48928, 113–14, Cobham to D'Abernon, 4 January 1881. D'Abernon (Vincent) had been offered a student dragomanship at Constantinople.

41 Bryant, *Imagining the Modern*, 34, 276.

42 N. Kizilyurek and S. Gautier-Kizilyurek, 'The Politics of Identity in the Turkish Cypriot Community and the Language Question', *International Journal of Society and Language (IJSL)*, CLXVIII, 2004, 37–54.

43 CO883/4/5, 22a, Warren Memorandum, 25 August 1885.

44 Katsiaounis, *Labour, Society and Politics in Cyprus*, 25–8.

45 Orr, *Cyprus Under British Rule*, 160; Hill, *A History of Cyprus*, IV, 297.

46 K.M. Karamanos, Κύπρος, Athens, 1954, 68; P.G. Epeirotou, Η Μάχη της Κύπρου] *1878–1956*, Athens, 1956, 11; Papadopoullos, «Εθναρχικός Ρόλος της Ορθοδόξου Ιεραρχίας», 95–141; P.N. Vanezis, *Pragmatism v Idealism*, London, 1974, 1–4; Z. Stavrinides, *The Cyprus Conflict*, England 1976, 17–29; H.I. Salih, *The Impact of Diverse Nationalism on a State*, Tuscaloosa, 1978, 5; Georghallides, *A Political and Administrative History*, 39, 81–2; P. Oberling, *The Road to Bellapais*, New York, 1982, 9–21.

47 S. Papageorgiou, 'The Genesis of the Greek and Turkish Nationalism in Cyprus, 1878–1914', *CR-2*, IX, 1, 1997, 56–65; Panteli, *A History of Cyprus*, 57–9; K. Hadjidemetriou, *A History of Cyprus*, Nicosia, 2002, 336, 362–9; Leventis, *Cyprus*, 47–8; Mallinson, *Cyprus*, 10.

48 CO67/134, 42, Haynes Smith to Chamberlain, 28 March 1903, with Greek memorial.

49 *The Times*, 7 August 1878, 10a–b.

50 Glenbow Archives, Calgary, Canada, M1332, 'Nicosia Address, 1878'.

51 FO Correspondence, 4319, June–December 1879, Memorial (French) to Wolseley, 16 February 1879.

52 Sinclair, *Camp and Society*, 143–4.

53 Cannadine, *Ornamentalism*, 58–64; J.M. Gullick, *Malaya*, London, 1964, 38–40; Gallant, *Experiencing Dominion*, 77–8, 92–3.

54 Gallant, *Experiencing Dominion*, 178, 185, 188, 196, 207.

55 FO421/32, Salisbury to Biddulph, 4 July 1879.

56 Kizilyurek, 'The Turkish Cypriot Upper Class and Question of Identity', 22.

57 G.S. Georghallides, 'British Rule in Cyprus, 1878–1960: A Short Re-appraisal', *Pacific Quarterly*, IV, 2, 1979, 153; H. Faustmann, 'Clientelism in the Greek Cypriot Community of Cyprus Under British Rule', *CR-2*, X, 2, 1998, 43; H. Faustmann, 'Conflicting Nationalisms During British Rule in Pre-1974 Cyprus', in R. Stupperich (ed.), *Nova Graeca*, Mannheim, 2004, 205–6.

58 R. Coughlan and W. Mallinson, 'Énosis, Socio-Cultural Imperialism and Strategy: Difficult Bedfellows', *MES*, XXXXI, 4, 2005, 575, 580.

59 M. Herzfeld, *Anthropology Through the Looking-Glass*, Cambridge, 1987, 28–30.

60 *The Graphic*, 10 August 1878.

61 Salisbury to Smith, 21 October, Viscount Chilston, *W.H. Smith*, London, 1965, 127.

62 Gladstone, 'England's Mission', 568–9.

63 *The Times*, 25 March 1880, 7f.

64 Lang, *Cyprus*, 204.

65 Hussein Sed Alatas, *The Myth of the Lazy Native*, London, 1977.
66 Lang, *Cyprus*, 203.
67 Scott-Stevenson, *Our Home in Cyprus*, 300.
68 Gallant, *Experiencing Dominion*, 178.
69 Butler, *Far Out*, 328.
70 John Thomson, *Through Cyprus with the Camera in the Autumn of 1878*, London 1879 (Trigraph, London, 1985), 16.
71 Mike Hadjimike, 'Revisiting Thomson – The Colonial Eye and Cyprus', *Britain in Cyprus*, 61–78.
72 Reginald Stuart Poole, 'Cyprus: Its Present and Future', *CR–1*, August 1878, 137–54, 146; Donald Malcolm Reid, *Whose Pharaohs? Archaeology, Museums, and Egyptian National Identity from Napoleon to World War I*, Berkeley, 2002, 178.
73 M. Given, 'Inventing the Eteo-Cypriots', *Journal of Mediterranean Archaeology (JMA)*, XI, 1, 1998, 3–29.
74 Anderson, *Imagined Communities*, 6.
75 Gourgouris, *Dream Nation*, 16, 28.
76 Ibid., 49, 90–112; Herzfeld, *Ours Once More*, 40; V. Calotychos, '(Pre)occupied Spaces: Hyphens, Apostrophes, and Over-sites in the Literary Imagining of Cyprus', *Step-Mothertongue*, 51.
77 *Le Telegraphe*, Athens, 'Foreign Views of our Occupation of Cyprus', *Littell's Living Age*, 1878, 575.
78 *Correspondence respecting the Cyprus Ordinance 'Regarding the Sale of Land to Subjects of Foreign Countries'*, confidential, 4077, February 1880, 41, Consul (Corfu) Sir. C. Sebright to Salisbury, 27 August 1878, with, most confidential, vice-consul Onorfio to Sebright, 14 August 1878; 46, private and confidential, Sebright to Salisbury, 3 October 1878; 552, Edwin Corbett, Athens, to Salisbury, 12 December 1878.
79 Hill, *A History of Cyprus*, IV, 497, footnote 1.
80 FO421/32, 37, secret, Salisbury to Biddulph, 4 July 1879.
81 CO67/18/1274, Biddulph Memorandum, undated.
82 Luke, *Cyprus under the Turks*, 8–9; A. Koudounaris, «Η Κάθοδος των Επτανησίων εις Κύπρο» *ICCS-2*, III, A, Nicosia, 1987, 89–98; Kyrris, *History of Cyprus*, 319–20; Gallant, *Experiencing Dominion*, 5–6; Bryant, *Imagining the Modern*, 33, 276.
83 Karpat, *An Inquiry into the Social Foundations of the Ottoman State*, 113–14.
84 *BLC*, 64. The Ottomans beheaded their grandfather in 1821.
85 Katsiaounis, *Labour, Society and Politics in Cyprus*, 27–8.
86 C.2324, Wolseley to Salisbury, 11 April 1879, 16.
87 P. Persianis, *Church and State in Cyprus' Education*, Nicosia 1978, 47.
88 A. Pollis, 'Intergroup Conflict and British Colonial Policy: The Case of Cyprus', *Comparative Politics (CP)*, 1973, 575–99.
89 Kyrris, *History of Cyprus*, 303; see the following entries in *BLC*: Euripides Antoniadis, Eleni Antoniadou, Stilianos Apostolides, Philip Bardas, Geronimo Barlaam, Evthemia Eustratiou, Andreas Themistocleous, Christodoulos Ioannides, Nicholas Lanitis, Polixeni Loizias (or Loiziados), Pericles Michaelides, Demetrios Nikolaides, Sophocles Pavlides, Corinna Sountia, Ephrosene Tarsis, 28–30, 39–40, 86, 99, 120, 169, 177, 190, 233–4, 254, 296, 348, 365.
90 *BLC*, 196.
91 G. Loukas, *Φιλολογικαί Επισκέψεις των εν τω βίω των Νεωτέρων Κυπρίων Μνημείων των Αρχαίων*, Athens, 1874.
92 Vizetelly, *From Cyprus to Zanzibar*, 14–15; M. Gialouraki, *Η Αίγυπτος των Ελλήνων*, Athens, 1967, 310; Sophocleous, *Συμβολή στην Ιστορία του Κυπριακού Τύπου*, I, 11; *BLC*, 170, 274.
93 CO67/5, Biddulph to Salisbury, 28 July 1879, enclosures, including court extracts, statements and letters.
94 M. Herzfeld, 'Hellenism and Occidentalism', in J.G. Carrier (ed.), *Occidentalism*, Oxford, 1995, 220.

95 Harry Luke, *Malta: An Account and an Appreciation*, London, 1967, 122; J. Aquilina, *Papers in Maltese Linguistics*, Valletta, 1970, 180.
96 Bryant, *Imagining the Modern*, 33–7, 45.
97 C.2930, Biddulph to Granville, 27 July 1880, with Spencer report, 16 July 1880; Biddulph to Kimberley, 21 December 1880; Biddulph to Kimberley, 28 January 1881; Biddulph to Kimberley, 17 February 1881, with, Spencer to Warren, undated; Cobham to Warren, 26 January 1881; Biddulph to Kimberley, 1 April 1881, with, Spencer to Warren, undated.
98 Gallant, *Experiencing Dominion*, 178.
99 C.2930, Kimberley to Biddulph, 10 June 1881.
100 Frederick Madden and David Fieldhouse (eds), *The Dependent Empire and Ireland, 1840–1900*, New York, 1991, 315.
101 Κ. Amantos, *Σύντομος Ιστορία της Κύπρου*, Athens, 1956, 121, 128.
102 *The Times*, 24 August 1881, 5d.
103 Nikolaos Klitos Lanitis, *Ο Ακρίτας του Ελληνικού Νότου*, Athens, 1945, 38.
104 *The Times*, 8 October 1881, 5.f; 20 October 1881, 10.c; Donne Journal, 6 October 1880.
105 *The Times*, 20 October 1881, 10.c.
106 Ibid., 21 October 1881, 7c–d.
107 CO67/20/16207, minute, Kimberley, 19 September 1881.
108 Th. Papadopoullos, *Κώδιξ Σχολείων Λευκωσίας*, Nicosia, 1991, 157. My translation.
109 P.K. Peristianis, *Church and State in Cyprus Education*, Nicosia, 1978, 158–9.
110 Spencer quoted, Bryant, *Imagining the Modern*, 125.
111 Katsiaounis, *Labour, Society and Politics in Cyprus*, 94–5.
112 Ioannis Economides, a Cypriot, worked for *Clio*. His family left Cyprus after the 1821 massacres, *BLC*, 267.
113 C.2930, Biddulph to Kimberley, telegraphic, 12 May 1881, 105; Biddulph to Kimberley, 14 April, 113.
114 CO537/23/6650, confidential, Biddulph to Kimberley, 12 April 1881. Many Liberals belonged to the Reform Club, including Dilke, William Harcourt and Bernhard Samuelson.
115 Gladstone papers 44226, *Syllogue Chypriote*, Nicosia, 9 April 1881; Le President (Pavlos) Valsamaki, Larnaca, 9 April 1881; inhabitants of Limassol, 10 April 1881; Biddulph to Kimberley, telegraphic, 12 May 1881, C.2930, 105; Kimberley to Biddulph, telegraphic, 13 April 1881, C.2930, 105; *The Times*, 15 April 1881, 3.e.
116 *BLC*, 38; Gallant, *Experiencing Dominion*, 78, 91–2.
117 CO67/17/17819, 450, Biddulph to Granville, 30 October 1880; Kypros Chrysanthis, «Σωματεία και Οργανώσεις της Κύπρου από το 1878–1955» *Kypriaka 1878–1955*, Nicosia, 1986, 274; *BLC*, 222–3.
118 C.2930, Gladstone to Biddulph, 19 April 1881, 105.
119 Gladstone papers, MS ADD 44544, 155, Gladstone to Kimberley, 14 April 1881.
120 Ibid., 93, 44226, Kimberley to Gladstone, 16 April 1881.
121 Ibid., 44227, Granville to Gladstone, 25 October 1881.
122 D.K. Fieldhouse, 'Sir Arthur Gordon and the Parihaka Crisis 1880–1882', *Historical Studies Australia and New Zealand (HSANZ)*, X, 37, 1961, 34.
123 Gladstone papers, MS ADD 44227, Granville to Gladstone, 25 October 1881.
124 Ibid., 44321, Gordon to Gladstone, 26 August 1878; M. Francis, 'Gordon, Arthur Charles Hamilton, first Baron Stanmore (1829–1912)', *ODNB* (www.oxforddnb.com/view/article/33459, accessed 22 Feb 2005).
125 Cannadine, *Ornamentalism*, 59.
126 Gladstone papers, 44227, Granville to Gladstone, 25 October 1881.
127 Madden and Fieldhouse, *The Dependent Empire and Ireland*, 129, 692.
128 C.3211, Kimberley to Biddulph, 10 March 1882; C.4264, 1881 Census; *The Times*, 6 April 1882, 4.a.
129 Anagnostopoulou, *The Passage from the Ottoman Empire to the Nation-States*, 183–4.
130 *The Times*, 27 March 1882, 5.e.

131 C.3384, Sophronios to CO, 23 March 1882; Kimberley to Biddulph, 29 March 1882, 84.

132 Madden and Fieldhouse, *The Dependent Empire and Ireland*, 303, 306.

133 M. Attalides, 'Forms of Peasant Incorporation in Cyprus during the Last Century', in E. Gellner and J. Waterbury (eds), *Patrons and Clients in Mediterranean Societies*, London, 1977, 137–55; P. Servas, *Κυπριακό: Ευθήνες*, Athens, 1980, 68–9; R. Katsiaounis, «Εκλέγειν και Εκλεγέσθαι στις Πρώτες Βουλευτικές Εκλογές της Αγγλοκρατίας το 1883» *Epeteris*, XX, 1994, 309–45; Faustmann, 'Clientelism in the Greek Cypriot Community of Cyprus Under British Rule', 41–77.

134 *The Times*, 27 March 1882, 5.e; ibid., 28 March 1882, 5.e.

135 Biddulph to Kimberley, 10 April 1882, C.3384, 99–100; C.3384, Muslim Representatives to CO, 26 March 1882, 84, signed by Esseïd Ahmed Assim and Nakib-ul-Eshraf, Hadji Ahmed Raïf, and the 'Deputies', Mustafa Fuad, Mustafa Safvet, Esseïd Mehmed Raif, Baroutdji-Zadeh Hadji Ali, Husseïn Niazi, Ibrahim Zihni, Ali Rifki, Osman Enveri, and Vehid.

136 C.3384, Kimberley to Biddulph, 31 March 1882, 85; C.3211, Kimberley to Biddulph, 28 April 1882, 105.

137 CO67/35/15475, confidential, Biddulph to Derby, 29 August 1884; CO67/38/10499, confidential, Biddulph to Derby, 29 May 1885; ibid., confidential, Sophronios and Bishops to Wolseley, 5/17 March 1885.

138 CO67/41/2184, confidential, Biddulph to Stanley, 25 January 1886, with Sophronios' proposed bill.

139 P. Zannettos, *Ιστορία της Νήσου Κύπρου από την Αγγλική Κατοχή Μέχρι το 1911*, II, Larnaca, 1911, 375.

140 CO67/38/10499, confidential, Biddulph to Derby, 29 May 1885, with confidential, Sophronios, Chrysanthos and Neophytos to Biddulph, 5/17 March 1885.

141 *BLC*, 418.

142 CO67/41/2184, confidential, Biddulph to Stanley, 25 January 1886, with Sophronios' proposed bill.

143 CO67/43/19416, telegram, Bulwer to Stanhope, 7 December 1886.

144 CO67/43/19416, minute, Fairfield, 7 December 1886.

145 CO67/61/15276, 243, Bulwer to Knutsford, 18 July 1889; CO67/61/15233, confidential, Bulwer to Knutsford, 18 July 1889.

146 CO67/60/11489, confidential, Bulwer to Knutsford, 23 May 1889.

147 A. Hourani, 'Ottoman Reform and the Politics of Notables', in W. Polk and R. Chambers (eds), *Beginnings of Modernization in the Middle East*, Chicago, 1968, 46.

148 CO67/52/10499, 142, Bulwer to Knutsford, 15 May 1888; CO67/63/10849, D.S. Cramby to Knutsford, 22 May 1889; CO67/63/10849, D.S. Cramby to Knutsford, 26 June 1889. Gregory Demetriades, the director of the Imperial Ottoman Bank in Kyrenia, asked Cramby to represent Kyrenia because they had no political demands; CO67/52/11085, minute, Fairfield, 4 June 1888; CO67/52/11514, 166, Bulwer to Knutsford, 28 May 1888; CO67/53/13442, 212, Bulwer to Knutsford, 25 June 1888; CO67/54/18571, 253, Bulwer to Knutsford, 27 August 1888.

149 CO67/53/13442, 212, Bulwer to Knutsford, 25 June 1888.

150 CO67/59/9383, 123, Bulwer to Knutsford, 30 April 1889, enclosure, Sophronios, Peristiani, Constantinides to Bulwer, 24 April 1889, with Memorial to the Queen, 20 April 1889, unsigned.

151 CO67/61/14066, confidential, Bulwer to Knutsford, 1 July 1889, includes Sophronios memorandum.

152 *The Times*, 2 July 1888, 6.d; ibid., 4 September 1889, 13.e; ibid., 17 June 1878, 6d; *Hansard* (Commons), CCCXXIII, 8 March 1888, 569–70; CCCXXIV, 26 March 1888, 260–1; CCCXXX, 22 November 1888, 1811–12; CCCXXXI, 26 November 1888, 132–3; CCCXLI, 4 March 1890, 1767; CCCLI, 10 March 1891, 585–7; Report of the Council of the Cyprus Society presented at the Second Annual Meeting, at the Church House, 25th June 1890, London, 1890, Hereafter Cyprus Society Report II–1890.

153 Cyprus Society Report II–1890, 5–6.
154 S. Runciman, *The Great Church in Captivity*, Cambridge, 1968, 289–318; V.T. Istavridis, *Orthodoxy & Anglicanism*, London, 1966, 1–19; H.R. Trevor-Roper, *From Counter-Reformation to Glorious Revolution*, London, 1992, 63–111.
155 Istavridis, *Orthodoxy & Anglicanism*, 3.
156 M.D. Chapman, 'Benson, Edward White (1829–1896)', *ODNB* (www.oxforddnb.com/view/article/2139, accessed 1 April 2005).
157 Istavridis, *Orthodoxy & Anglicanism*, 3, 6–14, 146.
158 Tillyrides, 'Archbishop Sophronios III (1865–1900) and the British', *KS*, 1978, 137.
159 Sinclair, *Camp and Society*, 167–8.
160 Tillyrides, 'Archbishop Sophronios III', 138.
161 Ibid., 139–40; *The Times*, 25 June 1889, 5.e; *The Guardian*, 26 June 1889, 969.
162 *The Oxford* Review, 27 June 1889, 2; Duckworth, *Some Pages of Levantine History*, 25.
163 *The Guardian*, 3 July 1889, 102.
164 *The Times*, 21 August 1889, 8.a; Tillyrides, 'Archbishop Sophronios III', 136.
165 *The Times*, 11 December 1890, 9e.
166 SA1/1452/1893, William Sinclair, Archdeacon of London, to His Excellency the Governor of Cyprus, 5 May 1893.
167 Cyprus Society Report II–1890.
168 Florence Nightingale papers 45810, ff. 224, 233, Sarah Chapman Hand to Florence Nightingale, 29 June 1891.
169 SA1/3397/91, Kenyon to Bulwer, 15 September 1890.
170 Ibid.
171 Ibid.
172 SA1/3397/91, Bulwer to Kenyon, 23 December 1890.
173 SA1/3397/91, Kenyon to Bulwer, 21 January 1891.
174 Ibid.
175 SA1/3397/91, Kenyon to Bulwer, 25 May 1891.
176 SA1/3397/91, Kenyon to Bulwer, 17 September 1891. Newton's daughter ran a hospital at Zalta and was willing to come out and help.
177 SA1/3397/91, Fisher to Chief Secretary, 18 January 1892.
178 SA1/3397/91, Fisher to Chief Secretary, 18 January 1892; SA1/3397/91, minute, Bulwer, 17 March 1892.
179 SA1/3397/91, Fisher to Bulwer, 8 March 1892.
180 SA1/3397/91, Bulwer to Fisher, 23 March 1892.
181 See SA1/331/1896.
182 *The Times*, 23 August 1924, 6d.
183 Ibid., 14 July 1890, 9f.
184 SA1/16/1892, Spencer to Chief Secretary, 2 January 1892.
185 SA1/1452/1893, William Sinclair, Archdeacon of London, to His Excellency the Governor of Cyprus, 5 May 1893; SA1/1452/1893, Chief Secretary to Sinclair, 30 June 1893; SA1/1452/1893, G.A.K. Wisely to Chief Secretary, 29 December 1893.
186 Poole, 'Cyprus', *CR–1*, August 1878, 151; Lang, *Cyprus*, 331–2; R.S. Merrillees, 'T.B. Sandwith and the Beginnings of Cypriot Archaeology', in Veronica Tatton-Brown (ed.), *Cyprus in the 19th Century AD*, Oxford, 2001, 222–35.
187 Lang, *Cyprus*, 332.
188 M. Given, 'The Fight for the Past', Tatton-Brown, *Cyprus in the 19th Century AD*, 255–60.
189 Cohn, *Colonialism and its Forms of Knowledge*, 5.
190 Reid, *Whose Pharaohs?* 161–2.
191 *The Times*, 20 July 1888, 13f, 11 July 1889, 6d.
192 Gallant, *Experiencing Dominion*, 20–1.
193 *The Times*, 20 July 1888, 13f.
194 Ibid., 11 July 1889, 6d.
195 Ibid., 3 March 1888, 11f.
196 Ibid.

197 Ibid.
198 Ibid.
199 Ibid.
200 Cohn, *Colonialism and its Forms of Knowledge*, 79.
201 *The Times*, 2 April 1888, 4c.
202 Ibid., 20 July 1888, 13f.
203 Ibid., 24 September 1888, 4a.
204 D.G. Hogarth, *Devia Cypria*, Oxford, 1889.
205 C.6003, Knutsford to Bulwer, 22 March 1890.
206 CO67/58/2573, 16, Bulwer to Knutsford, 21 July 1889, with *Énosis* article.
207 *The Times*, 29 April 1897, 10d.
208 CO67/58/2573, minute, Fairfield, 6 February 1889.
209 CO67/58/2573, minute, Knutsford, 8 February 1889; 33, Knutsford to Bulwer, 9 February 1889.
210 CO67/71/22005, FO to CO, 11 November 1891.
211 CO67/71/22005, minute, Fairfield, 16 November 1891; CO67/71/22005, CO to FO, 20 November 1891.
212 Christoforos G. Toraritis, 'Freemasonry in Cyprus', *Builder Magazine*, XV, 7 July 1929.
213 S. Neilos, *Στα Παρασκήνια της Κυπριακής Μασονίας*, Athens, 1980, 45–63.
214 CO67/68/4593, confidential, Memorandum, Bulwer, 14 February 1891.
215 CO67/78/11399, confidential, Bulwer to Knutsford, 29 April 1892.
216 K. Kyrris, «Ἕνας Πολιτικός Λόγος του Λούκα Παϊσσίου», *Kypriaka Chronika*, 1964, 498–507.
217 CO67/52/11081, Young to Warren, 4 May 1888; CO67/51/6237; CO67/53/5834, Bulwer to Knutsford, 4 June 1888; Jan Asmussen, 'Life and Strife in Mixed Villages', *CR–2*, VIII, 1, 1996, 105.
218 CO67/78/11399, confidential, Bulwer to Knutsford, 29 April 1892.
219 CO67/61/15276, 243, Bulwer to Knutsford, 18 July 1889.
220 CO67/61/15233, confidential, Bulwer to Knutsford, 18 July 1889.
221 CO67/62/24263, 355, Hackett to Knutsford, 30 November 1889.
222 CO67/66/18021, minute, Fairfield, 1 October 1890.
223 T.G. Lekka, *Κύπρος: Η Κατεχομένη Ἑλλάς*, Athens, 1952, 32; Epeirotou, *Η Μάχη της Κύπρου 1878–1956*, 15.
224 See CO67/73/4383.
225 CO67/79/2436, confidential, Sendall to Ripon, 29 January 1893, with enclosures; confidential, Ripon to Sendall, 2 March.
226 Katsiaounis, *Labour, Society and Politics in Cyprus*, 188–9, 175–81, 241–3.
227 A. Lymbourides, *Η Κύπρος και ο Α' Παγκόσμιος Πόλεμος*, Nicosia 1999, 61; *BLC*, 170–1.
228 Eleni Antoniadou, 'The Theatre in Cyprus', *Five Short Essays on Cypriot Literature*, ed. Andreas Sophocleous, Nicosia, 1981, 55–63.
229 CO67/91/8534, 97, Sendall to Ripon, 6 May 1895, with memorial, 22 April 1895.
230 CO67/91/8547, 110, Sendall to Ripon, 7 May 1895, with memorials and signatures.
231 CO883/5/7, Fairfield to FO, 15 June 1895.
232 CO67/107/16141, 172, Sendall to Chamberlain, 15 July 1897, including enclosed petitions and signatures.
233 CO67/107/22899, 232, Sendall to Chamberlain, 14 October 1897, with Limassol petitions.
234 Ibid.
235 CO67/108/25593, 262, Sendall to Chamberlain, 14 November 1897, with Nicosia and Varosha petitions.
236 Ibid.
237 CO67/108/26678, 274, Sendall to Chamberlain, 3 December 1897, with Kyrenia petition.
238 CO67/104/4968, confidential, Sendall to Chamberlain, 26 February 1897; CO67/105/8190; CO67/106/12697, 127, Sendall to Chamberlain, 4 June 1897.

239 CO67/105/8189, confidential, Sendall to Chamberlain, 7 April 1897; P. Papapolyviou, *Φαεινόν Σημείον Άτυχους Πολέμου: Η Σημμετοχή της Κύπρου στον Ελληνοτουρκικό Πόλεμο του 1897*, Nicosia, 2001.
240 CO67/67/3958, 53, British Ambassador Athens to Salisbury, 21 February 1890; to CO, 1 March 1890.
241 SA1:1259/1896, confidential, Merton King, Nicosia's commissioner, to Young, 4 July 1896; CO67/100/14824, 168, Sendall to Chamberlain, 4 July 1896.
242 Th. Theodotou, *A Cyprian Appeal to the British People*, London, 1893.
243 CO67/110/8723, FO to CO, 26 April 1897; CO67/154/3705, confidential, King-Harman to Crewe, 19 January 1909; Toraritis, 'Freemasonry in Cyprus'; *BLC*, 267–8.
244 CO67/114/619, confidential, Haynes Smith to Chamberlain, 27 December 1898; also CO883/6/5, Mediterranean 57, 7432, 58, Haynes Smith to Chamberlain, 15 March 1899.
245 CO67/113, confidential, Haynes Smith to Chamberlain, 3 October 1898, with Sophronios memorandum.
246 CO67/117/6013, confidential, Haynes Smith to Chamberlain, 27 February 1899; confidential, Chamberlain to Haynes Smith, 5 May 1899.
247 CO67/119, confidential, Tankerville Chamberlain to Young, 7 June 1899.
248 Gallant, *Experiencing Dominion*, 200–1.
249 CO67/117/6013, confidential, Haynes Smith to Chamberlain, 27 February 1899.
250 Ibid., 82–7.
251 Volume 7/2, Census 6 April 1891, 31; Bryant, *Imagining the Modern*, 83.
252 Ibid., 89–90.
253 C.D. Cobham, 'The Archbishopric of Cyprus', *Church Quarterly Review*, LXVII, 1908, 121–33; J. Hackett, 'The Archiepiscopal Question in Cyprus's, *Irish Church Quarterly (ICQ)*, I, 1908, 320–39.
254 CO67/125/768, Members of the Holy Synod to Haynes Smith, 13 December 1900; 266, Haynes Smith to Chamberlain, 24 December 1900; confidential, Haynes Smith to Chamberlain, 24 December 1900.
255 CO67/125/768, confidential, Haynes Smith to Chamberlain, 24 December 1900.
256 CO67/127, confidential, Haynes Smith to Chamberlain, 6 March 1901.
257 CO883/6, 45019, Mediterranean 57, confidential, A.E. Kershaw to Young, 14 November 1901; Gallant, *Experiencing Dominion*, 189.
258 Ibid., confidential, Haynes Smith to Chamberlain, 28 November 1901.
259 CO67/128/45019, minute, Collins, 18 January 1902.
260 Ibid., Anderson, 21 January 1902.
261 Ibid., Bertram Cox, 22 January 1902; H. Frendo, 'Maltese Colonial Identity: Latin Mediterranean or British Empire?' in V. Mallia-Milanes (ed.), *The British Colonial Experience, 1800–1964: The Impact on Maltese Society*, Malta, 1988, 199–201.
262 CO67/128/45019, minute, Ommanney, 1 February 1902.
263 CO883/6, 45019, confidential, Chamberlain to Haynes Smith, 19 February 1902.
264 For the flags see www.crwflags.com/fotw/flags/cy_br.html
265 He had also married Biddulph's daughter in 1888.
266 Persianis, *Church and State in Cyprus Education*, 62.
267 N. Katalanos, *Κυπριακό Λεύκωμα*, Nicosia, 1914; Karamanos, *Κύπρος*, 74.
268 Bryant, *Imagining the Modern*, 29–31.
269 Ibid., 110–14.
270 Ibid., 115–16; Deringil, *The Well-Protected Domains*, London, 1998, 94.
271 S. Mardin, *The Genesis of Young Ottoman Thought*, New Jersey, 1962.
272 CO67/9, 82, Salisbury to Biddulph, 19 February 1879; CO67/9, 115, Salisbury to Biddulph, 9 March 1879; ibid., 128, Salisbury to Biddulph, 17 March 1879; CO67/14, immediate, FO to Post Master General, 4 February 1880; ibid., Post Office, to FO, 3 March 1880; CO67/20/15727, 345, Biddulph to Kimberley, 25 August 1881; ibid., Kimberley to Biddulph, September 1881; Gazioglu, *The Turks in Cyprus*, 267.
273 CO67/115/25867, FO to CO, 16 November 1898.
274 CO67/117/1169, confidential, Haynes Smith to Chamberlain, 3 January 1899.

275 M.S. Hanioglu, *Preparation for a Revolution: The Young Turks, 1902–1908*, Oxford, 2001, 156–7; By World War I a Young Turk party was well progressed. CO67/173/35985, confidential, Goold-Adams to Harcourt, 4 September 1914.
276 Σsmail Sabahattin, *ΚΩbrΩs Sorununun Kökleri*, Istanbul, 2000.
277 Sophocleous, *Συμβολή στην Ιστορία του Κυπριακού Τύπου*, II, 233–78, 361–529.
278 Bryant, *Imagining the Modern*, 105–10.
279 Ibid.
280 Ibid., 239.
281 FO371/352/21509, memorandum, H.H. Lamb, 19 June 1907; FO371/352/21509, 372, O'Conor to Grey, 21 June 1907.
282 FO371/352/26316, confidential, King-Harman to Elgin, 9 July 1907; FO371/352/28030, King-Harman letter to Elgin, 31 July 1907; CO67/148, 267, King-Harman to Elgin, 16 May 1907.
283 SA1:2404/1907, confidential, Elgin to King-Harman, 12 July 1907.
284 M. Thomson, *Churchill: His Life and Times*, London, 1965, 84–5.
285 SA1:2404/1907, King Harman minute.
286 C.3966, King-Harman to Elgin, 21 October 1907.
287 Ibid.
288 Ibid.
289 *BLC*, 30.
290 C.3966, King-Harman to Elgin, 21 October 1907, 4.
291 Ibid.
292 All nine Greek members of the legislature signed the memorial.
293 C.3966, Greek Elected Members Memorial to Churchill, Bishop of Kitium, 12 October 1907, 6.
294 Ibid., 7–8.
295 Ibid., 6.
296 Ibid., 9–10.
297 Anagnostopoulou, *The Passage from the Ottoman Empire to the Nation-States*, 195.
298 C.3966, Churchill's Reply to the Greek Elected Members, 12 October 1907, 21.
299 Ibid.
300 R. Holland, 'Nationalism, Ethnicity and the Concert of Europe: The Case of the High Commissionership of Prince George of Greece in Crete, 1898–1906', *JMGS*, XVII, 2, 1999, 270.
301 Elgin papers, confidential, telegram, Churchill to Elgin, 13 October 1907.
302 CO883/7 Mediterranean 65, confidential, 19 October 1907; CAB37/89/83, recirculated, 21 June 1910; CAB24/89/457 GT 8285, recirculated, 7 October 1919. Hereafter, Churchill's 1907 Memorandum.
303 G.S. Georghallides, 'The Commutation of Cyprus's Payment of the Turkish Debt Charge', *Epeteris*, IV, 1970–71, 379–415.
304 Churchill's 1907 Memorandum.
305 Winston Churchill, *Liberalism and the Social Problem*, London, 1909.
306 Elgin papers, Hopwood to Elgin, 27 December 1907, R. Hyam, *Elgin and Churchill at the Colonial Office, 1905–1908*, London, 1968, 354, note 1.
307 Elgin papers, Sir George Murray to Elgin, 7 January 1907, ibid.
308 G.S. Georghallides, 'Lord Crewe's 1908 Statement on Greek-Cypriot National Claims', *KS*, 1970, 25–34.
309 SA1:3351/1907, confidential, King-Harman to Crewe, 8 May 1908.
310 CO67/151/14489, King-Harman to Elgin, 16 April 1908; *The Times*, 13 April 1908, 6b.
311 SA1:3351/1907, confidential, King-Harman to Crewe, 20 May 1908.
312 SA1:3351/1907, confidential, Crewe to King-Harman, 18 June 1908.
313 CO67/154/14682, 60, King-Harman to Crewe, 21 April 1909; CO67/158/8142, 52, King-Harman to Crewe 10 March 1910; J. Hackett, 'The Close of the Archiepiscopal Question in Cyprus', *ICQ*, 1910, 230–42.
314 CO67/158/8142, 52, King-Harman to Crewe, 10 March 1910.
315 CO67/158/8142, minute, Fiddian, 22 March 1910.

316 CO67/182/61311, confidential, Clauson to Bonar Law, 4 December 1916.
317 Anagnostopoulou, *The Passage from the Ottoman Empire to the Nation-States*, 191, 193.
318 CO883/7/5, 67, 25830, confidential, King-Harman to Crewe, 23 July 1909; CO to Treasury, 13 October 1909; 39078, Treasury to CO, 30 November 1909.
319 Ibid., CO to Treasury, 10 January 1910.
320 Ibid., 5687, Treasury to CO, 24 February 1910.
321 Ibid., 6956, Treasury to CO, 7 March 1910.
322 Ibid., 12695, 80, King-Harman to Crewe, 21 April 1910.
323 Ibid., 12712, confidential, King-Harman to Crewe, 21 April 1910.
324 Ibid., telegram, Crewe to King-Harman, 14 May 1910; confidential, Crewe to King-Harman, 19 May 1910.
325 Ibid., 17697, confidential, King-Harman to Crewe, 27 May 1910.
326 Ibid., 23934, confidential, CO to Treasury, 8 August 1910; 26830, Treasury to CO, 29 August 1910.
327 CO67/160/31642, minute, Fiddian, 18 October 1910; CO67/160/31642, minute, Seely, 19 October 1910.
328 CO883/7/10, 72, 7991, confidential, King-Harman to Harcourt, 25 February 1911.
329 Madden and Fieldhouse, *The Dependent Empire and Ireland*, 303, 306.
330 CO883/7/10, 72, 13884, note by W.D. Ellis, 5 May 1911.
331 CO67/164/32237, minute, G.I.H. to Harcourt, 29 September 1911.
332 CO67/164/32237, minute, Ellis, 2 October 1911.
333 Ibid., minute, Harcourt, 30 September 1911.
334 *The Times*, 2 August 1911, 9b.
335 *The Political Crisis in Cyprus, Official Papers, Nicosia, May 1912*, Nicosia, 1912, 6–15; CO883/7/10, 72, 41005, 228, Goold-Adams to Harcourt, 10 December 1911, with Memorial, Greeks of LC, 18/1 December 1911.
336 CO883/7/10, 72, 41005, 228, Goold-Adams to Harcourt, 10 December 1911; 41067, confidential, Goold-Adams to Harcourt, 14 December 1911.
337 Ibid., 6590, 34, Goold-Adams to Harcourt, 22 February 1912, with Goold-Adams to Constantinides, 10 January 1912.
338 Ibid., Memorial, signed, Greek elected members, 6 February 1912.
339 Ibid., confidential, Goold-Adams to Harcourt, 22 February 1912.
340 Ibid., 29, Harcourt to Goold-Adams, 27 March 1912; confidential, Harcourt to Goold-Adams, 27 March 1912.
341 Ibid., 11775, telegram, Goold-Adams to Harcourt, 17 April 1912; 11862, telegram, Goold-Adams to Harcourt, 18 April 1912.
342 Ibid., 12827, 57, Goold-Adams to Harcourt, 18 April 1912, with Greek memorial, 17 April 1912.
343 Ibid., 13699, confidential, Goold-Adams to Harcourt, 25 April 1912.
344 Ibid., confidential, Goold-Adams to Harcourt, 25 April 1912.
345 Ibid., Lukach order to commissioners of Nicosia and Famagusta, 5 April 1912.
346 P. Papapolyviou, *Η Κύπρος και οι Βαλκανικοί Πολέμοι*, Nicosia, 1997, 68–9, 237.
347 Sir Charles William James Orr, British Library, Manuscript Collections, Add MS 56100, Orr to Miss E. Leviseur, 8 April 1912, 68.
348 CO883/7/10, 72, 16830, 87, Goold-Adams to Harcourt, 21 May 1912, with resolution in Nicosia; 'Central Committee' to Goold-Adams, 11/28 May 1912; *The Political Crisis in Cyprus*, 60–4.
349 WO32/7534, Goold-Adams to Maxwell, 2 May 1912.
350 CO883/7/10, 72, 17665, 101, Goold-Adams to Harcourt, 30 May 1912; CO67/168/18972, Memorandum, Bucknill, 18 June 1912; Papapolyviou, *Η Κύπρος και οι Βαλκανικοί*, 238; Hadjidemetriou *A History of Cyprus*, 366.
351 Luke diary, 26 May 1912.
352 CO883/7/10, 72, 18715, 105, Goold-Adams to Harcourt, 4 June 1912, with Report, W.N. Bolton, Limassol's Commissioner to Goold-Adams, 2 June 1912; *The Times*, 28 May 1912, 3.b; 10 August 1912, 5.b; 20 August 1912, 3.d; 4 October 1912, 3.b; 12 October 1912, 5.c; also *The Times* (16 October 1912, 5d) published a letter from

a former high commissioner (only Sendall had died) claiming that there was no grass-roots desire for *énosis*.

353 CO883/7/10, 72, 16543, tel., Goold-Adams to Harcourt, 28 May 1912; 16605, tel., Goold-Adams to Harcourt, 29 May 1912; 16543, Harcourt to Goold-Adams, 29 May 1912; Luke diary, 1 June 1912; Goold-Adams appointed a mixed commission, comprising Bolton, Yorghanjibashizade Mustafa Sami Effendi and Stavros Stavrinaki. CO883/7/10, 72, 21104, 130, Goold-Adams to Harcourt, 27 June 1912. The commission was unable to agree, when Sami insisted that the riots were premeditated. SA1:876/1912, *passim*.

354 CO883/7/10, 72, 21104, 62, Harcourt to Goold-Adams, 11 June 1912.

355 CO67/168/18972, memorandum, John Bucknill, King's Advocate, 18 June 1912.

356 Ibid., 17 June 1912.

357 CO883/7/10, 72, 22775, 144, Goold-Adams to Harcourt, 12 July 1912, with Greek members to Goold-Adams, 13/26 June 1912; ibid., 25435, 151, Goold-Adams to Harcourt, 1 August 1912, Liassides and Oeconomides to Goold-Adams, 23 July 1912.

358 Ibid., 24695, confidential, Harcourt to Goold-Adams, 20 August 1912; 27100, CO, Fiddes to FO, 14 September 1912, with memorandum, 8 August 1912.

CHAPTER 7

Cyprus's strategic place in the British imperial structure: the backwater

> I went on spending the best years of my life in what was really for me a back-water, and caused me one great sorrow. (Hugh Sinclair, *Camp and Society*, 1926, 152)

Situating Cyprus within British imperial strategy will show that the island was useless and a liability. All war secretaries wanted the garrison withdrawn after 1888, resulting in a departmental battle, which had the War Office often confronting the Colonial and Foreign Offices, whose interests outweighed imperial strategy. But this did not alter Cyprus's status as a backwater.

The Carnarvon Commission reports

Gladstonian and Radical Liberals objected to the Carnarvon Commission on the defence of possessions, which the Conservatives established in 1879. The Colonial Secretary, Lord Kimberley, told the Cabinet in June 1880 that he was alarmed at its scope and departmental interference.[1] Kimberley was aghast at recommendations to fortify possessions, which, like Cyprus, would need local funding. But the new War Secretary, Hugh Childers, had served on the commission and successfully rebuffed Kimberley's assertions.[2] Conservatives, Liberals and government departments, excepting the Colonial Office, were represented on the commission. Carnarvon selected Thomas Brassey and Hugh Childers, Liberal navalists, and his Tory colleague, Sir Henry Holland, who had been his legal adviser at the Colonial Office and then the assistant under-secretary. General John Simmons represented the War Office, Admiral Milne the Admiralty and Robert Hamilton, who began his career at the War Office, before becoming the accountant to the Board of Trade and the Admiralty, represented the Treasury. But John Colomb, an imperial defence theorist, was adamant that the committee lacked someone like him.[3]

The places investigated were divided into first class – coaling stations and harbours of refuge; and second class – only coaling stations. Famagusta, the commissioners believed, was in the second-class category.[4] Gathering data was the problem. In December 1880 Carnarvon appealed to colonial administrators for information, but the reports which arrived in May 1881 were written in the office of the Inspector-General of Fortifications.[5] Famagusta's report echoed Admiral William Fanshawe Martin:

> Famagusta presents few natural facilities for defence and . . . no stationary defences alone can secure it from bombardment. It cannot therefore be made a harbour of refuge in which a vessel could refit in security.[6]

It recommended forts at the Quarry, Exonisi and Varosha sites and other defensive works at the Old Town Battery, and estimated that a 2,440-strong garrison and fortifications, costing £708,620, would secure a coaling station.

When *Superb* arrived in November 1881, Biddulph and Admiral Beauchamp Seymour assembled a committee comprising *Superb*'s captain, Thomas Ward, Lieutenant-Colonel H.W. Dumaresq, the commander of the Royal Engineers in Cyprus, and Major Falkland Warren, the Chief Secretary. The committee examined the measures, costs and manpower for defending the harbour and agreed with forts at Quarry and Exonisi (at another location), but the Varosha site was not good enough and a site 4,000 yards from Exonisi was considered better ('A'). The committee believed that the Old Town Battery was unsuitable and with the savings advised a revolving turret at the tip of the breakwater, when it was constructed (Appendix XI). It agreed that 2,440 men could defend the harbour. However, the *zaptieh* were preoccupied in civil duties and the Orthodox were 'unaccustomed to bear arms and devoid . . . of all the qualities necessary to form soldiers'. The Muslims were 'brave, sober and obedient', but only British gunners would do because they were 'far from intelligent'.[7]

For years, imperial defence theorists had wanted coal guaranteed to the navy and denied to the enemy. The Carnarvon Commission made this official. The three reports established that sea access was a matter of survival; it was the navy's duty to protect commerce; and local governments had to assume policing and coaling station defence with the aid of fortifications.[8] Almost every port was examined and decisions were made on whether to fortify them. Gibraltar and Malta were not examined. For Cyprus, the proposals were contingent on constructing a breakwater at Famagusta, but the Colonial Office had already rejected Samuel Brown's proposals before it received the Committee's report. The first two reports and extracts of the third were

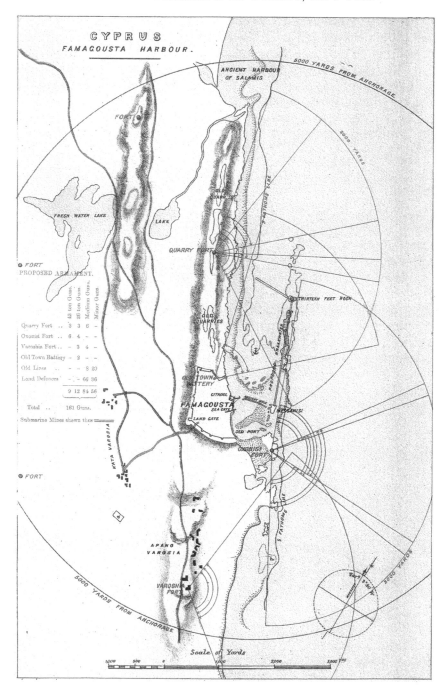

Figure 22 Map of Famagusta Harbour, Showing Defences, 1881
Source: MPG1/867/4.

not published until 1887, largely because Gladstone's government would not act on them.[9]

The Egypt and Sudan campaigns

The crisis in Egypt also overshadowed the reports. Although Egypt had gained from years of British and French investment in irrigation, railways, cotton plantations and schools, and, despite the Khedive selling his share in the Suez Canal to the British government in 1875, six months later he declared bankruptcy. Like the Sultan, he could not pay his creditors. London and Paris established dual control over Egypt's treasury, customs, railways, post offices and ports to secure their economic interests.[10]

Foreign interference provoked Egyptian popular mobilisation. Unpaid army officers, under Ahmad Urabi Pasha, and disaffected civilians, bitter at European and Turko-Circassian interference, declared that Egypt was for the Egyptians. The popular Urabi forced the new Khedive, Tawfiq, to replace his government with one that was favourable to him and in January 1882 he became War Minister.[11]

London and Paris perceived a threat to their strategic and financial interests and, under pressure from their representatives on the spot, sent a naval force to Alexandria in May.[12] Within weeks riots in Alexandria resulted in hundreds of casualties, including Europeans.[13] The Cabinet, excepting Gladstone, became more militant, but a new French government rejected military intervention and withdrew.[14]

As recently as 1878, Beaconsfield had sent the fleet to protect British interests from the Russians. In 1882, Gladstone, who had denounced Beaconsfield's actions, did likewise to Alexandria to protect British interests from the Egyptians. This time the British went further, bombarding Alexandria on 11 July.

In February 1879, Beaconsfield told Queen Victoria that he hoped to avoid occupying Egypt, but might have to and then 'almost in a night' Cyprus' vitality would be shown.[15] This *ex post facto* justification echoed Alexander the Great's words: 'Cyprus being in our hands, we shall reign absolute sovereigns at sea, and an easy way will be laid for making a descent on Egypt.'[16] These thoughts resonated in the corridors of a Liberal Whitehall in June 1882.

Cyprus figured in the plans for an expeditionary force. In June, Samuel Baker argued that it was ideally placed to launch an attack on Egypt.[17] Childers moved two infantry battalions and a company of Royal Engineers to Cyprus from Malta,[18] raised a transport corps there[19] and ordered Biddulph to prepare to encamp 10,000 troops. Biddulph had campsites measured near Limassol, mule tracks repaired, and purchased

1,000 donkeys.[20] But the infantry did not disembark at Limassol; instead, they waited for Major-General Sir Archibald Alison, the deputy quartermaster-general for intelligence, who arrived on 13 July, two days after Alexandria was bombarded. The two battalions at Limassol had remained idle, while chaos reigned at Alexandria.[21] Biddulph did not know about the bombardment, because the British-built cable from Alexandria to Zygi was cut and the Ottoman line from Syria to Cape Andreas was inoperative.[22] Allison sailed for Port Said, where he knew Wolseley planned to attack. Within hours, Biddulph received a mutilated telegram ordering Alison and the *Tamar* and the *Orontes*, which had just arrived, to Alexandria, because ships at Malta were too distant.[23] Meanwhile, the *Helicon* scurried after Allison, reaching him before he could betray Wolseley's plan. But the 48-hour delay meant that the troops arrived too late to save the city from being burnt by Urabi's retreating forces.[24]

Cyprus played a minor role in Wolseley's routing of Urabi's army. On 26 August the half-battalion of the Sussex Regiment in Cyprus left for Ismailia, as depots of regiments in Egypt arrived in Cyprus.[25] In September a hospital was established at Polymedia for 400 patients,[26] and officers arrived to purchase horses (after fatigue had decimated the cavalry's) and mules.[27] Biddulph also sent oxen, cereals, wood, food and munitions.[28] If the occupation continued, another 1,000 infantry depots would be based in Cyprus and if, as the government preferred, Ottoman forces replaced the British, the latter would be based in Cyprus.[29] In the event, 4,000 men were sent to recuperate at Troodos from Egypt's summer, providing the Cyprus government with respite from the monotony of working in such a backwater.[30]

During the war, Lord Waveney (Alexander Robert Adair), the Conservative member for Cambridge, suggested redeveloping Famagusta into a base because of its location between Constantinople and Cairo.[31] Kimberley acknowledged that Brown's report showed that Famagusta could be made a 'very useful and . . . commodious harbour' at little expense, but a military harbour needed costly forts and although Cyprus had 'some advantages as a military station', no money would be forthcoming.[32]

A month later, Major-General Charles Pasley, the Director of Works at the Admiralty, echoed Kimberley's statements to the War Office. Pasley had served in Canada, Bermuda and Victoria, as engineer and aide-de-camp to the commander of the assault on the Eureka stockade.[33] When Victoria became self-governing in 1855, he became public works commissioner. Back home he became the commanding Royal Engineer at Gravesend, supervised Chatham dockyard's extension and in 1873

became the director of works at the Admiralty, visiting and reporting on military ports. He retired weeks after his memorandum on
Famagusta.[34] Pasley had visited Cyprus and read Bocci's report, and
thought a redeveloped Famagusta could not compete with Malta
because, as Admiral William Fanshawe Martin had argued, the harbour was external, whilst Malta's was internal. Yet Pasley, like Adye
and Kimberley, thought that 'a much larger British force than can safely
be placed at Malta' could be gathered at Cyprus 'without having to
ask the permission of any foreign Government'. In a war against Russia
or the Ottoman Empire 'this would be of immense importance'.[35] But
how would the troops be promptly transported to battle without a
harbour that received warships?

The War Office warned the Colonial Office against selling land
at Famagusta without its consent.[36] This followed Childers' request
that the Cyprus government takeover the Polymedia–Troodos road
and pay construction costs.[37] The War Office wanted to restrict its
commitments in Limassol and keep its options open in Famagusta.
The Colonial Office was against a military move to Famagusta
because, as Fairfield revealed, 'much saleable land would be released
for sale, including the sea front of the ramparts, which would . . . fetch
a good price'.[38]

Inaction resulted in Samuel Baker renewing his call to make Cyprus
a strategic asset. On 26 January 1883, his speech 'Cyprus as a Strategical
Position' was read at the Royal United Service Institution. Baker wanted
secure bases throughout the Empire to form a chain for coal supply
and arsenals. Clearly he agreed with John Colomb, whose brother
Captain Philip Colomb, a naval strategist, attended the lecture. Baker
wanted Cyprus as one of the chain's links, so that ships based there
could protect Egypt by blocking the Syrian coast. Thus, a secure Cyprus
was needed to resist an attack in the fleet's absence. Baker argued that
Limassol was ideal for the garrison and trade.[39]

Some interested investors falsely believed that the Akrotiri Salt Lake
would make a good harbour. In December 1883, A.W. Maberly, a
Gloucester architect, proposed to construct it for unnamed investors
for £200,000. Samuel Brown laughed this off. He claimed that: 'if the
proposed breakwater were constructed of a similar economical type
to that adopted at Alexandria the cost . . . can hardly be put down
at less than one million pounds sterling'.[40] There was a misapprehen-
sion over Akrotiri's possibilities, no doubt because of perceptions over
Famagusta's insalubrity.

Cyprus' main role during the Egyptian War was as a haven for
refugees.[41] Whitehall chartered steamers to transport Europeans to
Limassol and Larnaca and others arrived after paying excessive fees.[42]

One ship arrived at Limassol with over 200 refugees[43] and Major Benjamin Donne, a *zaptieh* commandant, related that they 'continued to arrive every day in large numbers'.[44] But Cyprus received no help from Whitehall because Biddulph only needed 'very insignificant amounts'.[45] Biddulph formed local committees at Larnaca and Limassol with £100 at their disposal, London's Lord Mayor sent £300[46] and Cypriots housed refugees (many were Cypriots),[47] but local subscriptions were still needed.[48] Moreover, some refugees had smallpox. In August 1882 George Letts, a British contractor, informed Ellis that a violent form of the disease had broken out amongst the refugees near Troodos's military encampments and disorder was 'spreading rapidly' with 'three or four corpses . . . buried daily'.[49] Biddulph rejected that. There had been only eight cases and one casualty and he had passed an ordinance 'to prevent the spreading of epidemic, contagious or infectious diseases'.[50] In November Frederick Heidenstam, the Chief Medical Officer, reported that Limassol's sanitation was excellent.[51] Then cholera gripped Egypt in June 1883 taking 28,000 lives.[52] Biddulph feared for Cyprus' status as a sanatorium.[53] He made Larnaca the only port of entry and the Treasury funded a quarantine station at Ormideia, which was estimated at £500,[54] but cost £1,150.[55]

Cyprus' strategic role was even less during the Sudan campaign. In February 1884 the steering gear of *Alexandra* (the flagship of the Commander-in-Chief of the Mediterranean Station, Admiral Lord John Hay) broke down off Port Said and the only harbour in the vicinity able to accommodate its engineers was Famagusta.[56] Colonel Arthur Fyler of the West Kent's regiment, who witnessed it, asserted that it proved Famagusta's value as a naval station.[57] But it only proved its potential. An officer also recruited Cypriot Muslims for service under General Evelyn Wood and Cypriot muleteers served on six-month contracts.[58] Sinclair claimed that Cypriot muleteers 'were famous for horse-mastership . . . and the mules . . . unequalled for docility and endurance'.[59] Muleteers died in the line of duty, but those invalided were not compensated because they were not British subjects.[60] Even when the Cyprus government received medals for them, they had to travel to Troodos for the ceremony,[61] although most were unable to.

The island's main role was again as a refugee station and a sanatorium for invalided troops. Three contingents of officers and soldiers arrived from Alexandria in January, February and March and more in September. In September Admiral Hay asked Biddulph if Troodos had space for fifty invalids because of the quarantine at Malta. Biddulph had room for 100 men, but could not take those with heart disease or dysentery owing to the arduous journey and because they would be under canvas.[62]

Figure 23 General Simpson Hackett Presents Egyptian Medals to
1/2 Battalion Berkshire Regiment, Troodos, 1887
Source: J.P. Foscolo Collection: Courtesy of the Laiki Group Cultural Centre
Photographic Archive.

Egypt and the Troodos

Liberals and Conservatives agreed that the aim was to restore a stable
Egyptian government under the Khedive and withdraw; there were
over sixty official declarations to this effect.[63] The Conservatives did
not want a repeat of the Cyprus fever of 1878. After prodding, Lord
Hartington, the Liberal War Secretary, admitted that over 4 per cent
had fever in Egypt.[64] For this reason, and in order to protect British
interests in Egypt from internal unrest after the withdrawal, the
Conservatives planned to base troops in Polymedia and Troodos.[65]
In October 1885 London and Constantinople agreed to the military
withdrawal and in May 1887 Sir Henry Drummond-Wolff, the British
high commissioner in Egypt, negotiated for Ottoman troops to replace
the British within three years.[66]

Troodos's role as a sanatorium during the Egypt and Sudan wars
resulted in Cyprus figuring in Salisbury's plans for defending Egypt.

In July 1885, the 3rd Battalion Grenadier Guards, the 1st Battalion Coldstream Guards and the 2nd Battalion of the Scots Guards were comfortably encamped under the Troodos pines for the summer.[67] Biddulph had encouraged the establishment of Troodos as a sanatorium for Europeans living in Syria and Egypt and a company formed in Alexandria to construct a summer retreat, but the Egyptian war and cholera disrupted it.[68] In 1885 the War Office wanted land to establish a summer base for the troops in Egypt. But the High Commissioner, Sir Henry Bulwer, had reservations. The January 1886 plans (Figure 30) left him with land to encamp only four families (at 'A').[69] He wanted another site north of 'B'. Falkland Warren also warned Bulwer that the planned hospital and bazaar would pollute the springs that supplied water to the civilian and military camps and nearby villages.[70]

The conditions were no surprise. The Troodos Hill Station had become the summer capital where officers, their families and British residents lived for six months of the year. Warren even had his own residence overlooking Platres (Figure 24). It was only at Troodos's isolated confines that they could recreate and maintain a semblance

Figure 24 Falkland Warren's House overlooking Platres
Source: J.P. Foscolo Collection: Courtesy of the Laiki Group
Cultural Centre Photographic Archive.

Figure 25 Connaught Rangers playing polo on Cypriot mules, Photo *c*.1892
Source: J.P. Foscolo Collection: Courtesy of the Laiki Group
Cultural Centre Photographic Archive.

of 'British' country life away from the heat of the plains and the natives
(Figures 25 and 26).[71] Indeed, in September 1886 Bulwer entertained
the Duke of Edinburgh there.[72]

Bulwer's conditions were reasonable, but the War Office wanted an
unconditional agreement. It was further angered when Bulwer suggested
that the £5,000 sanctioned for the £43,000 Polymedia barracks project
should go to moving the garrison to Nicosia to unite the civilian and
military establishments.[73] Fairfield and Edward Stanhope, briefly the
Colonial Secretary in 1886, disagreed with Bulwer.[74] In order to have
unfettered control, the War Office decided to permanently station troops
at Troodos at a lower altitude to that previously investigated.[75] In April
1887 it proposed that if given exclusive rights it would 'always be open
to the Officer Commanding to allow civilians to camp within the lines,
if feasible, but it . . . considered [it] essential on sanitary and other
grounds that no such <u>right</u> should exist'.[76] Fairfield thought:

> It looks to me as if the War Department wanted to take all the avail-
> able camping land, and leave nothing for our officers, who it should be
> remembered go up on duty and for the restoration of their health.[77]

[211]

Figure 26 Government Cottage and Tennis Court, 1880
Source: J.P. Foscolo Collection: Courtesy of the Laiki Group Cultural
Centre Photographic Archive.

Clearly, the Cyprus government was reluctant to give land at
Troodos because of its socio-cultural and political importance. The War
Office had to accept land on the condition that it would remain the
Cyprus government's property and on 'ceasing to be required . . . for
Military purposes' it would revert.[78] But the land was not used. The
Anglo-Ottoman agreement was not ratified because of Franco-Russian
opposition and the troops stayed in Egypt.[79]

The Colonial Defence Committee report on Cyprus

With the British garrison staying in Egypt, the Colonial Defence Committee, which was formed in 1884 in the wake of Stead's naval scare, turned to determining Cyprus' strategic place. Between 1885 and 1887, it had produced 26 memoranda and 57 reports in order to streamline imperial and colonial defence.[80] Conservatives and Liberals wanted to reduce garrisons as Cardwell had.[81] But Beaconsfield's government had undermined this when it occupied Cyprus and then, paradoxically, Gladstone did so when occupying Egypt. There was no manpower to garrison both adequately. The worry was instability in Egypt which, unlike Cyprus, was strategically valuable. As one commentator asserted in 1887, Cyprus was 'practically a civil colony only'.[82]

In early 1888 the Colonial Defence Committee asked the Colonial Office to report on a scheme of defence for Cyprus. A local committee reported, but the Colonial Defence Committee thought it produced an outline of possible measures and promptly determined Cyprus' strategic place. It claimed its position was 'altogether anomalous' because it was 'defenceless except as regards the protection which could be afforded by the Mediterranean Squadron'.[83] Cyprus would be attacked 'only if a large force' was concentrated there and 'if garrisoned as at present, no military object whatever would be gained by attacking Cyprus beyond the destruction of . . . stores . . . and the effacement of the battalion'.[84] A defenceless Cyprus was no threat because no enemy would want to seize it – implying that Cyprus was of no strategic value in the hands of a foreign power. To use Cyprus as a base, it was 'necessary to create at least one port, and to defend it', because without naval protection, embarking troops would be unsafe.[85] While the present garrison was merely policing, and since the Carnarvon Commission had advised against British troops policing and the Colonial Defence Committee was told that the *zaptieh* could handle internal disorder, the troops should go.[86]

Salisbury, the Foreign Secretary and Prime Minister, objected. On 15 May, he had the War and Colonial Offices told that it 'cannot, on diplomatic grounds, be entertained so long as [the] British occupation of Egypt continues' because the effect would be 'very detrimental to British influence at Constantinople'.[87] In January 1887 Henry Brackenbury, who had organised the *zaptieh* in 1878 and now headed the Intelligence Branch of the War Office, warned that the British could not prevent the Russians advancing on Afghanistan or India without a base in the Black Sea, the eastern Mediterranean or the Persian Gulf.[88] This was one of the reasons for taking Cyprus in 1878, but no mention was made of the island. Salisbury thought that keeping troops there would demonstrate British military might, as in Egypt, where Evelyn Barring (Lord Cromer), the Consul-General, convinced politicians to retain a British army presence as a show of strength.[89] The Foreign Office was deciding imperial defence policy. Accordingly, Edward Stanhope, the War Secretary, retreated.[90]

A month later, Knutsford, believing that the troops would be 'removed in the event of war' to where their services would be needed,[91] told Stanhope that he would ask Bulwer if the *zaptieh* could maintain order.[92] The *zaptieh* were 650-strong in 1885 and comprised one-third mounted (216) and two-thirds foot (413).[93] By 1912, this had changed little (248 mounted, 434 foot), while 60 per cent of the force was still Muslim.[94] Bulwer replied that the 900-strong garrison 'could be considerably reduced', but not removed entirely because it was 'a visible representation of . . . British Power and . . . a moral support' to the government. In wartime it could go 'without danger to internal order', even if Orthodox–Muslim relations became strained, because the *zaptieh* could maintain order.[95]

Accordingly, in October 1888, Stanhope proposed to remove half the garrison and the headquarters to Malta. Salisbury agreed.[96] Fears of a French invasion had moved the focus to Gibraltar and Malta. If Russia joined France, Salisbury was advised that the Ottoman fleet and three British battleships could defend Constantinople.[97] The War Office wanted only three companies in Cyprus, but, on Knutsford's insistence, it agreed to four only if they were eventually removed to Malta.[98] Knutsford notified Bulwer and ordered him to reduce the *zaptieh* and lessen its military character.[99]

Imperial defence strategy was fixed until the Boer War.[100] In 1890 Charles Dilke, who according to one of his biographers had 'debated Cyprus in the House to the point of boredom, and beyond' in 1879,[101] wrote in *Problems of Great Britain*:

> It is difficult to write of Cyprus without raising party questions. The island is unfortified and virtually without a garrison, for the few British troops that are kept there would be wholly unable to defend it against serious attack. No money has been spent upon the harbour of Famagusta, which by a large expenditure might have been made into a good port, and Cyprus cannot be regarded as one of our chief military or naval stations.[102]

Indeed, British political and military authorities saw no benefit in keeping British troops in Cyprus. Nothing changed when in April 1890 Captain Arthur Young, Famagusta's commissioner, reported that a Russian Cruiser *Vladimir Monorornach* was taking soundings at Famagusta harbour.[103] The unflappable Fairfield thought there was 'no harm', as the Royal Navy did so all the time.[104] The Admiralty disagreed:

it is not usual now between civilised nations to send boats to deliberately sound or survey a port belonging to a foreign power without obtaining permission . . . but it might invoke awkward rejoinders if any notice is taken of this incident.[105]

Cyprus was not worth an 'awkward rejoinder'.

Withdrawing the garrison and the Cypriots

After the 1892 Liberal victory, the new War Secretary, Sir Henry Campbell-Bannerman, proposed to remove the entire garrison. Fairfield's absence panicked his colleagues. W.H. Mercer, a clerk new to Cyprus affairs, noted that from a 'military point of view the retention of the garrison . . . [was] condemned long ago', but there were political (*énosis?*) and economic reasons – the troops bought local produce – to oppose it.[106] The cool Fairfield thought the troops were unnecessary, but the Foreign Office had to sanction the proposal and the Foreign Secretary, Lord Rosebery, might want to avoid creating 'hopes in the Greek mind and correspondingly alarm in the Sultan's mind'.[107] Meade, who became the permanent under-secretary in 1892, agreed.

> The soldier is the visible mark of [the] British occupation; if he is removed, I should expect . . . [an] addition to the agitation of the Greeks for annexation to Greece; and it would certainly be taken as an intimation of the approaching abandonment of the island.[108]

The British army, although not needed to preserve order, provided a check on the Hellenists.

The Colonial Office used Hellenism in Cyprus to prevent War Office plans to remove the garrison. On 5 February 1894, a year after the previous debate, the War Office asked Lord Ripon, the Colonial Secretary, if the half battalion (Connaught Rangers) could join the other half battalion at Malta.[109] Five days later, the War Office told Fairfield that the Foreign Office agreed. Fairfield believed that the Headquarters and a wing of a regiment would remain, but recognised that reinforcing Malta was the priority.[110] Meade and Ripon agreed[111] and accordingly informed Sir Walter Sendall, Bulwer's successor, on 5 March 1894, that unless the *zaptieh* could not maintain order (Ripon thought they could) the withdrawal would occur.[112] A telegram on 12 March informed Sendall that the withdrawal was likely.[113]

After discussing the issue with his officers, Sendall, a robust man of great integrity,[114] concluded that there was 'no reason to think that [the] Government will not . . . maintain order if [the] proposed removal of troops [was] carried out'.[115] After receiving Ripon's telegram, Sendall still believed that, but was concerned that withdrawing the visible signs

[215]

of British power would result in discontent from merchants and those who might presume a sequel.[116] He thought that

> a sudden rupture, without any warning or preparation, of the relations which have subsisted for many years between the civil population and the military . . . would . . . [result in] much hardship to individuals, and . . . intensify the excitement and almost consternation which the measure will probably create.[117]

Trade at Limassol was declining and removing the troops would be 'a serious blow' that might result in anti-British activity.[118] Two weeks later, he supported his concerns with reports that jobs would be lost and traders could lose £14,500 a year in income.[119] It was clear, according to Sendall, how 'the material interests of the people are dependent upon the presence of the troops'.[120] Sendall warned Ripon that debate on Cyprus' future would renew the 'animosity between the Turks and the Greeks' as had transpired in 1893 when *Phoni tis Kyprou* published the letters between Dilke and Henry Labouchere supporting *énosis*. A handful of British troops would suppress 'slight collisions', but it 'might not be so easy to deal with it if the native police were the only available source'.[121] Sendall failed to mention that the army had not been needed at that time. He had back-tracked over the *zaptieh's* ability to maintain peace.

Fairfield relied on the Foreign Office to avert the withdrawal. He had discovered that Rosebery had privately agreed to the withdrawal, but his successor, Lord Kimberly, had not stated an official position.[122] Before the Colonial Office acted, Ralph Thompson, the under-secretary at the War Office, asked Meade if the Colonial and Foreign Offices would agree to caretakers staying and the Cyprus government keeping the military buildings repaired.[123] Thompson added that

> we – from a purely military point of view – don't want to have troops there, nor do we want it as a convalescent station as our doctors say that . . . it is much better that invalids should be sent home.[124]

Meade replied that the Colonial Office, with the Foreign Office's probable concurrence, would agree, but still wanted official Foreign Office agreement to a withdrawal.[125] But Meade advised Thompson:

> it would greatly tend to your getting a favourable reply from them (the Foreign Office) if you say that it is proposed to withdraw the Troops gradually & without attracting any attention.[126]

Meade told Sendall that a decision would 'probably be deferred for political reasons unconnected with Cyprus till later in the year', but he should expect the troops to go.[127]

In Cyprus, the Hellenists opposed the withdrawal and spread fear that Cyprus would be returned to the Porte. On 21 May, Sendall informed Ripon of rumours in the Greek-language press.[128] *Alíthia*, Aristotle Palaeologos' newspaper in Limassol, reported that Sendall had told London that Cypriots did not need troops to police them. Palaeologos called the move 'unreasonable and foolish . . . [because] cases of race conflicts . . . [made] their appearance every day' and there was 'great fear lest they should cause [the] most grievous consequences'.[129] The *zaptieh* were 'incapable' of stopping them and 'the departure of the army . . . would place the country in fearful dangers. Fanaticism is a strong weapon if placed in the hands of rude and ignorant people.'[130] Palaeologos, a Hellenist fanatic, was threatening 'race passions' if the troops were removed. Blackmail was the Hellenist response to the withdrawal. On 16 July, Sendall forwarded another article from *Alíthia*, which claimed that only sanguine people disbelieved that the withdrawal would not be 'followed by another more important event', Cyprus' return to the Porte.[131] On 20 July, the War Office informed the officer commanding the troops in Cyprus that the garrison would be reduced in January 1895 to one company. This was leaked.[132] Hellenists cried that Cyprus was being abandoned to the 'unspeakable Turk'. On 27 August, Sendall warned Ripon that a 'good deal of excitement' had spread. There was no cause for panic, but 'in the present depressed state of trade' the people were 'more receptive to unfavourable impressions and surmises', that is, to the Hellenist elite's intrigues.[133]

The debate on the withdrawal in *Alíthia* and *Phoni tis Kyprou* highlighted Hellenist and Orthodox-centric divisions. *Alíthia*, in typical Hellenist scaremongering, violently attacked their 'unfeeling masters' for the '*coup d'etat*' being planned against the 'Hellenes of Cyprus'.[134] The article announced:

> Let our master know it, let alas! The liberals learn it, let the world become aware of it. Then from end to end of Cyprus, there will be heard but one voice only, a thundering, imposing, manly, proud voice, a voice, strong in its right, and this voice will be 'give us over to Greece, our great country, our precious mother'.[135]

On the other hand, *Phoni tis Kyprou*, believing that its duty was to relieve anxiety, argued that the rumours about Cyprus's abandonment were 'entirely groundless and that there was no fear for a return of the *status quo ante*' because of the tribute's value.[136] Such rumours risked leading to disturbances with their Muslim co-inhabitants with whom they were 'living in peace and harmony'.

The contemplated reduction of the English troops in Cyprus has no bearing on the administration of the island, for it shows nothing else than that the peacefulness and law-abiding . . . Cypriot people have convinced the home government that the presence of a numerous army . . . is unnecessary.[137]

The differences in philosophy and approach between the Hellenists and the Orthodox-centric elite could not be more evident. But the rumours and anxieties only increased. On 8 September Sendall forwarded extracts from *The Times of Cyprus*, *Salpinx*, *Kipris*, *Alíthia* and *Evagóras*.[138] A. Turner, the editor of the first totally English newspaper, stated that trade would suffer 'so long as the intimidating, shilly shallying policy . . . continued'. Rumours at Larnaca that Sendall had arrived in a closed carriage and left for Beirut, where the British and Ottoman fleets lay, were not easily allayed, although Turner had just left him at Troodos: 'the panic that existed . . . and the demand for good old used Fezes was something most exciting.'[139] *Salpinx*, which had published Sophronios' church-state law proposal in 1885, did not joke, lamenting at how Cyprus went from one ruler to another without any pity on the people.[140] *Evagóras*, published in Nicosia since 1890 by Pericles Michaelides, formerly a teacher in Corinth,[141] called for armed resistance to returning Cyprus to the Porte.[142] Küfizade Mustafa Asaf Bey of *Kipris* disliked that thought, accusing the government of being indifferent to Hellenism.[143] But *Evagóras* believed that the British would return Cyprus to the Porte because it was

useless to England as a military station [and this] was shown from the very first months of the English occupation by the long discussions carried on in the English Parliament and the English Press and was confirmed . . . later by the interruption of all public works.[144]

After Egypt was occupied, whenever Parliament was asked to vote on a grant the politicians clamoured to declare that 'Cyprus is useless for England'.[145] The Hellenists reflected the two main British theses as to why Cyprus had not developed into a strategic asset: Gladstone coming to power and then occupying Egypt.

In the event, on 15 September the withdrawal was announced for January 1895.[146] Six days earlier, Ripon telegraphed Sendall: 'No intention of abandoning Island, no foundation for reports, movement of troops purely matter of military convenience, no political significance, give publicity.'[147] When the troops left, the 2nd Connaught Rangers from Cyprus and Malta replaced the 2nd South Lancashire in Egypt after it had reinforced India.[148] Ripon explained that he appreciated Cypriot disappointment and that the withdrawal would be a loss, but

Cyprus would 'be in no worse position than the great majority of the British Colonial Possessions'. It was no longer the norm to deploy forces in support of colonial governments and the army best served British interests concentrated where it could safeguard British trade and bases for the fleet.[149]

> In Cyprus Her Majesty's Government are confident that there is no section of the population which is disposed either to attack any other section of it, or to resist the Civil power, and they have therefore felt justified in adopting the recommendation of the Military Advisers of the Crown that the troops should be transferred to where they will be of more use for Imperial purposes.[150]

Ripon echoed *Phoni tis Kyprou*'s article of 18 August, thus the view of the Orthodox-centric leadership was adopted over Hellenist machinations.

Two months before the withdrawal, however, floods devastated Limassol. Much of it became uninhabitable and twenty-two people and many animals perished.[151] The cruiser, *Arethusa*, arrived from Alexandretta to aid the Connaught Rangers in clearing the debris and J. Williamson, the director of the Cyprus Company, described the traumatic events and the work of the troops in letters to *The Times*.[152] Limassol's Municipal Council and legislature members telegraphed the Colonial Office pleading for the troops to stay. They appealed to the sensitivities of the authorities,[153] as did the Cyprus Company, which established a relief fund, claiming that the people could not 'cope with a calamity of this magnitude'.[154]

Fairfield thought the floods were well-timed and that a private appeal to Thompson could overturn the decision.[155] Any appeal, if made, failed.[156] H.C.M. Lambert and F.W. Fuller, who were new to Cyprus affairs, debated with Fairfield how to approach Thompson. Various issues were canvassed and dismissed: Armenian revolutionaries and refugees in Cyprus; inter-communal Cypriot relations; and the Limassol flood (Sendall had forwarded more appeals on 3 December).[157] On 26 December, the Colonial Office forwarded the appeals to the War Office, with a draft of a letter to Sendall rejecting them.[158]

The War Office liked the draft.[159] It stated that 'for military reasons of much importance, they regret that they cannot meet . . . the desire of the inhabitants'.[160] Sendall was warned that Whitehall did not pledge to 'leave even one Company of troops permanently'.[161] On 13 February the four companies of the Connaught Rangers left on the hired transport *Jumma* for Alexandria. The Reuter reporter stated: 'the departure of the troops is greatly felt here.'[162]

Chamberlain and the strategist, traveller and backbenchers

The Tory-Unionist coalition from 1895 did not alter the desire to withdraw the military from Cyprus. On 22 February 1895, a week after the troop withdrawal, the War Office told the Colonial Office that troops were not required to guard the Limassol army stores. Limassol's commissioner, Roland Michell, suggested that the *zaptieh* take over, but they would need quarters.[163] Joseph Chamberlain, the Colonial Secretary, and Lord Lansdowne, a Whig who served as Canada's governor and India's viceroy before joining the Unionists and Salisbury's ministry as War Secretary, brokered an agreement between the War Office and the Cyprus government in early 1896. The latter took over the War Department buildings, barracks and yards except those that the War Office retained, which became the Limassol Depot.[164] Months later, the military contracted the Limassol–Platres Road to the Cyprus government for £700 over three years.[165]

Six months after coming to office, Lansdowne asked Chamberlain to confer with Salisbury on removing the entire garrison.[166] Fairfield, John Anderson, a colonial office clerk, and Meade thought that the Foreign Office would object because of the Ottoman atrocities in Armenia.[167] Pinning hopes on the Foreign Office paid off:

> in view of the condition of affairs … at Constantinople and in the Asiatic provinces of Turkey, Lord Salisbury considers that, from a diplomatic point of view, the present moment is not opportune for affecting the removal of the small British force still remaining in Cyprus.[168]

The question was postponed until affairs were 'quieter in the Turkish Empire'.[169] The military had no plans to use Cyprus as a base[170] and Salisbury's objections to a total withdrawal, which Lansdowne desired and to which Chamberlain agreed, show that he wanted a British armed presence in Cyprus to show British military strength. Imperial strategy and defence did not drive Joseph Chamberlain's development programme (Chapter 6), nor did defence advisers alter their view of Cyprus, even with the interest of strategists.

In 1899 Colonel Arthur Evelyn Fyler, who commanded the 50th Royal West Kent Regiment in Cyprus in 1882–83,[171] published a rare book *The Development of Cyprus*, in which he asserted that with Famagusta harbour's development it should be made into a defendable military and naval station.[172] Fyler combined his knowledge of Cyprus and imperial defence principles to argue that power should be concentrated at Famagusta bay because

> Fortifications are . . . made solely in preparation for a possible . . . war;
> at such a time Cyprus in its present state would be entirely dependent
> on our fleet for protection, but in war . . . there would be plenty of
> other work for the fleet . . . [and] it would therefore seem to be the
> highest wisdom, to make the important strategic points capable of
> self-defence . . .[173]

Thus, like Adye years earlier, Fyler wanted the garrison at Famagusta
in winter and in summer at Kantara.[174] Kantara captured a view of the
Karpass, Mesaoria and Famagusta, and had been a Byzantine, Lusignan
and Venetian fortress.[175] Fyler thought Kantara was ideal for a summer camp because the high tableland near the castle was perfect for
barracks. Kantara was only twenty-three miles from Famagusta, and
the Trikomo–Salamis road could be made into a military road, with
a light railway and heliograph connecting the camps.[176] Kantara was
724 metres high, making it perfect for a summer and winter station,
and was two miles from an anchorage (Davlos) to the north and another
in the south-east (Boghaz).[177] Fyler criticised Polymedia and Troodos
as military stations. Limassol's roadstead was still unsafe and the
march up the steep 6,000-foot ground to Troodos was physically hard
and costly.[178] Although Fyler's suggestion would mean an expensive
move, it was justified because only Famagusta could be made into a
coaling station. Fyler did not approach Whitehall with his proposals,
but the Colonial and Foreign offices knew of the book because he
had asked permission to quote data and publish maps from official
publications.[179]

Chamberlain's development agenda also impressed Rider Haggard,
the author of *King Solomon's Mines*. Haggard, a failed Unionist cand-
idate in East Norfolk in 1895, naturally praised Chamberlain as 'the
best Colonial Minister that we have had for many a long year'.[180]
Haggard had served as Sir Henry Bulwer's private secretary in Natal
in 1875, visited his old chief in Cyprus in 1887 and made a return
visit to the island in 1900.[181] In *A Winter's Pilgrimage* (1901), he
suggested that Cyprus could serve as a 'half-way house for troops
on their road to India' where they would grow accustomed to a warm
climate. Moreover, it was ideal as a training-ground for mounted
infantry, which were sorely needed in the Boer War. Cyprus had hardy
horses and mules, every conceivable physical difficulty on which to
train, and Chamberlain's schemes would afford them work.[182] Haggard
was unmoved by Famagusta's potential as a coaling station and
strongly argued that at Limassol (Akrotiri Salt Lake) a grand harbour
could be made with two entrances. He knew it could cost £2,000,000
to dredge, but was right in saying that that was equal to two
battleships.[183]

Cyprus' development was naturally debated in Parliament, where party affiliation continued to divide. Robert Pierpoint, the Tory member for Warrington, claimed that when Cyprus was occupied the people were promised 'a great many things . . . [but] we have never performed . . . Nothing whatever has been done towards making a naval station there, and as to the garrison . . . the soldiers there are practically reduced to a handful of caretakers.'[184] He thought the Cypriots would benefit from expenditure on naval works. He did not mention that his constituents, mostly engaged in iron making and transport work, would supposedly also benefit.[185] He urged Chamberlain and Goschen, the First Lord of the Admiralty, to start naval works because the navy needed a base (at either Famagusta or Limassol) other than Valletta, where medical officers reported fever.[186] Sir Albert Kaye Rollit, a steamship owner in Hull and the Conservative MP for Islington South, supported Pierpoint. He favoured Limassol Salt Lake probably because his brother-in-law was Roland Michell, Limassol's commissioner. Rollit consistently warned of the German menace to British trade in the Balkans, where he advocated commercial expansion.[187] He interpreted Chamberlain's initiatives as doing nothing to fulfil the original plan to convert Cyprus into a base.[188] Dilke objected, claiming that two successive governments had rejected converting Famagusta into a naval base because it would cost £2 million.[189] The Conservative Charles Bill rejected Dilke's searing exaggerations and referred to Dilke's comments in July's *Cosmopolis*:

> The British Government of 1880, containing . . . two prominent members of the present administration, put on record its opinion of the worthlessness of Cyprus as a military or naval station.[190]

Bill observed that Dilke proceeded to advocate ceding Cyprus to Greece.[191]

Chamberlain put the matter to rest: 'there is no intention to make a great naval and military harbour at Famagusta . . . [but] the harbour will be rendered more useful for commercial purposes.'[192] The Tory-Unionist coalition rejected Haynes Smith's belief that the Admiralty wanted a coaling station in the eastern Mediterranean. He produced reports on Famagusta's suitability as a coaling station and handed them to Prince Louis of Battenberg, commander of the battleship *Implacable* in the Mediterranean.[193] A civil engineer also produced a diagram demonstrating the project's feasibility, but this was not sent to London.[194] The Admiralty informed the Colonial Office that such a project was 'not one called for by naval interests'.[195]

'Martial races', Cypriot unity and imperial defence, 1898–1905

William Haynes Smith was 'notorious' for making proposals that were 'too much on the grand scale', asserted Frederick Graham, who replaced Fairfield as the assistant under-secretary after his untimely death.[196] Graham knew Haynes Smith from his days as the governor of British Guiana (1884–87), the Leeward Isles (1888–95) and Bahamas (1895–97). On 7 July 1898, in the comfort of Government Cottage at Troodos, Haynes Smith wrote to Chamberlain that he wanted to raise a local defence force

> which might be made a very fine body . . . at small cost, for all purposes of defence against anything except a large expedition. It would be a popular force . . . and both Turks and Greeks would willingly serve in it. It would not only be useful for the immediate object, but would . . . greatly tend to make the island a British island in sympathies and political aspirations.[197]

The Colonial Office hesitated. Graham claimed that 'no Cypriot army could defend Cyprus' and if the British fleet controlled the Mediterranean 'no power' would threaten it. A Cypriot army would be popular and there was 'good military material' there, better than at Malta, but unless Whitehall paid for it, as it had for the Malta regiment formed in 1889, the matter was beyond Cyprus.[198] Lord Selbourne, the parliamentary under-secretary at the Colonial Office, believed it might be used in the Mediterranean stations.[199] Graham suggested politely warning Haynes Smith against being 'too sanguine or too eager to embark on large schemes', which could 'only end in disaster'.[200]

The Colonial Defence Committee was not told of the proposal until August and it did not rush to examine it, prompting the impatient Haynes Smith, with Cretan autonomy resulting in similar demands from Hellenists in Cyprus, to repeat his idea twice.[201] Finally, in a general memorandum on the utilisation of native troops for colonial garrisons, the Colonial Defence Committee stated:

> At Cyprus it would certainly be advantageous if natives could be enlisted to take the place of British artillery or infantry in the Mediterranean stations, but the Committee are not aware whether this can be done under the existing political conditions of the island.[202]

The Committee wanted Cypriot troops in Malta or Egypt, as Selbourne had mooted, but wondered about the legality. If it were legal, it was recommended that 'two battalions of Mahommedans should be raised in Cyprus' to replace or augment Malta's garrison.[203]

Therefore, there were two differences from Haynes Smith's proposal: a Cypriot corps was seen as the solution to increasing or freeing up British troops at Malta or Egypt, as well as Cyprus, and the force was limited to Muslims, contradicting the initial proposal of a popular Muslim and Christian force to create loyalty to the Empire.

Limiting the force to Muslims was rooted in the theory of 'martial races'. Europeans utilised subject peoples that were inherently combative. The Dutch controlled the East Indies for over 300 years through the Royal Netherlands Indies Army and Portugal used locals for defence in Goa and Africa.[204] In 1857, the French recruited Senegalese into a West African colonial army, the *Tirailleurs Senegalais*, through local chiefs.[205] The British built their imperial defence around colonial manpower. The East India Company organised Bengalis, Tamils, Maharattas and Purbiahs into regiments under British and Indian officers. After India came under the Crown, in 1859, the Ghurkha and Burma Rifles were raised, and Sikhs, Rajputs, Jats, Kodavas and Mahars were designated martial races.[206] Troops from the sub-continent were used in local and imperial capacities, including Cyprus' occupation. Officers in India applied the theory in Africa.[207] Angolans were used against rebels in Mozambique in 1880 and, in 1896, the Central African Regiment was established and used in 1900 against the Somali 'Mullah' Mahommed Abdullah. In 1897, the Niger and West African Frontier Force was raised to protect British protectorates in West Africa from the French. In 1901, the British incorporated the various native units in West Africa into the West African Frontier Force and, the year after, did the same in East Africa, forming the King's African Rifles.[208]

The idea was to racially segregate such forces 'to strengthen the soldiers' ethnic awareness' and ensure that they 'would not make common cause against their European masters'.[209] Hence, the British theory was to raise troops in places where the notion of 'divide and rule' mostly applied.[210] So the War Office rejected raising a force of Chinese in Hong Kong because 'divide and rule' did not apply[211] and when the Hong Kong Regiment was raised in 1892, it was composed of Sikhs and Pathans. 'Divide and rule' contradicted Haynes Smith's aim to bring the Cypriots together. But the Colonial Defence Committee did not propose a segregated force in Cyprus: it already saw the Cypriots as segregated and considered the 'Turk' and not the 'Greek' to be a 'martial race'. The British identified the Cypriot Muslim with his Anatolian co-religionist, who was considered a fine soldier, but poorly led, and the Cypriot Orthodox as 'Greeks', who were disparaged as fighters.[212]

[224]

Sir Evelyn Wood, the Adjutant-General, asked Wolseley, who had proposed raising an Anatolian Muslim regiment in Cyprus when he was high commissioner and advocated African martial qualities,[213] if it was wise to raise a corps of Cypriot Muslims to serve in Egypt or Sudan.[214] Wolseley, the Commander-in-Chief of the army, wanted the issue raised with Lord Lansdowne. The War Secretary liked the idea, but could not fund it in 1899–1900.[215] Wood also read a report on the *zaptieh* by Captain William R. Robertson, who worked at the Intelligence Branch at the War Office, which claimed the Turks could form a corps because

> their staunch sobriety and extreme hardihood, together with an instinctive knowledge of arms and a natural capacity for a military profession, would render them most valuable in the organisation of a defence force.[216]

Attention was drawn to the *zaptieh* when some took part in Queen Victoria's Diamond Jubilee celebrations, in London, in 1897. When Wolseley presented them to the Duke of Cambridge he was stunned: 'You don't mean to tell me these people are white!'[217] Yet, the images of the *zaptieh*, which highlighted their strength, always portrayed them as dark – Oriental.

Figure 27 Mounted Zaptiehs of the Cyprus Local Military Police
Source: J.P. Foscolo Collection: Courtesy of the Laiki Group
Cultural Centre Photographic Archive.

While the debate over raising a regiment continued, Wood asked Wolseley about withdrawing the remaining troops.[218] Wolseley, as the first high commissioner, thought Cyprus would make a good sanatorium and London 'should not withdraw this last link between Cyprus and the army unless for cogent reasons'.[219] Nobody linked withdrawal with a Cypriot corps. Wood now doubted the value of the force because the *zaptieh* were established and increasing the garrison would only invite attack.[220] Wolseley thought the battalion could be used outside Cyprus,[221] but Lansdowne doubted 'that there would be room for a Cypriot battalion', but would consider it under the scheme for raising more colonial battalions.[222]

The *zaptieh* showed considerable 'racial' integration and affinity with British imperial aims. In January 1900 Haynes Smith informed Chamberlain that thirteen Orthodox and Muslim *zaptieh* wanted to volunteer for service in the Transvaal and that others would follow.[223] The War Office, however, could not find duties for them.[224] A mixed regiment was feasible. (During the First World War over 13,000 Orthodox and Muslim Cypriots served as muleteers in the British Army and in Second World War the Cyprus Volunteer Force and the Cyprus Regiment were the first colonial troops to fight the Nazis.)[225]

In February 1900, Haynes Smith suggested that the local force be mounted and wanted permission to pass an order-in-council to raise it.[226] In March, the Colonial Office forwarded Haynes Smith's letter to the War Office,[227] which replied that the legality of the proposition needed clarification.[228]

Meanwhile, the Colonial Office sought Salisbury's position. The Foreign Office asked the British Ambassador at Constantinople, Nicholas O'Conor, a career diplomat in China, Bulgaria and Russia, if Abdul Hamid would object. He asserted that the Sultan would worry that the Muslims would enlist more willingly, but he did not need consulting. O'Conor believed that 'a mobile and efficient military force in Cyprus, comprised to a large degree of Mussulmans, maybe a very important factor in the political situation . . . add[ing] to our prestige and influence'.[229]

Captain Guy H. Ivrea, of the Reserve Regiment of Dragoon Guards, put more pressure on the War Office when he volunteered to lead the corps. Ivrea thought the cost would be equal to the current company, with the advantage that the British troops would be freed.[230] He claimed that infantry were 'useless in Cyprus' because they were too far from Nicosia to suppress a disturbance there and it was strategically and economically sound to replace them with a local mounted corps.[231] Ivrea thought obvious the advantages of having 'several squadrons of light cavalry in the Eastern Mediterranean'.[232] Cyprus, which supplied donkey stallions to India, thousands of mules for the Boer War and had a hardy breed of ponies, could supply the horses.[233] The regiment would comprise one British commandant, three British squadron commanders and six Indian Muslim squadron officers, along similar lines as in Africa.[234] The 359-strong force would be at Nicosia or Polymedia.[235]

Lansdowne acted on Ivrea's reports, asking the Colonial Office, on 28 August and on 6 November, if it had resolved the legal issues.[236] This was not strange, but it was odd that the War Office did not check on Ivrea. By 1903, when he was still pushing for a Cyprus regiment, Ivrea, who had retired from the Royal Dublin Fusiliers in 1891 and the reserves of the Dragoon Guards in 1901, was being chased by creditors. He used multiple names: Guy Hardwin Gallenga, Guy Hardwin Ivrea and Marquis Ivrea or D'Ivrea.[237]

The Colonial Office replied to the War Office on 12 November that the law officers were asked on 27 June to report on whether an order-in-council could be passed to raise a local force for use elsewhere and the report had arrived two weeks later.[238] The Colonial Office sat on it for four months because it advised that the Cyprus government could not make laws to raise a force for service outside Cyprus.[239] Chamberlain asked the law officers to consider if section 176(3) of the Army Act 1881 allowed for a local law to raise a force of irregulars for general service. He thought the Anglo-Turkish Convention did not prohibit it and justified it in lieu of the military exemption tax the Cypriots paid. Since Britain occupied Cyprus to defend Ottoman Asia, it should use 'the resources handed over by the Sultan'. There were precedents in Weihaiwei and Bosnia. The Colonial Office cited Horace Rumbold, the former ambassador to Vienna, who revealed that the Bosnian force swore an oath to the emperor, but remained Ottoman subjects. Indeed it would have made a good model as it was composed of Orthodox, Catholics and Muslims.[240] The law officers reported that raising a regiment for service in Cyprus was possible, but could it not be used overseas because section 95 of the Army Act 1881 limited aliens serving in a corps to one for every fifty British subjects.[241]

The Colonial and War Offices agreed to amend the Army Act. Sir R.B. Finlay, a law officer, suggested removing the restrictions on aliens, which had caused 'trouble in the case of Cyprus'.[242] He was told that the Foreign Office would agree.[243] Clauson proposed allowing the enlistment of men under British rule.[244] The proposal for a Cyprus regiment was influencing imperial policy. Chamberlain told the War Office that there would be less criticism in Parliament if the provision stated that an inhabitant of a British protectorate was not an alien. The decision rested with St John Brodrick, the new War

Secretary.[245] A draft amendment from the Attorney-General's office stipulated that 'any person subject to the Government of Cyprus, any person enjoying His Majesty's protection and' so on, was not an alien.[246] The War Office clerks initially agreed,[247] but then opposed the mention of Cyprus.[248] Brodrick told the Colonial Office that owing to the Bill's late introduction and the difficulty of passing it by 30 April, he did not want changes that 'were not of immediate necessity'. The matter was deferred until the next parliamentary session.[249]

In July, O'Conor pursued the matter[250] and it was again referred to the War Office. E.A. Altham, the Adjunct Quarter-Master General, expressed on 27 July 1901 that

> it would be useless as well as unwise to attempt the defence of Cyprus on any minor scale. We have no troops to waste in places the defence of which is unnecessary to our strategic plans.[251]

Altham believed that there were two obstacles; the lack of power under the Army Act, only rectifiable by legislation, and Ottoman objections. He liked the idea of stationing it in Malta (to release two battalions to Egypt) because the 'loyalty of the semi-Turkish troops might be doubtful' if local disturbances occurred in Egypt.[252] If a European power attacked Egypt, the Cypriot and Egyptian regiments might turn hostile.[253] Altham suggested asking the Foreign Office to clarify the Sultan's position and asking the Colonial Office about the loyalty of the Cypriot Turks and whether placing them in Malta would be viable.[254] Lieutenant General William Nicholson, Director General of Military Intelligence, agreed.[255] But Lord Roberts, the new Commander-in-Chief of the army, wanted a postponement until a defence policy in Egypt was determined, and so the matter was held over until October.[256]

The proposal, however, was again forgotten as moves to remove the garrison were revived. In December 1901, Brodrick asked Chamberlain to consider removing the garrison to Malta since the *zaptieh* would uphold order and it was 'useless strategically' in Cyprus.[257] A.E. Collins, a Colonial Office clerk, argued that apart from the financial loss there was the rise of a hardcore *énosis* movement.

> Considerable agitation has been going . . . for union with Greece. This has been prominently to the front in the recent elections for the Legislative Council under the leadership of the Bishop of Kitium, who will in all probability be the new Archbishop . . . The possibility of actual disorder is perhaps much slighter than the H.C. supposes, and the Zaptieh force are loyal and capable of maintaining order, but the political effect of the withdrawal . . . would be unfortunate, more particularly since the agitation is very largely due to the supposition prevalent in the island that our occupation is not to be permanent. The withdrawal of the troops would add to this impression.[258]

Collins wanted London to announce that the government and garrison were staying – the garrison until the Army Act was changed to allow for the raising of a local corps.[259] Chamberlain informed the Foreign Office about the severity of the agitation, which made a withdrawal untimely. Lansdowne concurred[260] and the War Office agreed to postpone again.[261] Clearly, the Colonial and Foreign Office alliance was winning the day.

The question of raising a local force was not reconsidered. Haynes Smith raised it again on 25 January when proposing a breakwater at Famagusta.[262] The Colonial Office knew that an order-in-council was enough to raise troops for local use, but the War Office had to pay and it would not do so unless they were under the Army Act to serve elsewhere.[263] The War Office no longer liked the scheme and did not change the Army Act in 1902. Haynes Smith fumed. Much preparatory work was needed. He asked to raise a battalion of mounted infantry and two batteries of field artillery, through an order-in-council, to free the British troops and once the Army Act was amended it could be used generally.[264] But the War Office could not pay for it as it would have no funds until April 1903, which coincided with the next chance to alter the Army Act. But with the estimates due in November, little time was left to convince the War Office.[265] Haynes Smith no longer had Chamberlain's support. The latter told Brodrick that 'there would be no benefit . . . from the formation of such a corps which would justify any expenditure from Cyprus funds'.[266] Chamberlain knew Brodrick would not fund it, but believed a regiment for general service had merit and the force could be organised and funded in anticipation of changing the Army Act.[267]

But the issue was Egypt's defence. Lord Kitchener, the Commander-in-Chief in the Boer War, suggested reorganising four Sudanese battalions to ensure fidelity, but Altham thought:

> The old Roman maxim '*dive et impera*' still holds good; if reliance must be placed on foreign troops it is desirable that they should be intermingled and that garrisons should . . . be composed of men recruited at a distance from the localities . . . and thus unlikely to be in sympathy with local intrigues.[268]

A Cypriot regiment was better. The Turks 'despise' the Felaheen and Sudanese and would not join them in a mutiny, 'unless a wave of Mahommedan fanaticism' swept over North Africa. There were no hurdles once the Army Act was changed, unless the Sultan quibbled, so raising Cypriot battalions for Egypt was 'not impracticable' and would be '*prima facie* more likely than the Soudanese to be proof against local political intrigues'.[269] A Cypriot battalion with twelve British officers was estimated to annually cost £52,116. If two were raised, they could serve in Egypt or Malta, releasing two battalions for service in Egypt, or one in Egypt and one in Malta.[270] This was cost-effective, as the company in Cyprus cost £8,599 in 1902–03, and a full battalion would amount to nearly £70,000.[271] The proposal was sound, but Kitchener asserted that it would be inexpedient to station Cypriot Turks in Egypt because they had mutinied at Suakim.[272] Sir Evelyn Wood claimed to have raised two companies of Cypriot Turks, which were excellent until they refused to fight and he executed two.[273] This was an extraordinary revelation because Wood had not mentioned it before despite being part of the debate since April 1899.

The War Office consulted Lieutenant-Colonel James Henry Bor, an expert in leading semi-military forces, who had commanded the *zaptieh* for nine years (1884–92) and after, in Crete and Albania.[274] He argued that 'the courage of the Cypriot Moslems was very great, while that of the Christian . . . [was] inferior'. He thought they would fight well under English officers and agreed with Haynes Smith that the Cypriots were 'fearless horsemen . . . from childhood' and would make excellent mounted infantry, but their habits were too domestic and they were 'deficient in fighting instincts'.[275] Nicholson concluded that 'it would not be much use' to raise a Cypriot regiment for service outside the island until the Army Act was amended.[276] Roberts and Brodrick agreed, and accordingly informed Chamberlain.[277] This was the end of the scheme although Ivrea, Haynes Smith and O'Conor continued to push for it.[278]

The great debate over the military establishment in Cyprus

Cyprus, the military authorities believed, had so little value to imperial strategy and defence that they not only wanted to remove the British troops, but ignored Haynes Smith's urgings in April 1903, as his term as high commissioner drew to a close, that Cyprus should be used for manoeuvres, as Haggard had suggested. They were unmoved by his blandishments that the healthy climate made Cyprus ideal for convalescent troops; that it offered a more varied training ground than Egypt, which was flat, and was better for artillery training than Malta, which was overpopulated; that its roads were equal to South African wagon roads; and that ponies were hardy and cheap.[279] The War Office argued that the peacetime dispersal of the regular army was 'based on the strategical requirements of the Empire' and even if troops were available their 'allotment to Cyprus would not . . . secure any strategical advantage'.[280]

In May 1903, Major-General R.A. Talbot, the Commander-in-Chief in Egypt since 1899, determined after visiting Cyprus that the military establishment needed streamlining. He arranged with Haynes Smith for the Public Works Department to take over the duties of the Royal Engineers saving London £1,000 a year,[281] in exchange for a £125-a-year payment to Cyprus – a trifle, since Samuel Brown wanted £700 a year in 1884.[282] Talbot thought the stores and buildings were designed for more than one company and suffered from irregular shrinkage. He wanted a transit store at Polymedia to replace the Limassol depot and huts at Troodos to make it a sanatorium for Egypt, especially since it could be linked by rail to Famagusta. (Frederic Shelford, the railway's engineer, was in Cyprus at the time looking into its extension.) Talbot wanted the garrison enlarged to permit efficient training and provide officers for court martial.[283] Haynes Smith agreed, reminding Chamberlain: 'One desires a sufficient force to be able to prevent disturbances and not only to put them down after they occur.'[284]

Brodrick and his heir, Hugh Arnold-Forster, hailed the downsizing,[285] but rejected Talbot's vision for Troodos (although it was used during the 1895 and 1898 Sudan campaigns)[286] because invalids were better off returning home;[287] and the idea to increase the garrison only led to them pushing to remove it. Altham asserted: 'strategically, the detachment would be in a dangerous position on the outbreak of war' and the army was

> too small to permit our furnishing detachments to perform police duties in British possessions to which, for strategic reasons, no garrison would be allotted. If we yield to demands of this kind without increasing the establishments of the army the approved garrisons of extremely important places such as Malta and Egypt are encroached on, and undue risk is thus run.[288]

Nicholson, Roberts and Brodrick agreed.[289] So the War Office told the Colonial and Foreign offices that the garrison had only remained in 1894 because of internal political reasons and although arms had been smuggled into Cyprus from Brindisi, which Haynes Smith attributed to the 'growing truculence . . . of the Greek-speaking Cypriots towards British Officers and [the] British administration', the garrison had to go.[290]

The Colonial and Foreign offices favoured retaining and even increasing the garrison, having accepted Haynes Smith's position on the possible violence from Hellenic agitation. Adrian Fiddian, a new Colonial Office clerk, believed:

> From a civil point of view, we could not dispense with the presence of the military. The Pan-Hellenic propaganda is not likely to subside, and may at any moment take a very practical form.

[231]

> We should say at once that for civil reasons it is highly desirable (necessary) that no reduction should be made.[291]

O'Conor asserted that authority must be upheld 'in the face of the Hellenic propaganda' and 'the Mussulman inhabitants of the island are probably as fine military material as their co-religionists on the mainland'.[292]

To break the division, the matter was put to the Colonial Defence Committee.[293] John Clauson's memorandum of 30 December 1903 addressed the issues of maintaining, augmenting, substituting or removing the troops.[294] The committee considered the current company was a symbol of British authority and being at Limassol it did not prevent disturbances in Nicosia, even if doubled. It rejected a local force and withdrawing the garrison because

> the present agitation in Cyprus is serious and unscrupulous, and . . . any step which might be construed as a weakening of British control would encourage the elements of disorder and accentuate the difficulties.[295]

The *zaptieh*, Haynes Smith claimed in his 1901–02 report, were a fine body of men, but in a letter dated 24 June 1903 he stated that they could not prevent racial collisions even with the current garrison. To deal with disorder two changes were needed: substituting the regular infantry with mounted troops and providing combined training for the mounted *zaptieh*.[296]

The idea of upgrading to a mounted infantry surprised the War Office. Nicholson thought it was advantageous, but 'would entail considerable additional expenditure', which was militarily unjustified.[297] He estimated the initial charges at £3,000: £1,500 for 100 ponies and £1,500 for the saddlery and accoutrements. The annual charges for salaries and forage amounted to £3,000.[298] Although the Adjunct-General had agreed with the Colonial Defence Committee proposal, Roberts shared Nicholson's view.[299] Haynes Smith told the new Colonial Secretary, Alfred Lyttelton, that the Cypriots could provide their own horses,[300] thus halving the initial costs. But it made no difference to the War Office: one company of infantry detached from Egypt would stay;[301] and it ordered the speedy implementation of the recommendations for the *zaptieh* 'to facilitate the removal of the Regular troops as soon as the political situation' allowed.[302]

Lyttelton and the Admiralty had concurred with the Committee's proposals,[303] but the new War Secretary, Hugh Oakley Arnold-Forster, did not because of the 'considerable additional expenditure'.[304] Arnold-Forster, the ninth in a line of potential choices to replace Brodrick, was a well-known imperial strategist and a key figure behind Stead's 1884 'naval scare'. He tried to replace Cardwell's linked garrisons with large depots, hence his desire to withdraw the garrison from Cyprus, but the refusal of the Foreign Office to withdraw troops from Egypt and the Colonial Office to fund local regiments thwarted him.[305]

Clauson regretted that the War Office had 'jibbed on the ground of expense', because Cyprus was ideal for training mounted infantry and it was proving difficult to justify to Cypriot Hellenists that the British meant to stay: 'The foot company living at one end of the island in tumbledown huts conveys little to the local mind, and we have said . . . that it may go out at any time.'[306] Clauson hoped that the Colonial Office would reopen the question and asked for half a company of mounted infantry instead of one.

> The proper antidotes to picture postcards of charmed Paphian Aphrodites gazing wistfully at the Acropolis seem to me to be the bifurcation and specialisation in the Police of Hellenic detective guile and British-officered-Mussulman swoop and discipline.[307]

Arnold-Forster, however, insisted that the 132 troops had 'no Military duties', were 'merely a substitute for police' and only provided 'a guard on the Governor's House'. In fact, they did not even do the latter. In June 1904, he insisted on their withdrawal.[308]

Haynes Smith countered with calls for a mounted regiment and savaged Kitchener and Wood's evidence on the military qualifications of the Cypriot Muslims.[309]

> . . . no Cypriot was ever enlisted in Cyprus for military service in Egypt, or elsewhere. Two companies of Cypriot Turks never left Cyprus for military service, or were ever asked to fight. The experiment of raising a force of Cypriot Turks for military service outside the island has never been tried.[310]

Clauson clarified that the Cypriot Turks referred to formed part of a mixed Muslim corps raised in Egypt,[311] and a soldier who had seen a considerable number of them at Suakim in 1885 said that they behaved with 'considerable courage' compared with the natives and that his experiences of them in Cyprus showed him that they had 'soldierly qualities'.[312]

But the Colonial Office was ready to agree to the withdrawal. Fiddian believed that Haynes Smith was 'rather an alarmist' and having spoken with officers returning from Cyprus, he believed that there was no real use for troops in Cyprus.[313] So the new high commissioner, Charles King-Harman, was asked if the *zaptieh* could manage.[314] King-Harman was much more temperate than his predecessor. He rejected raising a Cypriot Muslim force because it was beyond Cyprus' means and it would be 'fraught with the greatest danger to the peace of the country'. The agitation it would excite among the

'Greek population would probably be unprecedented even in the history of Cyprus'.[315]

King-Harman claimed that the local factors that had kept the garrison from being withdrawn still applied: 'from a political point of view and for the sake of the peace of the island, the maintenance of the garrison is of paramount importance.' He claimed that the *énosis* movement was natural, harmless and controllable by a 'firm and absolutely impartial administration', but the Muslims were afraid and it excited 'feelings of retaliation between the two'. Withdrawing the garrison would cause panic and 'precipitate a conflict between the two sections of the population', which the *zaptieh* would struggle to suppress. The garrison, although small, was a real symbol of the British occupation, and so long as it remains there was little danger of civil war.[316]

The Liberal government of 1905 did not alter the War Office stance on withdrawing the garrison. Within months Lord Haldane, the War Secretary, asked the Colonial Office when the garrison could be withdrawn.[317] He was referred to King-Harman's despatch and told that nothing would change to permit its removal.[318]

The General Staff report of 1907

Haldane was an inspired choice as War Secretary: a Liberal imperialist who belonged to the Fabian Society and backed the Boer War. Britain's poor showing in South Africa stimulated him to pursue and achieve possibly the most vital reforms of the British military system: the institution of a General Staff (1906); the Territorial Army (1907); and the expeditionary force for employment on continental Europe.[319]

In 1907, the General Staff produced a military report on Cyprus, with others in 1913 and 1936.[320] The 'Military Qualities of Cypriots' was a feature of the report.

> the desperate and gallant defence of Nicosia and Famagusta against the Turks in 1570 shows that the Christian inhabitants were not devoid of martial qualities; while the opinion held regarding the Cypriot Turk... [is]that he is probably as fine military material as his co-religionists on the mainland. In the operation against the Mahdists at Suakin in 1885 a number of Cypriot Turkish muleteers were employed, and were reported on as having shown, though unarmed, considerable courage during one or two night alarms, where their conduct was in marked contrast to that of other natives similarly employed... both Mohammedans and Christians... would appear to offer useful material for cavalry or mounted infantry.[321]

The statements about the Christian inhabitants were bizarre, not least because many Orthodox had welcomed the 1571 Ottoman invasion. The perceived Muslim fighting abilities had become a received wisdom to the extent that the same paragraph was included in the two subsequent reports.[322] Clauson referred to them when, as high commissioner, he supported raising a Cypriot muleteer force in 1916.[323]

As for Famagusta harbour, it 'acquired some importance' since its redevelopment, but it is not clear how. It had a new water supply; it was as healthy as other towns in the island; and a fortnightly mail service from Alexandria and Port Said brought it within reach of troops wishing to escape Egypt's summer.[324] But there was no sanatorium and the outer harbour had not been touched. The development of the inner basin had not attracted much attention from naval authorities. But, in May 1906, Lieutenant-Commander Lancelot Napier Turton of the destroyer *Ariel* recommended Famagusta as a coaling station in two reports for Battenberg, now commander of the Second Cruiser Squadron. Turton argued that if sufficient coal was kept on the new wharf, ships with draft of 22 feet, and of any length and tonnage could be coaled alongside the wharf. He thought four cruisers and sixteen destroyers could berth simultaneously without affecting local traffic. The Lords of the Admiralty did not think the report was worth sending to the Board of Trade, nor was it used for the 1907 military report.[325] Since the General Staff report continued to assert the dangers of landing and embarking troops at Limassol,[326] Famagusta was better even without a breakwater.

Conclusion

Party affiliation determined, to a large degree, how Cyprus was viewed within British imperial strategy. Most Conservatives viewed Cyprus as valuable or potentially valuable, while most Liberals viewed it as inconsequential. Imperial defence strategy played a large part in Cyprus becoming an inconsequential possession. The British failed to forge a role for Cyprus after Beaconsfield's government postponed making it a military and naval base, despite its proximity to Egypt. Thus, it was logical that military advisers wanted to withdraw the garrison. Equally natural was the Colonial and Foreign Offices use of the growing truculence of the *énosis* movement that threatened Orthodox–Muslim relations. At first, the Colonial and Foreign offices failed to prevent a withdrawal – the garrison was too large to justify its presence in such an inconsequential station. Then they succeeded in thwarting the War Office, as high commissioners of Cyprus increasingly reported that the *zaptieh* could not maintain order in collisions between the Orthodox and Muslims.

A number of measures were proposed to give Cyprus some role in imperial strategy even with the inaction over a naval and military base. As a sanatorium it may have worked well, perhaps even showing that Cyprus had potential as an army base. The problem, however, was that the Troodos Hill Station, the preferred location, was to far from the only place to build a harbour – Famagusta – which the British did not want to build anyway. So for this and other reasons the idea was rejected. Another measure, which also hoped to nullify the *énosis* movement and allow for the British military withdrawal, was the proposal to raise a local regiment of Orthodox and Muslim Cypriots. Was this a missed opportunity to replace the British troops with local troops? Ultimately, the *énosis* movement resulted in a new Cyprus government rejecting this proposal.

This chapter has shown how ambiguous the label 'strategically important' can be when exploring the place of a supposed strategic possession to imperial strategy. Also, showing that a place was inconsequential demythologises the policies and geopolitics around its occupation and retention. The question remains, however: if Cyprus was so inconsequential, except as regards tribute money, why was it retained and not relinquished?

Notes

1 Schurman, *Imperial Defence*, 88–90.
2 Ibid.
3 Captain J.C.R. Colomb, *The Defence of Great and Greater Britain*, London, 1880.
4 CO67/25/2197, confidential, Report of a Committee held on board HMS Superb on 30 November and 1 and 2 December 1881. The committee seems to have made a mistake in saying that Famagusta was in the second-class category and thus desired as a coaling station and a port of refuge.
5 Schurman, *Imperial Defence*, 91–2.
6 CO67/25/2197, confidential, Memorandum on Famagusta Defences, J.H. Smith, IGF office, 25 May 1881.
7 CO67/25/2197, confidential, Biddulph to the Officer Commanding *Superb*, 28 November 1881; confidential, Biddulph to Kimberley, 20 January 1882; *Superb* Committee Report.
8 Schurman, *Imperial Defence*, 101–4.
9 Ibid., 107, 110–12.
10 Alexander Scholch, *Egypt for the Egyptians!* London, 1981, 43–63.
11 Ibid., 135–231; John Galbraith and A.L. al-Sayyid Marsot, 'The British Occupation of Egypt', *IJMES*, IX, 4, 1978, 471–88; A.G. Hopkins, 'The Victorians and Africa: A Reconsideration of the Occupation of Egypt, 1882', *JAH*, XXVII, 2, 1986, 363–91.
12 Galbraith and Marsot, 'The British Occupation of Egypt', 477.
13 Charles Royle, *The Egyptian Campaigns 1882 to 1885*, London, 1900, 57.
14 Galbraith and Marsot, 'The British Occupation of Egypt', 479–80, 484.
15 CAB41/12/7, Beaconsfield to Queen Victoria, 21 February 1879.
16 Alexander the Great, Arrian, *Book II*, 4.
17 *The Times*, 5 June 1882, 10.c.
18 CAB41/16/34, 5 July 1882.

19 WO to Queen Victoria, 10 July 1882, Childers, *Childers*, II, 95.
20 Sinclair, *Camp and Society*, 130; Storrs, *Chronology*, 31.
21 Childers, *Childers*, II, 90–1; Storrs, *Chronology*, 31.
22 Savile, *Cyprus*, 64; Sinclair, *Camp and Society*, 131.
23 ADM185/70. Quartermaster's Diary on the Battalion formed for special service in the Mediterranean on 26 June 1882; Childers, *Childers*, II, 90–1; Royle, *The Egyptian Campaigns*, 103–5.
24 Sinclair, *Camp and Society*, 131.
25 Donne Journal, 26 August 1882; SA1:7471 ML/48/6; *The Times*, 8 September 1882, 3e.
26 Ibid., 8f; G.C. Dawnay, *Campaigns: Zulu 1879, Egypt 1882, Suakim 1885: Being the Private Journal of Guy C. Dawnay*, Cambridge, 1989, 144.
27 Dawnay, *Campaign*, 104; Vogt, *The Egyptian War*, 159, 166; Wolseley to Childers, 1 September 1882, Royle, *The Egyptian Campaigns*, 165.
28 Sinclair, *Camp and Society*, 131–2.
29 CO67/29/14887/7699/921, immediate, Ralph Thompson, WO to CO, 21 August 1882.
30 Sinclair, *Camp and Society*, 133; Storrs, *Chronology*, 31.
31 *Hansard* (Lords), CCLXXIII, 28 July 1882, 17–18.
32 Ibid., 19–20.
33 The Eureka stockade was the setting of a gold miners' revolt in 1854, near Ballarat, Victoria, Australia, against the officials supervising the mining of gold in the area. For three years miners had debated the various expenses placed on them in executing their work, and their anger at the inaction of the authorities brought them to revolt. The 'rebellion', although swiftly and violently put down, was a watershed event in Australian political history. In Melbourne the miners had widespread public support and this resulted in the introduction of full white male suffrage for the elections for the lower house in the Victorian parliament. Thus the Eureka Stockade is identified with the birth of democracy in Australia.
34 R.H. Vetch, 'Pasley, Charles (1824–1890)', rev. Elizabeth Baigent, *ODNB* (www.oxforddnb.com/view/article/21499, accessed 23 Feb 2005).
35 CO67/28/19376, Major-General Pasley Memorandum, 24 August 1882; to CO, 7 November 1882.
36 CO67/29/16944, Cyprus 2/597, WO to CO, 25 September 1882.
37 CO67/24/14613, Childers to Kimberly CO, 15 August 1881.
38 CO67/28/19376, minute, Fairfield, 10 November 1882; on 8 December 1882 the CO asked the WO to decide, but there is no record of a reply. Ibid., confidential, CO to WO, 8 December 1882.
39 *The Times*, 27 January 1883, 5f.
40 CO67/34/2573, 33, Biddulph to Derby, 30 January 1884; CO67/34/2573, Brown Memorandum to Chief Secretary, 19 January 1884; CO67/36/3810, Maberly to Evelyn Ashley, 4 March 1884.
41 CO67/26/12239, 229, Biddulph to Kimberley, 1 July 1882.
42 Royle, *The Egyptian Campaigns*, 56; *The Times*, 14 June 1882, 5.e.
43 *The Times*, 16 June 1882, 5.e.
44 Donne Journal, 15 June 1882.
45 *Hansard* (Commons), CCLXXII, 24 July 1882, 1543.
46 CO67/26/13134, confidential, Biddulph to Kimberley, 15 July 1882; *The Times*, 9 January 1883, 8.c.
47 CO67/26/12815, 242, Biddulph to Kimberley, 8 July 1882; CO67/28/12888, minute, Fairfield, 21 July 1882; Fairfield opined that the Cypriots were 'finer fellows than the Maltese'. CO67/26/12239, minute, Fairfield, 11 July 1882; Kimberley thanked the Cypriots. Ibid., Kimberley to Biddulph, 15 July 1882.
48 *The Times*, 9 January 1883, 8.c.
49 CO67/26/16350, Geo Letts to Ellis, 13 August 1882.
50 Ibid., 298, Biddulph to Kimberley, 2 September 1882; CO67/26/17641, Ordinance 12A of 1882, 5 September 1882.

51 CO67/27/19941, CMO, Heidenstam to Chief Secretary, 2 November 1882; CO67/30/1566, Heidenstam to Chief Secretary, 30 December 1882.
52 Jacques Berque, *Egypt: Imperialism and Revolution*, London 1962.
53 CO67/31/11481, Biddulph to Derby, 4 July 1883; CO67/31/11481, CO to ADM, 7 July 1883; *The Times*, 6 July 1883, 5.d; *The Times*, 15 December 1883, 5.e.
54 T1/15476/17284, telegram, Biddulph to Derby, 30 June 1883; Biddulph to Derby, 30 June 1883.
55 Ibid., CO to Treasury, 21 July 1883; T1/15476/13349/83, Biddulph to Derby, 18 September 1883; ibid., Brown to Warren, 5 September 1883; Brown to Warren, 5 September 1883; Biddulph to Derby, 28 July 1883; Meade to T, 8 October 1883.
56 ADM50/277, Journal of Admiral Lord John Hay, Commander-in Chief Mediterranean Squadron or Station (CICMS), March 1883 to December 1885, 23 February 1884, 24 February and 1 March.
57 Arthur Evelyn Fyler, *The Development of Cyprus, and Rambles in the Island*, London, 1899, 45–6; *The Times*, 21 January 1884, 7d; 26 July 1884, 7a.
58 CO67/36/3748, 180, Sir E. Barring, Cairo to CO, 29 February 1884; minute, Fairfield, 4 March 1884; CO to Biddulph, 7 March 1884; SA1:762/85, Muleteers application form, 19 February 1885.
59 Sinclair, *Camp and Society*, 130; Storrs, *Chronology*, 135.
60 SA1:1957/85, Michael Kyriako invalided from Suakin pleaded for the Cyprus government to pay £4 compensation to his wife, which was being paid by Brigade-Major E.E.S. Swaine, Famagusta's first Commissioner; SA1:2670/1885, A muleteer from Nicosia, Costi Hadji Yanni, was fatally shot.
61 SA1:2549/1886.
62 SA1:16/1884, dates of arrival, 3 January 1884, 8 February 1884, 6 March 1884; *The Times*, 22 September 1884, 6.b; Baird, *General Wauchope*, 92; SA1:3604/84, Hay to Biddulph, 1 September 1884; *The Times*, 2 September 1884, 6.f.
63 Hopkins, 'The Victorians and Africa', 388.
64 *Hansard* (Commons), CCXCVII, 21 April 1885, 313.
65 Currie notes of a conversation with Bismarck, 28 September 1885, Rose Louise Greaves, *Persia and the Defence of India 1884–1892*, London, 1959, 251–3.
66 Salisbury to Victoria, 10 February 1887, *Letters to Queen Victoria*, 3rd series, I, 273. Drummond Wolff was appointed, along with an Ottoman, to oversee Egypt's reforms.
67 *The Times*, 4 July 1885, 1885, 8.d; *The Times*, 11 July 1885, 7.d.
68 C.3385, 171; Donne, *Records of the Ottoman Conquest of Cyprus*, 108. The only resort in the eastern Mediterranean was Alley, a Druze village on the treeless mountains near Beirut.
69 SA1:2045/86, 16–21, Bulwer minute, 6 October 1886.
70 Ibid.; SA1:2045/86, Warren to Bulwer, 23 July 1886; Warren minute, 9 October 1886.
71 Varnava, 'Maintaining Britishness'.
72 *The Times*, 2 September 1886, 6b.
73 CO67/43/340, confidential, Bulwer to Stanhope, 7 December 1886; minute, Fairfield, 14 January 1886; confidential, Stanhope to Bulwer, 19 January 1887.
74 Ibid., minute, Fairfield, 10 January 1886; minute, Fairfield, 14 January 1886; confidential, Stanhope to Bulwer, 19 January 1887.
75 SA1:1081/87, Bulwer to Hackett, 14 April 1887; Hackett to Bulwer, 16 April 1887; Warren to Bulwer, 26 May 1887; Bulwer to Stanhope, enclosures, 1 June 1887; SA1:2029/87, WO to Bulwer, 4 July 1887.
76 CO67/50/7731, Cyprus 8/53, WO to CO, 19 April 1887. Emphasis original.
77 Ibid., minute, Fairfield, 22 April 1887.
78 SAI:C.S/1558/88, Sketch of land the Cyprus government assigns to the War Department on Troodos, Major Ryder Main, RE, 14 July 1887.
79 Alfred Milner, *England in Egypt*, London, 1892, 124.
80 Schurman, *Imperial Defence*, 134–5.
81 Anthony Bruce, 'Edward Cardwell and the Abolition of Purchase', in I. Beckett and J. Gooch (eds), *Politicians and Defence*, Manchester, 1981, 24–46.

82 Harold Arthur Perry, 'England in the Mediterranean', *National Review* (*NR*), IX, 1887, 554–68.
83 CAB9/1/14, confidential, Local Committee Report, Cyprus, CDC remarks, G.S. Clarke, 1 March 1888.
84 Ibid.
85 Ibid.
86 Ibid.; Schurman, *Imperial Defence*, 135.
87 CO537/23/705, secret, FO, J. Paunceforte, to WO, 15 May 1888.
88 CAB37/19/8, Brackenbury memorandum, 25 January 1887.
89 Roger Owen, *Lord Cromer*, Oxford, 2004, 236–49, 282–3.
90 CO537/23/706, secret, WO to CO, 19 May 1888.
91 CO537/23/705, secret, CO to WO, 18 June 1888.
92 Ibid., secret, CO to Bulwer, 24 August 1888.
93 Donne, *Cyprus Guide*, 131.
94 General Staff, WO, *Military Report and General Information Concerning the Island of Cyprus*, London, 1913, 67.
95 CO537/23/448, secret, Bulwer to Knutsford, 29 September 1888.
96 CAB8/3/314, secret, Garrison of Cyprus, CDC memorandum, John Clauson, secretary, 30 December 1903. (Hereafter, Clauson 314 memorandum).
97 CAB37/22/32, Salisbury Memorandum, 6 November 1888; CAB37/22/44, Memorandum, A.W.A. Hood, A.H. Hoskins, W. Graham, C.F. Hotham, July 1888.
98 CO67/57/22877, WO to CO, 21 November 1888.
99 CO67/57/22877, 218, Knutsford to Bulwer, 27 November 1888; CO67/57/25765, WO to CO, 28 December 1888; CO537/23/448, secret, CO to Bulwer, 13 February 1889; CO to WO, 13 February 1889.
100 J.F. Beeler, 'Steam, Strategy and Schurman: Imperial Defence in the Post-Crimean Era, 1865–1905', *Far-Flung Lines*, 38.
101 David Nichols, *The Lost Prime Minister: A Life of Sir Charles Dilke*, London, 1995, 82.
102 Charles Dilke, *Problems of Greater Britain*, London, 1890, 666.
103 CO67/64/11086, confidential, Bulwer to Knutsford, 27 May 1890.
104 CO67/64/11086, minute, Fairfield, 10 June 1890.
105 CO67/67/12367, m.0202, ADM, Ewan Macgregor, to CO, 25 June 1890.
106 CO67/57/25765, minute, Mercer, 27 December 1892.
107 CO67/57/25765, minute, Fairfield, 28 December 1892.
108 CO67/57/25765, minute, Meade, 2 January 1893.
109 CO67/89/2225, confidential, Thompson, WO to CO, 5 February 1894.
110 CO67/89/2225, minute, Fairfield, 10 February 1894.
111 CO67/89/2225, minute, Meade, 13 February 1894; minute, Ripon, 16 February 1894.
112 CO67/89/2225, secret, Ripon to Sendall, 5 March 1894.
113 CO67/84/5122, secret, telegram, Sendall to Ripon, 23 March 1894.
114 C.A. Harris, 'Sendall, Sir Walter Joseph (1832–1904)', rev. Lynn Milne, *ODNB* (www.oxforddnb.com/view/article/36018, accessed 15 Aug 2005).
115 CO67/84/5122, secret, telegram, Sendall to Ripon, 23 March 1894.
116 CO67/84/6068, confidential, Sendall to Ripon, 26 March 1894.
117 Ibid.
118 Ibid.
119 CO67/85/6820, confidential, Sendall to Ripon, 10 April 1894; CO67/85/6820, confidential, Limassol Commission Memorandum, Roland Michell, 27 March 1894; CO67/85/6820, confidential, Receiver-General Taylor Memorandum, 9 April 1894.
120 CO67/85/6820, confidential, Sendall to Ripon, 10 April 1894.
121 Ibid.; CO67/79/2436, confidential, Sendall to Ripon, 29 January 1893.
122 CO67/79/2436, minute, Fairfield, 27 April 1894.
123 CO67/79/2436, confidential, Thompson to Meade, 27 April 1894.
124 Ibid.
125 CO67/85/6820, confidential, Meade to Thompson, 30 April 1894; minute, Ripon, 28 April 1894.

126 CO67/85/6820, confidential, Meade to Thompson, 30 April 1894.
127 CO67/85/6820, private, Meade to Sendall, 7 May 1894.
128 CO67/86/9566, confidential, Sendall to Ripon, 21 May 1894.
129 CO67/86/9566, translation, *Alithea*, 688, 18 May 1894.
130 Ibid.
131 CO67/86/13013, confidential, Sendall to Ripon, 16 July 1894; translation of extract from *Alithea*, 12 July 1894.
132 Clauson 314 memorandum.
133 CO67/86/15936, confidential, Sendall to Ripon, 27 August 1894.
134 CO67/86/15936, confidential, enclosure, translation, *Alithea*, 701, 16 August 1894.
135 Ibid.
136 CO67/86/15936, enclosure, translation, *Phoni tis Kyprou*, 18 August 1894.
137 Ibid.
138 CO67/87/16617, confidential, Sendall to Ripon, 8 September 1894.
139 CO67/87/16617, enclosure, *The Times of Cyprus*, 29 August 1894.
140 CO67/87/16617, enclosure, translation, *Salpinx*, 20 August 1894.
141 *BLC*, 233–4.
142 CO67/87/16617, confidential, Sendall to Ripon, 8 September 1894, enclosure, translation, *Kipris*, 27 August 1894.
143 CO67/87/16617, confidential, Sendall to Ripon, 8 September 1894, enclosure, translation, *Kipris*, 27 August 1894.
144 CO67/87/16617, enclosure, translation *Evagóras*, 20 September 1894.
145 Ibid.
146 CO67/89/16268, Meade, minute, 15 September 1894.
147 CO67/87/15879, telegram, Ripon to Sendall, 9 September 1894.
148 *The Times*, 23 January 1895, 10g.
149 Clauson 314 memorandum, Ripon to Sendall, 12 October 1894.
150 Ibid.
151 *The Times*, 15 November 1894, 3e; 29 November 1894, 10f.
152 Ibid., 26 November 1894, 6b; 5 December 1894, 12c.
153 CO67/89/20266, telegrams from Municipal Council and residents, 20 November 1894.
154 *The Times*, 27 November 1894, 5f; 14 December 1894, 14f.
155 CO67/89/20266, minute, Fairfield, 21 November 1894.
156 CO67/89/21457, confidential, WO to CO, 10 December 1894.
157 CO67/89/21457, minutes, 11 December 1894.
158 CO67/89/21457, immediate, CO to WO, 26 December 1894.
159 CO67/95/126, WO to CO, 2 January 1895.
160 CO67/89/21457, CO to Sendall, 4 January 1895.
161 Ibid.
162 *The Times*, 14 February 1895, 3b.
163 CO67/91/9513, 127, Sendall to Ripon, 20 May 1895; see also WO33/76.
164 CO67/103/1405, WO to CO, 18 January 1896; CO to Sendall, 28 January 1896.
165 CO67/103/8025, WO to CO, 14 April 1896; CO67/103/8025, Cyprus 2/1256, T to WO, 2 April 1896; CO67/99/13923, Sendall to Chamberlain, 19 June 1896.
166 CO67/95/22478, WO to CO, 16 December 1895.
167 CO67/95/22478, Anderson, minute, 18 December 1895; Fairfield, minute, 18 December 1895; Meade, minute, 20 December 1895.
168 CO67/103/593, FO to CO, 7 January 1896.
169 Ibid.
170 FO881/6656, secret, Sir P. Currie to Kimberley, 6 June 1895, enclosing, confidential, Colonel Chernside Memorandum on Naval Demonstration against Turkey, 5 June 1895.
171 *The Times*, 10 October 1882, 5a; 21 January 1884, 7d; 26 July 1884, 7a.
172 Fyler, *The Development of Cyprus*, 33–4, 44–58.
173 Ibid., 57.

174 Ibid., 45–58.
175 Robert Gunnis, *Historic Cyprus*, London, 1936, 252–5; L. and H.A. Mangoian, *The Island of Cyprus*, Bristol 1947, 64; K. Keshishian, *Famagusta Town and District Cyprus*, Limassol 1985, 273–5.
176 Fyler, *The Development of Cyprus*, 52–4.
177 Ibid., 53–4.
178 Ibid., 54–5.
179 CO67/116/27223, Fyler to FO, 2 December 1898; CO to Fyler, 9 December 1898.
180 Haggard, *A Winter's Pilgrimage*, 149.
181 D.S. Higgins, *Rider Haggard: The Great Storyteller*, London, 1981, 109, 111; W.R. Kotz, *Rider Haggard and the Fiction of Empire*, 1987, 14.
182 Haggard, *A Winter's Pilgrimage*, 134–5.
183 Ibid., 156.
184 *Hansard* (Commons), LXIV, 8 August 1898, 503.
185 Henry Pelling, *Social Geography of British Elections, 1885–1910*, London, 1967, 266.
186 *Hansard* (Commons), LXIV, 8 August 1898, 502–5.
187 P.A. Hunt, 'Rollit, Sir Albert Kaye (1842–1922)', *ODNB* (www.oxforddnb.com/view/article/47087, accessed 21 Aug 2005).
188 *Hansard* (Commons), LXIV, 8 August 1898, 512.
189 Ibid., 513.
190 Ibid., 515; Dilke, 'The Three Powers and Greece', *Cosmopolis*, XI, July, 1898.
191 *Hansard* (Commons), LXIV, 8 August 1898, 515.
192 Ibid., 519.
193 CO67/130/6606, private, Haynes Smith to Chamberlain, 25 January 1902.
194 SA1:C626/1902, 403/199, confidential, Suitability for naval station, Famagusta Harbour, 10 February 1902.
195 CO67/130/6606, private, ADM to Collins, CO, 22 February 1902.
196 CO67/112/16037, minute, Graham, 20 July 1898. Fairfield died of a stroke, perhaps brought on by the stress of the Jameson Raid, for which Chamberlain made him a scapegoat. Jeffrey Butler, *The Liberal Party and the Jameson Raid*, Oxford, 1968, 127–9. Unfortunately, Haynes Smith retained this characteristic. In 1921, aged 81, he was declared bankrupt. B9/912, Sir William Frederick Bart Haynes Smith (former) High Commissioner and Commander-in-Chief of Cyprus, 1920.
197 CO67/112/16037, confidential, Haynes Smith to Chamberlain, 7 July 1898.
198 CO67/112/16037, minute, Graham, 20 July 1898.
199 CO67/112/16037, Selbourne, note in the margin, 20 July 1898.
200 CO67/112/16037, minute, Graham, 20 July 1898.
201 CO67/114/619, confidential, Haynes Smith to Chamberlain, 27 December 1898; CO67/117/6016 & WO32/7519, secret, Haynes Smith to Chamberlain, 26 February 1899.
202 CAB8/2/173, secret, Colonial Garrisons: Utilisation of Native Troops, Colonial Defence Committee (CDC) Memorandum, M. Nathan, Secretary, 7 March 1899.
203 Ibid.
204 J.J. Johnson (ed.), *The Role of the Military in Underdeveloped Countries*, Princeton, 1962.
205 M.J. Echenberg, *Colonial Conscripts: The Tirailleurs Sınıgalais in French West Africa, 1857–1960*, London, 1991, 14.
206 B.R. Tomlinson, 'India and the British Empire 1880–1947', 1 & 2, *Indian Economic and Social History Journal*, XVII, 4, 1975, 337–80, & XIII, 3, 1976, 331–49; Nadzan Haron, 'Colonial Defence and British Approach to the Problems in Malaya 1874–1918', *MAS*, XXIV, 2, 1990, 272–95; Pradeep Barua, 'Inventing Race: The British and India's Martial Races', *Historian*, LVIII, 1995, 107–16; D.M. Peers, ' "Those Noble Exemplars of the True Military Tradition": Constructions of the Indian Army in the Mid-Victorian Press', *MAS*, XXXI, 1, 1997, 109–42.
207 Anthony H.M. Kirk-Greene, 'Damnosa Hereditas: Ethnic Ranking and the Martial Races Imperative in Africa', *ERS*, III, 4, 1980, 393–414.

208 V.G. Kiernan, 'Colonial Africa and its Armies', in B. Bon and I. Roy (eds) *War and Society: A Year Book of Military History*, I, New York, 1976; Risto Marjomaa, 'The Martial Spirit: Yao Soldiers in British Service in Nyasaland (Malawi), 1895–1939', *JAH*, XXXXIV, 2003, 413–32.
209 Marjomaa, 'The Martial Spirit', 419.
210 Haron, 'Colonial Defence and British Approach', 279.
211 CO537/210, Enlistment of Chinese and Malays, Hong Kong, 19 April 1879.
212 *The Times*, 21 July 1897, 5a.
213 Garnet Wolseley, 'The Negro as Soldier', *FR*, December 1888.
214 WO32/7520, minute, Wood, 4 April 1899.
215 WO32/7520, minute, Lansdowne, 11 April 1899; WO32/7519, minute, 15 May 1899; WO32/7519, minute, Wood, 18 May 1899.
216 WO32/7519, Captain W.R. Robertson Memorandum on the Cyprus Military Police, 13 May 1899. Robinson became the chief military adviser to the government during the First World War.
217 Basil Stewart, *My Experiences of the Island of Cyprus*, London, 1908, 259.
218 Clauson 314 Memorandum.
219 Ibid.
220 WO32/7520, minute, Wood, 23 and 27 November 1899.
221 WO32/7520, minute, Wolseley, 24 November 1899.
222 WO32/7520, minute, Lansdowne, 25 November 1899.
223 CO67/122/1498, 5, Haynes Smith to Chamberlain, 4 January 1900, including letter signed by the men, 24 December 1899.
224 CO67/126/2924, 079/917, WO to CO, 25 January 1900.
225 CO67/192/44124, 227, Malcolm Stevenson to Viscount Milner, 15 July 1919, enclosures; Leyla Tavsanoglu, *Cumhuriyet*, 31 July 2001; HS3/120 'Cyprus and the War', 14 September 1945; Christos Eleophotou, *Η Συμβολή της Κύπρου εις τον Β' Παγκόσμιον Πόλεμον*, Nicosia, 1975.
226 WO32/7521, secret, Haynes Smith to Chamberlain, 12 February 1900.
227 WO32/7521, 6394, CO to WO, 7 March 1900.
228 WO32/7521, 7690/1998, WO to CO, 21 March 1900.
229 CAB8/3/314, Appendix IV, confidential, 216, O'Conor to Salisbury, 20 June 1900.
230 WO32/7522, Captain Ivrea, 29 July 1900; undated memorandum, 'Cyprus', Captain Ivrea.
231 Ibid.
232 WO32/7522, undated memorandum, titled 'The Regiment to be raised', Ivrea to WO.
233 CO67/88/1532, IO to CO, 25 January 1894; CO67/127/6025, 22, Haynes Smith to Chamberlain, 7 February 1900; CO67/126/4415, WO to CO, 9 February 1900; CO67/126/4856, WO to CO, 19 February 1900; CO67/126/5439, WO to CO, 19 February 1900; CO67/126/6187, WO to CO, 24 February 1900; CO67/129/8515, WO to CO, 5 March 1901; CO67/127/6915, secret, Haynes Smith to Chamberlain, 9 February 1901; IOR/L/MIL/7/1009, Collection 14/9 Purchase of 14 Italian and 10 Cyprus donkey stallions, 1885–1886; IOR/L/MIL/7/1013, Collection 14/12A Purchase by the High Commissioner of 12 donkey stallions in Cyprus, 1886–1887; IOR/L/MIL/7/1015, Collection 14/13A Purchase by the High Commissioner of 10 donkey stallions in Cyprus, 1887–1888; IOR/L/MIL/7/1022, Collection 14/20 Purchase of 47 Italian and 10 Cyprus donkey stallions, 1894–1895; IOR/L/MIL/7/1024, Collection 14/22 Italian and Cyprus donkey stallions: payment of grooms and shipment, 1895–1898; IOR/L/MIL/7/1029, Collection 14/27 Purchase of 21 Cyprus and 15 Italian donkey stallions, 1897–1898; IOR/L/MIL/7/1033, Collection 14/31 Purchase and shipment of Italian and Cyprus donkey stallions, 1897–1898; IOR/L/MIL/7/1040, Collection 14/38 Deputation of Lieutenant Colonel Kuper R.A. to Cyprus and Italy to buy mules for India, date: 1899; IOR/L/MIL/7/1043, Collection 14/41 Cyprus mules, 1900; IOR/L/MIL/7/1045, Collection 14/43 Report on Cyprus mules used in South Africa, 1899–1900, 1900; IOR/L/MIL/7/1047, Collection 14/45 Purchase of Cyprus stallions, 1901–1902; IOR/L/MIL/7/1057,

Collection 14/55 Cyprus donkey stallions: 1904 purchase and quality of 1903 batch, 1904.

234 Marjomaa, 'The Martial Spirit', 419.
235 Ivrea 'The Regiment to be raised' Memorandum.
236 WO32/7522, WO to CO, 28 August 1900; WO32/7523, WO to CO, 6 November 1900.
237 *The Times*, 20 February 1883, 12a, 24 December 1884, 5a, 7 February 1885, 7a, 1 March 1889, 13c, 8 May 1889, 8b, 16 January 1901, 10b, 4 March 1891, 11a, 15 May 1901, 12c, 11 September 1903, 2f, 3 October 1903, 2f, 15 October 1903, 13a, 27 August 1904, 2f, 5 July 1952, 2a.
238 WO32/7523, CO to WO, 12 November 1900; WO32/7523, Bertram Cox to LO, 27 June 1900.
239 WO32/7523, LO to Chamberlain, 10 July 1900.
240 WO32/7523, draft, CO to LO, undated; WO32/7523, FO to CO, 6 March 1899; WO32/7523, Horace Rumbold to Salisbury, 28 February 1899; Emile de Laveleye, *The Balkan Peninsula*, London, 1887, 129.
241 WO32/7524, LO to CO, 28 December 1900.
242 WO32/7525, Finlay to Ilbert, 5 February 1901.
243 WO32/7525, Finlay to W.E. Davidson, 6 February 1901; ibid., Davidson to Finlay, 6 February 1901.
244 WO32/7525, Clauson, minute, 13 February 1901.
245 WO32/7525, Bertram Cox to WO, 16 February 1901; CO67/127/6915, secret, Chamberlain to Haynes Smith, 8 March 1901.
246 WO32/7525, note and draft amendment to WO, 25 February 1901.
247 WO32/7525, minutes, 26–27 February 1901.
248 WO32/7525, minute, 1 April 1901.
249 WO32/7525, R.H. Knox, WO to CO, 6 April 1901.
250 WO32/7526, private, O'Conor to FO, 10 July 1901.
251 WO32/7526, minute, Altham, 27 July 1901.
252 Ibid.
253 WO32/7526, draft letter to Sir Francis Reginald Wingate, 15 August 1901.
254 WO32/7526, minute, Altham, 27 July 1901.
255 WO32/7526, minute, Nicholson, 29 July 1901.
256 WO32/7526, minute, Roberts, 2 August 1901; WO32/7526, minute, Altham, 16 August 1901.
257 CO67/129/43086, Wood, WO to CO, 6 December 1901.
258 CO67/129/43086, minute, Collins, 10 December 1901.
259 Ibid.
260 CO67/129/43086, CO to FO, 18 December 1901; CO67/129/45793, Francis Bertie, FO to CO, 27 December 1901.
261 CO67/129/45793, CO to WO, 3 January 1902.
262 CO67/130/6606, private, Haynes Smith to Chamberlain, 25 January 1902.
263 CO67/130/6606, minute, Collins, 19 February 1902.
264 WO32/7527, secret, Haynes Smith to Chamberlain, 5 May 1902; also CO67/131/20576.
265 CO67/131/20576, minute, Clauson, 6 June 1902.
266 WO32/7527, Bertram Cox to WO, 18 June 1902; also CO67/131/20576.
267 Ibid.
268 WO106/41, secret, Memorandum on the Garrison of Egypt, Altham, 2 August 1902.
269 Ibid.
270 Ibid.
271 *Cyprus Blue Book 1902–03*, Nicosia, 1903, 74–5.
272 WO32/7526, minute, Altham, 12 August 1902.
273 WO32/7526, minute, Wood, 10 August 1901.
274 *The Times*, 6 February 1904, 10c.
275 WO32/7527, minute, Bor, 20 August 1902.
276 WO32/7527, minute, Nicholson, 21 August 1902.

277 WO32/7527, minutes, Roberts, Brodrick, 23 August 1902; CO67/133/37193, WO to CO, 5 September 1902.
278 WO32/7531, Ivrea to Roberts, 22 November 1903; WO to Ivrea, 26 November 1903; WO32/7530, Cyprus (Code 0 (D)):7690/2026, 767, O'Conor to Lansdowne, 17 November 1903.
279 CO67/134/15343, 54, Haynes Smith to Chamberlain, 15 April 1903.
280 CO67/134/15343, CO to WO, 4 May 1903; CO67/137/18399, 7690/2024, I(1), WO to CO, 18 May 1903.
281 WO32/7530, Cyprus (Code 0 (D)):7690/2026, Talbot to Haynes Smith, 3 June 1903.
282 Ibid., Talbot, to the IGF, 13 June 1903.
283 WO32/7529, Talbot to Adjunct-General, 13 June 1903.
284 CO67/135/24943, confidential, Haynes Smith to Chamberlain, 24 June 1903.
285 CO67/137/33861, 7690/2026 (I.G.F.2.), WO to CO, 10 September 1903; WO32/7530, Cyprus (Code 0 (D)):33861/1903, CO to WO, 12 September 1903; (Code 0 (D)):D/1237/9, Talbot to Haynes Smith, 11 December 1903.
286 WO32/7529, Cyprus (Code 0 (D)), Altham, minute, 2 June 1903; minute, 1 July 1903.
287 Ibid., Altham, minute, 3 July 1903.
288 Ibid., Altham, minute, 28 July 1903.
289 Ibid., Nicholson, minute, 29 July 1903; Roberts, 7 August 1903; Brodrick, 14 August 1903.
290 Ibid., minute, Altham, 3 October 1903; minute, Nicholson, 5 October 1903; WO to CO, 9 November 1903; WO to FO, 9 November 1903.
291 CO67/137/40991, minute Fiddian, 11 November 1903.
292 WO32/7530, Cyprus (Code 0 (D)):7690/2026, 767, O'Conor to Lansdowne, 17 November 1903.
293 CO67/137/40991, CO to WO, 18 November 1903; WO32/7530, immediate FO to WO, 4 December 1903.
294 CAB8/3/314, secret, Garrison of Cyprus, CDC memorandum, John Clauson, 30 December 1903.
295 Ibid.
296 Ibid.
297 WO32/7530, minute, Altham, 9 January 1904; minute, Nicholson, 20 January 1904.
298 Ibid., 7690/2026, estimated cost of mounted infantry, Nicolson, 20 January 1904.
299 Ibid., minute, Roberts, 26 January 1904.
300 Ibid., secret, Haynes Smith to CO, 12 January 1904.
301 Ibid., secret, CO to WO, 30 January 1904; Cyprus (Code 0 (D)), secret, WO to CO, 12 February 1904; WO to FO, 12 February 1904; WO to GOCE, 16 February 1904.
302 Ibid., secret, WO to CO, 12 February 1904.
303 Ibid., secret, CO to WO, 19 February 1904; WO32/7530, Cyprus (Code 0 (D)):M/0215, confidential, ADM to AC, 18 February 1904.
304 CO67/141/5102, 7690/2026 I(1), WO to CO, 12 February 1904; WO32/7530, Cyprus (Code 0 (D)):7690/2026 I(1), secret, AC to CO, ADM, and GOCE, 12 February 1904; WO32/7530, Cyprus (Code 0 (D)):7690/2026, Estimated cost of Mounted Infantry (100 all ranks), 20 January 1904.
305 Ian Beckett, 'H.O. Arnold-Forster and the Volunteers', *Politicians and Defence*, Manchester, 1981, 47–68; R.T. Shannon, 'Forster, Hugh Oakeley Arnold- (1855–1909)', *ODNB* (www.oxforddnb.com/view/article/30459, accessed 17 Nov 2004).
306 CO67/141/5102, Clauson, WO to Anderson, 17 February 1904.
307 Ibid.
308 Hugh Oakley Arnold-Forster, papers, Add MSS 50307, WO Papers, 1903–October 1904, VIII, 108, Schedule of Troops in the Colonies, 18 June 1904.
309 WO32/7532, secret, Haynes Smith to Lyttelton, 18 August 1904.
310 Ibid.
311 WO32/7532, Clauson, minute, 26 September 1904.
312 WO32/7532, illegible, minute, 5 October 1904.
313 CO67/141/3451, minute, Fiddian, 15 March 1905.

314 CO67/141/3451, CO to King-Harman, 24 March 1905.
315 CO67/142/12479, secret, King Harman to Lyttelton, 1 April 1905; also WO32/7533.
316 Ibid.
317 CO67/147/5092, confidential, WO to CO, 9 February 1906.
318 CO67/147/5092, H.F. Batterbee, minute, 14 February 1906; confidential, CO to WO 24 February 1906.
319 John Gooch, 'Haldane and the National Army', *Politicians and Defence*, 69–86.
320 General Staff, WO, *Military Report and General Information Concerning the Island of Cyprus*, London, 1907, 1913, and 1936. Hereafter, *MRC–I, MRC–II, MRC–III*, respectively.
321 Ibid., 82.
322 *MRC–II*, 17; *MRC–III*, 27.
323 CO67/181/32730, secret, Clauson to Andrew Bonar Law, 26 June 1916.
324 *MRC–I*, 31–2, 48–9.
325 CO67/147/27246, confidential, Reports, Lieutenant-Commodore Lancelot N. Turton to Prince Louis of Battenberg, 15 May 1906; M-6662, ADM to CO, 23 July 1906.
326 *MRC–I*, 47.

CHAPTER 8

'Cyprus is of no use to anybody': the pawn

> **Caesar:** Well, the little Ptolemy can marry the other sister; and we will make them both a present of Cyprus.
> **Pothinus:** [impatiently] Cyprus is of no use to anybody.
> **Caesar:** No matter: you shall have it for the sake of peace.
> **Britannus:** [Unconsciously anticipating a later statesman] Peace with honour, Pothinus.
> (George Bernard Shaw, *Caesar and Cleopatra*, 1899, Act II)

After ten years of Tory-Unionist rule the Liberals won office in December 1905. Six years earlier George Bernard Shaw, a socialist, journalist and playwright and the force behind the Fabian Society, a socialist group wanting to transform Britain through the 'permeation' of the nation's intellectual and political life, watched as his play *Caesar and Cleopatra* premiered. Shaw, who had visited Famagusta,[1] warned in his play that there were 'outrageous gags' about the foreign politics of the Beaconsfield 'period, which are . . . as "historical" as anything in [Joseph] Addison's *"Cato"*', a tragedy set in Rome that was an allegory of early eighteenth-century politics.[2] The Liberals and other European governments adopted Shaw's view that Cyprus would make a good bargaining chip.

The Liberals and the cession of Cyprus to Greece

After Cyprus was occupied, Gladstonian and Radical Liberals thought it would ultimately be ceded to Greece. At Berlin in 1878, Greece had been promised an unspecified area of Thessaly and Epirus. The Ottomans later refused to give up these territories and Greece mobilised in late 1880. In December, Gladstone told Granville, his Foreign Secretary, that Bismarck wanted to cede Crete to Greece instead of Thessaly or Epirus and it would then be worth ceding Cyprus to Greece 'in sovereignty not in mere occupation [but] of course it should not be thought of unless desired by the people [and] at present they can hardly have dreamt of it'.[3] Three days later Gladstone asserted that this was 'only an idea for the future'.[4] In January 1881, when redevelopment of Famagusta harbour was still being considered, the members of the Colonial Office, most of whom had Liberal tendencies, rejected spending imperial funds in Cyprus, not because it might be returned to Ottoman rule – as the Anglo-Turkish Convention stipulated – but because it might be ceded to Greece.[5] In February 1881, George Goschen, the temporary ambassador to Constantinople, proposed ceding Cyprus to Greece, or returning it to the Porte to resolve the territorial deadlock.[6] But Granville would only consult the Cabinet about ceding it to Greece.[7] Goschen then proposed handing Cyprus to Greece, instead of the part in Epirus Abdul Hamid would not cede, to end the stalemate and strengthen British prestige.[8] Gladstone's reply, that ceding Cyprus to Greece would violate the Anglo-Turkish Convention,[9] indicates his hypocrisy because he had contemplated it himself.

Many Liberals supported Cyprus joining Greece: Dilke, Labouchere and, most famously, Gladstone in 1897 during the Cretan crisis in a letter to the Duke of Westminster.

> I quote the case of Cyprus as a precedent, and I apprehend that so far it is good; while I subjoin the satisfaction I should feel, were it granted me, before the close of my long life, to see the population of that Hellenic Island placed by a friendly arrangement in organic union with their brethren of the Kingdom [of Greece] and of Crete.[10]

Two years later Sir Francis Allston Channing, a Liberal pro-Boer,[11] told Parliament that 'Cyprus should form part of the Hellenic kingdom of the future'.[12]

The pawn: Cyprus within the international alliance system

After the 1894 Franco-Russian alliance an isolated Germany sought to induce Britain into the Triple Alliance. Anglo-German relations were strained in 1896 over German policy in Transvaal, but improved in 1898 when they agreed to divide Portuguese Africa and Germany withdrew its patronage of the Transvaal before the Boer War.[13] In March 1901 'Oakleaf' (pseudonym) published 'Cyprus for German East Africa: A Fair Exchange' in the *United Service Magazine*.[14] Cyprus, Oakleaf thought, was of doubtful value and after Egypt was occupied there was 'an attitude of comparative indifference towards Cyprus'.[15] He, therefore, proposed giving it to Germany in return for German East Africa, in a similar deal to that which saw British Heligoland, a small island in the North Sea, exchanged for the larger German island of Zanzibar in 1890. By dominating Africa's resources from Egypt to South Africa, with a railway from the Cape to Cairo, Britain would be the pre-eminent power in Africa. But German East Africa dissected the proposed line and Britain would have to depend on German goodwill. Oakleaf asserted that Britain should support German interests in Asia Minor to 'check Russian aggression' against the Ottoman Empire and Cyprus was the ideal base for German operations in Asia Minor.[16]

Although the Cyprus for German East Africa proposal may have furthered Anglo-German relations, it was poorly conceived. Why would Cyprus be strategically important to Germany when it had not been to Britain who had had similar interests in Asia Minor in 1878? If building the Cape–Cairo line meant relying on German goodwill that also applied with Cyprus relative to Egypt.

In 1908 the French and Russian governments suggested returning Cyprus to Ottoman rule to solve the Cretan Question that had again become acute. A decade after the Franco-Russian alliance, Lord Lansdowne, the Foreign Secretary in the Conservative-Unionist coalition, and Paul Cambon, the French ambassador to London, signed the *Entente Cordiale*. The 'friendly understanding' was a bargain over informal and formal interests in Africa and Asia.[17] The Liberal government then signed an entente with St Petersburg in 1907, which delimitated interests in Persia, Afghanistan and Tibet.[18] Thus Britain, France and Russia formed the Triple Entente against the Triple Alliance.

When on 12 October the Cretan Assembly at Canea proclaimed union with Greece, Paris and St Petersburg saw no reason to prolong the inevitable and told London that the Young Turk government should be induced to cede Crete to Greece. As compensation and to stop them from drifting towards Germany they proposed that London restore Cyprus to the Porte. On 21 October Sir Francis Bertie, the British ambassador to Paris, informed Sir Edward Grey, the British Foreign Secretary, that his French counterpart, Stéphen Pichon, had said in a 'joking way' that Britain should return Cyprus to the Porte to counteract German intrigues: 'It was acquired for a reason which no longer exists. Now that England is in Egypt she can no longer require Cyprus. It is of no use to her.'[19] Three days later, Pichon told Bertie that his Russian counterpart, Aleksandr Isvolsky, thought the 'reasons for taking the Island had disappeared' and returning it could resolve the Cretan question.[20] Pichon mentioned that the Ionian Islands were given to Greece for sentimental reasons. Bertie replied that besides Gladstone (more of the received wisdom!) Corfu had not developed into the strategic asset originally hoped.[21] Pichon claimed that Cyprus was of no use to you now for you are in Egypt, and when it was taken on lease it was a sort of satisfaction obtained for the concessions made to Russia at the close of the war and as by way of being a point of observation opposite Scandiano, but it had not . . . come up to expectations not even in the matter of excavations.[22]

Charles Hardinge, the under-secretary at the Foreign Office, thought Pichon was 'very mischievous'.[23] It would be 'impossible' to return an island mostly of 'Greeks' to 'Turkish rule, since it would . . . create another Cretan question, and would be considered a breach of faith on the part of three-quarters of the population'.[24] Grey told Bertie

> I believe Cyprus is of no use to us and the Convention respecting it an anachronism and encumbrance, I would therefore give the island away in return for any better arrangements we could obtain. Indeed bargain or no bargain we should be better without Cyprus.
>
> But I am told that, whatever may have been the case when Aphrodite could walk naked on its shore, there are now inhabitants on the island and that the large majority of these are Christians. An attempt to put it again under Turkish Administration would lead to a revolt, which could only be put down by bloodshed, and the Turks would have to garrison and hold the island by force.
>
> There is also, I believe, a strong desire on the part of Cyprus to be annexed to Greece and it would be a damnable gift to Turkey if while relieving her of the burden of Crete we gave her a new Cretan question in Cyprus. For these reasons 'L'Affaire ne marchera pas' or as we say here 'this cock won't fight'.[25]

Grey sent the Colonial Office the draft reply to Bertie rejecting the proposal because the Porte would see it as a sequel to the Anglo-Russian *Entente* and an abrogation of the Cyprus Convention; there was no precedent to return predominantly Christian territory to Ottoman rule; and it would create another Crete.[26] Lord Crewe, the Colonial Secretary, was reluctant to admit to a foreign government that the case for returning Cyprus to Ottoman rule was arguable, but agreed to a casual reply.[27] Then Arthur Nicolson, the British ambassador to Russia, informed Grey that Isvolsky now insisted. Nicolson agreed with Isvolsky that Cyprus was useless, but doubted that the British public would accept the retrocession.[28] The Foreign and Colonial offices agreed to put the issue to rest,[29] telling the Russians that the Porte would reject the proposal because returning Cyprus would not increase its sovereignty, but losing Crete would reduce it.[30]

The Foreign Office was right. In 1910 Ahmed Riza, the President of the Chamber of Deputies of the Ottoman government, replied to the proposal, which was repeated by Joseph Reinach (a follower of Leon Gambetta and famous for championing Captain Dreyfus), that

'experience had shown that it could not play the role as a base of operations' for Britain and the Porte would happily reoccupy it, but not
under such circumstances.[31]

But if this was anathema, the warning from Baron von Wangenheim,
the German ambassador to Athens, to the German Chancellor, Prince
von Bülow, in June 1909, that both could ultimately join Greece, would
not have gone down well at all. Wangenheim thought that London's
opposition to Crete's union with Greece stemmed from the 'old
British longing for Suda Bay'. He claimed that during Crete's occupation the British troops had treated it as 'part of the Cretan coast
entrusted' to them and tried to 'keep the troops of the other Powers
away'. London could not demand it for delivering Crete to Greece, thus
it had 'little inducement' to solve the crisis when there was no profit
and was 'waiting to see what price Greece will offer'. Athens would
cede Suda Bay for Crete and 'England could easily cloak the transaction
by later taking Suda bay in exchange for Cyprus, which is useless for
British purposes and has long been yearning for union with Greece'.[32]

Five governments agreed that Cyprus was useless for strategic
purposes and that Britain should eventually relinquish it, which it eventually offered to do in 1912.

The Mediterranean war strategy

The context of the proposal was a possible war against the Triple
Alliance. In 1911 there were two dangerous crises that exposed the
unreadiness of the Admiralty for war and its weakness in the eastern
Mediterranean: the Agadir issue and the Tripolitanian War.

The Agadir crisis increased British anxiety over German naval
power. At the 1906 Algeciras conference, Paris received a sphere of
influence in Morocco, which it wanted to develop into a protectorate.
Some Moroccans resisted and Paris occupied Fez in May 1911. But
Berlin wanted a slice of the mineral-rich Sous and sent the gunboat
Panther to Agadir in July. Whitehall asked Berlin to explain. Talks
ensued. Grey claimed an attack on the British fleet during the talks
was a real possibility.[33] In November, after intense diplomacy, the Kaiser
accepted territory in the Congo to leave Morocco alone.[34]

The German challenge roused two Liberal pacifists. The pro-Boer
David Lloyd George, the Chancellor of the Exchequer since April 1908,
warned Germany in a speech at the Mansion House on 21 July not
to take Britain for granted,[35] echoing Disraeli from 1875.[36] Liberal
pacifists were stunned as Lloyd George joined the Liberal imperialists
Asquith, Grey and Haldane.[37] In 1904 Winston Churchill crossed the
floor in 1904 and sat beside Lloyd George. His speech inspired him.[38]

On 23 August they attended their first Committee of Imperial Defence meeting called after Berlin criticised Lloyd George's speech.[39] General Henry Hughes Wilson asserted that six British divisions were needed on the French-Belgian border to stop Germany marching to Paris.[40] But the First Sea Lord, Admiral Sir Arthur Wilson, reported that there was no plan to transport the army to France.[41] The Admiralty was unprepared and Asquith looked to replace its head, Reginald McKenna. Haldane volunteered[42] but on Lloyd George's suggestion Asquith chose Churchill, who had written a report on Britain's role in a Franco-German war.[43]

Churchill made immediate changes. Admiral John Fisher, a dominant naval figure, became his chief adviser, and he replaced Wilson with Admiral Sir Francis Bridgeman, and Vice-Admiral Sir George Egerton (the Second Sea Lord for only ten months), with Fisher's choice for the top job – Vice-Admiral Prince Louis of Battenberg, Prince Alexander of Hesse's elder son.[44] Churchill's former Tory colleagues worried about a 'Radical' reforming the navy, while his militancy stunned his party.[45] In November 1911 pacifist Gladstonians, Lord Morley, Lord Loreburn and McKenna disrupted Cabinet meetings, demanding to know about the secret military talks with France that had started in 1906. The Cabinet agreed not to negotiate further without Cabinet consent.[46] But Churchill was unfazed, telling a crowd at Glasgow in February 1912 that Britain's navy was 'a necessity' but the German was 'a luxury'.[47] He wanted battleships and despite Lloyd George's opposition the Cabinet agreed, provided that the Germans were approached to end the naval race. Haldane left for Berlin, but Churchill's speech enraged them and he returned with the new expansionist German Navy Bill,[48] which increased the 'striking force of ships of all classes'. British naval advisers were confronted with eight more German battleships and six cruisers.[49] Churchill perceived a German naval threat to home waters and suggested returning home the Atlantic Fleet at Gibraltar and replacing it with four pre-dreadnoughts from Malta. The War and Foreign offices objected to denuding the Mediterranean, wanting to maintain naval supremacy in the Mediterranean.[50]

The Italian invasion of Ottoman Libya in September 1911 coincided with German threats over Morocco,[51] showing London who the aggressors were. Salisbury had informed Rome in 1878 that Britain would not object to it taking Libya.[52] Months before attacking Libya, the Cyprus government had allowed three Italian warships to conduct manoeuvres off Larnaca.[53] But London fumed when Italy took the Dodecanese Islands.[54] Although promising not to annex them, Rome swiftly fortified them. In May Sir Arthur Nicolson, now the permanent under-secretary at the Foreign Office, warned that Britain now faced a 'very formidable naval and military combination' in the Mediterranean.[55] The Admiralty claimed that British interests had been safe because no power had taken territory east of Malta. If Italy kept any of the Dodecanese it could control the Levant and Black Sea trade and threaten Egypt and the route east. The Admiralty wanted the Italian retention of the Dodecanese 'strenuously oppose[d]'.[56]

The Foreign and War offices objected to Churchill's redistribution policy because of Italy's emergence as a threat, condemning the proposals before the Committee of Imperial Defence meeting at Malta in May 1912. Haldane warned that war plans needed changing if the Admiralty was right and command of the Mediterranean was lost for two months once war started. Malta would be open to attack, Egypt and Cyprus would need increased garrisons (which was impossible), and Indian, Australian and New Zealand troops would need re-routing round the Cape.[57] Grey thought Italy had joined the Triple Alliance because it feared the British navy, and retreating from the Mediterranean would encourage Rome to view London as 'soft' and turn it into an enemy. The Foreign Office proposed cooperation with the French in the Mediterranean to 'make Italy think twice' about falling into Habsburg arms.[58]

Churchill expected an attack from Kitchener, the Consul-General of Egypt,[59] who was armed with the Foreign Office memorandum. So he offered a compromise solution: to station three battle-cruisers and four armoured cruisers at Malta to secure British commerce and elude Austro-Hungarian and Italian dreadnoughts. He also agreed to finance submarine defences at Malta and Alexandria, where a new fort and wireless station would be constructed.[60]

The inability to defend British Mediterranean interests risked a 'permanent abandonment' of eastern links, which would 'break up the Empire'. Flotillas and fortifications would make seizing Gibraltar, Malta and Alexandria 'very hazardous', but they would not protect shipping.[61] Traversing the Mediterranean was vital: almost half Britain's food supplies entered the Mediterranean via the Suez Canal.[62] If the route was closed for two months, trade would divert to the Cape of Good Hope route and rely on Australasian produce.[63] Churchill thought Britain could not build and man the battleships to protect shipping in the Mediterranean, making an Anglo-French agreement necessary.[64]

London and Paris agreed on 23 July that the British navy would protect Anglo-French interests in the eastern Mediterranean and the French in the western.[65] So the British Fourth Squadron at Gibraltar was responsible for Malta, Egypt and Cyprus, the Adriatic, Ionian and Aegean seas and the North African, Syrian and Asia Minor coasts. Paris moved its six battleships from the Atlantic to the Mediterranean,[66] leaving the North Sea to the British, but London insisted that the agreement did not bind them to war.[67]

Britain's responsibilities to Cyprus were based on decisions taken in April 1912 by the Foreign Office and the Committee of Imperial Defence,[68] only a week before the Greek members resigned en masse.

> Cyprus, although technically Turkish territory, is for practical purposes a British Crown Colony, held on lease from Turkey, and as such will certainly be liable to attack by any enemy of Great Britain.[69]

Cyprus could not be defended from an Austro-Hungarian attack if command of the Mediterranean was lost for two months.[70] Defence would consist of one company (100 rifles) of British infantry; 250 mounted and 500 dismounted *zaptieh*; and two units of British Army Service and Medical Corps. The General Staff believed that Austrian planners could gather, dispatch and land a force (the fifteenth and sixteenth Austrian Army Corps in Bosnia-Herzegovina, trained in mountainous warfare, was perfect) within fifteen days without imperilling Balkan defences or European war plans. With the troops at Limassol, Nicosia, via Famagusta, was open to attack.[71] The General Staff knew that the garrison was 'maintained . . . as a symbol of British authority' and could not oppose a landing. So the capture of the island was 'inevitable'.[72]

The Cyprus for Argostoli proposal

Churchill proposed ceding Cyprus to Greece in return for the right to use Argostoli harbour on Cephalonia (one of the Ionian Islands) so as to improve the position of the navy. Historians of Cyprus barely mention the offer, falsely attributing its origin to Lloyd George and preferring to discuss, instead, the official October 1915 offer,[73] claiming that the offer of 1912 was not serious.[74] This will be disproved. Military historians of the First World War have not mentioned it either, nor the proposed Anglo-Greek *entente*, although the aim was to strengthen British naval power against Austria-Hungary and Italy and secure an ally in the eastern Mediterranean.

Churchill's proposal was possible because of Greece's development under Eleutherios Venizelos. After studying law in Athens, Venizelos founded the Cretan Liberal Party and in 1896 led the revolt against Ottoman rule. In 1905 he become Crete's first prime minister under Prince George, but Venizelos forced him out after the prince assumed absolute power. His star rose internationally, as did his ambition.[75] In 1909 Venizelos decided to enter the Greek parliament, but in August Greek military officers demanding military and political reorganisation brought down the government and chaos resulted. The officers called upon Venizelos. He established a National Assembly that revised the constitution and when the old leaders obstructed him, he called an election and won 300 of the 364 seats.[76] He began reform in earnest: in 1911 he contracted the British to reorganise the navy, the French the army and the Italians the gendarmerie. Venizelos wanted to build Greece into a Mediterranean power.[77]

In October 1912 Montenegro, Greece, Serbia and Bulgaria attacked the Ottoman Empire to achieve their conflicting irredentist ambitions, and the eastern Mediterranean was thrust into the spotlight for British and French naval planners. French pressure resulted in an Anglo-French agreement in November that bound each party to aid the other if another power attacked either or threatened the general peace.[78]

On 22 October Churchill told Grey and Asquith that he wanted Corfu because it was the key to the Adriatic. Only a large submarine and torpedo build-up on Corfu could meet the Austro-Hungarian fleet. Churchill thought the Ottoman collapse in Europe was inevitable and it was the chance to give Cyprus to Greece for a lease on Corfu. Grey believed it was possible, but that would take time to negotiate.[79] A few weeks later Grey told Rome's ambassador to London that Cyprus was 'of no use as a naval base' and naval advisers wanted one in the Aegean.[80] By then the Greek army had seized Salonica, and the navy – Mytilene, Chios and Samos. Churchill took notice as Constantinople sued for peace.

A month before peace talks began Lloyd George approached John Stavridi, the Greek Consul-General in London, with Churchill's proposal. Stavridi, a lawyer and Lloyd George's friend from his days as a practising solicitor, could 'mediate between the worlds of Greek and British politics'.[81] On 10 November he began a diary which reveals the Cyprus for Argostoli proposition.[82] Lloyd George knew Greece wanted to unite the 'Greeks' under Ottoman rule and told Stavridi:

> If the [Balkan] allies are in agreement they can divide up European Turkey as they think best . . . You may consider Crete as yours . . . England will not fire a shot or move a single ship to prevent you[83]

Lloyd George was a Gladstonian Philhellene and had no qualms about Ottoman rule leaving Europe 'bag and baggage': 'Personally I don't want him even to keep Constantinople', he told Stavridi.[84] Rome promised in the October 1912 Treaty of Lausanne to restore the Dodecanese to Constantinople when Ottoman troops left Libya, but Greece now claimed the mainly Orthodox-populated islands.[85] In November Grey discovered that the Italian Foreign Minister had made a démarche in Berlin and Vienna for Rhodes's retention.[86] Lloyd George called this a 'disgrace' and told Stavridi that Greece should demand all the islands as a *sine qua non* of peace terms.[87]

Over breakfast on 18 November Lloyd George told Stavridi about ceding Cyprus to Greece for an island in the Ionian Sea. Stavridi met Churchill that afternoon.

> Churchill went straight to the heart of the question . . . [and] explained the organisation of the British fleet in the Mediterranean and the working thereof in conjunction with the French fleet. As the powers were grouped . . . the enemies were Italy and Austria, and in any future war if they could close up the Adriatic they could bottle up the whole of the Austrian and part of the Italian fleets . . . Provided England had a base close enough to the Adriatic.[88]

Churchill named Argostoli in Cephalonia as the preferred base,[89] after realising that Corfu had been ceded to Greece on the condition that it would remain demilitarised.[90] He did not suggest its cession or lease, but the right to use its harbour in a secret treaty. Lloyd George asked how Cyprus' surrender would be justified if the use of Argostoli were secret. Churchill thought the public would understand once the Conservative leadership and the editor of *The Times* knew the facts. He recalled his 1907 trip to Cyprus, when he saw the 'great desire to be reunited to the mother country, and if it lay in his power he was going to see justice done'. Churchill was no Philhellene; this was the politician talking. The Cypriot Muslims were collateral damage. As the meeting ended, Churchill remarked: 'What a day this would have been for Byron if he was alive'.[91] Gladstone too would have been happy.

Churchill acted promptly. Two days after meeting Stavridi, an Admiralty report warned against engaging the Austro-Hungarian fleet in open waters and that it had to be bottled up in the Adriatic with submarine or destroyer action. This hinged on 'obtain[ing] a secure base as a starting point not more than 200 miles distant'.[92]

> The Island of Cephalonia would answer this purpose admirably, and if this Island was available as a base for Flotillas of 20 'D' class Submarines and 20 Destroyers, the Austrian Battle Squadron would be compelled to face a serious risk.[93]

On 22 November, Lloyd George informed Stavridi that Asquith and Grey agreed with the proposal. Stavridi proposed an Anglo-Greek understanding that gave Britain use of the Aegean islands Greece had occupied.[94]

Churchill then replaced Admiral Bridgeman, who questioned his Mediterranean strategy, with Battenberg.[95] Four days before Churchill met Stavridi, he told Battenberg of the change.[96] On 9 December, two days after replacing Bridgeman, Battenberg and Churchill discussed how to prevent the Austro-Hungarian and Italian fleets from meeting through the Malta channel, which would imperil British shipping and communications. They doubted that the fleet could block the Austro-Hungarian fleet in the Adriatic from Malta and the navy could not engage it in open waters.[97] The answer was to 'contain the Austrian Fleet in the Adriatic'.[98]

Venizelos was approached during the peace talks concurrently being held with the meeting of ambassadors chaired by Grey. On 10 December, Lloyd George told Stavridi that Asquith and Grey wanted negotiations started.[99] Two days later Stavridi briefed Venizelos.[100] On the morning that the peace conference opened at St James's Palace, Lloyd George entertained Venizelos and Stavridi over breakfast.[101] Venizelos approved of the exchange and the *entente* and thought King George would too. But he pointed out that Greece would breach neutrality laws if the British used Argostoli and the agreements were kept secret.[102] At breakfast the next day Churchill, Lloyd George, Battenberg, Venizelos and Stavridi agreed to make public the Cyprus for Argostoli deal and keep separate the *entente* because it affected France and Russia. Battenberg emphasised that the Greek navy was stronger than the Ottoman, but needed to focus on mobility. Stavridi wondered about the Ottoman reaction, but Churchill reassured him that London would arrange that.[103]

Two weeks later, Lloyd George told Venizelos that Churchill had prepared a report on the Anglo-Greek *entente* for Paris.[104] Instead, he was shown a memorandum advising him to develop a mobile navy, because the Porte was preoccupied with battleships, which were unsuitable in the island-dotted Aegean.[105] Churchill advised Venizelos to cancel the German dreadnought and order destroyers.[106] With Greece outmanoeuvring the Ottoman fleet, the Admiralty could assign it responsibility for patrolling the eastern Mediterranean. Churchill revealed that Asquith and Grey thought it would be difficult to justify giving up Cyprus unless it was made public. All agreed to delay until the Balkan-Ottoman peace negotiations had ended.[107] Three weeks later the five men met again. Churchill revealed that three French ministers (including Théophile Delcassé, the Navy Minister, who as Foreign Minister had pushed for the *Entente Cordiale*) liked the proposals.[108]

Why the Cyprus for Argostoli exchange failed

In January 1914 Venizelos returned to London hoping to resume talks, but Lloyd George warned him against raising the Cyprus for Argostoli deal with Grey because 'owing to the acute political crisis on the Home Rule Bill, nothing whatever would be done at the present time to carry into effect the proposals'.[109] On 21 January Venizelos met Grey and agreed in a meeting with Churchill, Lloyd George,

Battenberg and Stavridi to postpone until August. But the First World War intervened.[110]

The failure to realise the proposals has not been examined. Hill argued that George Streit, the Greek Foreign Minister, rejected them because they tied Greece to the *entente*.[111] But Streit, a diplomat of German ancestry, who served as ambassador to Vienna (1910–13), was not the Foreign Minister until 1914, and then only briefly, and was irrelevant given that the British postponed the talks in 1914. Another theory held that the Treaty of Bucharest (August 1913), which concluded the second Balkan War, had reduced the likelihood of a general war, and 'there was no longer any need for a British base at Argostoli'.[112] This can be challenged when exploring the view of Evdoros Ioannides (pseudonym Doros Alastos) that Grey's absence from the talks suggested that they were exploratory and did not have Cabinet consent,[113] implying that Grey or the Cabinet were obstacles.

No sources show Grey's view on the proposals and although he denied to the Colonial Office and the Cypriots that there had been discussions with Venizelos on handing Cyprus to Greece, he did not reject *énosis* outright as previous governments had. The denial was made after the *énosis* hopes of Greek Cypriot leaders soared with Greece's triumphs in the Balkan Wars. In early December the mischievous Theophanis Theodotou told Goold-Adams that Venizelos wanted to discuss *énosis* during the peace negotiations, but was hesitant to damage Anglo-Greek relations.[114] George Vandeleur Fiddes, the assistant under-secretary at the Colonial Office, thought that if Greece grabbed all the Aegean islands *énosis* would 'become much stronger' because it could be claimed that if Britain had not occupied Cyprus it would belong to Greece.[115]

Both the Muslims and Orthodox reacted to *énosis* rumours. The three Muslim legislature deputies petitioned Harcourt rejecting *énosis*, independence and self-rule, fearing Greek domination.[116] The Greek Cypriot leaders sensed the moment to demand *énosis*.[117] But as Fiddes recognised, the Colonial Office was powerless because *énosis* 'depend[ed] on questions of "high policy" and has not yet come under consideration, so far as we are aware'.[118] On 7 January 1913 Archbishop Kyrillos, after chairing a meeting of notables, publicly proclaimed *énosis*.[119] Within a week rumours spread that Britain would cede Cyprus to Greece and they were widely reported in Paris.[120] On 18 January the Greek newspaper *Eleutheria* (founded by Kyros Stavrinides, whose mother was from Mesolonghi, where Byron had died),[121] reported that 'a well-informed person of Cairo' claimed that *énosis* was imminent.[122] If Harcourt revealed this despatch to Churchill or to Lloyd George it did not affect their meeting with Venizelos on 29 January.

Meanwhile, Goold-Adams was on the verge of a breakdown.[123] His health was not helped when on 15 February *Alithia* alleged, uncannily close to the facts, that 'some talk has . . . been made *officially* between the Greek Prime Minister and the British Minister of Foreign Affairs about Cyprus'.[124] The resumption of Greco-Ottoman hostilities in February 1913 resulted in disturbances in Lefkara and Maroni, villages in Larnaca, when the Greeks took Janina.[125] The next day Goold-Adams took extended leave. Dr Eyioub Moussa, a new member of the legislature, telegraphed the Colonial Office: 'News for union with Greece causing much panic. Mohammedans preparing for flight. We earnestly await your assurance by telegram.'[126]

On 28 March Harcourt sought representation from Grey.[127] The day before, J. Arnold Goodwin, a Liberal Imperialist and friend of Grey's from Balliol College,[128] asked him:

> Is Cyprus important to us? Is it of value? Is it not more likely to be a source of anxiety? While the condition of the whole eastern Mediterranean is being discussed and settled, there is an opportunity of settling our relations with Cyprus and . . . perhaps of following the precedent of the Ionian Islands.[129]

There is no record of a reply from Grey, but he replied to Harcourt that if an answer was necessary it should be that 'the union of Cyprus with Greece has not been considered'.[130] This was the first time that London had not rejected *énosis* outright.

Why would Grey go cold about the Cyprus for Argostoli exchange? Churchill had dismissed Ottoman views, but a foreign secretary might not so easily, especially one who had opposed diminishing Ottoman sovereignty in Crete. But the Balkan Wars had changed that as Crete joined Greece in 1913 and he pushed for Greece to keep the other islands it seized. Anglo-Ottoman relations also deteriorated. In December 1913 the Porte announced that a German officer would command the Constantinople garrison, despite London, Paris and St Petersburg objecting.[131] Also, within weeks of the First World War starting, the Cabinet agreed to cede Cyprus to Greece at the first chance.[132] Since the Ottomans had not joined the Central Powers yet, there was no fear of antagonising them.

Grey's anxiety had been over upsetting Rome, which felt strongly about the Corfu Straits. In December 1912 the London Conference of Ambassadors accepted Albanian autonomy, but not independence, and the borders became contested. Greece wanted southern Albania, which had an Orthodox minority and in the second Balkan War seized parts of 'North Epirus'. Serbia wanted an outlet to the Adriatic. Italy and Austria-Hungary perceived a threat to their strategic interests and insisted that the territory opposite Corfu be in Albania. Austria-Hungary successfully forced a Serbian withdrawal, but Greece would not budge, so Rome sent 7,000 troops to Brindisi.[133] Grey wondered what the fuss was about.[134] Churchill believed that Rome had nothing to fear from a weak power such as Greece, which could threaten Italy from Argostoli and told Battenberg:

> It is extraordinary that the Italians should use such extreme language on the subject . . . It looks therefore as if it were not so much Greece but some stronger Naval Power that the Austrians and Italians have in mind. I wonder which? If it should turn out to be us there would not appear to be any special reason why we should support them . . . I am in favour of getting as much as possible for Greece now and making an alliance with her afterwards.[135]

Grey, however, wanted to use Italian anxieties in the Adriatic to remove them from the Aegean. He wanted Rome to make concessions to Athens in the Aegean in return for getting its way in Albania.[136] But Rome rejected returning the Dodecanese to the Porte.[137]

In July 1913 the Admiralty obtained the Italian naval staff secret paper on the value of the Corfu channel. Battenberg noted that 'the co-operation of Austrian and German ships in the mouth of the Adriatic is spoken of as an established fact', but Italy's partaking was uncertain. Germany hoped to coerce Rome into 'drawing the sword', but Berlin realised that 'the British Fleet at Malta stands between Italy and her large African Army'.[138] Churchill wanted to instil more fear into the Italians and in August 1913 directed the Commander-in-Chief of the Mediterranean Station, Admiral Sir Archibald Berkeley Milne, to stay at Malta, where he would be reinforced when war started, to watch the Adriatic and make proposals

> for securing an advanced temporary base in the Ionian Islands . . . but not actually violating neutral territory without direct permission from the Admiralty, who are fully alive to the advantage of using such a base and will use every effort to facilitate your obtaining one.[139]

The Cyprus for Argostoli deal was one way of obtaining such a foothold.

The concern over Italian reaction created uncertainty at the Foreign Office. Grey wanted diplomatic outcomes to diffuse tensions. His proposal for an international commission to delineate the southern Albanian border was accepted. Venizelos told Grey, however, that he could only withdraw from 'Northern Epirus' and remain in office if Greece were ceded all the islands it had occupied and Italy returned the Dodecanese to the Porte. Grey thought this fair, but the Triple Alliance did not. Venizelos was weakened when the international committee declared on 19 December 1913 that Albania would include territory Greece claimed. Then on 11 January Rennell Rodd, Ambassador to Italy, told Grey that Italy would not leave the Dodecanese unless it was given an economic sphere of influence in Asia Minor.[140] Despite Rome's provocative policy, Grey would not upset it because he thought it was uncommitted to the Triple Alliance, so he told Venizelos on 21 January: 'It would be undesirable to enter into a separate arrangement about the Mediterranean which must offend the susceptibilities of other Powers interested in it.'[141] Grey was trying to accommodate Italy and Greece. Although the former was being provocative, any British reciprocal provocation (like a base at Argostoli) would have severely jeopardised his mission. Thus, Grey's interests conflicted with Churchill's. In the end, Italian fears of the British navy prevented it from joining the Triple Alliance and it supported the French and British seizure of Corfu in January 1916.[142]

Churchill also may have reconsidered the Cyprus for Argostoli exchange because Greece failed to follow Admiralty advice on naval policy. Relinquishing the security of the Aegean and the waters around Cyprus to Greece was a gamble and hinged on the mobility of the Greek navy. The British naval mission under Rear-Admiral Mark Kerr, whom Fisher proposed as Fourth Sea Lord in November 1911, ended in December 1913 having technically improved the Greek navy.[143] Kerr also urged Venizelos to build a fleet of cruisers, destroyers and submarines and not battle-cruisers. But Venizelos insisted: as symbols of power he perceived them as vital for a powerful Greece.[144] This was of no use to the Admiralty, while the Foreign Office was alarmed lest Greece became too strong.[145] Meanwhile, London encouraged the Porte to buy battleships.[146] In October 1913 Venizelos discovered that the Porte was trying to buy a British dreadnought and tried to purchase it,[147] but failed.[148] Commentators have thought that London was trying to nullify German influence at Constantinople.[149] The move aided foreign policy, but the Admiralty was not trying to boost the Ottoman fleet, but weaken it against Greece's. The Admiralty was advising, on sound naval practices, that Greece establish flotilla defences and a mobile navy, yet it was helping the Porte to acquire battleships, which were useless in the Aegean.[150] But Venizelos failed to heed the advice, undermining a main reason for the Anglo-Greek *entente*.

Home Rule, although dismissed by commentators because of its detachment from the Near East,[151] was another factor. It split Liberals and Conservatives like few other issues. Andrew Bonar Law, the Conservative leader, was passionate about it because of family ties to Ulster. Ending British control of Ireland, especially in Protestant Ulster, was anathema to Tories and they could have seen handing Cyprus to Greece as further diminishing the Empire. Bonar Law adopted a radical stance in rejecting Home Rule, arguing that the Ulster Protestants were a distinct community with an equal right as the Catholics to self-determination. Nothing was said about Muslim minorities in the Aegean and Crete – they were not British territory – but such a comparison may have been made with the Cypriot Muslims (as it was in 1956). In October 1913 Asquith and Bonar Law began talks on the Irish issue, but they fell apart in January, as Venizelos arrived in London. The Liberals considered using the army to suppress a Protestant revolt and Churchill planned a naval show off the Ulster coast. The loss of a British overseas possession, albeit a valueless one, would have elicited Tory opposition.[152]

There were also divisions in the Asquith Cabinet with Lloyd George and Churchill clashing over the navy estimates from November 1913 to February 1914. In November Lloyd George agreed to the estimates in return for Churchill supporting his land campaign.[153] But the economisers and pacifists in the Cabinet outvoted them.[154] Herbert Samuel, John Simon, Walter Runciman and J.A. Pease, dubbed the 'Samsimon quartette' by Lloyd George, agitated for Churchill's head unless he cut the estimates. McKenna, Morley and Harcourt, who were in revolt against the 'scare press' over the alleged German menace, backed them.[155] They would have opposed the Cyprus for Argostoli deal because of the cost of developing Argostoli and the provocativeness of the move. The quarrel between Lloyd George and Churchill would have also jeopardised the success of the scheme. On 18 December Churchill told Asquith that he would resign if the quota of capital ships for 1914–15 were reduced below four,[156] and in an interview in the *Daily Chronicle* on 3 January Lloyd George virtually threatened to resign unless naval spending was reduced.[157] The Liberals were about to disintegrate on 19 January when Venizelos arrived. The next day, Asquith told his wife that he was confronted with many Cabinet resignations and would dissolve Parliament.[158] A week later Lloyd George told him that he had not compromised with Churchill and would leave the matter to the Cabinet.[159] It would not be resolved until early February. These divisions boiled behind the scenes when Lloyd George and Churchill gave Venizelos the 'now is not a good time' speech.

'Mother' rejects the pawn

The failure to realise the Cyprus for Argostoli deal did not end the policy to cede Cyprus to Greece: an official offer was made, but rejected, in October 1915. The policy of holding Cyprus as a pawn had a harmful impact on its rule. Also, before and after the October 1915 offer, men on the spot, and imperialists, questioned it and the rejection galvanised them into regurgitating the same imagined advantages used to justify the occupation in 1878.

In November 1913, Harcourt sent J.C.C. Davidson, his private secretary, later Conservative Party chairman, on a secret mission to investigate the 'weakness in the quality of the administration'.[160] After revealing that Goold-Adams was hated by his officers and the Greeks because, under Harry Lukach's influence, he had shown anti-Greek sympathies, Davidson opined that only by fostering 'purely Cypriot ideals . . . as opposed to Greek and Turkish', with a view to establishing a Cypriot government, could peace reign.[161] If possible or not, it would mean generational change in the Orthodox leadership, which was saturated with Hellenism, having even called one of their own, Christodoulos Sozos, Limassol's mayor, a traitor for suggesting they fight for temporary independence in 1912. He became an 'ethno-martyr' that same year (and was celebrated in a postcard) when he died at Bizani fighting the Turks.[162] But 'Cypriotness' contradicted the island's status as a pawn and accordingly Harcourt granted, in March 1914, proportional representation by *equally* increasing the official members.[163] The British fanned the flames of *énosis* by confining the Cypriot Greeks to a mere opposition.

On 5 November 1914, upon the Ottoman government joining the Central Powers, London annulled the Anglo-Turkish Convention and annexed Cyprus. Nine days later Goold-Adams was appointed governor of Queensland, a demotion,[164] and on 27 November John Clauson, the former chief secretary, succeeded him.[165] *The Times* greeted the annexation with a degree of fanfare, focusing on 'A Memory of Coeur de Lion' and the fact that Cyprus was again under an English king.[166]

As mentioned, in August 1914 the Asquith Cabinet decided to cede Cyprus to Greece at the first chance. When Athens remained neutral, owing to the German sympathies of its new king, Constantine, Grey thought offering Cyprus might alter that. In January 1915 Grey told Harcourt that he wanted to discuss giving Cyprus to Greece in the next Cabinet meeting so that country would enter the war and he told Kitchener, the new War Secretary, that 'surely Cyprus of which the Admiralty have never been able to make a proper use, would be a cheap price to pay if we could get Greece and Rumania on such terms with Bulgaria as would secure their active participation'.[167] But Kitchener rejected the proposal at the Cabinet meeting because 'under present and probable conditions Cyprus has some strategic value',[168] hinting at his desire for a landing at Alexandretta.[169] Grey held off.[170]

The British focus turned to the Dardanelles after Churchill, who favoured a landing there, won over Kitchener's Alexandretta proposal. The Venizelos government allowed Britain to occupy Mudros harbour at Lemnos as a base for the allied fleet[171] and in February 1915 Admiral Arthur Limpus, the commander of the Malta squadron, told Churchill that Britain 'ought to acquire Lemnos' – it 'is more valuable to us as a Sea Power than is Cyprus'.[172] Churchill told Fisher that 'if Russia has C'ple & Straits, we ought to have Lemnos'[173] – somebody had to watch them. This prompted Fisher, who had replaced Battenberg in October 1914, to tell Kitchener that 'we don't want a barren island in the Mediterranean'.[174]

Harcourt objected and distributed a note by Josiah Wedgwood as evidence.[175] While stationed at the Dardanelles, Wedgwood had spoken with Lukach, the civil 'governor' at Mudros[176] and Harry Pirie-Gordon, an intelligence officer in the Levant, who had travelled with Lukach to Syria and Cyprus in 1908 and later served together on the cruiser *Doris*.[177] Wedgwood (grandson of the famous potter) was a naval architect and had been a Liberal MP since 1906. His niece described him as 'an individualist rather than a party man' who believed that 'only in an atmosphere of freedom can man develop as a responsible political being'.[178] Lukach described him as 'politically muddled'.[179] They argued that Britain should take Alexandretta and a strip of land to Mesopotamia, to check Russia in the north and France to the south and balance Greek and Italian claims in Asia Minor. German rail and harbour works could be expanded to give Britain the overland route to India.[180] The old Baghdad railway dream was being regurgitated. In January 1915 an officer in the Intelligence Department of the War Office argued that 'so far from Cyprus menacing it, the Power that held Alexandretta would control Cyprus (Cyprus is nil)'.[181] But the three amateur strategists asserted that 'Cyprus should be retained and not 'swapped off' against Lemnos' because of the 'loyal' Muslims and the coming importance of Alexandretta.[182]

Although the Foreign Office wanted to bring Greece into the war throughout 1915 the focus had been on Sofia, but in the first week of October Bulgaria attacked Serbia and King Constantine forced Venizelos to resign, despite Parliament sustaining his policy to intervene against Bulgaria. Whitehall decided to offer Cyprus to Greece, but Grey bungled it. Despite Harry Luke (Lukach) later claiming that the offer was made to placate the French, it emanated from Ronald Burrows, a Greek classics professor, who as the Principal of King's College (1913–20) established the Koraes Chair for Modern Greek and Byzantine studies. He was passionate about self-determination and was involved in the Serbian Society, the Anglo-Romanian Society and others and was the Chairman of the Anglo-Hellenic League. In his drawing room 'one met Cabinet ministers, bishops, members of the diplomatic corps . . . scholars and historians'.[183]

[263]

The catalyst for Burrows' proposal was Professor Thomas Masaryk, the future president of Czechoslovakia, who was due to give a paper on 19 October entitled 'The Problem of the Small Nations in the European Crises'. On 12 October Masaryk told Burrows that he thought Asquith's presence would send the wrong message to a besieged Serbia. Burrows and Dr Robert Seton-Watson, a lecturer in Slavic history, visited the Foreign Office to ask what was being done for Serbia. After being told that the Foreign and War offices opposed sending troops to Macedonia, they went to see Asquith the next day.[184] They told Maurice Bonham-Carter, Asquith's private secretary, that Greece had to help Serbia now and that the only way to make the neutralist government of Alexandros Zaimis (his fourth stint as prime minister, his first was in 1897) do so was to offer it Cyprus in a way that it could not refuse it. Clauson was to be instructed to inform the Archbishop and the Greek members of the Legislative Council that London would give Cyprus to Greece at once on one condition: that Greece entered the war immediately on the Entente side. Clauson was to enable the Archbishop to go to Athens and appeal to the king and Parliament, informing them that the offer would never be repeated. The British ambassador in Athens was also to ensure that the offer was published in the Venezelist press before the government could give its answer.[185]

Burrows put his plan to Lord Cecil, the under-secretary at the Foreign Office, on 14 October and Cecil suggested to Grey that southern Thrace and Smyrna should be promised to Greece after the war – and Cyprus, now.[186] The Cabinet accepted Burrows' scheme the next day.[187] That evening, Asquith, Bonar Law, the Colonial Secretary, Arthur Balfour, the First Lord of the Admiralty, Sir Austen Chamberlain, the India Secretary, Kitchener and King George V, approved Grey's cable to Athens.[188] As soon as Greece's army gave full support to Serbia, Cyprus would be transferred, and was offered independently of territory obtained after the war.[189] The Foreign Office informed Burrows and cabled Clauson, ordering him to announce the offer and assist the Archbishop to head for Athens to press its acceptance.[190]

But Clauson refused to cooperate. He told Bonar Law that he found it difficult to tell the 'loyal Muslims' because they were hostile to Constantinople and feared for their lives under Greek rule.[191] Clauson was clearly ignorant of Muslim loyalties; British intelligence found that many (including Abdul Hamid Bey, a member of legislature for the Larnaca district, 1906–8, 1911–14, 1917–18) aided the Ottoman cause financially and with vital intelligence.[192] Instead of ordering Clauson to follow his orders, Bonar Law asked Grey what to do. On 18 October Grey, who was increasingly lacking in confidence according to his colleagues,[193] opted to wait for Athens.[194] So only half of Burrows' plan was implemented.

At Masaryk's lecture the next day, Cecil told Burrows of Clauson's protest. Burrows rushed to the Colonial Office, where he spoke to J.C.C. Davidson, now Bonar Law's private secretary, and at 10 Downing Street he urged Bonham-Carter to act. On 20 October Burrows found the clerks at the Foreign Office indignant at Grey. Burrows suggested getting Venizelos to send for Kyrillos. A cable was sent,[195] but within hours Sir Francis Elliot, the British minister in Athens, cabled that Zaimis' government had rejected the offer because its military advisers thought joining the Allies would imperil Greece.[196]

With the rejection, Cyprus' place within the British imperial structure entered a new phase. London stated that the offer had lapsed and would not be repeated.[197] The offer galvanised imperialists. In February 1916, when the War Committee sanctioned the Anglo-French discussions, which had started in autumn 1915, on the division of Ottoman Asia between Britain and France (later the Sykes-Picot Agreement), imperialists objected to London's promise not to give Cyprus to a third power without consulting France. The most vociferous and influential opponent of ceding Cyprus to Greece was Lord Curzon, who became a member of the Imperial War Cabinet in 1916 and Foreign Secretary in 1919. He told Grey in February 1916: 'I regard Cyprus as a most valuable possession not to be parted with in any circumstances now above the horizon.'[198] Curzon and the Colonial Office solicited the support of the military departments to thwart Lloyd George's efforts to cede Cyprus to Greece at the Paris Peace Conference.[199] Exaggerated advantages were once again invented to justify the maintenance of British rule; while the new phase saw little sympathy to Hellenism and few attempts to try to justify ceding Cyprus to Greece.

Conclusion

This chapter has shown that only when strategy demanded it and there was something to gain did the Liberals, some of whom had considered Cyprus a useless acquisition and associated it with Greece, view the island as a pawn to be parted to Greece with – and not to its legal owner. Although the policy originated with the Admiralty, the Foreign Office was the pivotal department determining its course. The offer of October 1915 was not an isolated event, but the outcome of years of seeing Cyprus as strategically useless and a pawn.

The two efforts to cede Cyprus to Greece failed because Grey did not grasp the opportunities presented. The first time the advantages were the naval upper hand in the Mediterranean vis-à-vis the Austro-Hungarian fleet, instilling fear into the Italians over the strength of the British navy and obtaining Greece as an ally. Many issues combined to scuttle that proposal, not least of which was Grey trying to placate Italy instead of giving a firm commitment to Greece to make Italy think twice about moving closer to Austria-Hungary. The second time, when the proposal was officially made, Britain stood to gain only the last advantage – Greece's entry into the war – and although the proposal was well thought out, it did not go to plan and Grey did not enforce the original order to a high commissioner that had once made his view quite clear about the British mission in Cyprus.

Notes

1 S.G. Lazarides, *Theodoulos N. Toufexis: The Award-Winning Photographer of Cyprus, 1872–1948*, Nicosia, 2004, 133.
2 Shaw to Golding Bright, 15 December 1898, *Caesar and Cleopatra*, ed. Gale Lawson, Indianapolis, 1974, 167.
3 Gladstone papers, Gladstone to Granville, 17 December 1880.
4 Granville papers, Gladstone to Granville, 20 December 1880.
5 CO67/22/74, minute, Meade, 7 January 1881; Herbert, 8 January 1881.
6 PRO30/29/189, secret, Goschen to Granville, 25 February 1881; Spinner, *George Joachim Goschen*, 79.
7 PRO30/29/210, Granville to Goschen, 2 March 1881; private, Granville to Goschen, 3 March 1881.
8 PRO30/29/189, personal, Goschen to Granville, 25 March 1881; Lawrence, *The British Administration of Cyprus*, 47.
9 C.2930, Gladstone to Biddulph, 19 April 1881, 105.
10 Gladstone, papers, ADD MSS 44337, 409–26.
11 Stephen Koss, *The Pro-Boers*, Chicago, 1973, xxvi.
12 *Hansard* (Commons), 75, 4 August 1899, 1522.
13 John Lowe, *The Great Powers, Imperialism and the German Problem, 1865–1925*, London, 1994, 100–1, 106.
14 Oakleaf, 'Cyprus for German East Africa: A Fair Exchange', *United Service Magazine* (*USM*), XXII, October 1900–March 1901, 357.
15 Ibid.
16 Ibid., 357–61.
17 P.J.V. Rolo, *Entente Cordiale*, London, 1969, 205–70.
18 C.3750, Parliamentary Papers, London, 1908, CXXV.
19 CO67/153/40302, 417, confidential, Bertie to Grey, 21 October 1908.
20 Ibid.; FO800/172, private and confidential, Bertie to Hardinge, 26 October 1908.
21 FO800/172, private and confidential, Bertie to Hardinge, 26 October 1908.
22 Ibid.
23 FO800/172, private, Hardinge to Bertie, 29 October 1908.
24 Ibid.; Alastos, *Cyprus in History*, 340.
25 FO800/172, private, Grey to Bertie, 29 October 1908.
26 CO67/153/40302, 36765, Mallet, FO to CO, 2 November 1908; CO67/153/40302, confidential, FO draft reply to Bertie.
27 CO67/153/40302, confidential, CO to FO, 10 November 1908; CO67/153/42548, 39349, Mallet, FO to CO, 19 November 1908; confidential, CO to FO, 30 November 1908.
28 CO67/157/6978, 75, confidential, Nicolson to Grey, 1 February 1909.

29 CO67/157/6978, minute, Bertram Cox, 27 February 1909.

30 CO67/157/6978, confidential draft, FO to Nicolson.

31 FO371/882/7771, confidential, Sir G. Lowther to Grey, 28 February 1910, with article in *Samedi* of Ahmed Riza's speech, 26 February 1910; Joseph Reinach, *La Cretoise Question seen Peak*, Paris, 1910.

32 Wangenheim to Bülow, 6 June 1909, *German Diplomatic Documents, 1871–1914*, III, London, 1930, 381.

33 FO800/87, private, FO to Sir A. Wilson, 19 September 1911.

34 I.C. Barlow, *The Agadir Crisis*, Durham, 1940.

35 Thomson, *Churchill*, 121; Don Cregier, *Bounder from Wales: Lloyd George's Career Before the First World War*, London, 1976, 172–4.

36 *Manchester Guardian*, 22 July 1911.

37 Bentley Gilbert, 'Pacifist to Interventionist: David Lloyd George in 1911 and 1914. Was Belgium an Issue?' *Historical Review (HR)*, XXVIII, 4, 1985, 863–85.

38 Winston Churchill, *The World Crisis 1911–1918*, I, London, 1923, 43.

39 Edward Goschen, *The Diary of Edward Goschen, 1900–1914*, ed. Christopher Howard, London, 1980, 242.

40 CAB2/2/9, Committee of Imperial Defence (CID) Minutes, 23 August 1911.

41 Ibid.

42 R.B. Haldane, *An Autobiography*, London, 1926, 227; N. D'Ombrian, 'Churchill at the Admiralty and the Committee of Imperial Defence, 1911–14', *Journal of the Royal Services Institute for Defence Studies*, 1970, 38–9.

43 Cregier, *Bounder from Wales*, 220.

44 Lord Fisher to Churchill, 26 October 1911, Note, Churchill, November 1911, on Fisher's letter to J.A. Spender, 25 October 1911, Churchill to Asquith, 16 November 1911, Randolph Churchill, *Winston S. Churchill*, II, 2, 1907–1911, London, 1969, 1298–1300, 1316–17, 1335–6.

45 Thomson, *Churchill*, 127–8.

46 J.A. Pease, diary, 1 November 1911, Gilbert, 'Pacifist to Interventionist' 878.

47 Churchill Papers, CHAR9/43/41–4.

48 Geoffrey Miller, *The Millstone*, Hull, 1999, 234–8.

49 CAB37/111/84, Minute, Churchill to CID, accompanying translation of German Navy Law, 2 July 1912.

50 Churchill Memorandum, 15 February 1912, Randolph Churchill, *Winston S. Churchill*, II, 2, 1519.

51 William Askew, *Europe and Italy's Acquisition of Libya, 1911–1912*, Durham, 1942.

52 Gladstone to Granville, 22 April 1881, Low, *Reluctant Imperialists*, 15; PRO30/29/210, private, Granville to Goschen, 13 May 1881; Francesco Crispi, *The Memoirs of Francesco Crispi*, II, London, 1912, 118.

53 SA1:1108/1911, Arrival of three Italian warships, 6 June 1911.

54 Richard Bosworth, 'Britain and Italy's Acquisition of the Dodecanese, 1912–1915', *HJ*, XXIII, 4, December 1970, 683–705; and *Italy, the Least of the Great Powers*, London, 1979, 299–336.

55 FO800/356, Nicolson to Bertie, 23 May 1912.

56 ADM116/3109, secret, Italian occupation of Aegean Islands and its effect on naval policy, E.T.T., 20 June 1912. It was recognised that Cyprus was the exception, but the naval advisers had opposed its occupation.

57 CAB37/110/68, Haldane Memorandum, 9 May 1912.

58 CAB38/20/14, Memorandum, Crowe, 8 May 1912; FO800/48, Grey to Kitchener, 8 May 1912; FO800/48, Kitchener to Grey, 19 May 1912.

59 See 'The Geography Lesson', *Punch*, 5 June 1912.

60 FO800/48, Kitchener to Grey, 2 June 1912; CAB38/21/25, Churchill note on arrangements with Kitchener, undated; CAB37/111/76, Memorandum, Churchill, 15 June, 1912.

61 ADM116/3109, secret, War Staff Memorandum, 21 June 1912.

62 ADM116/3109, Memorandum, Captain W.A.H. Kelly, 3 July 1912.

63 ADM116/3493, secret, Memorandum, Board of Trade, May 1912.

64 ADM116/3109, Admiralty War Staff Memorandum, 21 June 1912; CAB37/111/78, Memorandum, Churchill, 22 June 1912.
65 ADM116/3109, Draft, Anglo-French Naval Agreement, 23 July 1912.
66 *The Times*, 11 and 16 September 1912.
67 Churchill to Grey and Asquith, secret, 23 August 1912, Randolph Churchill, *Winston S. Churchill*, II, 3, London, 1969, 1638–9; FO371/1368, Grey to Bertie, 7 and 21 November 1912.
68 116th meeting of the CID, 25 April 1912; FO371/1866/4484/23077/1912, secret, 453.M., Memorandum, 30 December 1912, S.H. Wilson, Secretary of the ODC.
69 FO881/10014, Memorandum, 10 April 1912; CAB 38/20/8.
70 CAB38/20/16, Note, CIGS covering General Staff reports on the attack and defence of: Malta (92C); Cyprus (93C); and Egypt (149B), 9 May 1912; CAB38/20/13, 1. Austrian attack on Cyprus; 2. Defence of Cyprus, 9 May 1912.
71 Ibid.
72 Ibid.; CAB38/21/24, Memorandum, General Staff, 1 July 1912.
73 I.P. Pikros, *Ο Βενιζέλος και το Κυπριακό*, Athens, 1980, 4–10; Purcell, *Cyprus*, 231; Georghallides, *A Political and Administrative History of Cyprus*, 92–3, 88–102; Panteli, *A History of Cyprus*, 68–9, 81; Loukis Theocharides, *The British Offer of Cyprus to Greece (1915)*, Nicosia, 2000, 12–13.
74 Hadjidemetriou, *A History of Cyprus*, 366–7.
75 Doros Alastos, *Venizelos: Patriot, Statesman, Revolutionary*, London 1942, 56–6; Venizelos had at least three biographies from Western authors (S.B. Chester, H.A. Gibbons, V.J. Seligman) by 1921.
76 E.J. Dillon, 'Foreign Affairs', *CR–1*, XCVII, Jan 1910, 110–28, 113–14; Mavrogordato, *Modern Greece*, 82–3; S.V. Papacosma, *The Military in Greek Politics: The 1909 Coup d'etat*, Kent, 1977, 38–156.
77 Alastos, *Venizelos*, 80; Maurice Pearton, 'Britain and Greek Naval Defence 1910–1916', *Greece and Great Britain During World War I*, Thessaloniki, 1985, 17–47.
78 Miller, *The Millstone*, 317–19.
79 CAB1/34, most secret, Churchill to Grey and Asquith, 22 October 1912; minute, Grey, 22 October 1912.
80 C. Svolopoulos, 'Anglo-Hellenic Talks on Cyprus During the Axis Campaign Against Greece', *BS*, 1982, 199–208. Geography was clearly not Grey's strong suit.
81 Michael Llewellyn Smith, *Ionian Vision: Greece in Asia Minor, 1919–1922*, London, 1973 (2000), 13.
82 J.T.A. Koumoulides edited the diary and the *Journal of Modern Hellenism* published it, IV–V, 1987–1988, 93–119 and 85–121. The diary is cited as 'Stavridi diary', with the date and the subsequent part and page number referring to the Koumoulides publication.
83 Stavridi, quoting Lloyd George, diary, 10 November 1912, I, 99.
84 Ibid., 98.
85 Bosworth, *Italy, the Least of the Great Powers*, 306–7.
86 FO286/552, 49789, 75, Grey to Elliot, 20 November 1912.
87 Stavridi, diary, 10 November 1912, 1, 99.
88 Ibid., 18 November 1912, I, 100–1.
89 Ibid.
90 *Protocols of Conferences between Great Britain, Austria, France, Prussia, and Russia relative to the Union of the Ionian Islands to Greece, and the Succession to the Greek Throne*. London, January to March 1864.
91 Stavridi diary, 102–3.
92 ADM116/3099, secret, memorandum, 20 November 1912.
93 Ibid.
94 Stavridi diary, 22 November 1912, I, 103.
95 J.S. Saunders to A.J. Balfour, reporting a conversation with Bridgeman, 10 October 1912, Churchill, *Winston S. Churchill*, II, 3, 1663–4.
96 See Battenberg and Churchill and Bridgeman and Churchill exchanges, ibid., 1675–9.

97 ADM116/3109, minute, Churchill, 9 December 1912.

98 ADM116/3109, minute, Battenberg, 9 December 1912.

99 Stavridi diary, 10 December 1912, I, 105.

100 Ibid., 12 and 13 December 1912, I, 106.

101 Ibid., 16 December 1912, 1, 107.

102 Ibid.

103 Ibid., 17 December 1912, I, 108–9.

104 Ibid., 5 January 1913, I, 110.

105 Ibid., 7 January 1913, I, 111–12; ADM116/3098, 'Greece. Naval Strength – Present and Future', 24 December 1912.

106 Pearton, 'Britain and Greek Naval Defence 1910–1916', 17–47.

107 Stavridi diary, 7 January 1913, I, 111–12.

108 Ibid., 29 January 1913, I, 117.

109 Ibid., 20 and 21 January 1914, II, 85.

110 Ibid., 22 January 1914, II, 86.

111 Hill, *A History of Cyprus*, IV, 520. This was based on reports in the Greek newspaper *Ethnos* in 1934.

112 Theocharides, *The British Offer of Cyprus to Greece*, 13, fn. 10; also, E. Hatzivassiliou, *The Cyprus Question, 1878–1960*, Minnesota, 2002, 32. Hatzivassiliou cites *Ionian Vision*, thereby implying that this is Llewellyn Smith's view when in fact it is not.

113 Alastos, *Cyprus in History*, 340–1.

114 CO883/7/10, 72, 38496, confidential, paraphrase, Goold-Adams to Harcourt, received 4 December 1912.

115 Fiddes wondered: 'Then what will become of the tribute?' CO67/167/38496, minute, Fiddes, 5 December 1912; CO67/168/40614, Alison Russell to Ellis, 12 December 1912. Russell, who had replaced Bucknill, agreed.

116 CO883/7/10, 72, 41168, Orr to Harcourt, 19 December 1912, enclosing letter and petition from Mehmed Shevket, Mustapha Hami and Mehmed Ziai to Harcourt, 13 December 1912.

117 CO883/7/15, 77, 493, Orr to Harcourt, 24 December 1912, to FO 9 January 1913, with Greek letter and petition from a meeting on 19 December at the Archiepiscopal Palace and signed by over 30 leaders.

118 CO67/167/41168, minute, Fiddes, 28 December 1912.

119 Georghallides, *A Political and Administrative History of Cyprus*, 93; Panteli, *A History of Cyprus*, 68–9.

120 Epeirotou, *Η Μάχη της Κύπρου 1878–1956*, 18.

121 *BLC*, 355, 281.

122 CO883/7/15, 77, 3780 confidential, Goold-Adams to Harcourt, 21 January 1913, enclosure, extract from *Eleutheria*, 18 January 1913.

123 CO67/171/3961, Goold-Adams to Ellis, 22 January 1913.

124 C067/169/9530, 59, Goold-Adams to Harcourt, 13 March 1913, enclosure, article from *Alethia*, 15 February 1913. The words were emphasised in the translation.

125 SA1:691/1913, 6–7, confidential report, Police inspector to Larnaca's Commissioner, 19 April 1913.

126 CO883/7/15, 77, 10069, telegram, Eyioub to CO, 25 March 1913.

127 CO883/7/15, 77, 10069, Read to FO, 28 March 1913.

128 H.C.G. Matthew, *The Liberal Imperialists*, Oxford, 1973, 300.

129 FO71/1764/14866, Goodwin to Grey, 27 March 1913.

130 CO883/7/15, 77, 11684, Louis Mallet, FO to CO, 7 April 1913.

131 Joseph Heller, *British Policy Towards the Ottoman Empire, 1908–1914*, London, 1983.

132 FO800/91, Grey to Harcourt, 19 January 1915; Philip Magnus, *Kitchener*, London, 1958, 313–14.

133 FO371/1801, 128, confidential, Rodd to Grey, 16 May 1913.

134 FO371/1801, 223, Grey to Bertie, 29 March 1913.

135 Quoted by Miller, *The Millstone*, 357.

136 FO371/1818/21566, Grey to Rodd, 7 May 1913.

137 FO371/1764/25846, Grey to Rodd, 2 June 1913.

138 CAB1/33, Battenberg memorandum, 19 June 1913.

139 ADM137/819, *Mediterranean War Orders No. 1*, August 1913.

140 FO371/2112/2179, Rodd to Grey, 11 January 1914.

141 FO800/63, private & secret, Grey to Elliot, 21 January 1914.

142 George Leon, *Greece and the Great Powers 1914–1917*, Salonika, 1973, 315–16.

143 Fisher to Churchill, 2 and 9 November 1911, Churchill, *Winston S. Churchill*, II, 2, 1318–20, 1325–26.

144 G. Miller, *Superior Force*, Hull, 1997, 150–1; Pearton, 'Britain and Greek Naval Defence 1910–1916', 39–40.

145 FO371/1381/55766, 216, Elliot to Grey, 25 December 1912; minute Nicolson.

146 J. Heller, *British Policy Towards the Ottoman Empire, 1908–1914*, London, 1983.

147 Stavridi diary, 9, 11, 12, and 29 December 1913.

148 Admiral Limpus to Churchill, 3 and 29 December 1913, Churchill, *Winston S. Churchill*, II, 3, 1800–1.

149 B. Kondis, 'The Problem of the Aegean Islands on the Eve of World War I and Great Britain', *Greece and Great Britain During World War I*, 49–63, 51.

150 ADM116/3493, Remarks on Shipbuilding Policy for Greece, 7 January 1913.

151 Theocharides, *The British Offer of Cyprus to Greece*, 13, note 10.

152 D. Brooks, *The Age of Upheaval*, Manchester, 1995, 141–50; J. Smith, *The Tories and Ireland 1910–1914*, Dublin, 2000.

153 B.B. Gilbert, *David Lloyd George: A Political Life – Organiser of Victory, 1912–16*, London, 1992, 70.

154 Cregier, *Bounder from Wales*, 222–3.

155 Ibid., 224.

156 Churchill to Asquith, 18 December 1913, Churchill, *Winston S. Churchill*, II, 3, 1834–5.

157 *Daily Chronicle*, 3 January 1914; George Riddell, *More Pages from My Diary, 1908–1914*, London, 1934, 196–7.

158 Asquith to Margot Asquith, 20 January 1914, J.A. Spender and C. Asquith, *Life of Herbert Henry Asquith, Lord Oxford and Asquith*, II, London, 1932, 72; Asquith to Venetia Stanley, 6 January 1914, Churchill, *Winston S. Churchill*, II, 3, 1844.

159 Lloyd George to Asquith, 27 January 1914, Churchill, *Winston S. Churchill*, II, 3, 1855; Cregier, *Bounder from Wales*, 228–9.

160 J.C.C. Davidson, *Memoirs of a Conservative: J.C.C. Davidson's Memoirs and Papers, 1910–1937*, ed. R.R. James, London, 1969, 13. Douglas Jardine, a junior in the secretariat in Cyprus, was Davidson's friend and so the mission was hidden behind a holiday to catch up. Jardine also criticised the Cyprus regime, telling Davidson: 'the old representatives of the Service that I have met are certainly the most incompetent and evil-doing creatures I have ever clapped eyes on'. Jardine to Davidson, 28 July 1913, 13, fn. 1.

161 Ibid., 16–17.

162 G. Papadopoulos et al., *Χριστόδουλος Σώζος: Μια Μεγάλη Μορφή της Νεώτερης Κυπριακής Ιστορίας*, Nicosia, 8 December 2002, 9–10.

163 CO67/172/7481, minutes and correspondence; CO67/172/9309, confidential, Harcourt to Goold-Adams, 27 March 1915; CO67/172/18111, minutes and correspondence.

164 *The Times*, 14 November 1914, 7e; David Cannadine, *Aspects of Aristocracy*, New Haven, 1994, 117.

165 *The Times*, 27 November 1914, 7c.

166 Ibid., 6 November 1914, 7e.

167 FO800/91, Grey to Harcourt, 19 January 1915; Magnus, *Kitchener*, 313–14; On 18 January Grey told Bertie that Serbia needed Greek and Romanian help and to secure Greece's entry into the war he wanted to offer Cyprus. FO371/2241, 105, very confidential, Grey to Bertie, 18 January 1915.

168 CAB37/123/33, Cabinet Meeting, 20 January 1915; Montagu papers, Asquith to Venetia Stanley, 20 January 1915, Gilbert, *Winston S. Churchill*, III, 1, 431.

169 WO106/1570, Proposed Attack on Alexandretta, January–November 1915; WO157/689, secret, Notes on Alexandretta, Catoni (British Consul at Alexandretta) and Kennedy, Additional to the Military Report on Syria, 20 January 1915; WO157/689, secret, Alexandretta, 19 January 1915.

170 FO371/2242, Grey to Elliot, 23 January 1915.

171 FO800/63, private and secret, Elliot to Grey, 5 February 1915.

172 Churchill papers, 13/47, Limpus to Churchill, 19 February 1915, Gilbert, *Winston S. Churchill*, III, 300.

173 Churchill to Fisher and Oliver, 2 March 1915, Gilbert, *Winston S. Churchill*, III, 300.

174 Magnus, *Kitchener*, 314.

175 CAB37/127/36, Wedgwood to Harcourt, 22 April 1915. Hereafter Wedgwood to Harcourt.

176 ADM137/96, Churchill and Oliver to Carden, 16 February 1915.

177 CAB37/124/13, Report, Captain Frank Larkin, with note, Vice-Admiral R.H. Peirse, CIC.

178 C.V. Wedgwood, *The Last of the Radicals: Josiah Wedgwood, MP*, London, 1951, 9.

179 Luke, *Cities and Men*, II, 17.

180 Wedgwood to Harcourt.

181 WO157/689, Intelligence Department, WO, Cairo, 5 January 1915.

182 Wedgwood to Harcourt.

183 George Glasgow, *Ronald Burrows: A Memoir*, London, 1924, 198–9.

184 Ibid., 228.

185 Ibid.

186 FO371/2273, 152128, minute, Cecil, 14 October 1915.

187 Lord Maurice Hankey, diary, 15 October 1915, Stephen Roskill, *Hankey*, I, London, 1970, 227.

188 FO371/2273, 902, 72, Grey draft, 16 October 1915; 68, Grey to Elliot, 16 October 1915; 67, secretary to King George V to FO, 16 October 1915.

189 Ibid., 65, telegram, Grey to Elliot, 16 October 1915.

190 Glasgow, *Burrows*, 229–30; FO371/2273, 153141, 96, Bonar Law to Clauson, 16 October 1915.

191 FO371/2273, Clauson to Bonar Law, 17 October 1915.

192 KV1/18, Imperial Overseas Intelligence 1918: Cyprus Section and Appendices, 1921; SA1:669/15, Collaborating with enemy, Abdul Hamid Bey, file missing.

193 Keith Robbins, 'Grey, Edward, Viscount Grey of Fallodon (1862–1933)', *ODNB* (www.oxforddnb.com/view/article/33570, accessed 22 Aug 2005).

194 FO371/2273, 153141, Grey note, 18 October 1915; FO to CO, 18 October 1915; CO to Clauson, 19 October 1915.

195 Glasgow, *Burrows*, 235–6.

196 FO371/2273, 1073, Elliot to Grey, 20 October 1915.

197 *Hansard* (Commons), LXXV, Grey to Philip Magnus, 26 October 1915, 5.

198 FO800/106, Curzon to Grey, 3 February 1916.

199 Fisher, 'The Cyprus Proposition'.

CONCLUSION

Venus Loquitur

No pilgrim to my Paphian shrine
Now gather as of yore:
The gems, that through this isle of mine
Once sparkled, shine no more.

But more than all its gems of old,
My Garnet, comes with you,
Whose Government brings British gold,
My Cyprus to renew!

Emblem of might and right at home,
Emblem abroad, of 'Swag',
Le Venus, daughter of the foam,
Draped in the British flag!

(*Punch*, 3 August 1878)

'Venus (Aphrodite) speaks', according to the title of this satirical poem in *Punch*. She pronounces on the good fortune of her island as it comes under British rule. This, of course, is a conceit: it is not Aphrodite who speaks, but an unnamed Briton who wrote the poem that accompanied Edward Linley Sambourne's cartoon 'Wolseley Courts Cyprus' (Figure 20) that claims to speak in Cyprus's name. For all its classical imagery this was a thoroughly Victorian era piece of doggerel and yet an excellent statement about Cyprus's occupation and the justifications of imperial expansion based on the renewal of acquisitions.

In Cyprus's case, renewal and future prosperity under imperial rule was cast in terms of its past. It was a familiar past to *Punch* readers: educated boys and girls studied the classics and ancient Greece represented one of the poles of English intellectual culture. The other was Latin and here Aphrodite is given her Latin name of Venus and even speaks in Latin, though only twice. Most knew the tradition that Aphrodite, which in Greek means 'risen from the sea,' did exactly that from the foamy waves of Paphos. They might also have known another tradition, that this took place off Kythera, one of the Ionian Islands. Unlike the huge tracts of Empire in Asia, Africa and Oceania, Cyprus was on the periphery of Europe and, like the Ionian Islands, it carried the huge weight of a Greek past on the nineteenth-century British mind.

[272]

These are only the first inconsistencies that this rhyme illustrates. As this study has shown, the Ionian Islands preceded Cyprus as a rather inconsequential imperial possession. Both became Hellenised during British rule and both were disappointments. British perceptions surrounding Cyprus's occupation and its administration between 1878 and 1915 were characterised by conceptual and organisational confusion, resulting from conceiving the future strategic and economic value of the island in a distant past and an overly optimistic future.

This book has examined the tensions underlying British imperialism in Cyprus: its place in the imperial imagination and imperial structure. So much has been written about the British empire's construction outside Europe and about how it was administered and conceived, yet so little has been written about the same themes in Britain's tiny empire in 'Europe'. This study has tried to rectify this by looking at whether the assumptions made about imperial rule outside Europe hold true in a 'European space'.

The obvious answer is that they did. Yet the tension between the process of ruling a foreign people and the perception that they were Europeans and that their ancestors lay at the heart of modern British intellectual and political culture deformed the British encounter with Cyprus. The 'natives' of Africa and Asia could hardly be equated with the citizens of Athens and Sparta.

Such ironies resonate through the poem. Aphrodite laments that for centuries no pilgrims had visited her shrine in Paphos and that Cyprus once was rich. But for centuries it had been in a miserable condition; presumably, because of the rule of the 'unspeakable Turk'. The British pilgrims have now awakened her; she can speak again and her first words are of welcome. Cyprus's supposed prosperity in antiquity and medieval times was a useful myth for English imperialism, but *Punch* knew the irony of using the classical past to justify imperial acquisition in the present.

This book has shown that the initial reasons for occupying Cyprus lacked foundation. Like many other acquisitions Europe made, the British claimed it as an Eldorado. The British public were told that the island was to be enriched; harbours were to be made, roads built, irrigation works undertaken, its famous forests replenished and capital attracted. But these projects had no existence in fact. *Punch's* Venus has some fun with this. The gems of old are replaced by a modern gem, a garnet. Or rather a Garnet Wolseley who, if he is a precious stone at all, could be only a British stone, not a Greek one. Wolseley brings British gold to renew Cyprus in a reverse of the Eldorado thesis – if Cyprus was so rich, why would the British need to import gold? *Punch*, in the traditional Radical mistrust of imperial renewal, knew that

Cyprus would need British gold to renew it, but would not get it. Because the British did not find Cyprus an 'Eldorado' of boundless wealth, they did not invest the energy or funds to 'renew' it. Cyprus' case contradicts the economic theory of imperialism. The island attracted investors, but the climate and insalubrity, and the Colonial Office preference for the Crown Agents discouraged them. Then when the imperial interest in Cyprus waned, so did that of investors. Imperial funds were also rejected, until Joseph Chamberlain entered the picture. But that was late – by the turn of the century there was little imperial interest in Cyprus. The Eldorado thesis applies well to Cyprus, as it does to western and central Africa for the French, Libya for the Italians and Palestine for the British. The Eldorado thesis applies well where imperialism needs justifying: because it was in 'Europe', the taking of Cyprus needed explaining to the other European powers and the British public; while French and Italy imperialism was never so popular and always needed justifying.

Cyprus was occupied at the start of the period of 'new imperialism' and in order for the other European powers to agree to it, London agreed to them occupying Ottoman territory. Paris and Rome could look to Ottoman Africa for compensation. So the scramble for Africa did not start because the British occupied Egypt. Indeed, Cyprus' occupation also resulted in King Leopold occupying the Congo after he missed out on Cyprus, which he long harboured ambitions to occupy.[1] The failure to make Cyprus valuable did not prevent the subsequent expansion or force the British to make Cyprus a stronghold either.

British aims in Cyprus were not lost on the author of the poem, and Sambourne. Wolseley's presence in the poem and cartoon, where he courts Cyprus with flowers while carrying his helmet and lance, was a reference to the British military agenda in Cyprus. First and foremost the British wanted Cyprus for strategic purposes. It was going to fit nicely into imperial strategy as an appendage to Gibraltar and Malta, a watchtower over the informal empire in Egypt and the 'sick man of Europe' and as the basis for a new empire in the Levant, which would guard against Russian moves into western Asia and potentially India, the jewel of the British Crown. Cyprus' perceived strategic value and the desire for an empire in the Levant were rooted in the Crusades, which were an imperial fight to 'liberate' the Holy Land from the Muslims. Christianity forms a major component of modern English cultural identity and imperialism forms a major part of British nationalism. Cyprus was for centuries a crusader kingdom; it had a role in early Christianity and was adjacent to the Holy Land. The British wanted to revitalise western Asia by establishing informal control over it through the establishment of Cyprus as a *place d'armes*, an entrepôt and an example of good government to the Porte. Europe would be fearful of the British stronghold of Famagusta, while the Near East would marvel and rejoice at the spectacle of the fertile soil, lush green pastures and abundant crops. All of this was to follow the supplanting of the Crescent by the standard of St George on the island where Richard *Coeur de Lion* had once roamed.

But fitting Cyprus into the British imperial structure overnight was an exaggerated expectation. Its state disheartened those employed in surveying its potential, as well as those at home awaiting results. Within months of the occupation, Cyprus had a reputation as a pestiferous hell-hole that lacked a harbour for warships. At first, London tried to convince the military men sent to rule Cyprus that it was a strategic pearl: it failed. Then when civilian personnel replaced the military, some tried to convince the metropolis of that; and failed too. Cyprus' vision within imperial strategy had been misconceived. There was no longer a threat through Armenia and the Porte would not cooperate to establish informal British control in Asia Minor. Force to do so was unjustified, as the Russian threat bypassed Mesopotamia and moved to Afghanistan within a year of Cyprus' occupation. Ottoman financial problems also resulted in the Conservative government thinking twice about sponsoring new imperial interests in western Asia. Moreover, the British did nothing to make their position in Cyprus strong enough to guard against instability in Armenia or Egypt, necessitating the latter's military occupation, while resulting in massacres and genocide in the former. The focus on Egypt also explains why the imperial interest in western Asia subsided. Although the British said they did not want to stay permanently in Egypt, proposals to evacuate to Cyprus were never taken up. It was far better to dominate a place you had significant interests in than a place detached from its periphery where you had few, even if you enjoyed its occupation and administration.

The failure of the Cyprus venture raises questions on the decision-making process. It was the men at the highest levels of office – Beaconsfield and Salisbury – who were dazzled by the historical associations of the island and convinced a willing Cabinet on the need to occupy it and not the departments of state. Cyprus was celebrated as a Phoenician outpost, when they held the trade of the Mediterranean and Zeno – the Cypriot – founded stoicism; in Greek mythology, as the birthplace of Aphrodite and the kingdom of Pygmalion; as a vital place of early Christianity, where the Apostle Barnabas was born and where St Paul and he converted the first Roman proconsul; and during the Crusades, as a theatre of adventure to the most romantic of English kings. It seemed hardly worth asking if so interesting an island was fit for the use to which those that selected it wanted to put it. Certainly, only a few advisers of state were asked. The departments – the Admiralty and War Office and then the Colonial Office after 1880 – were saddled with the consequences of fashioning a role for Cyprus within imperial strategy and ruling an island which had lost the imperial interest that had underpinned its occupation. The only interest was the tribute, which resulted in limiting local funds for development, especially in Famagusta: improving its harbour for local purposes might reawaken the imperial interest in its capabilities and required the spending of local funds to make it healthy for imperial purposes, thus threatening the payment of the tribute. In a reverse of the idea of renewal, stagnation was purposefully adopted. In the hands of a few Colonial Office officials, most of whom (apart from Edward Fairfield) had not even visited Cyprus, modernity was imposed unwittingly. Then, it was the politicians that decided to withdraw from the island; the officials in the Colonial Office had no idea about it. Nevertheless, the politicians were reflecting the military advisers who had consistently pronounced against the island's strategic value, but had been thwarted in their efforts to remove the military establishment by the Colonial and Foreign Offices warning that the result would be inter-communal disturbances. The Mediterranean naval crisis of 1912 and then the First World War did not revise its status as a backwater; instead they were the catalysts behind Cyprus becoming a pawn. There could not have been a greater statement against its strategic shortcomings.

British nationalism and imperialism, as the poem suggests, were interconnected, helping to explain the euphoria (except from many Liberals) that greeted Cyprus' occupation. Aphrodite recognises the contradiction that in Britain there are free institutions, justice and open government – broadly, democracy. But abroad the British government has a different reputation: it has an emblem of 'swag' that represents the heap of acquisitions and the vastness of the British empire, built on the subjugation of people. The draping of Aphrodite, the daughter of the foam, in the British flag is a powerful nationalist and imperialist representation. The British empire itself sprang from the sea and it was the potential of the sea to engender power that was the focus of imperial policy. Certainly, there was nothing strange in personifications draped in the British flag: there were equivalents for India, Malaya, South Africa, Canada, Australia and elsewhere. But what is being draped in Cyprus' case? Aphrodite: an enduring symbol of ancient Greece, which was usurped as a spiritual ancestor and the basis of modern European political culture. The British had occupied a vital part of their own political and cultural mythology. Cyprus' perceived

European identity set it apart from the rest of the Empire: the tension of governing an inferior breed of people, while situating them within the unitary ideals of ancient and modern Greece. Where else in the Empire was there a colony that could be claimed by two competing cultural hegemonies, one of which, Greece, was a protégé of the coloniser?

The British, Hellenic settlers and many Orthodox Cypriots educated abroad, usurped the topological dream of Hellenism and imposed it on the existing elite and population. Cypriot Orthodox identity was altered, as the British failure to dramatically improve the quality of life propelled the *énosis* demand. The failure to situate Cyprus within imperial structures was reflected in the failure of British methods of rule as well. The British rejected undertaking the paternalistic respons-ibilities that the Cypriots were accustomed to under Ottoman rule and which they craved from the British. They even refused to replace them with similar structures, such as the co-option of the local elites, which was policy in Africa and Asia. But distancing themselves from the Ottomans was important – indeed vital for the Eldorado thesis to apply. The irony of the result was that the British contributed to the manifestation of a challenge to their rule. They achieved this by facil-itating the imposition of a national identity on the Cypriot Orthodox through applying political modernity to the restructuring of govern-ment and society. Alongside the growth of Hellenism, there also grew disaffection with the constitution because it did not grant the politicians real power. The carrot on a string approach was a recipe for disaster. The refusal to grant more power to the local politicians resulted in them using the failure of British economic policy to pursue their Hellenist agenda against those that called for cooperation with the British and the Muslims to improve the quality of life of all Cypriots. It is thus possible to make a number of conclusions about the vari-ous received wisdoms about identity development in Cyprus. First, that the nationalist discourses are wrong and need replacing with a new awareness of identity formation in Cyprus, which corresponds to the 'modernist' school of thought on identity-formation/nationalism. Second, the idea that the British treated the Cypriot Orthodox Christians as 'African natives' and implemented a policy of divide and rule is wrong, because as has been shown above that the British policy-makers in London saw the Cypriot Orthodox Christians as Europeans and applied modernity in their approach to governing.

Cyprus' Muslims did not sit idly watching the growth of Hellenism or the imposition of modernity. Many embraced the modernity of the Young Turks, but the real battle for the Muslims was *énosis*. They naturally reacted to the threat to their existence. For as long as London was confused about what to do with Cyprus, it would remain British. But when a role for Cyprus was found, as a pawn, the Muslims were the casualties.

The Ottoman empire had become inconsequential to London after the agreements of 1878. The failure of the Cyprus venture was partly responsible; a stronghold may have made the Porte think twice about not intervening in Egypt when London urged it to in 1882; it may also have prevented the escalation of violence in Crete. Perhaps too, it would have averted the massacre of Armenians in the 1890s; and further even, it may possibly have made Britain and not Germany the main player at Constantinople. But the old faith in the Ottomans had faded. London was more than happy to collect the Cyprus tribute to cover their liabilities to the bondholders of the Ottoman defaulted loan than to aid the Porte to open up its economy and increase production and, thus, revenue. This approach lacked the dynamism of Beaconsfield's policy of 1878 and the morality that characterised Gladstone's foreign and imperial politics and contradicted the aim to show the Porte how to govern by making Cyprus the example.

The British introduction of modernity and sympathy with the Hellenists created a rift that was not apparent between the Orthodox and Muslim Cypriots and which positioned the British in the middle. The British justified keeping troops in Cyprus because of the potential violence between Orthodox and Muslim Cypriots – even though no such violence had existed. Crete was the example and it was implied that the violence there would manifest itself in Cyprus. It did, albeit to a much lesser extent, because the British let it. The failure to do anything – like fostering the commonalities of the two communities, developed so well during the later stages of Ottoman rule – resulted in inter-communal clashes in 1912. If the troops stayed to prevent this, then presumably a British withdrawal would lead to a civil war. This was one of the British arguments for refusing to grant *énosis* after the Second World War.

The confusion over what to do with Cyprus and the confusion that the British brought to bear on the Cypriots provides the setting from which to appreciate the violence that gripped the island in the mid-1950s. The difficulty in subjugating a people that the coloniser had helped to become Greek was a problem faced during the first phase of British rule and which was not reconciled. The offer of 1915 saw to that, as Hellenists cried that the offer recognised their right as the majority to self-determination.

One other reason for rejecting *énosis* in the 1950s was the British belief in Cyprus' strategic value after the Second World War. This resulted in the policy to fight EOKA. Although Cyprus had finally become important when the British moved their Middle East head-quarters from Egypt to Cyprus in 1952, Cyprus' new-found import-ance was grounded on exaggerated strategic perceptions: during the Suez campaign, Cyprus failed as an airbase; as a naval base it was worse, as Malta, which was 1,000 miles from Alexandria, had to be used.[2] The failure to situate Cyprus within the British imperial picture was evident from the start, notwithstanding the opinion of some imperial strategists that maintained that it was, or had the potential to be, a very significant strategic asset.

Nationalism, which has plagued the stability of Cyprus, started manifesting itself in the 1890s in the Cypriot Orthodox community and was not instituted as a 'national policy' until 1910. The Cypriot Orthodox may not have become 'Greeks' if the British and the Hellenist leaders, which replaced, marginalised and absorbed the leaders that preached good relations with the British and Muslims, had not imposed it on them. The parallels with the present day are clear: most Cypriot Orthodox question the motives of the 'Anglo-Americans' and consider them and the Turks the enemy; while those that want to work with the Turkish Cypriots are marginalised. Even the leaders of these two factions – the nationalist and the Cypriotist – today, share the names of those that did battle between 1900 and 1910; Tassos Papadopoulos, the Hellenist, and George Vasilliou, the Cypriotist, compare admirably to the volatile Kyrillos Papadopoulos and the stoic Kyrillos Vasilliou.

This study has shown that the imperial venture in Cyprus failed: the strategic, commercial and political advantages could not sustain the imperial interest and the island became a pawn to be ceded to Greece.

In 'Venus Loquitur' *Punch* mocked the imperialist notion of renewing the prosperity of acquisitions and making them into assets in the traditional Radical mistrust of imperial adventure. Cyprus, it thought, was simply another possession added to the swag of other inconsequential possessions and its renewal was an empty imperialist rant. *Punch* was right. Cyprus, the eligible strategic asset, which had been the cause of the negotiated European partial-partition of the Ottoman Empire in 1878, became a pawn by the eve of the First World War. A British government had finally decided what to do with the island.

In Greek mythology, Pygmalion, the King of Cyprus, sculpted a beauti-ful ivory statue of a woman, which he fell in love with. Eventually, Aphrodite gave it life. The British sculpted two incompatible ima-ginaries of Cyprus. The first was the Christian Crusader, which was spiritual, imperial and strategic; the second was the Grecian, which was cultural and imperial, but also anti-imperial in the context of

Philhellenism. Of these, the British gave life to only the second and they embraced it as the answer to the failure to bring life to the first. Their failure to ultimately hand Cyprus to Greece, however, awakened the imperial interest in Cyprus and served as the catalyst for a new effort to bring to life the imperial and strategic and to deny the cultural. British rule needed justifying somehow.

Notes

1 R.P.A. Roeykens, 'The Historical Context of the Ephemeral Project to take as a Colony the Island of Cyprus (1876)', *Bulletin Des Seances Academie Royale Des Sciences D'Outre Mer Bruxelles*, VIII, 1962, 362–79.
2 Varnava, *The Cyprus Problem and the Defence of the Middle East, 1945–1960*, 50–2.

APPENDIX I

Beaconsfield poem

Right Hon. The Earl of Beaconsfield, KG, etc. etc. etc.

Hail to the Chief who in triumph returns;
'Peace,' but 'with honour,' his footsteps attends:
Heart of Old England with gratitude burns;
   City with Country its welcoming blends.

Shines here no helmet, here glitters no sword;
   Trumpet sounds none in the long crowded street;
Citizens only his cavalcade guard;
Flowers from fair hands this new conqueror greet.

Brighter the hope that his victories fill
   Than trophies won hard on the red battle-field;
A sword in his voice, and a hoist in his will
That daunts all aggression, and dares – not to yield.

Genius prepared both for faction and fighting;
   Patriot on fire for a land not his own;
Eastern and Western in Congress uniting,
Swayed by his counsel, their quarrels condone.

Hence rise the cheers of a Senate that listens
   To a tale yet more wondrous that that of 'Alroy';
Hence on his bosom the Star that outglistens
   'Tancred's' wild vision and 'Coningsby's' joy.

Banquet on banquet, and toast upon toast,
   Fill up the measure of praise and of glory;
Tell us, at last, without braggard or boast,
   The moral of all this magnificent story.

Let others shun the hazards and the falls,
And shrink the steep when Duty calls;
Or, safe within the streak of silver sea,
Live for themselves and for the passing day.

England! For thee a nobler task we find –
To lead the nations, not to lag behind;
Be thine the praise, in every time and peace,
To ennoble, kindle, purify our race!

Henceforth (blest omen!) thine happy isle
On which the Queen of Love first deigned to smile;
Mother of those whose laws, whose arms, whose arts
Subdued from clime to clime the wildest hearts.

But nobler than that old imperial Rome
Is to thy sons their own inspiring home;
Wealth, Freedom, Justice, as thy dower are given,
And Gospel Truth, the last best boon of Heaven.

Then onwards to 'fresh woods and pastures new;'
O'er earth and sea to thine own self be true;
The ancient East, through thee with light divine
Once more imbued, shall still 'arise and shine.'

Like that 'good man,' the Cypriot saint of yore,
On friendless souls sweet consolations pour;
Catch from the genius of the neighbouring strand
The holy stirrings of that Sacred Land;
Whilst the bright Day-star sees the Crescent wane,
Be thine this glorious Cross, not borne in vain.

A.P.S.
(*Source*: Disraeli papers, Box 73)

APPENDIX II

Ormiston estimates

If the breakwater were 1¼ miles long the works proposed would cost:

Breakwater	£126,478
Dredging and plant	£70,687
Removing mole	£10,000
Wharf	£14,000
Lighthouse on end of breakwater	£2,000
Seven moorings	£10,500
Contingencies, 10 per cent	£23,366
Engineering, 6 per cent	£15,422
Total	£272,453

If the breakwater were 1⅔ miles long the works proposed would cost:

Breakwater	£192,174
Dredging and plant	£70,687
Removing mole	£10,000
Wharf	£14,000
Lighthouse on end of breakwater	£2,000
Ten moorings	£15,000
Contingencies, 10 per cent	£30,386
Engineering, 6 per cent	£20,054
Total	£354,301

(Source: Ormiston Report, 5)

APPENDIX III

Bocci recommendations and cost

the desiccation of Lake Paralimni;
the purification of Famagusta Harbour and Lake John;
the purification of the lakes of Famagusta and Xerolimni;
the desiccation of Lake George;
the purification of the lake of St. George-Spathariko-Arnadi and the grounds of Trikomo;
and the purification of the lower grounds of the Mesaoria.

The mean total of these works came to £111,500.

(*Source*: Bocci report, 50)

APPENDIX IV

'What shall we do with Cyprus?', 1879

1

Here's another little baby Queen Victoria has got,
Another little Colony, although she has got a lot,
Another little Island, very wet, and very hot,
Whatever will she do with little Cyprus?
Already she has Colonies the names I quite forget,
For on Victoria's family, the sun can never set,
She'll surely never manage them, if troublesome they get,
So I'll tell you I'd do with little Cyprus.

Chorus

There was once a little lady, who had lodgings in a shoe,
She had so many babies that she didn't know what to do,
Queen Victoria's the lady, Old England is the shoe,
And the latest baby's little Master Cyprus.

2

I'd make it a Sanatorium, for Dipsomaniacs,
I'd make that Island happy, with a British Income Tax,
Tho' it's no use sending Gladstone, with his handy woodman's axe,
For there is little timber left in Cyprus.
We could send them sev'ral ironclads, all warranted to sink,
And a glorious aristocracy, with lives as black as ink,
We could send Sir Wilfred Lawson, just to show them how to drink
The water; that's so nasty, out in Cyprus.

Chorus

There was once a little lady, who had lodgings in a shoe,
She had so many babies that she didn't know what to do,
Queen Victoria's the lady, Old England is the shoe
And I'll tell you I'd do with little Cyprus.

3

I'd send them a German Admiral, who's ill when on the main
I would send the Duke of Cambridge, for he doesn't mind the rain
With a Magna Charta Doctor; and the Dewdrops on his mane,
He'll make it pretty warm for them in Cyprus.
We can part with all our statues, and the posters on our walls,
The can have a 'Woolwich Infant', with some powder and some balls
And if they're good we'll send a minor Canon of St. Pauls,
To blow up all the wicked ones in Cyprus

Chorus
There was once a little lady, who had lodgings in a shoe,
She had so many babies that she didn't know what to do,
Queen Victoria's the lady, Old England is the shoe
And I'll tell you I'd do with little Cyprus.

4

Now that Cyprus has been rescued from the bonds of Mr Turk,
She can rescue us from 'Turkish Bonds' that 'Bulls' would gladly shirk,
And we've sev'ral thousand Jingoes, who are lately out of work,
But perhaps, they wouldn't care for *them* in Cyprus.
We'd part, tho' most unwillingly, with Bishops, half a score,
And Ritualistic parsons, who have lately proved a bore,
There's Tooth and *Machonockie, may go knocking* at the door,
But they'd never let them in the *aisle* of Cyprus.

Chorus
There was once a little lady, who had lodgings in a shoe,
She had so many babies that she didn't know what to do,
Queen Victoria's the lady, Old England is the shoe
And I'll tell you I'd do with little Cyprus.

5

The Cypriotes, will find that we, our babe will not forget,
We'll send them several palaces, that lately are 'to let,'
And if they're very good, we'll let them pay our National Debt,
We mean to do the fatherly by Cyprus.
We can give them the Permissive, and the Sunday Closing Bills,
And lots of Irish Members, who will cure their island's' ills
And we'll send them Captain Burnaby, with tons of Cockles Pills,
To cure the collywobbles, out in Cyprus.

Chorus

There was once a little lady, who had lodgings in a shoe,
She had so many babies that she didn't know what to do,
Queen Victoria's the lady, Old England is the shoe
And I've told you what I'd do with Baby Cyprus.
W&Co. 1247.

(*Source*: 'Comical Topical Song', written by E.V. Page, composed by
Vincent Davies and sung by Arthur Roberts, J.W. Rowley and H.P.
Matthews, at Willey & Co., 7 Argyll Place, Regent Street, W.1.)

APPENDIX V

Cyprus finances as of 31 March 1914

Local revenue since the British occupation	£7,636,739	
Imperial grants-in-aid	£1,197,085	
Total		£8,833,824
Local expenditure since the British occupation	£5,345,967	
Tribute payments	£3,254,739	
Total		£8,600,706
Surplus		£233,118

(*Source*: Annual Report for Cyprus 1913–14, C.7643, 1914, 7)

APPENDIX VI

Imports and exports, 1901–18 (incomplete)

	Larnaca	Limassol	Kyrenia	Paphos & Latsi	Famagusta & Karpass	Nicosia & Karavostasi
1901–2	244,805/111,617	87,366/121,298	11,647/12,878	10,448/30,126	7,192/31,159	2,634/4,052
1902–3	235,296/100,957	116,469/106,010	17,873/16,898	12,843/28,619	13,324/15,819	7,156/2,795
1903–4	234,128/149,660	84,582/97,541	8,903/17,909	6,363/27,613	12,694/67,306	7,852/14,410
1904–5	253,501/197,377	79,331/125,145	7,028/18,517	4,920/41,662	39,443/68,541	4,682/14,888
1905–6	284,449/188,912	79,917/101,559	7,653/18,195	5,683/33,067	45,752/70,788	7,018/11,542
1911–12	263,350/232,488	144,509/212,427	6,536/23,083	8,975/47,908	95,032/103,276	29,370/7,375
1914–15	197,447/175,479	115,344/157,412	9,067/13,854	15,014/41,343	119,938/99,942	39,934/8,746
1915–16	176,671/173,552	132,603/215,239	1,542/16,320	21,864/65,509	211,730/172,717	43,589/7,153
1916–17	262,032/251,495	204,502/227,657	393/8,687	42,475/42,309	379,451/171,960	78,927/6,338
1917–18	257,428/170,274	197,186/261,199	643/162	17,033/64,541	427,114/288,231	68,764/3,515

(*Source*: Cyprus Blue Books)

Words in the Cypriot language, still commonly spoken today

Word in Cypriot (Greek Lettering)	Word in English	Origins	Meaning
Άππαρος	Aparos	Medieval Greek	horse
Αρτιρώ	Artiro	Turkish	left-over/increase bid
Βαζάνια	Vazania	Arabic	eggplant
Βάρτιτζια	Vartija	Arabic	white figs, red on the inside
Βλαντξίν/Φλαντξίν	Vlanjin/Flanjin	Old French	lungs
Βούρκα	Vourka	Turkish	leather backpack
Ζάβαλλιν	Zavallin	Turkish	poor man!
Ζορλής	Zorlis	Turkish	a difficult person
Ζούρα	Zoura	Italian	grime
Καραόλος	Karaolos	Venetian	snail
Καρκόλα	Karkola	Italian	bed
Κατσέλλα	Katsella	Arabic	cow
Κκελλέ	Kelle	Turkish	head
Κοπέλλιν/α	Kopelli/a	Italian	boy/girl
Κόρτα	Korta	Latin	piece
Κουβέλλα	Kouvella	Latin	female sheep
Κουρτέλλα	Kourtella	Venetian	knife/blade
Λόττα	Lotta	Latin	pig
Λούντζα	Lountza	Italian	smoked pork
Μάντξιπας	Manjibas	Latin	baker
Μάτσα	Matsa	Venetian	bunch/bundle
Ματσούκα	Matsouka	Latin	shepherd's staff
Μουτσούνα	Moutsouna	Italian	face
Μπουκκώννω	Mboukono	Latin	snack
Παττίχα	Batiha	Arabic	watermelon
Πελλετώ	Belleto	Turkish	observe
Πελλός	Bellos	Medieval Greek	crazy/idiot
Πετσέττα	Betsetta	Italian	napkin/kitchen towel

Word in Cypriot (Greek Lettering)	Word in English	Origins	Meaning
Πλαζίριν	Plazirin	French	grateful/thankful
Ππουνιά	Pounia	Venetian	hit
Πομυλόρι	Bomilori	Italian	tomato
Πότσα	Botsa	Italian	jug
Πουρνέλλα	Pournella	French/Italian	plum/prune
Πράτσο	Pratso	Venetian	measurement with cloth
Πρόκκος	Brokkos	Italian	signal to start a game
Πρότσα	Protsa	French	fork
Ρεζίλιν	Rezilin	Turkish	embarrassment
Ρέμπελος	Rembelos	Venetian	bad character
Ροτσιά	Rocca	Italian	hit
Σαγιά	Sagia	French	long dress/priests garb
Σιόρ	Sior	Venetian	sir
Σκαρπάρης	Skarparis	Venetian	shoemaker
Στετέ	Stede	Turkish	grandmother
Τάβλα	Tavla	Latin	slab
Τίτσιρο	Titsiro	Italian	naked
Τουρτουρώ	Tourtouro	Medieval Greek	freezing
Ταβλίν	Tavlin	Latin	table with food
Τζαμούζα	Jamouza	Turkish	cow that gives much milk
Τσαέρα	Tsa-era	Old French	chair
Τσάκρα	Tsakra	French	trap
Τσάμπρα	Tsambra	French	chamber
Τσαττάλιν	Tsatallin	Turkish	pants
Φανέλλα	Fanella	Italian	vest or t-shirt
Φάουσα	Faousa	Medieval Greek	someone who talks to much
Φκιόρο	Fkioro	Italian	flower
Φλόκκο	Flokko	Italian	tassel, mop
Φουστάνι	Foustani	Italian	dress
Χαΐριν	Ha-irin	Turkish	suitable
Χαλλούμι	Halloumi	Arabic	Cypriot cheese, usually salty
Χαπάριν	Habarin	Turkish	discover/realise/ notice

(Source: Theodore Papadopoullos, Δημώδη Κυπριακά Άσματα εξ Ανεκδότων Συλλογών του ΙΘ' Αιώνος, Nicosia, 1975; Constantine G. Giakoullis, Θησαυρός Κυπριακής Διαλέκτου, Nicosia, 2002)

APPENDIX VIII

Address of Archbishop Sophronios III to Sir Garnet Wolseley, 1878*

Your Excellency,

The unexpected news that Cyprus has been placed under English protection has spread like lightning, and has made a profound impression on the population. Subsequently we discovered that as a result of a convention between Turkey and England, Her Majesty Queen Victoria's government has sent your Excellency as Governor General of the island. We would like therefore to say: 'Welcome among us.'

The island of Cyprus, Your Excellency, although located in the furthest corner of the Mediterranean, carries a high value in the eyes of the English, for a number of reasons. But she has the further advantage of a population which is peaceful and easy to govern, and which, without renouncing its origin or its aspirations, will be faithful and devoted to its new and paternal authority. Unfortunately, for a very long time, any factors, both physical and political, have combined to keep this land in a far from prosperous state, from a material and intellectual point of view. But it seems divine Providence, in her bounty, has decided that this unfortunate island should at last come to enjoy the benefits of good administration and true civilisation. It is of course indubitable that the great, generous, and enterprising English nation, supported by her enlightened and humane government, should govern the peoples who find themselves under her powerful aegis with liberal laws appropriate to the development of their resources and their well-being. We therefore hope that this moment heralds a new life and a new era of prosperity for this land, which will mark a new epoch in its annals; that we will all, Christian or Muslim, learn that the law is sovereign of all; that we are all equals in the eyes of the law, that is to say that we all have the same rights and the same duties; that, in one word, we will be guided in the way of truth, duty and liberty. When justice reigns in the courts; when notions of honour and humanity inspire those who govern, all institutions feel it, and peoples prosper. Cyprus, to whom nature has given a rich and fertile soil, has to this day only lacked the steady hand needed to take full advantage of these resources. We are certain, however, that your Excellency's will be able to fill that void.

*translated from the French original by Dr Ian Coller

If, after this, the inhabitants of this island who are most distinguished by their intelligence and experience should be called to the councils of the Government, to consult on questions regarding customs, ways of life, forms of government, language, legislation and the needs of the country, it is to be hoped that helpful advice will be ready in coming forth, as much in the interest of the government as in that of the governed.

> Long Live Her Majesty Queen Victoria!
> Long Live the English Nation!
> Long Live our Governor General!

(*Source*: Glenbow Archives, Wolseley fonds (M-1332–os-26)).

APPENDIX IX

Greek Brotherhood of the Cypriots of Egypt

Frantziskos Grollos

Born in Larnaca in 1831, his father was from Corfu and his mother was related to Petros Oikonomides, who perished in the massacres of 1821. He settled in Egypt and was the president of the Alexandria branch of the Greek Brotherhood (1875–76).

Nikokles Grollos

Born in Larnaca in 1833, he is the brother of Frantziskos. He was the president of the Alexandria branch from 1874–75.

Euthemios Orastis

Born in Larnaca but moved to Limassol and then became a trader in Alexandria. He was a founding member of the Alexandria branch of the Greek Brotherhood of the Cypriots of Egypt in 1873.

Anastios Orastis

The nephew of Euthemios, Anastasios studied in Athens and Paris. He served as Vice-President of the Alexandria branch of the Greek Brotherhood of the Cypriots of Egypt at its founding, and as President in 1877–88, and again in 1894–95. Anastasios Orastis was a close associate of Kyprianos, the Bishop of Kitium.

Charalambos Mavroskoufes

Born in Marathasas (near Kykkos) in 1843 and worked in Limassol from a young age before settling in Egypt, and was one of the founding members of the Alexandria branch of the Brotherhood of Cypriots. Mavroskoufes made substantial donations to the Greek military, especially during the Balkan Wars. Neoklis Michaeilides

Born in Larnaca, Michaeilides became a trader in Alexandria and was a founding member of the Alexandria branch of the Greek Brotherhood of the Cypriots of Egypt and its President in 1876–77.

Demosthenes Mitsis

Raised in Larnaca, Mitsis studied foreign languages at the French Academy in Lebanon and returned to Larnaca and worked in trade with merchants based in Alexandria. He moved to Alexandria and became a trader and factory owner. From 1901 to 1908 he was the President of the Greek Brotherhood of the Cypriots of Egypt, when he funded the establishment of schools in Nicosia, Larnaca, Limassol and Trikomo. His wife was Italian.

Lambros Groutas

Born in Cyprus, Groutas moved to Alexandria when he was young and became a merchant. He was one of the founders of the Alexandria branch of the Greek Brotherhood of the Cypriots of Egypt and served as its President between 1888 and 1894 and from 1895 to 1901. His wife was from Mykonos.

Nikodemos Georgiades

Born in Paphos, Georgiades was a cousin of Archbishop Damaskinos (1924–27). He studied theology and philosophy at the University of Athens before moving to Egypt where he was a teacher. He was one of the founders of the Alexandria branch of the Brotherhood and was president of the Cairo branch from 1884 to 1887.

George Kypiades

Born in Larnaca and studied law in Athens. He later also studied theology, physics, philology and history. He became a lawyer in Alexandria, where he lived until 1876, when he returned to Cyprus, until 1891, later returning to Alexandria, where he died in 1910. He actually founded a 'Cypriot Brotherhood of St John's' in Alexandria in 1861 and became its president and when the Alexandria branch of the Greek Brotherhood of the Cypriots of Egypt was founded he became its secretary.

Alkiviades Ieronimides

Born in Larnaca. Related to Dranet-Pasha, who fled Cyprus after the events of 1821 and settled in Alexandria, where Mohammed Ali gave him sanctuary. Ieronimides traded in France and settled in Alexandria, where he became a merchant. A member of the Cairo Branch.

Vasilios Sivitanides

Born in Alexandria to Cypriot parents, he studied French and became a merchant. He was one of the founding members of the Alexandria branch of the Brotherhood. A diehard nationalist, he left his entire estate to the Greek state to use to found a technical school in Athens, which was achieved and was opened in 1930.

Sotirios Violaras

Parentage unknown. Koudanris claimed to be a Cypriot. Merchant in Alexandria. President of Cairo Branch (1881–83).

Alexandros Karatzas

Parentage unknown. Koudounaris claimed to be a Cypriot. He married a Grollo. A banker in Cairo. Served as President of the Cairo Branch (1888–97).

Nicholas Christofidou

Born in Oreines, father from Rizokarpaso. Member of Cairo Branch. Not a prolific figure in Cyprus. Major benefactor of a church in Cairo.

Michael Samolis

Cairo Branch. No further information.

S. Averkiadou

Cairo Branch. No further information.

(*Sources*: E. Th. Soulogiannis, «Έλληνες Κύπριοι στην Αίγυπτο (1826 Μέχρι Σήμερα)», ICCS-2, 171–200; Entries in BLC; copy of Kypros newspaper, Andreas Sophocleous, Συμβολή στην Ιστορία του Κυπριακού Τύπου, I, Nicosia, 1995, 253, 34).

APPENDIX X

Members of the Cyprus Society in 1890

President: HRH Princess Christian

Patrons:
His Beatitude the Archbishop of Cyprus
Lord Brassey
Lord Randolph Churchill
M. Gennadius, the Greek Minister resident in London
Lady Charles Beresford
Lady Bowen
Lady Elizabeth Dugmore
Lady Lechmere
The Hon. Mrs W. Lowther
The Countess of Meath
Lady Laura Ridding
The Dowager Lady Waterpark

Vice-Presidents:
The Right Rev. Bishop Blyth, Bishop of the Church of England in Jerusalem
and the East
Bishop of Carlisle
Bishop of Durham
Bishop of Gibraltar
Bishop of Lichfield
Bishop of Salisbury
Bishop of Southwell
Bishop of Wakefield
The Very Rev. the Dean of Lichfield
The Very Rev. the Dean of Norwich
The Venerable the Archdeacon of London
The Rev. Canon Duckworth
The Rev. Prebendary Eyton
The Right Hon. Earl Nelson

Sir George Arthur Bart
The Right Hon. Sir George Bowen
Sir Algerton Borthwick, MP
Colonel Hon. F. Bridgeman MP
Sir Dyce Duckworth, MD
Major-Gen. Sir Frederic J. Goldsmid
Stanley Leighton, MP
Lieut.-Gen. Sir John Stokes

Council:
Chairman: Major-Gen. Sir Frederic J. Goldsmid
The Rev. Brymer Belcher
The Rev. J. Crosthwaite Bellett
The Rev. R. Milburn Blakiston
The Rev. E. Hamilton Blyth
The Rev. H.B. Chapman
George Cowell
Mrs Finn
Dr Freshfield
D.G. Hogarth
Mrs Vaughan
F.G. Kenyon (wife of E.R. Kenyon)
Miss Kerr
Mrs Lewis (??)
General Lowry
General Maclagan
Mrs Milton
Rev. H. Bickersteth Ottley, Bishop Blyth's Commissary for Cyprus and Syria
Athelstan Riley
Mrs Sandford
Rev. Canon Scarth
Rev. C.A. Solbé
Major Watson, RE
The Rev. Frederick Whitfield
The Rev. Forbes E. Winslow

Correspondent in Cyprus:
The Rev. J. Spencer, MA, Inspector of Schools in Cyprus

Hospital Committee:
Chairman: Captain E.R. Kenyon, RE, late Commissioner of Kyrenia
Dr Abraham, MA, MD
F.W. Barry, MD, Late Sanitary Commissioner with the Government of Cyprus
Mrs Burt
H.B. Cholmeley, MA, MB
George Cowell

Dr Bedford Fenwick
Mrs Vaughan Instone
W. Johnstone, MD, AMS, Late District Medical Officer of Kyrenia
Mrs Milton
Mrs Mylne
C.E. Newton
Athelstan Riley
Mrs Sandford
P. Gordon Smith
C. Stevens
Major Watson
Miss Watson
Rev. F. Whitfield

Educational Committee:
Chairman: Major-General Sir F.J. Goldsmid
The Rev. Brymer Belcher
W.J. Birkbeck
The Rev. E. Hamilton Blyth
The Rev. H.B. Chapman
Mrs Finn
The Rev. G.C. Fletcher
Sir Craven Goring
Sir Theodore Hope
Captain E.R. Kenyon
The Venerable the Archdeacon of London
General Maclagan
Rev. H. Bickersteth Ottley, Bishop Blyth's Commissary for Cyprus and Syria
Rev. Brisco Owen
Rev. Salisbury Price
Athelstan Riley
Rev. Canon Scarth
Reginald Soames
Rev. C.A. Solbé
G.A. Spottiswoode
Major-Gen. Harding Steward

Honorary Treasurer:
Captain G.A.K. Wisely

Honorary Secretaries:
Miss S. Chapman Hand (sent the letter to Florence Nightingale)
William White, FSA

(*Source*: Report of the Council of the Cyprus Society presented
at the Second Annual Meeting, held at the Church House,
25 June 1890, George Pulman & Sons, London, 1890)

APPENDIX XI

Recommendations of local committee

Works	43-ton guns	26-ton guns	medium guns	remarks
Quarry Fort	3	3	6	
Exonisi Fort	6	4	0	
Varosha Fort	0	0	0	abandoned
3-gun battery	0	3	0	
Old Town battery	0	0	0	abandoned
Breakwater turret	2	0	0	
Total	11	10	6	

(*Source*: CO67/25/2197, confidential, Report of a Committee held on board HMS Superb on 30 November and 1 and 2 December 1881)

SELECT BIBLIOGRAPHY

The original bibliography to the dissertation was over seventy pages. Owing to space constraints, the following list does not include all references but the archival sources, a selection of government documents and a very select list of primary and secondary sources. All sources are listed in full the first time they are referenced in the footnotes.

Primary sources

Official unpublished documents

National Archives, Kew, London

Departments
Admiralty (ADM); Air Ministry Papers; Board of Trade (BOT); Cabinet (CAB); Colonial Office (CO); Crown Agents for Overseas Governments and Administrations (CAOG); Foreign Office (FO); Intelligence (KV); Treasury (T); War Office (WO).

Private papers
Disraeli, Benjamin (Lord Beaconsfield), papers, National Archives, Kew, London.
Granville, Lord, correspondence and papers, National Archives, Kew, London; Reference: PRO30/29, NRA 8654 Leveson-Gower.
Grey, Edward, Viscount Grey of Falloden; correspondence and papers, National Archives, Kew, London, Reference: FO800/35–113, NRA 23627 Foreign Office (FO800/106 folio 526).
Kitchener, Lord, correspondence and papers, National Archives, Kew, London, Reference: PRO30/57/77, PRO30/57/1.
Simmons, Sir John Lintorn Arabin, Knight Field Marshal; correspondence and papers, 1857–96, National Archives, Kew, London, Reference: FO358, NRA 23627 Foreign Office.

British Library
Arnold-Forster, Hugh Oakley; Papers; War Office Papers, 1903 – October 1904, VIII, Barracks, Depots &c. Stations & Garrisons (Colonial &c.), Somaliland, Foreign Preparations, British Library, Manuscript Collections, Reference: Add MSS 50307.
Bertie, Sir Francis Leveson, 1st Viscount Bertie of Thame; correspondence and papers, British Library, Manuscript Collections, Reference: Add MSS 63011–53 (63040 folio 193).

D'Arbernon, Lord; Papers and Correspondence; British Library, Manuscript Collections, Reference: Add MSS 48928.

Escott, Thomas Hay Sweet; Papers and Correspondence; British Library, Manuscript Collections, Reference: Add MSS 58774–58801.

Gladstone, William E., papers and correspondence; British Library, Manuscript Collections, Reference: Add MSS 44086–835, 44900–1, 45724 and 56444–53.

Martin, Sir William Fanshawe, 4th Baronet, Admiral; correspondence and papers, 1816–95; British Library, Manuscript Collections, Reference: Add MSS 41408–62.

Nelson papers, Vol. VI, General Correspondence Vol. V, 1 June – 15 October 1798, British Library, Manuscript Collections, Reference: Add MS 34907.

Nightingale, Florence; Papers and Correspondence, British Library, Manuscript Collections, Reference: Add MSS 45810.

Orr, Sir Charles William James, Knight Colonial Administrator; Letters to E. Leviseur, 1900–14, British Library, Manuscript Collections, Reference: Add MS 56100.

Wolseley, Lieutenant-General Sir Garnet (later Lord), 41324, Letter Book containing copies of his semi-official correspondence as High Commissioner and Commander-in-Chief in Cyprus 2 Aug. 1878–11 May 1879. Paper; ff. 97. Folio.

Oxford University

Luke, Sir Harry Charles, Knight Colonial Governor; diaries and papers, 1903–59, Oxford University: St Antony's College, Middle East Centre, NRA 20811 St Antony's College.

Stavridi, Sir John, Knight Consul-General for Greece, papers, St Antony's College, Oxford.

Cambridge University

Churchill, Sir Winston Leonard Spencer, Knight Statesman and Historian; correspondence and papers, 1884–1945, Cambridge University, Churchill Archives Centre, Reference: CHAR and WCHL, NRA 20556 Churchill.

Glenbow Library and Archives, Calgary, Canada

Wolseley papers, M1332, box 6, 'Nicosia Address, 1878'.

Secretariat Archive (SA1), State Archives, Nicosia

SA1:2464, SA1:2484, SA1:2491, SA1:2492, SA1:2691, SA1:2710, SA1:2711, SA1:2712, SA1:2715, SA1:2718, SA1:2748, SA1:2809, SA1:2810, SA1:2811, SA1:2812, SA1:2813, SA1:2814, SA1:2815, SA1:2816, SA1:2817, SA1:2843, SA1:2846, SA1:2850, SA1:2858, SA1:7402, SA1:7471, SA1:7480, SA1:7489, SA1:7493, SA1:14390, SA1:14543, SA1:14544, SA1:14545, SA1:14549, SA1:14550, SA1:14560, SA1:14574, SA1:14575, SA1:14663, SA1:14664, SA1:14675, SA1:14889, SA1:14891, SA1:15143, SA1:15144, SA1:15195, SA1:15320, SA1:15321, SA1:1884, SA1:1885, SA1:1886, SA1:1887, SA1:1888, SA1:1889, SA1:1890, SA1:1891, SA1:1892, SA1:1893, SA1:1895, SA1:1902,

SA1:1903, SA1:1904, SA1:1905, SA1:1906, SA1:1907, SA1:1908, SA1:1910, SA1:1911, SA1:1912, SA1:1913, SA1:1914, SA1:1915, SA1:1916, SA1:1917, SA1:1918, SA1:1919, SA1:1920, SA1:1921, SA1:1922, SA1:1923, SA1:1924, SA1:1926, SA1:1927, SA1:1937, SA1:1938.

Official published documents

Parliamentary Papers

Cyprus. Translation of a Report Forwarded by Mr. Campbell, British Consul at Rhodes, upon the Island of Cyprus, for the Years 1854–8, XXX, London, 1859.

Cyprus. Report. General and Statistical, by Mr. Vice-Consul White, LXX, London, 1863.

Cyprus. Commercial Report by Vice-Consul White of the Island of Cyprus for the Year 1862, LXX, London, 1863.

Cyprus. Report by Mr. Vice-Consul Sandwith on the Trade of Cyprus for the Year 1865, LXXII, London, 1867.

Island of Cyprus. Report by Acting Consul Lang upon the Commerce of Cyprus for the Year 1870, LXVI, London, 1871.

Report by Consul Lang, LX, London, 1872.

Correspondence Respecting the Convention Between Great Britain and Turkey of June 4, 1878, C. 2057, London, 1878.

Correspondence Respecting the Island of Cyprus, C. 2229, London, 1879.

Reports Made to the Admiralty on the Anchorages etc. of the Island of Cyprus, C. 2244, London, 1879.

Correspondence Respecting Complaints Made Against the Government of Cyprus, C. 2324, London, 1879.

Correspondence Respecting the Island of Cyprus, C. 2543, London, 1880.

Report by Mr. Ormiston on Improvements Proposed at the Harbour of Famagusta dated January 10, 1880, C. 2544, London, 1880.

Returns Connected with the Payment to the Porte out of the Revenues of Cyprus, C. 2628, London, 1880.

Correspondence respecting the Cyprus Ordinance 'Regarding the Sale of Land to Subjects of Foreign Countries', confidential, 4077, February 1880.

Correspondence Respecting the Financial State of the Island of Cyprus, C. 2629, London, 1880.

Correspondence Respecting the Affairs of Cyprus, C. 2930, London, 1881.

Further Correspondence Respecting the Affairs of Cyprus, C. 3091, London, 1881.

Cyprus. Report by Her Majesty's High Commissioner for 1880, C. 3092, London, 1881.

Constitution and Function of a New Legislative Council, C. 3211, London, 1882.

Further Correspondence Respecting the Affairs of Cyprus, C. 3384, London, 1882.

Cyprus. Report by Her Majesty's High Commissioner for 1881, C. 3385, London, 1882.

Papers Relating to the Administration and Finances of Cyprus, C. 3661, London, 1883.

Papers Relating to the Constitution of a New Legislative Council, C. 3791, London, 1883.

Correspondence Respecting the Affairs of Cyprus. C. 4188, London, 1884.

Report on the Census of Cyprus, 1881, C. 4264, London, 1884.

Correspondence Respecting the Affairs of Cyprus. C. 4694, London, 1886.

Correspondence Respecting the Affairs of Cyprus. C. 4961, London, 1887.

Correspondence Respecting the Affairs of Cyprus. C. 5251, London, 1888.

Correspondence Relating to the Affairs and Finances of Cyprus, C. 5523, London, 1888.

Correspondence Relating to the Affairs of Cyprus, C. 5812, London, 1889.

Further Correspondence Relating to the Affairs of Cyprus, C. 6003, London, 1890.

Drought in Cyprus, Cmd. 1434, London, 1903.

Correspondence Respecting the Affairs of Cyprus, Cmd. 1465, London, 1903.

Correspondence Relating to the Affairs of Cyprus, C. 3966, London, 1908.

Unofficial published sources

Baker, Sir Samuel W., *Cyprus as I Saw it in 1879*, Macmillan, London, 1879 (repr. IndyPublish, Virginia, 2001).

Brassey, Lady Annie, *Sunshine and Storm in the East or a Cruise to Cyprus and Constantinople*, Longman, London, 1880.

Butler, William Francis, *Far Out: Rovings Retold*, W. Isbister, London, 1880.

Butler, W.F., *An Autobiography*, Charles Scribner's Sons, London, 1911.

Cecil, Lady Gwendolyn, *Life of Robert Marquis of Salisbury*, 2 Vols, Hodder & Stoughton, London, 1922.

Churchill, Randolph, *Winston S. Churchill*, Vol. II, Companion Part 1, 2, and 3, Heinemann, London, 1969.

Cobham, C.D., *Excerpta Cypria*, Cambridge University Press, Cambridge, 1908 (Kraus, New York, 1986).

Collen, Capt. E.H.H., *Report on Cyprus, based on information obtained chiefly from Consular Reports, Foreign Office, 1845–1877*, Intelligence Branch, Q.M.G. Department., Horse Guards, London, 18 May, 1878.

Derby, 15th Earl of, *The Diaries of Edward Henry Stanley, 15th Earl of Derby (1826–93), Between September 1869 and March 1878*, ed. John Vincent, Offices of the Royal Historical Society, London, 1994.

Dilke, Charles Wentworth, *Greater Britain: A Record of Travel in English-Speaking Countries During 1866 and 1867*, Macmillan, London, 1868.

Dilke, Charles Wentworth, *Problems of Greater Britain*, Macmillan, London, 1890.

Disraeli, Benjamin, *Tancred: or, The New Crusade*, Henry Colburn, London, 1847.

Dixon, W. Hepworth, *British Cyprus*, Chapman & Hall, London, 1879.

Donne, Major Benjamin Donisthorpe Alsop, *Records of the Ottoman Conquest of Cyprus and Cyprus Guide and Directory*, J.W. Williamson & Co., Limassol, Cyprus, 1885 (enlarged edition, incl. Donne's journal, ed. Philip Christian, Laiki Group Cultural Centre, 2000).

Ellis, Tristan, *Twelve Etchings of Principle Views and Places of Interest in Cyprus*, Gammon & Vaughn, London, 1879.

Farley, James Lewis, *Egypt, Cyprus and Asiatic Turkey*, Trübner & Co., London, 1878.

Flinn, W.H., *Cyprus: A Brief Survey of its History and Development*, C.W. Archer, Nicosia, 1924.

Fyler, Arthur Evelyn, *The Development of Cyprus, and Rambles in the Island*, Percy Lund, Humphries & Co., London, 1899.

Gladstone, W.E., *Midlothian Speeches, 1879* (intro.) M.R.D. Foot, Leicester University Press, Leicester, 1971.

Greaves, George Richards, *Memoirs of Sir General George Richards Greaves*, John Murray, London, 1924.

Green, Colonel A.O., *Cyprus: A Short Account of its History & Present State*, M. Graham Coltarat, Scotland, 1914.

Haggard, Rider H., *A Winter Pilgrimage in Palestine, Italy and Cyprus*, Longman, London, 1901.

Hamilton, Sir Edward Walter, *The Diary of Sir Edward Hamilton 1885–1906*, ed. Dudley W.R. Bahlman, The University of Hull Press, Hull, 1993.

Hogarth, D.G., *Devia Cypria*, Henry Frowde, Oxford, 1889.

Hogarth, D.G., *The Nearer East*, Heinneman, London, 1902.

Kinneir, J.M., *Journey Through Asia Minor, Armenia and Koordistan in 1813–14*, London, 1818.

Lang, R. Hamilton, *Cyprus: Its History, its Present Resources and Future Prospects*, Macmillan, London, 1878.

McCalmont, Hugh, *The Memoirs of Major-General Sir Hugh McCalmont*, ed. Major-General Sir Charles Edward Callwell, Hutchinson, London, 1924.

Mallock, W.H., *In an Enchanted Island; or a Winter's Retreat in Cyprus*, Richard Bentley & Son, London, 1889.

Orr, Sir Charles W.J., *Cyprus Under British Rule*, Robert Scott Roxburghe House, London, 1918 (reprinted, Zeno, London, 1972).

Sandon, Dudley Ryder, Viscount, *The Cabinet Journal of Dudley Ryder, Viscount Sandon*, eds Christopher Howard and Peter Gordon, University of London, Institute of Historical Research, London, 1974.

Scott-Stevenson, Esme, *Our Home in Cyprus*, Chapman and Hall, London, 1880.

Seeley, John Robert, *The Expansion of England*, London, 1883.

Sinclair, Hugh Montgomerie, *Camp and Society*, Chapman and Hall, London, 1926.

Stewart, Basil, *My Experiences of the Island of Cyprus*, Skeffington & Son, London, 1906.

Storrs, Sir Ronald, *Orientations*, Ivor Nicholson & Watson, London, 1937 (repr., Readers Union, 1939).

Thomson, John, *Through Cyprus with the Camera in the Autumn of 1878*, London, 1879 (Trigraph, London, 1985).

Vizetelly, Edward (Bertram H. Clere), *From Cyprus to Zanzibar by the Egyptian Delta*, C. Arthur Pearson, London, 1901.

Wolseley, Sir Garnet, *Cyprus 1878: The Journal of Sir Garnet Wolseley*, ed. Anne Cavendish, Cyprus Popular Bank Cultural Centre, Nicosia, 1991.

Secondary sources

Monographs

Alastos, Doros, *Cyprus in History: A Survey of 5,000 Years*, London, 1955 (Zeno, 1976).

Anagnostopoulou, Sia, *The Passage from the Ottoman Empire to the Nation-States*, Isis Press, Istanbul, 2004.

Anderson, Benedict, *Imagined Communities: Reflections on the Origin and Spread of Nationalism*, Verso, London, 1983.

Anderson, M.S., *The Eastern Question 1774–1923*, Macmillan, London, 1966.

Andrew, C.M. and Kanya-Forstner, A.S., *The Climax of French Imperial Expansion, 1914–1924*, Stanford University Press, California, 1981.

Attalides, M.A. (ed.), *Cyprus Reviewed*, Jus Cypri, Nicosia, 1977.

Attalides, M A., *Cyprus: Nationalism and International Politics*, Q. Press, Edinburgh 1979.

Bar-Yosef, Eitan, *The Holy Land in English Culture 1799–1917: Palestine and the Question of Orientalism*, Oxford University Press, Oxford, 2005.

Blake, Robert, *Disraeli*, Eyre & Spottiswoode, London, 1966.

Bryant, Rebecca, *Imagining the Modern: The Cultures of Nationalism in Cyprus*, I.B. Taurus, London, 2004.

Cain, P.J. and Hopkins, A.G., *British Imperialism: Innovation and Expansion, 1688–1914*, Longman, London, 1993.

Cannadine, David, *The Decline and Fall of the British Aristocracy*, Yale University Press, New Haven, 1994.

Cannadine, David, *Ornamentalism: How the British Saw Their Empire*, Penguin, London, 2001.

Chakrabarty, Dipesh, *Provincializing Europe: Postcolonial Thought and Historical Difference*, Princeton University Press, New Jersey, 2000.

Cohn, Bernard S., *Colonialism and its Forms of Knowledge: The British in India*, Princeton University Press, New Jersey, 1996.

Cregier, Don M., *Bounder from Wales: Lloyd George's Career Before the First World War*, University of Missouri Press, Columbia and London, 1976.

Deringil, Selim, *The Well-Protected Domains: Ideology and the Legitimation of Power in the Ottoman Empire 1876–1909*, I.B. Taurus, London, 1998.

Dietz, Peter, *The British in the Mediterranean*, Brassey's, London, 1994.

Eldridge, C.C., *Disraeli and the Rise of a New Imperialism*, University of Wales Press, Cardiff, 1996.

Fieldhouse, D.K., *Economics and Empire 1830–1914*, Weidenfeld & Nicolson, 1973.

Frendo, Henry, *Party Politics in a Fortress Colony: The Maltese Experience*, Malta, 1979.

Gallant, Thomas W., *Experiencing Dominion: Culture, Identity, and Power in the British Mediterranean*, University of Notre Dame Press, Notre Dame, Indiana, 2002.

Gellner, Ernest, *Nations and Nationalism*, Blackwell, Oxford, 1983.

Georghallides, G.S., *A Political and Administrative History of Cyprus 1918–1926*, Cyprus Research Centre, Nicosia, 1979.

Glasgow, George, *Ronald Burrows: A Memoir by George Glasgow*, Foreword by E.K. Veniselos, Nisbet & Co., London, 1924.

Gole, Susan, *Maps of the Mediterranean Regions Published in British Parliamentary Papers 1801–1921*, The Bank of Cyprus Cultural Foundation, Nicosia, 1996.

Gourgouris, Stathis, *Dream Nation: Enlightenment, Colonisation, and the Institution of Modern Greece*, Stanford University Press, California, 1996.

Haddad, William W. and William Ochsenwald (eds), *Nationalism in a Non-National State: The Dissolution of the Ottoman Empire*, Ohio State University, Columbus, 1977.

Harfield, Alan (ed.), *The Life and Times of a Victorian Officer*, Wincanton Press, Somerset, 1986.

Herzfeld, Michael, *Ours Once More: Folklore, Ideology, and the Making of Modern Greece*, University of Texas Press, Austin, 1982.

Herzfeld, Michael, *Anthropology Through the Looking-Glass: Critical Ethnography in the Margins of Empire*, Cambridge University Press, Cambridge, 1987.

Hill, Sir George Francis, *A History of Cyprus*, IV, *The Ottoman Province the British Colony, 1571–1948*, ed. Sir Harry Luke, Cambridge University Press, London, 1952.

Hobson, J.A., *Imperialism*, Cosimo, London, 1902.

Hughes, Quentin, *Britain in the Mediterranean and the Defence of Her Naval Stations*, Penpaled, Liverpool, 1981.

Karpat, Kemal, *An Inquiry Into the Social Foundation of Nationalism in the Ottoman State: From Social Estates to Classes, From Millets to Nations*, Princeton, 1973.

Katsiaounis, Rolandos, *Labour, Society and Politics in Cyprus During the Second Half of the Nineteenth Century*, Cyprus Research Centre, Nicosia, 1996.

Kedourie, Elie, *Nationalism*, Hutchinson, London, 1960.

Koss, Stephen, *The Rise and Fall of the Political Press in Britain*, I, Hamish Hamilton, London, 1981.

Koudounaris, Aristedis, *Βιογραφικόν Λεξικόν Κυπρίων, 1800–1920* (*Biographical Lexicon of Cypriots, 1800–1920*), Nicosia, 2001.

Kyrris, Costas P., *History of Cyprus*, Nicocles, Nicosia, 1985.

Lee, Dwight E., *Great Britain and the Cyprus Convention Policy of 1878*, Harvard University Press, Mass., 1934.

Lewis, Bernard, *The Multiple Identities of the Middle East*, Schocken Books, New York, 1999.

Luke, Harry C., *Cyprus Under the Turks 1571–1878*, Oxford University Press, London 1921.

Luke, Sir Harry C., *Cyprus: A Portrait and an Appreciation*, Harrap, London, 1957 (revised 1965).

Macfie, A.L., *The Eastern Question, 1774–1923*, Longman, London, 1989 (revised, 1996).

MacKenzie, John M. (ed.), *Imperialism and Popular Culture*, Manchester University Press, Manchester, 1986.

MacKenzie, John M., *Orientalism: History, Theory and the Arts*, Manchester University Press, Manchester, 1995.

Marriott, J.A.R., *The Eastern Question: An Historical Study in European Diplomacy*, Clarendon, Oxford, 1924.

Medlicott, W.N., *Bismarck, Gladstone and the Concert of Europe*, London, 1956.

Miller, Geoffrey, *The Millstone: British Naval Policy in the Mediterranean, 1900–1914, the Commitment to France and the British Intervention in the War*, University of Hull Press, Hull, 1999.

Monypenny, W.F. and Buckle, G.E., *The Life of Benjamin Disraeli Earl of Beaconsfield*, Vols I–VI, John Murray, London, 1929.

Owen, Roger and Sutcliffe, R.B. (eds), *Studies in the Theory of Imperialism*, Longman, London, 1972. ·

Owen, Roger, *The Middle East in the World Economy 1800–1914*, Methuen, London, 1981.

Pamuk, Sevket, *The Ottoman Empire and European Capitalism, 1820–1913: Trade, Investment and Production*, Cambridge University Press, Cambridge, 1987.

Panteli, Stavros, *A History of Cyprus: From Foreign Domination to Troubled Independence*, East West Publications, London, 2000.

Papadakis, Yiannis, *Echoes From the Dead Zone: Across the Cyprus Divide*, I.B. Taurus, London, 2005.

Persianis, Panayiotis K., *Church and State in Cyprus' Education: The Contribution of the Greek Orthodox Church to Cyprus' Education During the British Administration 1878–1960*, Nicosia, 1978.

Pratt, Michael, *Britain's Greek Empire: Reflections on the History of the Ionian Islands from the Fall of Byzantium*, Rex Collings, London, 1978.

Purcell, H.D., *Cyprus*, Ernest Benn, London, 1969.

Reid, Donald Malcolm, *Whose Pharaohs? Archaeology, Museums, and Egyptian National Identity from Napoleon to World War I*, Berkeley, 2002, 161–2.

Robinson, R.F. and Gallagher, J., *Africa and the Victorians*, Macmillan, London, 1961.

Rose, Jonathon, *The Intellectual Life of the British Working Class*, Yale University Press, New Haven, 2002.

Roussou-Sinclair, Mary, *Victorian Travellers in Cyprus: A Garden of Their Own*, Cyprus Research Centre, Nicosia, 2002.

Said, Edward, *Orientalism*, Vintage Press, New York, 1978.

Schumpeter, Joseph A., *The Sociology of Imperialism*, A.M. Kelley, New York, 1951.

Schurman, Donald M., *Imperial Defence 1868–1887*, ed. John Beeler, Frank Cass, London, 2000.

Seton-Watson, R.W., *Disraeli, Gladstone and the Eastern Question: A Study in Diplomacy and Party Politics*, F. Cass, London, 1962.

Severis, Rita G., *Travelling Artists in Cyprus, 1700–1960*, Philip Wilson, London, 2000.

Shirley, Rodney W., *Kitchener's Survey of Cyprus 1878–1883: The First Full Triangulated Survey and Mapping of the Island*, Bank of Cyprus Cultural Foundation, Nicosia, 2001.

Smith, Michael Llewellyn, *Ionian Vision: Greece in Asia Minor, 1919–1922*, Allen Lane, London, 1973.

Stephens, Robert, *Cyprus: A Place of Arms*, Praeger, New York, 1966.

Varnava, Andrekos, *The Cyprus Problem and the Defence of the Middle East, 1945–1960: Britain's Reluctant Relinquishment of a* Place d'Armes, Andrekos Varnava, Melbourne, 2001.

Wasserstein, Bernard, *Divided Jerusalem: The Battle for the Holy City*, Yale University Press, New Haven, 2001.

Waterfield, Gordon, *Layard of Nineveh*, John Murray, London, 1963.

Yapp, Malcolm, *The Making of the Modern Near East*, Longman, London, 1987.

Yashin, Mehmet (ed.), *Step-Mothertongue From Nationalism to Multiculturalism: Literatures of Cyprus, Greece and Turkey*, Middlesex University Press, London, 2000.

Journal articles on Cyprus

Demetriou, Kyriacos, 'Victorian Cyprus: Society and Institutions in the Aftermath of the Anglo-Turkish Convention, 1878–1891', *Byzantine and Modern Greek Studies*, 1997, 1–29.

Faustmann, Hubert, 'Clientelism in the Greek Cypriot Community of Cyprus Under British Rule', *Cyprus Review*, X, 2, 1998, 41–77.

Georghallides, G.S., 'Churchill's 1907 Visit to Cyprus: A Political Analysis', *Epeteris*, III, 1969–70, 167–220.

Georghallides, G.S., 'Lord Crewe's 1908 Statement on Greek-Cypriot National Claims', *Kypriakai Spoudai*, 1970, 25–34.

Georghallides, G.S., 'Memorandum by Mr Headlam-Morley and Mr Childs Respecting Cyprus', *Epeteris*, V, 1972, 189–240.

Given, Michael, 'Inventing the Eteo-Cypriots: Imperialist Archaeology and the Manipulation of Ethnic Identity', *Journal of Mediterranean Archaeology*, XI, 1, 1998, 3–29.

Given, Michael, 'Maps, Fields, and Boundary Cairns: Demarcation and Resistance in Colonial Cyprus', *International Journal of Historical Archaeology*, VI, 1, March 2002, 1–22.

Harfield, Major A.G., 'The Cyprus Pioneer Corps and the Cyprus Military Police During 1879–1882', *Bulletin Military Historical Society*, XXVI, 101, August 1975, 1–8.

Harfield, Major A.G., 'British Military Presence in Cyprus in the 19th Century', *Journal of the Society for Army Historical Research*, 1978, 160–70.

Katsiaounis, Rolandos, «Εκλέγειν και Εκλεγέσθαι στις Πρώτες Βουλευτικές Εκλογές της Αγγλοκρατίας το 1883» ('Voting and Elections in the First Legislative Elections during British Rule in 1883'), *Epeteris*, XX, 1994, 309–45.

Kitromilides, Paschalis M., 'Greek Irredentism in Asia Minor and Cyprus', *Middle Eastern Studies*, XXVI, 1, 1990, 3–17.

Kizilyurek, Niyazi, 'From Traditionalism to Nationalism and Beyond', *The Cyprus Review*, V, 2, 1993, 58–67.

Kyrris, Kostas P., 'Symbiotic Elements in the History of the Two Communities of Cyprus', *Kypriakos Logos*, VIII, 1976, 243–82.

Lee, Dwight E., 'A Memorandum Concerning Cyprus', *The Journal of Modern History*, 1931, 235–41.

Medlicott, W.N., 'The Gladstone Government and the Cyprus Convention, 1880–85', *The Journal of Modern History*, 1940, 186–208.

Papadopoullos, Theodore, «Εθναρχικός Ρόλος της Ορθοδόξου Ιεραρχίας» ('The Ethnarchic Role of the Orthodox Heirachy'), *Kypriakai Spoudai*, XXXV, 1971, 95–141.

Pollis, Adamantia, 'Intergroup Conflict and British Colonial Policy: The Case of Cyprus', *Contemporary Review*, 1973, 575–99.

Sant Cassia, Paul, 'Religion, Politics and Ethnicity in Cyprus During the Turkocratia (1571–1878)', *European Studies of Sociology*, 1986, 3–28.

Sant Cassia, Paul, 'Banditry, Myth, and Terror in Cyprus and Other Mediterranean Societies', *Comparative Studies in Society and History*, 1993, 773–95.

Temperley, Harold, 'Disraeli and Cyprus', *English Historical Review*, XLVI, April 1931, 274–9.

Temperley, Harold, 'Further Evidence on Disraeli and Cyprus', *English Historical Review*, XLVI, July 1931, 457–60.

Tillyrides, Andreas, 'Archbishop Sophronios III (1865–1900) and the British', *Kypriakai Spoudai*, 1978, 129–52.

Varnava, Andrekos, '*Punch* and the British Occupation of Cyprus in 1878', *Byzantine and Modern Greek Studies*, XXIX, 2, 2005, 167–86.

Yavuz, M. Hakan, 'The Evolution of Ethno-Nationalism in Cyprus under the Ottoman and British Systems', *The Cyprus Review*, III, 2, Autumn 1991, 57–79.

Essays in collected works and chapters in selected works on Cyprus

Headlam-Morley, Sir James, 'The Acquisition of Cyprus in 1878', in Sir James Headlam-Morley, *Studies in Diplomatic History*, Methusen, London 1930, pp. 193–211.

Pollis, Adamantia, 'International Factors and the Failure of Political Integration in Cyprus', in Stephanie Neuman (ed.), *Small States and Segmented Societies*, Praeger, New York, 1976, 44–83.

Varnava, Andrekos, 'Maintaining Britishness in a Setting of their Own Design: The Troodos Hill Station in Cyprus during the Early British Occupation', in Kate Darian-Smith, Patricia Grimshaw, Kiera Lindsey and Stuart Macintyre (eds), *Exploring the British World*, RMIT Publishing, Melbourne, 2004, pp. 1102–33.

Unpublished sources (theses and papers)

Lawrence, Lee Edward, *The British Administration of Cyprus, 1878–1914*, unpublished PhD dissertation, University of Wisconsin, Madison, 1935.

Wosgian, Daniel Stepan, *Turks and British Rule in Cyprus*, unpublished MA dissertation, Columbia University, 1963.

INDEX